Developing the Physical Education Curriculum
An Achievement-Based Approach

Luke E. Kelly, PhD
University of Virginia

Vincent J. Melograno, EdD
Cleveland State University

Human Kinetics

Library of Congress Cataloging-in-Publication Data

Kelly, Luke E.
   Developing the physical education curriculum: an achievement-based
approach / Luke E. Kelly, Vincent J. Melograno.
         p. cm.
Includes index.
   ISBN 0-7360-4178-8
   1. Physical education and training--Curricula--United States. 2.
Curriculum planning--United States. I. Melograno, Vincent. II. Title.
   GV365.K45 2004
   796'.071--dc21

                                                2003012466

ISBN-10: 0-7360-4178-8
ISBN-13: 978-0-7360-4178-2

Copyright © 2004 by Luke E. Kelly and Vincent J. Melograno

The Web addresses cited in this text were current as of October 15, 2003, unless otherwise noted.

Acquisitions Editor: Scott Wikgren; **Developmental Editor:** Melissa Feld; **Assistant Editors:** Susan C. Hagan, Anne Cole, and Amanda Gunn; **Copyeditor:** Patsy Fortney; **Proofreader:** Kathy Bennett; **Indexer:** Betty Frizzéll; **Permission Manager:** Dalene Reeder; **Graphic Designer:** Nancy Rasmus; **Graphic Artist:** Dawn Sills; **Photo Manager:** Kareema McLendon; **Cover Designer:** Jack W. Davis; **Photographer:** © Human Kinetics; **Art Manager:** Kelly Hendren; **Illustrator:** Argosy; **Printer:** Sheridan Books

Printed in the United States of America   10 9 8 7 6 5 4

Human Kinetics
Web site: www.HumanKinetics.com

United States: Human Kinetics
P.O. Box 5076
Champaign, IL 61825-5076
800-747-4457
e-mail: humank@hkusa.com

Canada: Human Kinetics
475 Devonshire Road, Unit 100
Windsor, ON N8Y 2L5
800-465-7301 (in Canada only)
e-mail: info@hkcanada.com

Europe: Human Kinetics
107 Bradford Road
Stanningley
Leeds LS28 6AT, United Kingdom
+44 (0)113 255 5665
e-mail: hk@hkeurope.com

Australia: Human Kinetics
57A Price Avenue
Lower Mitcham, South Australia 5062
08 8372 0999
e-mail: info@hkaustralia.com

New Zealand: Human Kinetics
Division of Sports Distributors NZ Ltd.
P.O. Box 300 226 Albany
North Shore City, Auckland
0064 9 448 1207
e-mail: info@humankinetics.co.nz

In loving memory of my wife, Eileen, and to my children,
Luke Andrew, Zachary, and Melissa.

Luke E. Kelly

To the fond memory of Mom & Dad and Nan & Pop and to a
bright future for Craig & Natalie and Laura & Bill.

Vincent J. Melograno

Contents

Preface

A truly functional and accountable physical education curriculum clearly communicates to teachers and other stakeholders (such as parents and administrators) what students will learn, how the curriculum will be taught, and when and how teachers and administrators will know the students have achieved the intended outcomes. The purpose of this book is to provide an integrated process that addresses the broad range of challenges physical educators face in building such a curriculum to meet the diverse needs of their students.

Staff in schools today are being asked to address an ever increasing array of educational and social issues. These increasing demands are competing for already limited instructional resources and valuable instructional time. Concurrently schools are increasingly pressured to be more accountable and more productive by having higher percentages of their students meet established national, state, and local outcomes and learning standards. For example, No Child Left Behind legislation was built on accountability and assessment principles including setting standards, measuring student progress against the standards, providing intervention for struggling students, and holding schools responsible for results. For physical education, the National Association for Sport and Physical Education (NASPE) suggested content standards and corresponding grade-level benchmarks as a basis for quality physical education programs.

The current trends in education have direct implications for the physical education curriculum. Many excellent physical educators are conducting exemplary programs designed to meet the needs of their students, yet many of these programs are being cut because decision makers do not understand or value them. Physical educators are also facing increasing demands to do more with less. Teachers are commonly being asked to handle increases in class size and diversity in abilities while at the same time having to justify their programs and defend them from cuts. Although this increased pressure and demand for accountability are affecting all content areas, physical education is frequently one of the first content areas reduced to address the needs of others. To respond to these new demands, physical educators need a wide range of skills beyond knowing how to teach their content. Teachers need to know how to do the following:

- Promote the value of their programs and the impact they are having on their students' current and future wellness

- Justify keeping their instructional time from being reduced by showing the impact it will have on students' mastery of content in their curriculum and on other aspects of the overall school curriculum

- Know what support services are reasonable to request to accommodate the needs of a student with special needs and how to request these services

- Acquire the confidence and skills needed to be effective members of the overall school curriculum committee so they can play an active role in both promoting physical education and educating others about the value of physical education

This book is designed for physical education teacher candidates and practicing physical educators interested in professional development. It is recommended to higher education personnel for use in undergraduate and graduate curriculum courses and for teacher inservice seminars and workshops. For teacher candidates, it should be used in upper-level courses prior to student teaching, preferably in conjunction with field experiences. For graduate courses and inservice programming, professionals will find the book useful in designing, revising, and evaluating physical education curricula. As resource material, the book is valuable to school personnel (administrators, supervisors, and physical education teachers) looking to improve their existing physical education programs.

Historically, an inseparable link has always existed between curriculum theory and curriculum design. The uniqueness of this book is that it builds on the rich history of curriculum theory in physical education and provides the first systematic achievement-based curriculum (ABC) model for translating curriculum theory into a functional curriculum. The ABC model is unique in that it is independent of any particular curriculum theory or model. As such, it does not dictate what content to include in the curriculum or how to teach it. Instead the ABC model provides a systematic decision-making process that allows you to develop a physical education curriculum that addresses your unique needs and concerns. Because the ABC model is a dynamic process, it also allows you to easily incorporate national, state, and local outcome-based and performance-based standards into your curricula.

The ABC model presented in this book is not revolutionary; it is a logical process that guides you through the integrated steps of program planning, assessing, implementation planning, teaching, and evaluating a functional curriculum. What is unique is that this book takes you step by step through these decision processes and provides actual examples to illustrate each step. Some of you may possess some of the skills and the knowledge needed to use the ABC model but need to be shown how to use this information to address curricular problems. Because the ABC model is a process and not a static solution to an existing problem, you can use it repeatedly to address the ongoing problems that will emerge to challenge your physical education programs. The ultimate goal of the ABC model is to empower you with the skills you need to document, promote, and justify your programs so that both your students and the community at large understand the value of daily physical education and the need for it to be an integral part of the school curriculum.

This book is divided into four parts. **Part I** develops your understanding of curriculum development. **Chapter 1** offers a foundation for the physical education curriculum; **chapter 2** reviews the impact of educational mandates and standards; **chapter 3** describes some physical education curriculum models; and **chapter 4** introduces the ABC (achievement-based curriculum) model. Part II deals with planning decisions. **Chapter 5** establishes program philosophy, goals, objectives, and policies; **chapter 6** details planning at the program level; and **chapter 7** helps you devise functional assessments. **Part III** covers the implementation of the physical education curriculum. **Chapter 8** summarizes how to organize instruction for maximum learning and the principles for effective teaching; **chapter 9** provides a comprehensive analysis of learning experiences; and **chapter 10** introduces teaching templates and student learning formats that are new schemes for curriculum designers. **Part IV** focuses on evaluating and communicating the physical education curriculum. **Chapter 11** looks at student evaluation and grading; **chapter 12** outlines program evaluation; and **chapter 13** covers aspects of your professional role in establishing program effectiveness. **Appendix A** is a program planning case study; it illustrates the first nine steps of the planning-down process. **Appendix B** contains the reproducible forms you will need to develop your own curriculum.

Each chapter contains special features. Chapter-opening scenarios establish the need for the information that follows by presenting real-life, practical physical education settings that place you in a problem-solving situation. The chapter contents help you deal with these scenarios. Then, a set of expected outcomes identifies the knowledge and skills you will acquire by completing the chapter. Finally, each chapter ends with a section called "Making It Work," in which issues and practical considerations are addressed. This section will answer some of the lingering questions you may have after reading the chapter.

In summary, think of curriculum designing as answering three questions: Where am I going? How will I get there? and, When will I know I've arrived? We do not provide final answers in this book because they vary from one educational setting to another. Instead, we present a rationale and process by which these questions can be answered. Clearly, this is not a cookbook for a physical education curriculum. There is no single recipe for such a design. However, when you have finished this book, you will understand the ingredients, and you will be able to design a meaningful and effective achievement-based physical education curriculum.

Acknowledgments

There are two remarkable women who have had a significant impact on my life and professional work that I would like to acknowledge. First and foremost is my wife, Eileen. Although unfortunately she is not able to see this book in its final form, she contributed in countless ways to its creation and development. As an elementary physical educator for more than 20 years, she kept me in tune with the issues in the field and let me know when I needed to get out of the ivory tower and back in touch with the realities being faced by physical educators. She provided the love, support, patience, and encouragement needed for me to develop and write this book. Finally, she was and always will be my inspiration. Eileen was an advocate for every student she taught. She taught me that if you fight for what is best for the students you never lose! I would also like to acknowledge Dr. Janet A. Wessel, professor emeritus from Michigan State University. I had the honor of working with Janet in my first position in higher education. Janet was a pioneer, a visionary, and as hard a worker as I have ever met. Janet created the precursor of the achievement-based curriculum in the 1960s while creating a physical education curriculum for individuals with mental retardation, and she called it objective-based instruction. Janet has been an exemplary mentor, a model of dedication to the profession, and a relentless advocate for improving the quality of our school physical education programs.

This book would not have become a reality without the dedication, patience, perseverance, and attention to detail of my coauthor, Vince Melograno. Vince is the consummate professional and epitomizes the concept of collaboration. I thank him for his friendship, insight, selflessness, and thoughtfulness.

I would like to thank Scott Wikgren of Human Kinetics for seeing the merit of this project and working with us from its inception to completion. While his title is acquisitions editor, he is in touch with the needs of the field and is a physical educator at heart. I am particularly grateful for Scott's sensitivity and understanding while I dealt with some personal issues. I would also like to thank Melissa Feld, developmental editor, for making this the most painless editing process I have ever experienced. Melissa was a pleasure to work with and added many little details that enhanced the overall quality of the book.

Finally, I would like to thank my colleagues, former students, and the numerous physical educators I have had the pleasure to collaborate with over the years. I thank them for their dedication, professionalism, and willingness to share their views and field test new ideas. There is not one aspect of the ABC model that has not been improved due to their input.

Luke E. Kelly

This book reflects the contributions of many others including colleagues, master teachers, and teacher candidates. Their creative ideas are proudly represented throughout the book. As curriculum designers, they truly practice what this book preaches—a sincere belief in and commitment to achievement-based physical education.

In addition, the book could not have been written without certain people. First, special thanks and respect are reserved for Luke Kelly. We were brought together on this project somewhat unexpectedly. What started out as a professional relationship has evolved into a valued friendship. It is very satisfying to look back at our give-and-take, good-natured debating, helpful critiques, and hours spent on a single idea and know that we produced something that we hope will be meaningful. All of this was accomplished while Luke overcame some personal hardships.

Appreciation and thanks are also extended to Scott Wikgren, acquisitions editor at Human Kinetics, who supported this book from beginning to end. His understanding, patience, and sensitivity during some difficult times was a source of strength and encouragement. Having worked with Scott on other projects, I can attest to his professional style and personable manner. He is a distinct asset to the team at Human Kinetics.

Finally, I would like to thank Melissa Feld, developmental editor, whose dedication to this book was evident during all phases of manuscript review, editing, production, and marketing. Her organizational skills, attention to detail, and suggestions for improving the book were much appreciated. Melissa always approached her role in a persistent yet timely and pleasant way. Her leadership of the staff at Human Kinetics who worked on this book was outstanding.

Vincent J. Melograno

PART I

Understanding Curriculum Development

This introductory section lays the groundwork for developing the physical education curriculum. Although this background material may seem overwhelming, it is essential to establish the reasons for the curriculum and the basis for curriculum decision making. The section is broken down into four chapters. Chapter 1 offers a foundation for developing the physical education curriculum. Chapter 2 is a review of the educational mandates and standards and discusses their direct impact on the physical education curriculum. Chapter 3 describes some known curriculum models for physical education. Finally, chapter 4 addresses the achievement-based model that serves as the process for developing the physical education curriculum. A brief description of each chapter follows.

Chapter 1

Foundation for Curriculum Development

What is a curriculum, and why do we need one? Where does physical education fit in? How are all of the curriculum areas connected? In this chapter we explore the nature of curriculum including the meaning of curriculum, important curriculum perspectives, the concept of planning down and implementing up, and achievement education. The role of the curriculum *designer* is contrasted to the role of the curriculum *consumer*. In this chapter we also establish three contemporary contexts that could influence physical education curriculum development: (1) we discuss the importance of understanding the dynamics of change to avoid defensive reactions to new ideas, (2) we outline some ways that learning and teaching have been redesigned, and (3) we identify several popular education trends (culturally responsive teaching, inclusive education, developmentally appropriate practices, outcome-based education, advances in technology). Finally, we present several philosophical perspectives because values and beliefs affect the development of curriculum. The chapter concludes with a description of recent viewpoints in physical education and raises various issues in reference to curriculum development in physical education.

Chapter 2

Physical Education Mandates and Standards

Increasing demands for accountability in education have led to widespread curriculum reform efforts. At the center of this educational redesign are sets of mandates related to legal actions, state-level requirements, and aspects of diversity. As a curriculum designer, you must know what is being imposed on the physical education curriculum. Because standards-based education is a significant part of school restructuring, we present national content standards and corresponding grade-level benchmarks in physical education in this chapter. We also illustrate state-level and district-level standards and analyze the impact of these factors on designing the physical education curriculum.

Chapter 3

Physical Education Curriculum Models

Models of physical education curriculum that represent different value orientations and purposes have evolved over time. A knowledge of these models can help you determine your own direction in designing a physical education curriculum. This chapter describes various widely accepted models, including movement education, fitness education, developmental education, activity-based education, humanistic and social development, sport education, wilderness sports and adventure education, conceptually based education, and personally meaningful education. In reality, most schools today reflect eclectic models that contain aspects of several of these models. Also, available time limits the full implementation of the models. For these reasons, we recommend the achievement-based curriculum model as the *process* for making curriculum development decisions.

Chapter 4

Achievement-Based Physical Education Curriculum

We refer to the recommended curriculum design for physical education as the achievement-based curriculum (ABC) model. In this chapter, we identify and illustrate the principles and concepts of the achievement-based model. This construct serves as the focus for the remaining aspects of curriculum design.

one

Foundation for Curriculum Development

In a fairly large city school district, a school community action group believes that the K-12 curriculum needs a major overhaul. The student population is culturally diverse, ranges from low to high socioeconomically, and demonstrates mixed abilities across all grade levels. The school curriculum, in the opinion of the action group, no longer fits the students. In addition, the action group cites the following discoveries as reasons for change:

- Proficiency test scores placed the district in academic emergency according to state performance standards.

- Growth in education increased from $198 million in 1998 to over $3 billion in 2002.

- The number of children in home schools increased from 301,000 in 1990 to nearly 2 million in 2002.

- In 1990 charter schools did not exist; over 2,000 charter schools existed in 2002.

- The percentage of U.S. households with personal computers increased from 2.3% in 1982 to 51% in 1998; by 2002, over 50% of U.S. households had Internet access.

An oversight curriculum design team is formed, and you are asked to represent physical education. Your role is to serve as an advocate for physical education as well as to convey the characteristics and features of a contemporary physical education curriculum. You bring the following knowledge about the patterns and trends in physical activity:

▌ The percentage of young people who are overweight more than doubled in 35 years from about 5% in the late 1960s to about 14% in 2002.

▌ Inactivity and poor diet cause at least 300,000 deaths a year in the United States; only tobacco causes more preventable deaths.

▌ About 30% of adults report no physical activity at all in their leisure time.

▌ Among high school students, daily attendance in physical education has declined from approximately 42% in the first half of the 1990s to 15% today.

▌ Only 19% of all high school students report being physically active for 20 minutes or more in daily physical education classes.

At times, you wonder if the task is too overwhelming. You realize that you are faced with a difficult challenge to contribute to the development of the overall school curriculum and to establish physical education as a viable subject area. What does all of this mean when it comes to developing the physical education curriculum? Is change possible given some of the more traditional practices in physical education? How are different values and beliefs considered when developing the physical education curriculum? What are the standards and outcomes of a quality physical education program?

EXPECTED OUTCOMES

This chapter will help you establish the foundation for curriculum development. After reading this chapter, you will be able to do the following:

1. Describe the meaning of curriculum, important curriculum perspectives, the concept of planning down and implementing up, and the achievement cycle

2. Accept the role of designer in creating a contemporary physical education curriculum

3. Recognize the dynamics of change and the redesign of learning and teaching that has occurred in education

4. Determine the influence of education trends on the development of physical education curricula

5. Develop a philosophical viewpoint to guide you in your development of a physical education curriculum

6. Resolve curriculum issues that relate to physical education

Developing a curriculum for the purpose of meeting intended student outcomes is an essential act of teaching and includes designing assessments to diagnose student needs. Assessments help to guide teaching and enable teachers, students, and others (parents, school officials, the public) to determine whether they have reached their intended outcomes. To begin, you should know what is meant by curriculum and the role of the teacher in its development. You should also understand the rationale for the physical education curriculum from various sources. This chapter addresses the cultural context for designing curriculum, including schools and society as well as students and their families. Philosophy serves as another source because curriculum is an extension of one's values and beliefs. Therefore, this chapter is organized around three questions:

▌ *What is the nature of curriculum?* To answer this question, we (1) define curriculum, (2) introduce important curriculum perspectives, (3) recommend the concept of planning down and implementing up, (4) identify achievement education, and (5) describe the role of the curriculum designer.

- *What are the contemporary contexts for curriculum development?* To answer this question, we (1) review the dynamics of change, (2) summarize attempts to redesign learning and teaching, and (3) outline education trends.

- *How does philosophy fit into curriculum development?* To answer this question, we (1) revisit traditional values and beliefs, (2) present curriculum value orientations, (3) analyze recent viewpoints in physical education, and (4) discuss curriculum issues.

Nature of Curriculum

In this section we propose a systematic approach to curriculum development. We begin by presenting the meaning of curriculum and several perspectives that are important to curriculum designing. Then, we explain the notion of planning down and implementing up because of its significance to the proposed designing process. This section also provides the background knowledge for using achievement as the focus for school curricula. Last, we describe the role of the curriculum designer and explain why we recommend it for those interested in developing a physical education curriculum that is personalized and responsive to the contemporary needs of learners.

Meaning of Curriculum

The school curriculum reflects the role of education in society. It combines public policy and professional judgment. Definitions of curriculum vary greatly. Defined broadly, curriculum includes all of the experiences a student has in school. Defined narrowly, curriculum is a plan or set of outcomes. Any practical definition should reflect the general understanding of the term as used by educators, and it should be useful in making operational decisions. Some distinguish between the plans made for learning and the actualization of those plans as experienced by the students (Glatthorn, 1994). Therefore, we will define curriculum here as the planned sequence of (1) what students are to learn, (2) how students acquire that learning, and (3) how students' learning is verified.

Physical education is unique because it contributes to all three learning domains—cognitive, affective, and psychomotor. Your challenge is to fulfill this potential by creating a physical education curriculum that guides and facilitates student achievement. Because the emphasis is on planning, you will need a systematic process to design the physical education curriculum. This designing process should not be confused with instruction, which is defined as the delivery system for implementing the curriculum.

Instruction also involves planning followed by teacher–student interaction. During the planning phase of instruction, teachers make several decisions regarding daily plans, teaching materials, audiovisual materials and technology, facilities and equipment, time allocation, organizational schemes, management procedures, discipline strategies, and teaching methods. The range of actual teacher and student behaviors occurs during the interactive phase of instruction. Although curriculum and instruction can be analyzed separately, in practice they are inseparable. For this reason, we address both *designing* and *implementing* the curriculum in this book.

Currently, two competing forces are at work regarding the extent to which teachers determine the school's curriculum. On the one hand, state departments of education and school districts attempt to control the curriculum. Curriculum guides might indicate specifically what is to be taught grade by grade in a given subject. Some states and districts use curriculum monitoring systems and end-of-course tests to ensure that the approved curricula are implemented. The emphasis on national performance standards and high-stakes testing has created the need for a prescriptive curriculum. At the same time, others argue that teacher autonomy is needed to reform schools. They assert that teachers alone should be responsible for curriculum development. We recommend a balanced approach in which the state identifies a curriculum framework or model that includes a set of general goals, and the school district develops, with considerable teacher input, grade-level outcomes. Teachers can enrich and adapt the curriculum and determine appropriate instructional strategies. This means that you need to be competent in your ability to *design* curriculum. That is the purpose of this book!

Curriculum Perspectives

To extend the meaning of curriculum, we will examine several viewpoints that will further explain the nature and extent of curriculum development. This section presents information about the hidden curriculum, curriculum alignment, integrating the curriculum, and curriculum mapping. Keep in mind these concepts and the principles underlying them as you proceed through this book.

Hidden Curriculum

Students learn a great deal from aspects of schooling other than the intended curriculum. These kinds of unintended learnings are referred to as the hidden curriculum. The hidden curriculum comprises what students learn from the school's culture—its values, norms, and practices (Glatthorn, 1993). It consists of unplanned and unrecognized values that are taught and learned through the process of education. In other words, students are repeatedly exposed to unconscious acts that are consistent in meaning, such as gender role modeling by teachers. These representative acts, which communicate implicit values to the student, may or may not be consistent with the explicit philosophy of the teacher or school.

Although the term *hidden curriculum* is often viewed as negative, learnings can be both desirable and undesirable depending on one's viewpoint. For example, organizing and managing the physical education environment exposes the hidden curriculum. In a crowded gymnasium, control often becomes dominant through different uses of power. The teacher controls the selection of activities, methods, and movement around the gym as well as how much time is spent giving feedback and assessing students. As a result, students unconsciously learn traits found in the larger culture. They learn how to be punctual, docile, and conforming and how to stand in line, take turns, and wait. As a curriculum designer you should be aware of the subtle and pervasive influence of these behaviors (Glatthorn, 1994).

Curriculum Alignment

A major objective of any curriculum is to guarantee agreement among what is designed, what is implemented, and what is assessed. We should not assume that the translation of the written curriculum to the taught curriculum to the attained curriculum happens without a focused effort. A curriculum should reflect the most generally accepted research bases, programmatic scope (K-12), effective developmental processes, and relevant assessment practices. In other words, the curriculum should be internally aligned.

External alignment seeks agreement between the curriculum and other sets of criteria such as competencies, outcomes, content standards, grade-level benchmarks, proficiencies, subject matter strands, or performance objectives. Whatever the criteria, alignment involves a process to identify discrepancies between what is intended and what actually happens. This process is sometimes referred to as a performance audit. When applied to the curriculum, an audit reveals the discrepancy (match) between the curriculum goals, objectives, assessment, learning experiences, and evaluation and the external set of criteria. For example, many states administer statewide tests to measure student performance in various subject areas. The tests are normally based on preapproved curriculum models. A common practice in schools is to determine the degree to which the local curriculum is aligned with the approved model, which in turn should reveal the degree of alignment with the test itself. Although mandated state-level tests in physical education do not exist, state-level curricula in physical education do exist. Attempting to align schools' physical education curricula with the state model is a common practice.

Curriculum Integration

Our rapidly changing, information-based society has resulted in an overloaded school curriculum. Because the school day is normally divided into small blocks of time, the curriculum becomes fragmented, rarely providing connections between subjects or establishing how material is relevant to students' lives. In the real world, people make decisions, solve problems, and deal with issues in a combined manner. They do not use subject matter separately in isolation (Jacobs, 1989).

Curriculum integration responds to the need to make students' learning relevant and to encourage critical thinking. Teachers collaborate to make connections across subject areas. This requires careful planning to link appropriate concepts, outcomes, and activities within the organized curriculum. Teachers from different subject areas cross-reference lessons to expose natural relationships. The following examples illustrate the potential of this integrated model (Christie, 2000):

- *Language arts.* Write about a positive sport, fitness, or dance role model; maintain an activity and nutrition journal with health-related reflections.
- *Social studies.* Create a sports time line that corresponds with the historical period being covered; play games from different time periods or cultures.
- *Mathematics.* Calculate point scoring in sports; calculate averages and percentages in sports; work with formulas to determine accurate personal training zones.
- *Science.* Explore movement principles and the respective actions of muscles and levers

as physics concepts; learn the functioning of the human organism and the effects of exercise and diet in biology.

- ▌ *Music.* Create sound accompaniment to guide movement patterns (e.g., clapping, singing, recorded music, student-made instruments); create instruments for performing rhythmic activities.

- ▌ *Art.* Draw various symmetrical and asymmetrical shapes that the body can make; depict shapes through movement sequences; use drawings to label body parts.

Curriculum Mapping

To make sense of students' experiences over time, both horizontal (one academic year, across subjects) and vertical (over the K-12 experience) views are needed. The classroom level or subject matter (micro view) is dependent on the site and district level (macro view). Although the micro and macro levels are connected, teachers usually have sketchy knowledge of what goes on throughout the curriculum. With data from curriculum mapping, however, teachers can review and revise the curriculum within a larger, much-needed context (Jacobs, 1997).

Calendar-based curriculum mapping relies on technology to collect real-time information about the actual curriculum, including content, skills, and assessment data. Curriculum mapping includes seven phases:

1. *Collecting the data.* Each teacher describes three major elements that make up the curriculum on the curriculum map: (a) the processes and skills emphasized, (b) the content in terms of essential concepts and topics, and (c) the products and performances that are the assessments of learning.

2. *First read-through.* Each teacher becomes an editor for the maps by looking for repetitions, gaps, meaningful assessments, matches with standards, potential areas for integration, and timeliness.

3. *Mixed group review session.* Small groups (of six to eight) composed of teachers who do not ordinarily work together share their findings from the individual review of the maps. This is a reporting procedure.

4. *Large group review.* Findings are gathered in a chart encompassing all of the reporting sessions. Participants comment on emerging patterns, both general and specific.

5. *Determining points that can be revised immediately.* Teachers begin to sift through the data and determine areas that can be handled right away. For example, a few teachers can address glaring repetitions through an exchange of ideas.

6. *Determining points that will require long-term research and development.* Teachers will find areas that require more in-depth investigation before a solution can be produced. Problems could encompass a range of grade levels or subject matter. For example, a major gap may exist in a series of assessments between the elementary and middle school program.

7. *Continuing the review cycle.* Curriculum review should be dynamic. With the help of technology, teachers have the means for ongoing, systematic, immediate, and long-range planning. The idea of reviewing the curriculum on a four-year cycle, for example, makes little sense given the rapid changes in any subject area.

Planning Down and Implementing Up

The ongoing reform of education is based on specific learning outcomes that students should achieve. Curriculum is the means to these ends. The ongoing reform of education challenges us to think differently about how we plan, instruct, and assess our students. What do we expect students to know, feel, and be able to do as a result of their physical education experience?

Many teachers use favored lessons and time-honored activities rather than derive their curricula from targeted goals or standards. We advocate the reverse. Start with the end in mind—the desired outcomes, goals, or standards—and then derive the curriculum that will achieve them. This design may seem backward, but in fact it is logically forward (Wiggins & McTighe, 1998).

Another way to think of this concept is "designing down and delivering up" (Hopple, 1995). After determining exit-level outcomes, you "design down" by deciding the lower-level outcomes for the program, course, unit, and lesson levels. Once you have established the benchmarks or enabling outcomes at these levels, you can "deliver up" your instruction. Students progress from entry ability toward target outcomes. This approach to curriculum development departs from the common practice of creating assessments near the end of teaching. Instead you begin with what you would accept as evidence that students have attained the desired outcomes. This concept, as used throughout this book, is referred to as *planning down and implementing up*.

Achievement Education

Quality education is a professional imperative. It has set us in pursuit of curriculum and instruction programming that can be designed and implemented for all students. To design quality programs in physical education, we must address issues of individualization, accountability, and effective practices. High-quality programming, which accommodates the needs, performances, and interests of a diverse group of students, is the precursor to superior results—student *achievement* (Wessel & Kelly, 1986).

More recently, the systematic approach to curriculum, assessment, instruction, and learning was called the achievement cycle (Glatthorn, 1998). The key concept of the cycle is the interactive relationships of four elements: standards-based curricula, performance evaluation, assessment-driven instruction, and authentic learning. The primary aim of all curricula, assessments, and instruction (the contributing components) is authentic learning (the central outcome).

Normally, the cycle begins with curriculum development, proceeds to performance assessments based on the curriculum, and then moves to assessment-driven instruction to maximize authentic learning. These three contributing components can be ordered in different sequences. You might begin with assessments, derive the curriculum, and then move to assessment-driven instruction. The key is to maintain congruence among the contributing components and to focus on the learning outcome. This approach also emphasizes the importance of ongoing monitoring of both the contributing components and the central outcome.

Our discussion of achievement education in this section constitutes merely an overview. The organizing framework of this book is an achievement-based approach to developing the physical education curriculum, which is fully described in chapter 4. Its key concepts are addressed throughout this book.

Role of the Designer

The *contexts* for developing curriculum—the dynamics of change, education trends, values and beliefs, philosophical viewpoints, and curriculum issues—are covered in this chapter. Together they serve as the foundation for curriculum designing. Ultimately, you should consider them all when establishing the foundation for your own physical education curriculum. Before doing so, however, you should have a clear understanding of the role you need to play in the curriculum development process.

As a curriculum designer, you have two options. You can take the easy way and use the intuitive approach to curriculum design. Many do, and the result is often a curriculum with ambiguous purposes, inappropriate content, ignored learning sequences, casual forms of evaluation, and limited kinds of learning activities. The other option is to develop the competencies needed to translate the meaning of curriculum and its principles and concepts into a viable physical education curriculum. If you select the second option, this book is for you.

The realities of our culturally pluralistic society require the continued reform and improvement of American education *including physical education.* Because of prevailing social and educational forces, you must incorporate the following into your curriculum designs:

- Appropriate programming, designed and conducted in the least restrictive environment, to meet the specific and unique needs of students with disabilities
- Coeducational programming that is gender-neutral in design, gender-integrated in practice, and congruent with current legislation
- Multicultural learning experiences designed to consider and validate each person's cultural heritage and individual potential
- Racial integration that recognizes the diversity and multiplicity of values, beginning with genuine concern and respect for each student's worth and uniqueness
- Basic education that should develop greater competence in academic skills by raising expectations in terms of academic performance and student conduct

Although teachers are a diverse group, they share two basic needs: to have control over their teaching environments and to have an impact on their students. Control over curriculum development will help you meet these two basic needs. *Designing* curriculum that is responsive to contemporary student needs, rather than *consuming* someone else's philosophy, program, materials, and strategies, is essential to your feeling of efficacy. The law of effect is operational. Success, as determined by student achievement, is a highly positive reinforcement for your curriculum decisions.

Thus, the key to educational reform is for teachers to be curriculum designers rather than curriculum consumers. Traditionally, as consumers, teachers have been locked in a bureaucratic tangle in which they are forced to spend almost all of their creative energy making instantaneous decisions. "Consumer teachers" neither desire nor expect to be involved in any creative process of curriculum development. On the other hand, as designers, teachers choose and plan day-to-day activities that assume accountability for student learning. "Designer teachers" can create curricula tailored to the existing abilities and interests of their students. Many teachers, however, are not able to design curricula that are personalized and responsive to the contemporary needs of students. With this book, you can develop the skills you need to design your physical education curriculum.

Curriculum designing is no doubt a challenge. When carried out correctly, it can be complex and time intensive. Physical educators, in particular are continually bombarded with a wealth of content options. Nevertheless, you must decide *what* to teach and *why* to teach it. Your curriculum design should reflect your basic philosophy. It consists of many interrelated components that must function together. Once we have established the foundation of curriculum design in this chapter, we will be in a position to explore the various components of curriculum design in the remainder of the book.

What Is Your Knowledge Base?

- Foundation for curriculum development (chapter 1)
- Physical education mandates and standards (chapter 2)
- Physical education curriculum models (chapter 3)
- The achievement-based physical education curriculum (chapter 4)

Where Are You Going?

- Establishing the philosophy, goals, objectives, and policies (chapter 5)
- Program planning (chapter 6)

When Will You Know You've Arrived?

- Developing functional assessments (chapter 7)
- Student evaluation and grading (chapter 11)

How Will You Get There?

- Maximizing learning and effective teaching (chapter 8)
- Learning experiences (chapter 9)
- Planning for learning and teaching (chapter 10)

How Will You Continually Improve?

- Program evaluation (chapter 12)
- Professionalism (chapter 13)

The model in figure 1.1 illustrates the relationship among the curriculum components. Note that the concept of planning down and implementing up is also depicted. The answers to the questions represent a systematic approach to designing curriculum. To answer the first question, you must establish the program philosophy, goals, objectives, and policies. Learning objectives provide specific direction for the intended outcomes, and they are useful in developing the remaining curriculum components. Then you need to determine the scope and sequence of the curriculum (program planning). Because of the link between objectives and criterion standards of performance (assessment), the second question is answered by developing functional assessments for the objectives and determining evaluation and grading procedures. The third question is answered in several ways: (1) maximizing learning and observing principles of effective teaching, (2) developing appropriate learning experiences, and (3) planning for learning and teaching. To answer the final question, you evaluate and modify the curriculum for continual improvement and maintain professional responsibilities.

We do not provide final answers to these questions in this book. Instead, we offer a rationale and process to help you answer these questions using an achievement-based curriculum model. Clearly, this is not a cookbook for a physical education curriculum. There is no single recipe for such a design. However, when you are finished with this book, you will understand the ingredients, and you will be able to design meaningful and effective curricula.

You shouldn't view this system of planning as a mechanical process of education. On the contrary, the rationale for what students learn and how and how well they learn it is organized in a way that clarifies curricular planning and enhances the sequence of learning. A wide spectrum of imaginative and creative educational experiences can be designed for the full range of learning objectives—from simple behaviors (e.g., recall, listen, jump) to

What Is Your Knowledge Base?

- Foundation for Curriculum Development
  (Chapter 1)
- Physical Education Mandates and Standards
  (Chapter 2)
- Physical Education Curriculum Models
  (Chapter 3)
- The Achievement-Based Physical Education Curriculum
  (Chapter 4)

IMPLEMENT
UP

Where Are You Going?

- Establishing the Philosophy,
  Goals, Objectives, and
  Policies (Chapter 5)
- Program Planning
  (Chapter 6)

- Professionalism
  (Chapter 13)
- Program Evaluation
  (Chapter 12)

**How Will You
Continually Improve?**

- Planning for Learning and
  Teaching (Chapter 10)
- Learning Experiences
  (Chapter 9)
- Maximizing Learning and
  Effective Teaching
  (Chapter 8)

**When Will You Know
You've Arrived?**

- Developing Functional
  Assessments (Chapter 7)
- Student Evaluation and
  Grading (Chapter 11)

How Will You Get There?

PLAN
DOWN

▌ Figure 1.1   Model for designing the physical education curriculum using the achievement-based approach.

complex mental tasks (e.g., create a dance routine), values development (e.g., fair play), and advanced movement patterns (e.g., hit a golf ball).

Contemporary Contexts

Our earlier definition of curriculum (see page 5) emphasized the role of education in society and the blending of public policy and professional judgment. Although you should make every attempt to be up-to-date or current, sustaining the momentum of change that is found in society and schools is difficult. For that reason, it is important to recognize

the dynamics of change and our natural reaction to change. This section begins with an analysis of change as growth and renewal (the public ideal) and change as a conservative impulse (our private reality).

The school curriculum is often criticized for its lack of relevance. However, a challenging national standards movement has established the roots for a redesign of learning and teaching in this century. We will explore this redesign effort in this section along with some education trends that could potentially influence the nature of physical education curriculum.

Dynamics of Change

Have you ever tried to look ahead 5 or 10 years? What kind of world might we face given expected changes in technology, biology, social values, demography, and education? Popular in today's education, for example, is the notion of preparing students to participate in the global economy of the "Information Age." As educators, we face a daunting task; we are engaged in a great venture of exploration, risk, discovery, and change without a comprehensive map for guidance. According to Senge and colleagues (1999), profound change sometimes refers to external changes in technology, customers (students), or the social and political environment. But change also refers to internal attempts to adapt to changes in the environment. The timeless concern is whether internal changes in practices, views, and strategies are keeping pace with external changes.

Change is riddled with paradox; we both embrace and resist it. We know change is inevitable and needed, but our natural reaction to it is often defensive. Change is more difficult than we think for several reasons. It provokes *loss,* challenges *competence,* creates *confusion,* and causes *conflict* (Evans, 1996).

For example, suppose that, after years of teaching a required personal fitness course for high school seniors, you are suddenly forced to eliminate it in favor of an elective program consisting of alternative activities (e.g., cycling, in-line skating, and rock climbing).

▪ Significant change almost always results in a loss of some kind. In the case of the preceding example, it would be hard to deny your feeling of loss.

▪ Change immediately threatens your sense of competence. New practices, procedures, and routines can make you feel inadequate and insecure. It is understandable that a different approach might make you feel that the personal fitness course is outmoded and that you have been ineffective.

▪ Whatever improvements change may promise, it almost always increases confusion. The previous roles, rules, and policies of the required fitness course are replaced with the confusion, loss of control, and politics associated with completely different kinds of elective activities. With this uncertainty, it is often unclear who is responsible for what. You become confused and often distressed.

▪ Innovation is supposed to be better for everyone, but the reality is quite different; it often leads to conflict and friction. Changing from a required fitness-based course to an elective, alternative activities program invariably produces winners and losers, at least initially. Conflict is both natural and inevitable when resources are limited and competing priorities are at stake.

Change exposes you to risks and failures. How do you respond to potential failure? Do you cope, or do you try to avoid the situation? Although there may be no external rewards for change, the internal reward is knowing you are honoring the professional imperative to change and your own need to be a change agent.

As a change agent you must first make the case for innovation by emphasizing the seriousness of the problem and the rightness of a solution. You must challenge other teachers' acceptance of and comfort with the status quo. Those who may be resisting change need help, however difficult and unpleasant it may be to provide, to move from loss to commitment, from old competence to new competence, from confusion to coherence, and from conflict to consensus. Your goals as a change agent are to (1) make change meaningful (through the use of continuity, time, and personal contact); (2) develop new behaviors, skills, beliefs, and ways of thinking (by providing training that is coherent, continual, and personal); (3) realign structures, functions, and roles (by clarifying responsibility, authority, and decision making); and (4) generate broad support for change (with critical mass, pressure, and the positive use of power).

Redesign of Learning and Teaching

In the 1980s a federal report titled *A Nation at Risk: The Imperative of Educational Reform* (National Commission on Excellence in Education, 1983) raised public concern about the condition of education in the United States. Overall, the quality of education was rated as poor. Supposedly, students were not learning, and teachers were not teaching effectively. As a result, the 1980s saw massive school improvement efforts through legislation at all levels, school effectiveness projects, and instructional intervention approaches. Many so-called reforms that became popular included magnet schools, proficiency testing, school choice, alternative schools, vouchers, charter schools, and year-round schools.

Just three years after *A Nation at Risk,* another pivotal report was issued titled *A Nation Prepared:*

Teachers for the 21st Century (Carnegie Task Force on Teaching as a Profession, 1986). One of its recommendations led to the creation of the National Board for Professional Teaching Standards (NBPTS) in 1987. The mission of the NBPTS was to (1) establish high and rigorous standards for what accomplished teachers should know and be able to do; (2) develop and operate a national voluntary system to assess and certify teachers who meet these standards; and (3) advance related education reforms for the purpose of improving student learning in U.S. schools (National Board for Professional Teaching Standards, 1994).

An overwhelming set of expectations, it seemed, had been placed on schools in general, and on students and teachers in particular. It prompted a historic education summit in 1989 involving the president and the nation's governors. Educational goals were adopted, and a National Education Goals Panel was established to measure their progress. *America 2000: An Education Strategy* (U.S. Department of Education, 1991) delineated the elements needed to ensure that students would be prepared to function in our diverse society and to compete in a global economy. The goals stated that by 2000 (1) children would enter school ready to learn; (2) the high school graduation rate would be 90%; (3) students would leave 4th, 8th, and 12th grades having demonstrated competency in challenging subject matter; (4) teachers would receive the professional development needed to help students reach the other goals; (5) U.S. students would be first in the world in math and science; (6) every adult would be literate; (7) schools would be free of drugs and violence; and (8) schools would promote partnerships to increase parent involvement.

The other critical element of the education equation—the teacher—was not forgotten. The Interstate New Teacher Assessment and Support Consortium (INTASC) developed model standards for teachers (Darling-Hammond, 1992).Because of the general applicability of the standards for teachers of all disciplines and all levels, many professional societies, state departments of education, and university schools of education have used the standards in their attempts to define teaching excellence.

Ultimately, the shift toward student and teacher competencies led to the passage of the Goals 2000: Educate America Act (PL 103-227) in March 1994. With educational standards written into federal law, a national standards movement emerged. The National Education Standards Improvement Council (NESIC) demanded that all students achieve the standards, given adequate support and sustained

effort. Voluntary content standards were developed on a kindergarten through 12th grade (K-12) continuum across various school subjects, including physical education. In addition, a National Commission on Teaching & America's Future was appointed in 1994. After two years of intense study, it concluded that "the reform of elementary and secondary education depends first and foremost on restructuring its foundation—the teaching profession" (National Commission on Teaching & America's Future, 1996, p. 5). The commission recommended that rigorous standards be developed and enforced for teacher preparation, initial licensing, and continuing development.

Then, despite the unprecedented challenges of an economic recovery and the war on terrorism following the events of September 11, 2001, President George W. Bush secured passage of the landmark No Child Left Behind Act of 2001 (PL 107-110). The NCLB Act was the most sweeping reform of the Elementary and Secondary Education Act (ESEA) since it was enacted in 1965. This reauthorization of ESEA was built on the accountability and assessment requirements established in 1994 and the overall direction of states' education policy initiatives over the past decade: (1) setting standards, (2) measuring students' progress against standards, (3) providing help for struggling students, and (4) holding schools accountable for results. It redefined the federal role in K-12 education to help close the achievement gap between disadvantaged and minority students and their peers.

The NCLB Act (accessible through its official Web site, www.NoChildLeftBehind.gov) requires statewide accountability systems covering all public schools and students. These systems must be based on challenging state standards in reading and mathematics, annual testing for all students in grades 3 through 8, and annual statewide progress objectives ensuring that all groups of students reach proficiency within 12 years. Assessment results and state progress objectives must be broken down by economic status, race, ethnicity, disability, and English proficiency to ensure that no group is left behind. School districts and schools that fail to make adequate yearly progress (AYP) toward statewide proficiency goals will, over time, be subject to improvement, corrective action, and restructuring measures aimed at getting them back on course to meet state standards.

Clearly, student learning and teaching practices of the past are not adequate to meet the demands of the 21st century. Standards are now the cornerstone of educational reform. The questions that arise are,

What should students know and be able to do as a result of their physical education program? and, What knowledge and skills are essential for effective teaching in physical education? Answers to these questions are offered in chapter 2, which provides comprehensive sets of content standards for the K-12 physical education curriculum and standards for physical education teachers.

Education Trends

Education responds constantly to societal forces that operate in the larger culture. Many people expect schools to solve our "social ills." We are confronted with substance abuse, changes in family patterns, violence, terrorist-related threats, poor fitness among youth, childhood obesity, sexually transmitted diseases, greater inequities between the "haves" and the "have-nots," a TV and video game generation, high crime rates, poor school performance, abused children, teenage suicide, disruptive behavior, changing ethnic and linguistic diversity, and high dropout rates, to mention a few. The increased demand for accountability that has resulted from these challenges has changed education through curriculum reform, school restructuring, and teacher empowerment for school-based management decisions. For example, along with programming for students with disabilities, special attention is being given to new categories, such as students from diverse ethnic groups, at-risk students, and gifted students.

Although there are many hopeful trends in education, five major trends are particularly relevant to curriculum design. As a professional educator, you need to acknowledge, respond to, and become a part of these trends, which are addressed throughout this book. Your own beliefs and values should be challenged as you review these trends. Try to imagine how each might influence your physical education curriculum design.

Culturally Responsive Teaching

Experts in the field continually call for a "culturally responsive pedagogy" (Villegas, 1991); that is, teaching that considers cultural differences. Skills are needed to accommodate the diversity found in cross-cultural school settings. For example, language differences are evident in school systems. Ethnic minorities account for over 20% of the school-age population. In the year 2000, two-fifths of all school-age children were minorities.

Teachers don't need to be members of students' cultural groups, but they must be sensitive to the cultural characteristics of learners and accommodate these characteristics in the classroom. In addition to being knowledgeable about various cultures, teachers need to be aware of their own biases. They must also realize that bias and prejudice are learned responses.

Teachers should respect cultural differences, believe that all students are capable of learning, and see themselves as capable of making a difference in their students' learning. These competencies could serve as performance criteria to ensure that teachers can instruct effectively in a multicultural society.

Current research also shows that students need a fast-paced curriculum that actively engages their attention. It should be stimulating rather than over-simplified, especially for those students performing below expectation. This does not mean that drill, practice, and rote-learning activities should be rejected, but that they should be integrated into realistic learning experiences. The curriculum should challenge students to develop higher-order skills and knowledge. In physical education, for example, students might invent their own games or develop original sport strategies on their own or as part of a team.

Curriculum goals should enrich students' past learning, not correct deficiencies. When teaching familiar material, teachers should use several approaches so that students can monitor their own learning. Because active participation is a stimulus for learning, activities should involve *all* students. To accommodate cultural differences, flexible and varied teaching styles are needed. Whereas some students learn well through direct instruction, others benefit more from self-directed activities, cooperative group projects, and reciprocal (peer) tasks.

Physical education, because of its social orientation, can play a leading role in eliminating discriminatory practices and promoting multicultural understanding. Physical education and sport have a rich heritage that has evolved from cultures throughout the world. The different racial and ethnic contributions or the unique contributions of women could be highlighted. A collection of articles edited by Chepyator-Thomson (1994) in the *Journal of Physical Education, Recreation & Dance* can help you develop strategies for addressing multiculturalism in physical education programs. This focus on culturally responsive teaching will assist you in responding to the issues of diversity raised by the wave of social and cultural change in the United States.

Inclusive Education

The concepts presented here are usually associated with special education categories. However, they are applicable to students for whom a "regular" education is not considered appropriate, regardless of the reasons. The *full inclusion* model places and instructs all students in regular settings regardless of the type or severity of disability. Multidisciplinary teams of professionals representing different specialties (e.g., reading, math, motor development) bring their collective skills and knowledge together to provide personal programs for each student. The full inclusion model completely eliminates special education, which some view as an unnecessary "second system" (Villa & Thousand, 1990).

The legislation that guides policies and practices for educating students with disabilities is the Individuals With Disabilities Act (IDEA), first passed in 1970 and has been reauthorized ever since. IDEA mandates that placement of students with disabilities be based on the concept of the least restrictive environment (LRE). This means that, to the maximum extent appropriate, students with disabilities are educated with students without disabilities. Separate programming should occur only when the nature or severity of the disability is such that education in the regular setting cannot be achieved with the use of supplementary aids and services (Block, 1994).

Inclusion has implications for subject areas such as physical education (motor development) because of the need to create an individualized curriculum.

Unfortunately, many schools interpret least restrictive environment as a continuum of placements rather than as a mandate to provide appropriate support in the regular setting. Inclusion focuses on everyone's abilities and possibilities, not on deficiencies and limitations. A collection of articles edited by Craft (1994) in the *Journal of Physical Education, Recreation & Dance* offers ideas and strategies to help you meet the challenge of inclusion.

Developmentally Appropriate Practices

Many factors determine the quality of educational programs (e.g., cost-effectiveness, range of activities, satisfaction, achievement). A primary determinant, however, should be the degree to which teachers apply principles of child and adolescent development. In other words, is the program *developmentally appropriate?* By definition, developmental appropriateness is two-dimensional. Age appropriateness depends on universal, predictable sequences of growth and change that occur in all dimensions—physical, intellectual, emotional, and social. These typical developments provide a framework for program planning. Individual appropriateness refers to each person's pattern and timing of growth, as well as personality, learning style, and family background. The curriculum and instruction should be responsive to individual differences.

In physical education, developmentally appropriate practices recognize each student's changing abilities to move; they accommodate individual characteristics such as previous movement expe-

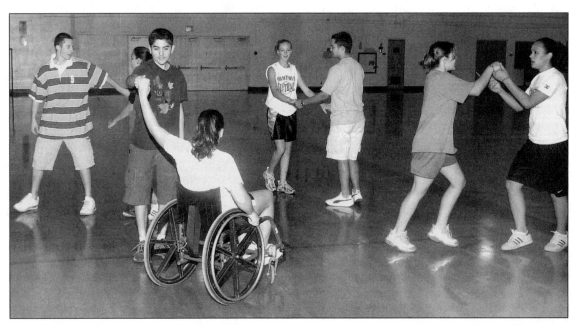

Inclusive physical education means students with disabilities are educated with students without disabilities.

riences, fitness and skill levels, and body size. Guidelines developed through the Council on Physical Education for Children (Graham, Castenada, Hopple, Manross, & Sanders, 1992) make a distinction between practices that are in the best interests of children (appropriate) and those that are counterproductive, or even harmful (inappropriate). For example, appropriate practice means that the physical education curriculum has an obvious scope and sequence based on goals and objectives appropriate for all children. It includes a balance of skills, concepts, games, educational gymnastics, rhythms, and dance experiences designed to enhance cognitive, motor, affective, and physical fitness development. Inappropriate practice means that the physical education curriculum lacks developed goals and objectives. Inappropriate curricula are based primarily on teachers' interests, preferences, and backgrounds rather than on students'. Additional information is provided in a collection of articles edited by Graham (1992) in the *Journal of Physical Education, Recreation & Dance*. Appropriate practices related to the design of physical education curriculum are identified throughout this book.

Outcome-Based Education

Excellence in education is in the spotlight; it is a national priority. Everyone seems to know how to improve schools. One idea that is ready for widespread use is the outcome-based approach, a comprehensive design for teaching and learning and instructional management. It has its roots in the earlier mastery learning and competency-based education movements. The premise is that student success is reflected in "goals reached" rather than in the student's relative advantage over other students' performances or in completion of a prescribed set of courses. The system recognizes the limitations of a fixed-time, one-shot instructional delivery approach that assumes that students who don't do well within the time allowed for initial learning are inherently incapable of doing well at all.

Clearly developed, publicly stated outcomes provide the focus for curriculum organization. The critical first step is to define desirable learning outcomes. Next, appropriate curriculum materials (learning units) are adopted. The third step is to "link," or align, exit outcomes with objectives and then with assessment instruments. Establishing this kind of congruency is a complex task when carried out correctly. The last step is to devise a way of managing the curriculum. During this phase, learning units are monitored and formal procedures are developed for revising the curriculum based on student achievement and teacher experience

The Physical Education Outcomes Project of the National Association for Sport and Physical Education (NASPE) is consistent with the described model. The guide created by the project, *Outcomes of Quality Physical Education Programs* (Franck et al., 1992), included outcome statements and grade-level "benchmarks" (competencies) that define the *physically educated person.* Then, NASPE appointed a standards and assessment task force to develop content standards and assessment material based on the *Outcomes* publication. Work of the task force was published in *National Standards for Physical Education: A Guide to Content and Assessment* (Rink et al., 1995). The document established content standards for the physical education school program (grades kindergarten, 2, 4, 6, 8, 10, and 12) and teacher-friendly guidelines for assessing the content standards. It was designed to expand and complement, not replace, the *Outcomes* publication. A general description of each content standard follows. (The revised NASPE content standards and grade-level benchmarks, expected in 2004, were not available for use in this book.)

A physically educated person

1. demonstrates competency in many movement forms and proficiency in a few movement forms;
2. applies movement concepts and principles to the learning and development of motor skills;
3. exhibits a physically active lifestyle;
4. achieves and maintains a health-enhancing level of physical fitness;
5. demonstrates responsible personal and social behavior in physical activity settings;
6. demonstrates understanding and respect for differences among people in physical education settings; and
7. understands that physical activity provides opportunities for enjoyment, challenge, self-expression, and social interaction.

Specific outcomes are associated with each part of the definition. Because the outcomes and benchmarks offer a viable framework for designing curriculum, they are treated in greater detail throughout this book, particularly in chapter 2.

Advances in Technology

Our lives are being transformed by technology. The World Wide Web has created new ways to gain information and communicate. In business, education, and everyday life, people are using personal computers, notebook computers, handheld computers, digital videodiscs (DVDs), pedometers, digital cameras, camcorders, and other technologies. Many participate regularly in electronic message systems such as interactive newsgroups, bulletin boards, chat rooms, and listservs. Software programs for word processing, databases, spreadsheets, and teacher utilities (e.g., grading programs, sign makers, awards, desktop publishing) offer practical applications for curriculum development and computer-assisted instruction (CAI).

Understanding and analyzing movement and sport skills are important aspects of physical education. Computer-based video analysis is a good technological fit because it facilitates the process of assessing and manipulating video images. It requires a VCR or camcorder, a video-capture board, and movement-analysis software, all of which is now reasonably priced (Bolt, 2000). Handheld computers (data-entry devices) are also becoming popular in physical education because of the need to collect data (e.g., attendance, scores, anecdotal notes) in the field. Data can be easily transferred to a desktop computer and stored in some type of database or spreadsheet file.

Even our means of physical activity is being transformed by technology. High-tech exercise equipment is widely available, and virtual-reality technology creates virtual activity experiences such as mountain climbing, scuba diving, or skiing without having to leave home. Following are some other examples of technology used to enhance and improve the physical education curriculum (Siedentop, 2001):

- Heart monitors track exercise patterns; collected data are downloaded to a personal computer for graphic display and analysis.

- Teachers and students use the Internet to participate in newsgroups that address the needs and interests related to physical activity.

- Teachers use videotaping to analyze and improve students' performances and their own teaching strategies.

- Courses are offered on various topics (e.g., fitness testing) that require an Internet connection, e-mail account, and Web browser.

- Companies offer complete computer-based health management systems that provide exercise evaluation, nutrition evaluation, health risk assessments, and much more.

Imagine the physical education setting of the future. Middle school students have met a series of performance criteria for tumbling skills (e.g., forward and backward rolls, headstands, cartwheels, handstands). Now they are expected to learn the roundoff, review skills, and create a routine. The following learning centers (stations) are used: (1) a DVD player to show sample floor exercise routines, (2) a camcorder to provide review and verification

Technology can enhance and improve the physical education curriculum.

of skill levels, (3) aerobic activity areas where students wear heart monitors, (4) video recording areas where students can attempt to perform the roundoff and receive feedback, (5) computers to create and display graphic representations of students' routines, (6) a DVD video camera and recorder to record routines for immediate playback and review, and (7) software programs to provide the biomechanical principles of the roundoff. The data collected at each learning center are entered into networked computers where students store individual folders (Mohnsen, 2001).

Philosophical Perspectives

A sound, basic philosophy (defined as the search for reality, truths, and proper conduct) is needed for consistency of behavior. It is made up of value assumptions that direct and guide decision making. These ultimate inferences and principles determine one's thinking and action. Thus, philosophy is important to curriculum design.

Some people view philosophy as having little practical value. This raises the question, then, On what basis are decisions made regarding daily tasks within the learning environment? Frequently, educational decision making is based on "common sense" that is inconsistent, illogical, and confusing to the student, a haphazard collection of concepts acquired unconsciously and uncritically. The resulting practices may be educationally sound, but directed toward objectives that are philosophically incompatible. Common sense is then reduced to doing what requires the least effort or what current pressures for conformity demand.

For example, attempts to integrate physical education by gender have placed males and females in the same educational setting (conformity) with a "throw out the ball" program (least effort). This so-called commonsense approach is acclaimed for its contribution to self-directed learning, independence, social responsibility, and self-confidence. Obviously, any learning gains in these aspects are unplanned and incidental at best. This trend may explain the downward trend from kindergarten to 12th grade in students' "liking" physical education. Unfortunately, in many cases negative learning accumulates across the K-12 continuum.

A solid philosophy of physical education is fundamental to quality programming. Educational philosophy should be action oriented and dynamic. It should inform an assessment of what you're doing and why you're doing it. Without a sound educational philosophy, what you're doing may actually be counterproductive to what you hope to attain. Moreover, teachers who struggle with inconsistencies between what they believe and the direction education is taking are usually unhappy, less productive, and overly critical. If the question, Where are you going? is a valid one, then so is the question, On what basis (philosophy) are you making decisions about where you are going?

All teachers should establish their own *tenets* of physical education. This section will help you do so by reviewing traditional values and beliefs, curriculum value orientations, and recent philosophical viewpoints in physical education. In addition, we present several curriculum issues in physical education that are sufficiently controversial to warrant resolution within a philosophical context. Try to determine your values. Exactly what do you believe? Ultimately, any curriculum you design should reflect your beliefs and values.

Traditional Values and Beliefs

Physical educators should ask themselves, Which philosophies merit my energy and commitment? and, Which educational goals should I pursue? Answers seem even more elusive given the accelerated rate of change in society described in the previous section. In light of change, a philosophy is needed to provide meaning to physical education. Sound educational programs will not just evolve by themselves. Physical education—all of its parts, episodes, and individual actions—must relate to a grand plan, an overall purpose.

Over the years, prevailing philosophies have been applied to educational thinking. Traditional philosophies, such as idealism, realism, naturalism, pragmatism, and existentialism, continue to influence curriculum design. They are described in table 1.1 in terms of underlying concepts (values and beliefs), general education emphases, and implications for physical education (Annarino, Cowell, & Hazelton, 1980; Bucher, 1983; Freeman, 1982).

As an outgrowth of traditional philosophies and historical events, the early 20th century was dominated by two philosophies of physical education: education *of* the physical and education *through* the physical. Education *of* the physical focused on physical fitness and its outcome of strength, power, cardiorespiratory efficiency, and agility. This narrow theory viewed bodily development and health as ends, not means. From the Civil War to the end of the 19th century, a variety of physical education programs competed for supremacy in what was

Table 1.1   Traditional Philosophies

Traditional philosophy	Underlying concepts	Educational emphases	Implications for the physical education curriculum
Idealism	■ Mind is more real than anything else. ■ Thoughts and purpose are central ("idea-ism"). ■ Mind and spirit are keys to life; people are more important than nature. ■ Values exist independently and are permanent; people have free will. ■ Reasoning and intuition help people find truth; scientific methods may be used.	■ Development of moral and spiritual values (whole, individual personality). ■ Development of mind (rational powers and reasoning). ■ Education process originates within self (student); learning is self-initiated. ■ Development of essential personality qualities (self-reliance, self-responsibility, self-direction). ■ Teacher guides development of creativity through various methods and learning environments.	■ Must contribute to intellectual development. ■ Strength and fitness acceptable if contribution is made to personality development (self-discipline). ■ Play and recreation important for well-balanced personality. ■ Activities centered on ideals (courage, honesty, fair play). ■ Teacher serves as a positive role model. ■ Teacher is responsible for program effectiveness; guidance more important than equipment and facilities. ■ Reflective thinking and analyzing problems are more important than knowing rules/terms.
Realism	■ Physical world is real; world is made up of matter. ■ Physical events result from the laws of nature. ■ Truth is determined by using scientific method. ■ Mind and body have a close and harmonious relationship; they are inseparable and neither is superior. ■ Philosophy and religion can coexist; either can be used to determine individual beliefs.	■ Development of reasoning powers. ■ Education is basic to life; develop ability to understand and make adjustments to *real* world. ■ Education is objective (teaching, testing, evaluation). ■ Educational process proceeds in a step-by-step fashion; inductive reasoning is used. ■ Scientific orientation (experimentation, demonstration, observation). ■ Measurement techniques are standardized, including testing.	■ Prepare students to adjust to the world; emphasis placed on the *outcome* of an activity. ■ Values physical fitness because of intrinsic contribution to greater productivity. ■ Activities selected on basis of scientific evidence of their worth. ■ Learning process emphasizes drill and orderly progression; skills separated into component parts. ■ Desirable social behaviors can be developed through sports programs; winning is *not* stressed. ■ Play and recreation contribute to life's adjustments because of contact with real world.
Naturalism	■ Physical world is the key to life; everything we experience is part of nature. ■ Nature, as the source of value, is reliable and dependable; anything is of value if it is workable.	■ Satisfy basic, inborn needs of the individual. ■ Educational process governed by each person's rate of mental and physical development; learning "readiness." ■ Education considers physical and moral development, not just mental; balanced learning.	■ Activities are a source of overall development, not just the physical. ■ Self-directed activities primary for an adjustment to environment. ■ Play, resulting from children's interests, teaches desirable social behaviors.

Traditional philosophy	Underlying concepts	Educational emphases	Implications for the physical education curriculum
Naturalism		▪ Students are involved in own education; self-activity and self-expression. ▪ Teacher guides by example and demonstration; use of informal inductive methods. ▪ Use of rewards and reprimands as part of learning process.	▪ Self-improvement rather than competition; people compete against themselves. ▪ Development of whole person. ▪ Students develop at their own rates. ▪ Teacher must know students' needs and rates of development.
Pragmatism	▪ Basic reality is change caused by human experience; experience is the only way to seek truth. ▪ Success is the only judge of the value and truth of a theory; a workable theory is a true theory.	▪ Learning occurs through experience (inquiring, observing, and participating). ▪ Education is for social efficiency; prepare students to take their places in society. ▪ Education is child centered rather than subject centered; individual differences are important (learning rates). ▪ Problem solving necessary to face world of change; learning is purposeful and creative. ▪ Evaluation of adjustment to environment. ▪ Education is a broad process to develop *total* person (mind, body, soul).	▪ Varied activities result in more meaningful experiences; creative problems and challenges are encouraged. ▪ Emphasis on social value of physical activities (interaction). ▪ Needs and interests of students determine curriculum. ▪ Problem solving and self-discovery develop creativity (dance and movement education). ▪ Teacher is a motivator while student is "learning by doing." ▪ Standardization discouraged; individual differences stressed in spite of goal to integrate individual into society.
Existentialism	▪ True reality is human existence; people are what they cause for themselves. ▪ Persons determine their own systems of values; values must be self-disciplined.	▪ Discovery of inner self; develop one's own beliefs. ▪ Individual process used because of different rates and ways of learning; schools provide environment only. ▪ Curriculum is centered on individual student who selects subjects and methods. ▪ Teacher serves as a stimulator; encourages students to discover their own truths. ▪ Teach personal responsibility; students learn to assume responsibility for the consequences of their decisions. ▪ Affective approach (attitudes and appreciations); difficult to measure.	▪ Freedom to choose activities and programs. ▪ Balanced and varied activities to satisfy individual needs and interests; diversity. ▪ Play is used to develop creativity; "winning" has little value. ▪ Self-knowledge is important (individual/dual activities, self-testing); through self-discovery, students know themselves. ▪ Teacher serves as counselor and guide; shows students available options; students feel more responsible for education.

called the "battle of the systems." Several European systems, more appropriately called gymnastics or physical training, had been introduced in the United States, in the process discarding a nationalistic goal (i.e., military training, the well-being of the state) in favor of an emphasis on physical and health benefits. This functional approach maintained its importance into the 20th century. The contemporary education-of-the-physical philosophy is represented by the concept of physical fitness.

Many of the late 19th- and early 20th-century programs were rivaled by the "new physical education." Known as the natural program or natural gymnastics, it represented the education-*through*-the-physical philosophy, a sharp contrast to education *of* the physical. Achieving the general goals of education through physical activity became the dominant theme during the first half of the 20th century, and remains in the minds of many as the philosophical basis for action. Nineteenth-century terms such as *physical culture, physical training*, and *gymnastics* gradually disappeared in favor of terms such as *citizenship, social values, character development*, and *intellectual functioning*.

The education-through-the-physical philosophy gained considerable acceptance as a result of Americans' valuing of individualism and competitiveness, the democratic principles of American society, and the broad goals of education. These factors transformed physical education from a one-dimensional gymnastics program to a multidimensional sport-activity program. Although this approach would seem to hold much potential, it has not produced the desired results. By trying to satisfy all of the goals of education—that students become physically fit, skilled, emotionally stable, knowledgeable, good citizens, and socially responsible—the meaning of physical activity has suffered. Unfortunately, attainment of these goals has been *implicit* (assumed) as a result of participation in physical activity. Education through the physical is realized only when physical activity is directed *explicitly* toward the accomplishment of such goals.

Curriculum Value Orientations

A value-free curriculum created through an objective, scientific approach is impossible to achieve. One's basic beliefs and philosophical perspective end up being reflected implicitly. Instead, one should recognize the importance of making values explicit in the curriculum development process. Traditionally, the sources of these values have been the needs and goals of society, the needs and interests of learners, and subject matter (physical education)

content. Curriculum designs vary depending on the value given to each of these sources. Jewett, Bain, and Ennis (1995) described different value orientations that consider the three curriculum sources. As you review these orientations, try to identify examples of how these values are reflected in actual practice.

Disciplinary Mastery

Knowledge of the important subject matter content is the top priority in the disciplinary mastery orientation. Schools transmit the cultural heritage and knowledge that is of most worth. The goal of the curriculum is to make students healthy, responsible citizens with the knowledge, competencies, and attitudes needed to participate in a free-market capitalistic society. The "back to basics" focus in the 1980s reflected this orientation. The current emphasis on proficiency testing and national achievement standards also shows a commitment to disciplinary mastery.

Evaluation of schools based on student performance in language arts (reading and writing), math, and science illustrates the importance of achieving competence in the identified disciplines. In physical education curriculum development, subject matter content is still the predominant value orientation. Emphasis is placed on basic movement skills, fitness content, and movement forms that constitute our popular sports, recreation, and athletic activities. This value orientation represents a philosophy that defines a body of knowledge. Some educators believe that school physical education should be organized around a more academic framework of sport sciences or sport studies, focusing on subdisciplines such as exercise physiology, kinesiology, motor learning and development, sport sociology, sport psychology, and sport humanities. Such an academic framework would certainly change the content and sequence of activities in physical education.

The concept of a body of knowledge in physical education is relatively new. The decade of the 1970s is often called the "disciplinary years." Subdisciplines emerged that are well established today, including exercise physiology; kinesiology and biomechanics; motor learning, control, and development; sport sociology; sport psychology; sport pedagogy; and sport humanities (history, philosophy, and literature) (Siedentop, 2004). Along these lines, the American Alliance for Health, Physical Education, Recreation and Dance (1987) published the *Basic Stuff* series, in which six disciplinary areas (exercise physiology, psycho-social, motor learning, motor development, kinesiology, and humanities) were used to structure the knowledge base for physical education along with corresponding concepts and learning activities.

Self-Actualization

Respect for the worth and dignity of the individual underlies the self-actualization value orientation. The curriculum is directed toward individual growth in self-direction and self-management abilities. A high priority is given to individual autonomy and the responsibility for setting personal goals. With a self-actualization orientation, individual excellence takes top priority over subject matter and social concerns. In physical education, developing self-confidence and a positive self-concept is often hidden within a more explicit focus on "playing the game." However, teachers who value self-actualization are skillful in designing movement, sport, and fitness tasks that increase student goal setting, self-understanding, and personal decision making.

Social Reconstruction

In this value orientation, social reform is an important goal. Societal needs take precedence over individual needs. Curriculum is seen as the vehicle for creating a better society. Vocational programs provided to develop occupational skills for jobs created by new technology are an example of the social reconstruction orientation. Other examples are special programs developed around social problems such as race relations, cultural diversity, gender identification, family living, drug use and abuse, and AIDS prevention. This orientation assumes that the curriculum is a bridge between what is and what might be. Physical educators who see sport as a microcosm of life, for example, would select goals for developing interpersonal sensitivity, awareness of others, and group social skills. Evaluation focuses on group interaction, cooperation, and responsibility.

Learning Process

From this value orientation, how we learn is as important as what we learn. One reason for this emphasis is the knowledge explosion. Because covering all of the important knowledge is impossible, developing the process skills for continual learning becomes a high priority. Greater use of high technology also highlights the need to focus on the learning process to cope with rapid change. The communications revolution is changing our lives as well as our schools and their curricula. Problem-solving abilities and higher-order thinking skills are increasingly needed. Physical educators who value learning processes use effective progressions for skills, sport, and fitness learning. They are skillful in designing movement, sport, and fitness problems and tasks within indirect or guided discovery formats. For example, students may examine ways of solving movement problems when they navigate an unfamiliar obstacle course that requires balancing, crawling, climbing, leaping, and jumping.

In the learning process value orientation, students solve movement problems in an obstacle course.

Ecological Integration

The primary goal of the ecological integration curriculum is the personal search for meaning. This value orientation incorporates the "celebration of self" and the holistic person integrated within the total environment. The ecology of the natural environment is respected and preserved. The curriculum is directed toward a social as well as biological ecology. The school is responsible for developing individuals who function effectively as citizens of a single world. Teachers with an ecological integration perspective attempt to balance the social, student, and subject matter emphases within the curriculum. Physical educators possess knowledge of a wide range of skill, sport, and fitness activities and the ability to select activities to meet the needs and interests of students within particular settings. The curriculum matches the right content to the right student at the right time.

Recent Viewpoints in Physical Education

Since 1950 a series of societal and professional developments (e.g., post-Sputnik education reform, the Civil Rights movement, the Vietnam War, the fitness renaissance, specialization in universities) has caused philosophical diversity and turmoil. Serious questions have been raised concerning the assumptions underlying physical education, sport, and fitness. Siedentop (2001) identified the major philosophical movements of the recent past.

As you read about them in the following sections, compare your philosophical beliefs and values to those implicit in these movements.

Human Movement

Since its development in England in the late 1930s, the concept of human movement has received wide acceptance. In the United States, this occurred from the late 1950s onward. Within a short time, human movement has gained significant recognition as a basic philosophical approach to physical education. Numerous terms have been used to describe this concept, such as, *movement education, movement exploration, educational dance, educational gymnastics,* and *developmental movement.*

This philosophy was the impetus for the disciplinary structuring of physical education. Subdisciplines such as sport physiology, biomechanics, sport sociology, and sport psychology developed under the human movement framework. Schools began to advocate a more open approach to teaching physical education. Exploration and guided discovery were promoted in a noncompetitive and success-oriented climate, particularly at the elementary level. In a contemporary curriculum, movement concepts and skills that provide the basis for understanding all movement are grouped as follows (Kirchner, 1992):

- *Body awareness:* what the body can do, the shapes it can make, the way it balances, and transfer of weight

Human movement viewpoint: students are exploring body and spatial awareness, qualities, and relationships through the use of body socks.

■ *Spatial awareness:* skills relating to moving in different directions, moving at different levels, and spatial aspects of movement

■ *Qualities:* how the body can move and skills relating to speed, force, and flow of movement

■ *Relationships:* the connection between the body and other bodies or objects

In chapter 3 you will see how the movement education curriculum model (page 57) reflects this philosophical viewpoint.

Humanistic Sport and Physical Education

The social turmoil of the 1960s and 1970s helped create humanistic psychology, which advocated the full development of individual potential. Personal growth and self-development were central to humanistic education. Affective learning, values clarification, and social development were considered as important as academic development.

For physical education, primary goals were organized around self-expression and interpersonal relations. This meant an emphasis on cooperation instead of competition, enjoyment instead of excellence, process instead of product, and expression instead of obedience. In chapter 3 you will see how the humanistic and social development curriculum model (pages 59-60) reflects this philosophical viewpoint.

Play Education and Sport Education

Educational psychologists regard learning that results from intrinsic motivation to be more substantial than learning brought about by external incentives. Intrinsic learning offers the best opportunity for retention, transfer, and positive self-concept. Learning that occurs naturally without the instruction of others is often called play, and interfering with or directing learners' play is thought to jeopardize natural development. To many, this philosophical viewpoint epitomizes the potential of physical education because a person at play is engaged in an inherently meaningful experience. The goal of play education, then, is skill acquisition and affection for the activity itself. However, play education was never really accepted as a prescription for the physical education curriculum.

A more recent philosophical orientation, sport education, is an extension of play education. Because sport is an institutionalized form of competitive motor play, it should be the subject matter of physical education. Sport education includes the organization of students into teams, scheduled competition among teams, a culminating event, and

record keeping. In chapter 3 you will see how the sport education curriculum model (pages 60-61) reflects this philosophical viewpoint.

Experiential and Adventure Education

Values such as challenge, compassion, personal development, and social and environmental responsibility are consistent with the current focus on experiential and adventure education. School physical education programs reflect these values by offering activities such as cycling, in-line skating, climbing, hiking, backpacking, and challenge courses. Many of these activities are conducted outside the regular class schedule and away from school facilities. The concept of "expedition" is central to this philosophy. Expeditions have clear goals, a series of challenges, an extended time frame, and an authentic form of assessment that is built into the challenge. In chapter 3 you will see how the wilderness sports and adventure education curriculum model (page 61) reflects this philosophical viewpoint.

Fitness Renaissance and the Wellness Movement

The popularity of fitness is probably connected to quality-of-life issues (e.g., consumer advocacy, ecological control, human rights). The philosophical foundation for this movement is the concept of wellness, a broad, holistic view of health. Instead of being defined as the absence of illness, wellness means that sickness and disease are prevented. This philosophy stresses that physical, mental, and emotional health are interrelated. In the same way, work, play, and social life need to be approached positively with appropriate balance. Positive criteria include coping with everyday stress, feelings of accomplishment, an active lifestyle, and feelings of contentment. Fundamental to this philosophy is the notion of lifelong involvement in fitness and sports. In chapter 3 you will see how the fitness education curriculum model (page 58) reflects this philosophical viewpoint.

Curriculum Issues

Whether you realize it or not, conflicts and problems are created by your beliefs about physical education. Conflicts are commonly referred to as issues. On the other hand, problems are situations that are perplexing or difficult. Issues, which generally appear in advance of problems, consist of two or more opposing views; issues are controversial. Although problems are not controversial, their solution could give rise to issues because several solutions may be possible. You can resolve them in advance by designing your curriculum so that what

A school physical education program values adventure education by offering in-line skating.

you believe (philosophy) and what you plan to do (practice) are congruent.

A controversial issue that has existed for a long time is whether physical education should be required or elective. There are at least three possible answers: that it should be required, that it should be elective, or some combination of the two. Regardless of the answer, however, problems are created. In a required program, teachers must determine what should be required. In an elective program, teachers must decide how to schedule a variety of activities. In a combined program, teachers must decide the ratio of required to elective hours. Clearly, resolving the issue can lead to many different problems.

Gender-integrated learning is another interesting example. Because most people agree that the concept of gender integration is a good one, no issue exists. Without an opposing view, there exist only problems, such as selecting gender-neutral activities, establishing fair performance standards, and creating equal competition.

Several issues can be raised with respect to curriculum design. Their resolution requires continual evaluation, analysis, reflection, and justification. Issues resolution also serves another useful purpose—as a basis for policy making. As we will see in chapter 5, deciding on policies is an extension of curriculum development. A distinction is made between student policies (i.e., grading, credit, dress, attendance, waivers, equivalencies) and organization and administration policies (i.e., frequency, class time, class size, "pull-out" from physical education,

access and control of facilities, transition, health and safety emergencies, and supervision).

The issues discussed in this section represent conflicting ideas and values specific to physical education. Ultimately, your curriculum should reflect your acceptance of one of the opposing views. For each of the issues addressed, you will notice that we support one of the opposing views. See if you agree. Which side of the issue do you really support?

Student vs. Content Emphasis

Attempts have been made to meet the needs and interests of students through changes in physical education class organization and processes. However, these changes (e.g., block scheduling, elective programming, independent study options, team teaching, minicourses, and differentiated staffing) have not necessarily focused on students' needs. Organizational changes do not ensure attention to needs. The issue is one of selection. Is content selected to meet cognitive, affective, and psychomotor needs, or is it assumed that these needs are satisfied by a content-based curriculum?

When a curriculum emphasizes content (activities), the chance of "cheating" students is increased. More likely, students will be expected to satisfy arbitrary content standards instead of having their needs met by the content. For example, we cannot assume that team sports will meet all students' needs for social adjustment and responsibility (e.g., teamwork, fair play, tolerance). Consider, for example, the way males treat females, particularly during the initial phases of a game. Males have learned to expect inferior performances from females. The experience of some students, then, may be poor self-image, lack of confidence, and dependence. In many instances, isolating those of lesser ability so they can experience success should take precedence over adhering strictly to a content-based curriculum.

Individualized vs. Group Focus

When someone says that a curriculum is "student centered," what exactly does that mean? The fact is, students can be addressed either individually or as a group. Locke and Lambdin (1976) distinguished between cohort and individualized instruction.

> Cohort instruction includes any pedagogical strategy in which the teacher teaches the same thing to all students at the same time by the same method and requires all students to practice in the same way, at the same pace, and for the same length of time. Students are subject to the same kinds of standards and the same criteria for evaluating achievement. (Locke & Lambdin, 1976, p. 13)

Presumably, in cohort instruction teachers can't attend to individual needs and interests that deviate significantly from those selected, which are usually the average of the group. Theoretically, subject matter and group characteristics are paramount in cohort instruction.

> Individualized instruction includes any pedagogical strategy in which the teacher adjusts objectives (ends) or content, instruction and practice (means), or all of those elements, to produce the most appropriate match with the characteristics of individual students. The process of matching educational ends and means to student needs and interests may be controlled by the teacher, the student, or both. In short, this process adjusts learning to the student. (Locke & Lambdin, 1976, p. 14)

In individualized instruction, teachers deal with students as individuals even though their unique needs and interests will be diverse. Theoretically, individualized instruction focuses on the learning characteristics of individuals. Class transactions, however, would not occur on a one-on-one basis. In a traditional physical education curriculum, individuals have been manipulated to satisfy group arrangements; organization by groups has been undisputed. Instead, physical education should represent equal opportunity for learning. When imposed, group values, group objectives, group arrangements, and group standards contradict the meaning of physical education.

Gender Integration vs. Gender Segregation

This issue shouldn't exist, but some teachers still believe in gender-segregated programming. Clearly,

Recognizing individual characteristics is an important consideration in large groups.

the separation of males and females belongs to the past. However, separatists will continue to perpetuate the myths and misconceptions associated with the separate domains of men and women. The conflict is created between those who want to examine sexuality, gain insights into self-concepts, and promote gender-neutral curricula and those who want to maintain the "folding curtain" separating the boys' gym from the girls' gym.

Inclusion vs. Exclusion

Although physical education has been acclaimed as providing "learning for all," this principle of inclusion is not borne out in practice. Instead, physical education has been designed for exclusion. Students are excluded when they stand in line waiting their turn, must meet some minimum standard based on chronological age, compete against someone of superior ability and inevitably fail, engage in tasks that require prerequisites not yet learned, and attempt activities in which entry-level abilities are deficient. Mosston and Mueller (1974) offer a vivid illustration of exclusion and inclusion:

> For example, let us look at the high jump as an educational experience. We are not concerned here with the use of the high jump in athletic competition, where the exclusion principle is congruent with philosophy and practice. We are examining the design of the high jump experience in light of the stated educational objective. After several "innings" the rope or bar excludes most participants. If the raising of the bar continues, it soon excludes all! The design of the activity is obviously hardly congruent with the philosophy of physical education. . . . Place the bar at a slant, so that it represents variable height; with its intrinsic quality of *inclusion*. (p. 100)

Multiple vs. Single Learning Modes

Individuals learn in a variety of ways, and some teaching approaches may actually interfere with a student's individual learning style. With this as the premise, value judgments need not be imposed about how people learn, and learning may be individually tailored. Many physical educators fail to realize that using only one style of teaching—particularly the direct style—excludes alternative student response and fails to accommodate variability in learning and performance.

Although all students should seek outcomes, physical educators must respect the diversity among learners. Not all students can achieve out-

comes in the same manner. The theory of multiple intelligences (Gardner, 1993) suggests that people possess several capacities for learning. The curriculum could be organized around the following seven domains of learning. Outcomes should be selected for each intelligence depending on content and individual student preferences.

- *Visual/spatial:* Relies on the sense of sight and the ability to visualize an object and create mental images (e.g., chart plays, sketch-out routine)
- *Verbal/linguistic:* Relates to written and spoken language (e.g., reactions to videos, written fitness program)
- *Logical/mathematical:* Deals with deductive thinking, reasoning, and recognition of abstract patterns (e.g., calculating energy expenditure, biomechanical analysis of sports skills)
- *Bodily/kinesthetic:* Involves using the body to solve problems, create products, and convey ideas and emotions (e.g., outdoor education challenges, designing free-exercise routine)
- *Musical/rhythmic:* Includes recognition of environmental sounds and sensitivity to rhythm and beats (e.g., creating a dance step, moving to a drumbeat)
- *Interpersonal:* The ability to understand and work effectively with others (e.g., planning a cooperative game, role-playing fair play)
- *Intrapersonal:* Refers to knowledge about and awareness of one's own emotions and self (e.g., reflective fitness journal, describing feeling of being a pro golfer)

In the main, physical educators still adhere to and defend the stimulus–response learning model; nonetheless, independent, alternative student response and discovery learning are preferable. Teachers must develop alternative teaching styles if the meaning of physical education is to become a reality.

Personalized vs. Authoritarian Approach

Meeting individual needs and interests may not be new, but problems have arisen regarding the approach. The dominant authoritarian style—direct teaching (highly structured, teacher-centered) and "throw out the ball" programming (teacher-directed, recreational) seems to conflict with individualized approaches. A more personalized style is desirable. A wide variety of personalized approaches can help you practice what you preach.

The change from an authoritarian style depends on a change in the assumptions underlying many programs. The actions of many physical educators reveal the following basic assumptions:

- Students must be required or forced to engage in physical activity (i.e., they are lazy).

- Students must be extrinsically motivated by grades, awards, and points (i.e., they are unconcerned about physical activity).

- Students must have decisions made for them, (i.e., they are incapable of making decisions regarding physical activity).

These assumptions should be dismissed. Physical education can develop students' abilities to direct themselves, make decisions, and accept responsibility for those decisions. The curriculum should move the student along a continuum from dependence and irresponsibility to independence and responsibility. The assumptions underlying such an approach are as follows:

- Students are interested in physical activity experiences.

- Students are by nature self-motivated and self-advocates.

- Students are self-reliant and assume personal responsibility for decisions.

- Students need a system of education to develop rational decision-making abilities.

Explicit vs. Implicit Learning

Quality learning occurs when experiences are planned and sequenced toward the attainment of desired behaviors. Some educational outcomes, particularly psychosocial outcomes, are concomitant with skill development and knowledge acquisition. This so-called concomitant learning addresses interests, attitudes, appreciations, respect for others, self-confidence, responsibility, decision-making ability, and independence. These qualities also fit the recent resurgence of character education in the school curriculum. On the other hand, disrespect for others, circumvention of rules to win, exploitation of others' weaknesses, intimidation, intolerance, poor self-image, irresponsibility, and dependence are also examples of concomitant learnings. Whether helpful or harmful, positive or negative, concomitant learnings are inevitable.

For example, a teacher might explicitly believe that differential treatment of students on the basis of ability, gender, race, or social class is unjustified. In basketball, the teacher may use drills and lead-up games that don't result in differential treatment.

However, during the game itself, the teacher may make no adjustment or modification that considers individual differences. The result might be that three out of five players dominate the game. Although the reason is likely to be ability, other factors such as gender and race compound the problem. When such distinctions are promoted, students may implicitly question the value of basketball as a "team" sport.

The issue here is whether students should learn educational outcomes explicitly or implicitly. For the most part, desirable psychosocial values are learned implicitly, supposedly as a result of participation in physical activities. However, unless the desired value is planned for and taught *explicitly*, its attainment is impossible to predict. It can't be learned by chance. Let's say you want to teach the concept of shared responsibility. You will have to select content and learning experiences that will enable your students to practice the concept. Simply playing doubles tennis may not be sufficient. Students should be taught the responsibility of partner play, the use of individual and partner strengths and weaknesses, and the consequences of failing to recognize each other's responsibilities.

Summary

If you believe in achievement-based education and the role of the *designer* in curriculum development, you have much to consider in terms of the foundation for the physical education curriculum. The contemporary contexts for change (standards-based education, high-stakes testing, and accountability) combined with highly significant trends in education (i.e., culturally responsive teaching, inclusive education, developmentally appropriate practices, outcome-based education, and advances in technology) suggest that we may need an almost total restructuring of learning and teaching. The implications for developing a relevant, results-oriented curriculum are somewhat staggering when you consider these demands.

Philosophy is an important context for curriculum designing. Ultimately, it provides the basis for making practical decisions. This chapter offered a review of traditional values and beliefs, curriculum value orientations, some recent viewpoints in physical education, and several curriculum issues that should help you establish your own tenets of physical education. After testing your beliefs and values against existing mandates and standards (in chapter 2) and some popular curriculum models (in chapter 3), you should have the knowledge and skills necessary to develop an achievement-based curriculum.

Making It Work

Have you achieved the expected outcomes (see page 4) for this chapter? You should be able to establish a foundation for your physical education curriculum. Still, you may have some practical questions that need answers, such as the following:

▌ *Where do I start when developing a curriculum?* Many teachers teach things they know or can do. The idea of developing a curriculum on the basis of values, beliefs, developmental needs, and standards seems far removed from personal likes and dislikes. Hopefully, you will develop your physical education curriculum in a more purposeful manner. The best place to start is with the end in mind. That is, what do you want kids to know, be able to do, and feel as a result of their physical education experience? The end you're seeking is relative. It could be at the end of elementary or middle school, or it could be at the end of fifth grade. Ideally, all of the physical education teachers in a school district should understand all of the "ends" that are being sought and plan down from there. This means that *achievement* can truly be central to the practical design of curriculum.

▌ *Do curriculum designers really exist?* If your K-12 experiences in physical education were negative, you probably have doubts. It's true that physical education is being reduced or eliminated in many schools, in part because of weak programs and poor teaching. However, it is strongly supported in just as many schools where teachers have assumed the role of designer. Although curriculum designing may be difficult and time-consuming *at first,* it will save you effort and time in the long run. Once students learn your "system," your task becomes primarily one of curriculum refinement and revision. Besides, the wave of social and cultural changes in the United States is so great that teachers need to develop programs for increasingly diverse groups of students. To survive as a teacher in the current atmosphere of accountability, you will need to be competent in the role of curriculum designer.

▌ *Can the physical education curriculum and physical educators really change?* We'd better! There are all sorts of messages out there, but it's a good news–bad news story. The bad news is that physical education continues to be attacked because of its lack of relevance, "throw out the ball" programs, and poor teaching. In this era of high-stakes testing, physical education is often seen as nonacademic, nonessential, noncore, and frivolous. On the good side, the need for physical activity has never been greater as evidenced by the surgeon general's report (U.S. Department of Health and Human Services, 1996), NASPE's report of the shape of the nation (National Association for Sport and Physical Education, 2002), and legislation such as the Physical Education for Progress (PEP) Act, reauthorized under the No Child Left Behind Act of 2001. Although there is a tendency to resist, change is a professional imperative for survival. To overcome feelings of loss, confusion, and conflict, develop new skills, clarify roles, and create a critical mass of support.

▌ *Why should physical educators be concerned with general education trends?* We need to stop thinking that we are "outside" the school curriculum. Granted, we may be somewhat physically separated, but we have allowed ourselves to become psychologically separated as well. The result is that physical education is excluded because it is labeled as a special subject. Theoretically, changes in education should have the same impact on physical education as any other subject, and the implications of recent trends for physical education have been clearly established. For example, physical education teachers can be leaders in the "culturally responsive" movement by taking advantage of our strong social orientation. Students come from radically different social, ethnic, and racial backgrounds. Physical education, through its various forms of movement, offers a unique opportunity for students to develop the understanding and sensitivity needed to function in a diverse society. Another trend that has an impact on physical education is inclusion. Because we alone represent the physical dimension of education, our contribution to an individualized, developmentally appropriate program should be distinct. And finally, student outcome standards seem to be everywhere—at national, state, and local levels. Parents, legislators, business leaders, and others are focused on the product (outcome) of education—that is, student achievement. Physical education has responded with its own set of standards as previously identified.

■ *Is my philosophical viewpoint really that important?* Without a set of beliefs and values, you run the risk of teaching by intuition. Usually, the result is inconsistent and illogical behavior leading to confusion. Curriculum designing is a conscious act. Given all of the available options, you should know what you believe and value and what you do not. If necessary, write down your beliefs and values as they come to mind. It might help to compare your list with known philosophies to see if there are any discrepancies within your viewpoints. Then, make sure that your curriculum decisions are a true extension of these beliefs and values. That's easier said than done! But if you subscribe to the achievement-based curriculum planning process proposed here, there are enough checks and balances across the curriculum components to give you some assurance.

■ *Can students' needs actually be used as a basis for curriculum design?* Of course, as long as these needs are satisfied explicitly. Cognitive and psychomotor needs are usually easier to satisfy than affective needs because they are more easily observed and measured. Don't make the mistake many physical educators make of establishing lofty affective goals (e.g., teamwork, fair play, tolerance), but not planning for them explicitly. These qualities are learned implicitly, if at all. The claim that students have met these affective needs is often false. Careful curriculum designing can help avoid this error. Without a doubt, students' needs are probably universal to any curriculum design. They may be called learner capabilities, developmental channels, or dimensions, but all of these terms are referring to the same thing. Kids *need* to develop and mature physically, intellectually, socially, and emotionally. It's difficult to argue against needs as the foundation on which curricula are built.

two

Physical Education Mandates and Standards

The following is written on the flip chart in the image:

A physically educated person

1. demonstrates competency in many movement forms and proficiency in a few movement forms

2. applies movement concepts and principles to the learning and development of motor skills

3. exhibits a physically active lifestyle

4. achieves an [...] -enhancing level of physical [...]

5. demonstra[...] [...]ial behavior in physical [...]

6. demonstrates [...] [...] for differences among people in phy[...]

7. [...] provides opportunities for

Tax levies have been defeated three consecutive times at a poor county school district. Voters claim they are disappointed with the overall quality of education and can identify with the national media attention on poor-performing schools. They are determined not to support any tax increase until there is improvement. In fact, some taxpayers are interested in seeking school vouchers or establishing charter schools as a better way to spend their tax dollars. School officials agree that a systematic approach is needed for curriculum revision. Furthermore, the state department of education has developed recommended courses of study for each subject area that include content standards and grade-level benchmarks.

32 Developing the Physical Education Curriculum

A general K-12 curriculum committee is established with subcommittees for each subject area. At the orientation meeting, it is announced that there may need to be a redistribution of time across the K-12 curriculum to accommodate those areas of greatest need. Time for language arts (reading and writing), mathematics, science, social studies, and technology would increase, but time for art, music, health, and physical education might decrease. Currently, physical education is offered 90 minutes per week (3 days, 30 minutes each) at the elementary level (grades K-5), 40 minutes daily at the middle school level (grades 6-8), and 135 minutes per week (3 days, 45 minutes each) at the high school level (grades 9 and 10 only).

Subcommittees in each subject area must propose the elements or concepts around which they will organize their curricula and the corresponding sets of goals and objectives. The physical education subcommittee, chaired by the county supervisor, includes two teachers each from the elementary, middle, and high school levels. Along with the other subcommittees, the physical education subcommittee is asked to review and become familiar with the state-level course of study. Another document is made available that outlines a set of national standards and grade-level benchmarks for physical education. Seven standards define "the physically educated person." So that the needs of all students can be addressed appropriately, the chair of the subcommittee also distributes summaries of federal mandates (Title IX, IDEA, Section 504) representing gender integration and the concept of inclusion.

Members of the physical education subcommittee realize for the first time that they have a difficult task ahead of them. How important is the amount of time allocated for physical education, and what should it be across the K-12 continuum? Should they give greater weight to the recommended state-level course of study than to the national standards and benchmarks? To what extent are these outside guidelines being imposed on the school curriculum? How can they factor the impact of federal mandates into the curriculum? What process should they use to identify the elements or concepts around which to organize the physical education curriculum?

EXPECTED OUTCOMES

This chapter will help you recognize educational mandates and standards that have an effect on the physical education curriculum. After reading this chapter, you will be able to do the following:

1. Identify the legal requirements that focus on providing opportunities for students regardless of race, gender, cultural background, socioeconomic status, or disabling condition
2. Acknowledge the role of contemporary trends and issues in society that influence curriculum decision making
3. Analyze the standards-based emphasis in education and the corresponding national content standards and benchmarks in physical education
4. Determine state-level standards that must be considered when designing the local (district, grade-level) physical education curriculum

Developing an achievement-based curriculum is a practical activity that reflects a set of values and beliefs about the role of physical education in society and schools. This philosophical perspective, and ultimately the curriculum itself, is challenged by the political, legal, social, and cultural contexts that affect schools and students. Schools are bombarded today with increasing legal mandates, national standards, state-level requirements, local initiatives, and demands for accountability. They are given the task of solving many of our social ills. Schools are expected to deal with, for example, many personal, family, and social factors and issues such as substance abuse, HIV/AIDS education, violence, child abuse, teen pregnancy, suicidal tendencies, character education, serving breakfast and lunch, literacy, unemployment, single-parent homes, gifted and talented programs, technology, career counseling, incarceration of students, economic survival, bilingual language development, inclusion of students with disabilities, high-stakes performance testing, cultural diversity, vocational training, and, maybe, maintaining a healthy and physically active lifestyle.

Expectations of schools, usually imposed without regard for cost and time, place extreme pressure on curriculum decision makers. That is, when unfunded mandates are issued, schools are forced to take on more responsibility, but the mandates do not address what should be replaced. Physical education faces a clear and present danger! The message to physical educators should be obvious: We can wait to be reduced (or eliminated), or we can be proactive by justifying our role in the overall curriculum and showing the viable use of school time. Two features of the achievement-based curriculum are its emphasis on superior results for all students and time analysis.

The curriculum designer should be an informed decision maker. The wave of reform initiatives in education was traced in chapter 1 (pages 11-12). Most recently, the No Child Left Behind Act of 2001 (NCLB Act) reflects a consensus on how to improve the performance of U.S. elementary and secondary schools while at the same time ensuring that no child is trapped in a failing school. The NCLB Act, which reauthorizes the Elementary and Secondary Education Act (ESEA), is based on the following set of principles and strategies: (1) increased accountability for states, school districts, and schools; (2) greater choice for parents and students, particularly those attending low-performing schools; (3) more flexibility for states and local educational agencies (LEAs) in the use of federal education funds; (4) a stronger focus on reading and math, especially for our youngest children; and (5) an emphasis on teaching practices that have been proven to work. For physical education, there are provisions for competitive grants to LEAs and community-based organizations for initiating, expanding, and improving physical education programs for kindergarten through 12th grade students to make progress toward meeting state standards for physical education. The money is for equipment and support to enable students to participate actively in physical education and for staff and teacher training and education.

You need to know what is being imposed on physical education from outside the school both for curriculum and *liability* reasons. We will present several legal requirements that deal with providing educational opportunities for all students. In all likelihood, you will also need to consider state-level requirements that are the result of legislative action, state departments of education policy, or both. Because the school curriculum is used to transmit and transform society, we will also introduce the aspects of a diverse society that influence curriculum decision making. We will explore the national standards movement in greater depth including an analysis of the national content standards and grade-level benchmarks in physical education. As a curriculum designer you should also be aware of existing state-level standards for physical education, some of which we identify for illustrative purposes. Finally, we provide a sample district-level physical education curriculum that takes into account these mandates and standards.

Education Mandates

As a curriculum designer you will be (and perhaps are already) confronted with a myriad of legal, education policy, and social mandates that you must factor in when designing your physical education curriculum. These mandates deal with the moral, ethical, and professional obligations to create a safe and appropriate learning environment that is responsive to all students regardless of gender, race, ethnicity, social class, physical and mental ability, and preferred learning style. This section provides a review of these legal requirements, state-level requirements, and selected trends and issues around student diversity.

Legal Requirements

The desegregation of schools probably represents the most significant legal act affecting all of education. More recently, other federal laws to eliminate discriminating practices were enacted that have a direct impact on physical education programs. Because of the nature of physical education, you have additional legal and professional responsibilities. This section covers each of these aspects.

Gender Integration
Nearly every segment of our society contributes to differential treatment of males and females. Unfortunately, teachers and schools transmit discriminatory attitudes and practices in settings that are supposed to provide the skills to live in a democratic manner. However, equal educational opportunity is clearly a slow and difficult process. Attempts to eliminate discrimination on the basis of gender have faced the same obstacles as the attempts to eliminate discrimination on the basis of race.

Title IX of the Education Amendments Act of 1972 prohibiting gender discrimination in education represented a positive action toward the elimination of arbitrary distinctions between boys and girls, men and women. Furthermore, the concept of physical coeducation is characterized by a changing view and commitment to equal opportunity. Although this change is mandated by the law, its impetus for action must come from the physical educator. Modifications of attitudes and practices are based on sound logic and scientific inquiry that lead to a clear rationale for curriculum design and implementation.

The reactions of physical educators to Title IX have been polarized. Those at one end of the continuum refuse to admit that discriminatory practices in physical education ever existed. They view the philosophy underlying Title IX to be highly inappropriate. Logistics, different interest patterns, and gender-related activities particular to physical education are often given as other reasons for the appropriateness of gender-separate classes. Those at the other extreme are convinced that blatant and conscious discrimination has occurred throughout the history of physical education. In particular, access to physical activities has been denied to females. Certain games, activities, and sports, for example, were considered more appropriate for males (e.g., football, soccer, weight training, wrestling, baseball), and others were considered more appropriate for females (e.g., dance, field hockey, volleyball, self-defense). Innovative curriculum reform lies somewhere between these extremes.

The physical education curriculum must comply with the moral, ethical, humanistic, and legal requirements of Title IX. Programs, courses, and activities may not be offered separately on the basis of gender, and students cannot be required to complete or be refused said programs, courses, or activities on such a basis. The following regulations influence the nature of physical education:

■ Students in physical education classes or activities may be grouped by ability as assessed by objective standards of individual performance developed and applied without regard to gender. For example, a pretest of tennis skills (forehand, backhand, serve) might reveal that students fall into one of four descriptive levels: novice, apprentice, proficient, or distinguishable. Instruction and activities could be focused on these levels.

■ Separation of students by gender is permitted *within* physical education classes or activities during participation in activities in which the purpose or majority of the activity involves bodily contact. For example, males and females can be separated during the application phase (game play) of football and basketball, but not necessarily during warm-up activities, lead-up games, drills, or practice routines.

■ Single standards of measuring skill or progress may be used only if they do not have an adverse effect on members of one gender. For example, if a standard results in one gender scoring high and the other scoring low, the standard is discriminatory and therefore inappropriate. Normally, the differences within genders are greater than the differences between genders. That is, the difference between the lowest- and highest-performing male and the difference between the lowest- and highest-performing female is often greater than the difference between the lowest and highest males and females.

Including Students With Disabilities

Physical education can help students with disabilities acquire critical lifetime leisure skills, including behavior skills, and encourage them to continue to participate in active recreational pursuits outside of school (Block, 1994). In landmark legislation, the Education for All Handicapped Children Act of 1975 (Public Law 94-142) mandated free and appropriate education, including physical education, for all eligible children ages 3 through 21. The reauthorization of this law as the Individuals With Disabilities Education Act (IDEA) provided specific guidelines and practices for educating students with disabilities. Another important mandate is Section 504 of the Rehabilitation Amendments (Public Law 93-112). It is often called the nondiscriminatory clause. Qualified students must be given access to school programs (e.g., interscholastic athletics, intramurals, clubs) with appropriate accommodations.

The individualized education program (IEP) is one of the most important aspects of IDEA. The IEP is a written statement for each child with a disability that details the specially designed instruction to meet that child's unique needs including present performance, annual goals, services to be provided, transition services as required, dates and duration, and evaluation procedures. The law requires that physical education services, specially designed if necessary, be made available to students declared eligible by the IEP process and that these be free, appropriate, and in the least restrictive environment (LRE). Because physical education was included as part of the special education definition, physical education is a *direct,* and therefore required, service.

Gender integration is one of the legal requirements a curriculum designer must address.

Basically, LRE means that, to the maximum extent appropriate, children with disabilities are educated in the same environment in which students without disabilities receive their education, including physical education. Appropriate placement in regular settings might require the use of supplementary aids and services (Sherrill, 1998).

LRE consists of a continuum of placements ranging from regular physical education to adapted physical education. If regular physical education is the appropriate placement, then accommodations must be determined (e.g., frequency of instruction, location, types of cues, equipment adaptations). Placement decisions are covered in greater detail in chapter 7.

Since the passage of PL 94-142, educators have made several attempts to operationalize the LRE concept. Most recently, the concept of inclusion has been popularized as the way to carry out LRE. Inclusion is the practice of educating all students, including students with significant disabilities, in regular education settings. Providing adapted equipment, specialized instruction, and personnel is critical. Also, regular and special education staffs work collaboratively to provide appropriate and meaningful programs for all students. The belief is that everyone belongs, is accepted, is valued, and is supported by peers, staff, and community members. Advocates of full inclusion point out the advantages of regular socialization experiences. In physical education, each student is viewed as simply another student in the class who may learn and move differently from others. All students are viewed as individuals with unique objectives who may be on different levels of the curriculum, need different challenges and different instruction to meet their unique motor and fitness needs, and need varying amounts of supports to ensure meaningful participation and success in all physical education activities (Block, 1994).

A discrepancy exists, however, between the intent and adoption of inclusion and its implementation. Many schools have embraced inclusion to reduce the cost of personnel, materials, and equipment. All students with disabilities are placed in the regular program, but then the school fails to provide the appropriate services. The challenge of LRE requirements and failed attempts at accommodating students with disabilities places additional responsibility on today's curriculum designer.

Professional Responsibility

Physical education teachers are concerned with other forms of legal responsibility. *Liability* means that schools assume responsibility for the well-being of their students. Because physical education often involves activities that carry some risk, teachers need to take proper precautions to safeguard students from those risks. If teachers act in reasonable, prudent ways, they minimize the chance of being found guilty of inappropriate practices or behavior. The present era of lawsuits has resulted in physical education teachers being even more attentive to potential areas of liability

Using adapted equipment allows students with disabilities to be included in physical education.

such as unclear procedures, lack of supervision, deviations from curriculum plans, safety aspects when designing instruction, the entry-level skills of students, grouping techniques, and equipment and facilities (Siedentop, 2001).

Several aspects of legal and professional responsibility have direct implications for designing the physical education curriculum. When designing a curriculum, you should give adequate consideration to the adequacy of your resources. By following a well-articulated curriculum, you are giving yourself important protection in terms of legal liability. Make sure you have the following as well (Jewett, Bain, & Ennis, 1995):

- Evidence that students are physically able to participate

- Activities that are appropriate to students' ages and abilities

- Professional endorsement of the activities and school board approval of the curriculum

- Qualified teachers and staff for instruction and supervision

- Correct instruction and warm-up prior to student participation, particularly in activities with inherent risks

- Adequate facilities and equipment

State-Level Requirements

The legislature, department of education, office of public instruction, and board of education in each state establish requirements, separately or in combination, that cover a broad array of policy areas such as curriculum content, instructional time, graduation requirements, special needs regulations, performance testing, number of school days, school funding formulas, and teacher licensure. These requirements vary significantly from state to state. As a curriculum designer you should be aware of those policies that affect the physical education curriculum. The purpose of this section is to illustrate how two relevant areas (model curriculum and performance testing) are handled in selected states. You will need to look carefully into your own state-level requirements.

Model Curriculum

A common practice at the state level is to provide a framework for the development of educational programs. The mandate usually comes in the form of legislative or state board of education action that requires local school districts to develop and implement said programs. The framework accommodates the flexibility needed to establish programs that are responsive to local needs. In this section we will discuss the frameworks from Michigan and Ohio.

If a high-risk activity is included in the curriculum, teachers need to be sure safety precautions are in place.

Michigan's exemplary physical education curriculum (EPEC) was developed under the guidance of the Michigan Governor's Council on Physical Fitness, Health and Sports (2000). The mission of EPEC is to develop, test, and disseminate materials and procedures that enable schools to achieve the public health goal of promoting lifelong physical activity. EPEC provides students with the fitness levels; motor skills; activity-related knowledge; and personal, social, and attitudinal characteristics they need to be active for life. The potential contributions of physical education in each of these four content areas are as follows:

Physical Fitness

∎ Development of fitness, especially aerobic capacity and strength of the low back and abdominal area, is essential to lowering the risk of disease and to lowering health care costs both now and in the future.

∎ The association between physical activity and physical fitness is strong. It is reasonable to assume that physically active (fit) children are more likely to become physically active (fit) adults.

Motor and Leisure Skills

∎ Movement ability is an essential prerequisite to seeking and obtaining fitness through participation in a broad range of activities.

∎ People who are unskilled tend to avoid participation in physical activity, thereby impairing their ability to obtain the beneficial effects of activity.

∎ Providing children with the skills to participate in a variety of physical activities is essential to the public health goal of promoting lifetime physical activity.

Cognitive Understanding

∎ Knowing the effects of physical activity and inactivity, how to prevent and care for activity-related injuries, and how to control the body in space contributes to an individual's motivation to be active and to manage movement safely and effectively.

∎ Preparing children to systematically plan and execute the right kinds and amounts of physical activity is essential to the public health goal of promoting lifetime physical activity.

Personal and Social Attitudes

∎ Physical education, though not alone in the responsibility to foster positive personal and social attitudes (e.g., cooperation, self-concept, responsibility, and best effort), provides a unique setting in which children can learn these key life skills and incorporate them into their daily lives.

The K-5 curriculum includes 35 objectives dispersed across the four content areas with 51 lessons per grade. At the middle school level (grades 6-8), the program assumes daily physical education with 45-minute classes. The personal conditioning unit, for example, provides 20 sessions. The objectives of this unit are reviewed, practiced, and reinforced in a personal conditioning "strand" for 15 minutes on the 115 days that are not part of the unit.

Ohio's model for competency-based physical education (Ohio Department of Education, 1999) is a resource tool that incorporates community-, district-, county-, and statewide expertise to foster high-quality, locally developed educational programs. The Ohio General Assembly directed that boards of education of city, local, and exempted village school districts implement competency-based education programs in mathematics, science, reading, writing, and social studies for grades K-12. The legislation further directed the state board of education to develop other curriculum areas as appropriate. The board determined that physical education was to be developed.

Legislation in Ohio requires that all state models provide the following components: (1) performance objectives (what students should know and be able to do), (2) instructional objectives (knowledge, skills, and concepts used for instructional plans), (3) assessment strategies and methods (to assure continuous monitoring of student progress), and (4) intervention services (supplemental activities to remediate, reinforce, or support student learning). The Ohio physical education model identifies four major competencies:

- *Overall challenges:* Defining questions, making decisions, and setting goals related to physical education challenges

- *Accessing information:* Assessing, evaluating, and using information, products, and services related to fitness

- *Refining skills (practice):* Developing, evaluating, and refining psychomotor knowledge and skills

- *Communication:* Reassessing, communicating, and reframing questions and advocating fitness

The Ohio model also identifies three content areas for physical education: total fitness, motor skill development and movement, and lifetime sport and leisure skill development. Subcategories (strands) expand the focus and serve as organizers for each content area. The competencies, content areas, and strands, which are all interrelated, are integrated throughout the physical education curriculum from pre-K to grade 12. Overall program-level objectives, strands, and student objectives and competencies for each content area are shown in table 2.1.

Performance Testing

Over $500 million is spent annually in the United States to develop, administer, and score statewide education tests. The nature of these high-stakes tests vary markedly in terms of the subjects and grade levels tested, types of test items, structure and frequency, and exit requirements. Regardless of any

differences, the primary intent is clear: to establish a strong foundation for a performance-based educational system that holds its schools accountable for student achievement. Although the most common areas of testing are reading, writing, mathematics, science, and social studies, other subjects are emerging as test areas including health and physical education. Curriculum designers must recognize any mandated performance tests because of the role of assessment in the achievement-based approach to curriculum design.

The Washington state assessment system (WSAS) includes a standardized testing program that focuses on essential academic learning requirements (EALRs), content standards that provide broad achievement indicators for the state, districts, schools, and individual students (www.k12.wa.us/assessment/AssessSyst.asp). The state also supports the development of classroom-based assessments, tied to the EALRs, that help guide day-to-day instruction. The Washington assessment of student learning (WASL) requires students to both select and create answers to demonstrate their knowledge, skills, and understanding in each of the EALRs. The assessments in health and fitness, available for use in 2005, will be structured around the following standards and components:

1. The student acquires the knowledge and skills necessary to maintain an active life: movement, physical fitness, and nutrition. To meet this standard, the student will

    1.1 develop fundamental and complex movement skills, as developmentally appropriate.

    1.2 safely participate in a variety of developmentally appropriate physical activities.

    1.3 understand the concepts of health-related physical fitness and develop and monitor progress on personal fitness goals.

    1.4 understand the relationship of nutrition and food nutrients to physical performance and body composition.

2. The student acquires the knowledge and skills necessary to maintain a healthy life: recognize patterns of growth and development, reduce health risks, and live safely. To meet this standard, the student will

    2.1 recognize patterns of growth and development.

Table 2.1   Ohio's Model for Competency-Based Physical Education

Content areas and strands	Competencies			
	Overall challenges	**Accessing information**	**Refining skills**	**Communicating**
Total fitness • *Physical activity and personal fitness:* Extend knowledge and skills in this area • *Cardiovascular health:* Examine various dimensions of cardiovascular health • *Flexibility:* Exhibit flexibility in movement forms • *Muscle strength/endurance:* Demonstrate competence in muscular strength and endurance	Achieve and maintain a healthy level of physical fitness	Correlate fitness-performance results with personal and lifetime health; evaluate current research on what is needed to maintain minimum fitness standards	Practice competencies that support lifetime wellness	Report how fitness affects overall wellness: disease protection and prevention, stress management, weight management, longevity, employability
Motor skill development and movement • *Body image:* Examine various dimensions of body image and self-concept • *Locomotor skills:* Demonstrate competence in locomotor skills • *Manipulative skills (through grade 3); motor skill analysis (grades 4-12):* Demonstrate manipulative skills • *General space:* Manage general space	Critique movements; apply lessons and offer feedback	Investigate what discipline-specific information will improve performance	Demonstrate movement competencies in a wide array of psychomotor skills	Report on knowledge and skills that will improve motor skills performance
Lifetime sport and leisure skill development • *Self and others:* Examine the benefits of social interaction on wellness • *Individual sports:* Demonstrate competence in individual sports • *Games and team sports:* Demonstrate competence in group games and team sports • *Lifetime activities:* Implement lifetime physical activities	Develop a personal lifetime health and fitness plan that incorporates physical, mental, emotional, and social components	Investigate rules, strategies, skills, and safety factors for physical activity—outdoor pursuits, individual, team; investigate participation *and* recreation options	Perform at best personal level in physical activities; be responsible for own actions in a social or sport setting	Advocate the benefits of life-long physical activity and its contribution to wellness

2.2 understand the concept of control and prevention of disease.

2.3 acquire skills to live safely and reduce health risks.

3. The student analyzes and evaluates the impact of real-life influences on health. To meet this standard, the student will

3.1 understand how environmental factors affect one's health.

3.2 gather and analyze health information.

3.3 use social skills to promote health and safety in a variety of situations.

3.4 understand how emotions influence decision making.

4. The student effectively analyzes health and safety information to develop health and fitness plans based on life goals. To meet this standard, the student will

   4.1 analyze health and safety information.

   4.2 develop a health and fitness plan and a monitoring system.

Trends and Issues of Diversity

The school setting has changed dramatically over the past several decades. The minority student population in schools is approaching 50%. Many adolescents maintain a physically inactive lifestyle, due in large part to an information-based, technological society. Teachers must be able to adjust their planning and teaching to accommodate the wide range of individual differences in terms of race, primary language, cultural values, religion, lifestyle, gender, sexual orientation, social class, physical and cognitive ability, and learning style (Jewett, Bain, & Ennis, 1995). Providing *total* equity in physical education is not easy.

Attempts to forge a society based on equality and mutual respect via the education system are obvious. Desegregation, legal mandates, and programming such as multicultural, bilingual, and character education make it clear that schools are playing a serious role in this *affirmative* action. Thus, designing an individualized curriculum for a diverse class is a difficult but essential task. The thought of an affirmative curriculum is even more challenging to the curriculum designer. Although many teachers perceive students to be alike, this illusion of homogeneity should be replaced by the reality of heterogeneity. Hellison and Templin (1991) illustrated the wide range of student skills, interests, attitudes, and backgrounds:

> Billy wants to be there, Mary doesn't. Suzi is an exceptionally skilled athlete, Joey has difficulty with any physical activity. Danny is back in school after two suspensions, Karen has a perfect attendance record. Pam is epileptic, Larry is learning disabled, and Dave has a congenital heart defect. Tom constantly complains, and Don brings the teacher an apple every day. Andrew is a 4-foot, 5-inch ninth-grader, and Jack is a 6-foot, 5-inch ninth-grader. Kay's father is the CEO of one of the country's largest companies, and they live in the suburbs; Sue lives with her divorced mother in the inner city, and they are on welfare. (p. 27)

Developing a knowledge and awareness of student diversity is one thing. Doing something about it is another. The physical education curriculum provides opportunities for all students to experience a wide range of activities that suit individual needs. To start, it's important to know the categories that define the common characteristics of people or groups. These general terms, which seem to be socially acceptable, are described in table 2.2 along with some implications for the physical education curriculum (Glatthorn, 1993; Jewett, Bain, & Ennis, 1995; Melograno, 1996). There is a tendency to deal with issues of diversity by looking at single categories. However, the problems facing students, and teachers, are really complex combinations of two or more of these elements. Remember that the proposed achievement-based approach to curriculum design focuses on quality programming that produces superior results for all students.

Standards-Based Movement

Chapter 1 addressed the redesign of learning and teaching, the roots of which have been established through the challenging national standards movement. Standards documents such as the ones published by national organizations and subject matter groups, and the federally funded documents in other subject areas, are now complete. The majority of these documents describe standards at levels of specificity that provide sufficient clarity for instruction; they serve as instruments of accountability even though the process used to validate standards is unclear and many standards are merely untested goals.

In an attempt to identify what students should know and be able to do, standards documents describe the requisite knowledge and skills, performance activities, curriculum goals, instructional strategies, and assessment options. Schools have adopted the standards, and parents want to know how their children are performing compared to the standards. In some cases, there are competing sets of standards, and they are too complex to be of any practical value. The public outcry for and political attention given to school improvement and high performance standards leaves us wondering if we are setting ourselves up for failure. However, standards may well serve as the organizing framework for curriculum development. This section presents the standards-based effort in physical education at the national level and illustrates the use of standards at the state and district levels.

Table 2.2   Student Diversity in Physical Education

Category	Description	Implications for physical education curriculum
Gender	Consists of socially and psychologically appropriate behavior for males and females sanctioned and expected within society; role expectations vary across cultures and change over time; differences in strength, size, and weight are often exaggerated and similarities ignored.	Provide opportunities for all students to experience a range of physical activities; use gender-neutral language (e.g., player) and avoid gender-negative descriptions (e.g., throw like a girl); encourage the development of skill and fitness levels that will earn the legitimate respect of students' peers and family.
Race	Socially constructed category that reflects the physical characteristics of people such as skin color, hair texture, and facial features; race does not contribute to cultural understanding since cultural groups define themselves by nationality, geography, language, and religion—factors that seldom correspond with race.	Avoid differences by the way students are grouped or the way students group themselves into squads or teams; be alert in planning and monitoring the racial composition in all activities; resist students' preference to interact with students of their own race as it is unlikely that teams made up of a single race will develop the understanding and attitudes desired to function effectively in a multiracial society.
Culture	Customary beliefs, social forms, and material traits of a racial, religious, or social group; learned, patterned ways in which a group of people think, feel, and act in solving problems of living in their environment; students are *not* "disadvantaged" or "culturally deprived" but experience *cultural discontinuity*; i.e., students with a particular set of cultural values and norms find themselves in a setting with very different values and norms.	Be aware of individualized and competitive group structures that are contrary to the more cooperative norms of some cultures; systematically vary patterns of learning experiences; empower students through experiences that involve decision making and social action skills; students from victimized groups will have higher expectations of themselves; challenge students to take learning risks and expand their horizons through problem-solving tasks; use alternative forms of assessment within learning experiences such as teacher and student as coevaluators of portfolios (e.g., logs, journals, self-checks, peer criteria task sheets).
Social class	Distinctions based on economic factors that facilitate or limit opportunities; identifies strata of society primarily on the bases of educational level, occupation of the head of the household, area of residence, and family income.	Provide access to quality programs for all students regardless of their financial ability; be sensitive to class and neighborhood differences that influence students' present skill levels and their willingness to participate in particular sports or activities.
Physical ability	Includes physically disabled, low-ability, average-ability, and physically gifted students; represents the full range of motor performance including coordination, control, and mobility.	Determine students' present level of performance; prioritize long-term goals and short-term objectives; plan and implement programs that reflect the concept of "least restrictive environment" for all students; incorporate the notion of IEPs for all students; provide appropriately challenging tasks for all ability levels; structure activities with small progressive levels of difficulty built into each task to increase each student's opportunity for success; anticipate and plan for needed interventions.
Cognitive ability	Includes mentally retarded, specific learning disabilities, slow learners, average ability, and intellectually gifted students; represents the full range of cognitive performance from simple recall to synthesizing and evaluating information.	Determine students' present level of performance; prioritize long-term goals and short-term objectives; plan and implement programs that reflect the concept of "least restrictive environment" for all students; incorporate the notion of IEPs for all students; provide appropriately challenging tasks for all ability levels; structure activities with small progressive levels of difficulty built into each task to increase each student's opportunity for success; anticipate and plan for needed interventions.

(continued)

Table 2.2 *(continued)*

Category	Description	Implications for physical education curriculum
Gifted/talented	Usually revealed by a high IQ test score; however, IQ tests are insensitive to creativity and focus on lower mental processes; other types of intelligence have emerged such as Gardner's multiple intelligences (1993) including visual/spatial, verbal/linguistic, logical/mathematical, bodily/kinesthetic, musical/rhythmic, interpersonal, and intrapersonal (see page 26 for descriptions).	Avoid the tendency to favor highly skilled students. Promote an atmosphere of inclusion rather than of elitism; entry appraisal provides the means for identifying gifted learners; select learning experiences that challenge gifted students in a mixed ability setting; recommended strategies are: • *Accelerate the pace:* Enable gifted students to progress more rapidly through learning tasks; use pace options through self-directed tasks, contracting, programmed learning, independent projects, learning activity packages, and computer-assisted learning. • *Provide for enrichment:* Offer greater depth or breadth than regular learning experiences; use content options and level-of-difficulty options; use reciprocal learning in "cluster" groups that work together in regular class on advanced topics or areas of special interest; use cooperative learning judiciously so as not to limit growth.
At-risk	Student who is in danger of failing to complete his/her education with an adequate level of skill or of dropping out of school before having achieved the skills needed for effective functioning in society; personal, family, school, and social factors include health problems, substance abuse, teen pregnancy, low self-esteem, low aspirations, suicidal tendencies, low socioeconomic status, single-parent home, low parental support, neglect and abuse at home, low academic achievement, community beset with stress and conflict, unemployment, and/or incarceration.	Learning progressively more complex skills is dependent on *success* during early stages; at-risk students often lack this prerequisite success since they resist common learning models; the humanistic/social development curriculum model (pages 59-60), with an emphasis on responsibility and decision making, has been advocated for at-risk students (Hellison & Templin, 1991); four approaches seem to be effective: • *Reciprocal learning:* This goes beyond receiving and giving feedback by peers; concept of "scaffolding" is advanced, a metaphor for support that is gradually removed when it is no longer needed. • *Cooperative learning:* Personal responsibility (individual accountability) and decision making are inherent to this approach. • *Tutoring*—One-on-one tutoring by teachers, aides, or peers is effective. • *Use of technology:* Decision making is enhanced through self-directed learning supported by technology (computers, videos, CD-ROMs).
Learning style	Ways in which students learn along continuums of dependence-independence or highly analytic-highly social; differences among students' ability to remember and follow instructions, focus on a problem, and work cooperatively.	Plan for a few highly analytical and a few highly social students, with the remainder falling somewhere in between; use analytic learning styles for problem solving and independent work, and social learning styles for cooperative learning, teamwork, and group activities; plan for and encourage students to work and learn within their nonpreferred style.

Adapted from Glatthorn, A.A. (1993). Learning twice: An introduction to the methods of teaching. New York: HarperCollins; Jewett, A.E., Bain, L.L., & Ennis, C.D. (1995). The curriculum process in physical education (2nd ed.). Boston, MA: WCB/McGraw-Hill; and Melograno, V.J. (1996). Designing the physical education curriculum (3rd ed.). Champaign, IL: Human Kinetics.

When planning their programs, teachers must address the diverse needs of their students.

National Content Standards and Benchmarks

Explicit standards for the physical education school program evolved through a series of projects. The Council on Physical Education for Children (COPEC) provided a set of developmentally appropriate practices that maximize opportunities for learning and success for all children (Graham et al., 1992). At about the same time, the outcomes project of the National Association for Sport and Physical Education (NASPE) defined the physically educated person. The definition, consisting of five major focus areas, was expanded to 20 outcome statements. This was followed by a set of attendant benchmark statements for grades K, 2, 4, 6, 8, 10, and 12 in the publication *Outcomes of Quality Physical Education Programs* (Franck et al., 1992). Each part of the definition and corresponding outcomes are shown in figure 2.1.

NASPE next appointed a standards and assessment task force to develop content standards and assessment material based on the *Outcomes* publication. Work of the task force was published in *National Standards for Physical Education: A Guide to Content and Assessment* (Rink et al., 1995). The document established content standards for the physical education school program and teacher-friendly guidelines for assessing the content standards. It was

designed to expand and complement, not replace, the *Outcomes* publication. The physical education content standards and corresponding benchmarks for grades K, 2, 4, 6, 8, 10, and 12 appear in table 2.3. They provide the answer to the question, What should students know and be able to do as a result of their physical education program? (Note: The revised NASPE content standards and grade-level benchmarks, expected in 2004, were not available for use in this book).

After reviewing table 2.3, you should realize that (1) the seven content standards serve as common themes across the curriculum, (2) the content standard is further defined within each grade level, and (3) sample performance benchmarks describe developmentally appropriate behaviors representing progress toward achieving the standard. This framework offers a vertical (sequential, progressive) and integrated structure of the physical education subject matter. We will use these standards and benchmarks throughout this book as the achievement-based approach evolves.

State-Level Standards

All states have developed or are developing standards of learning. In most cases, these standards are the foundation for statewide testing. In Virginia, for example, standards of learning (SOL) assessments are administered at different levels in reading, writing,

A Physically Educated Person

HAS learned skills necessary to perform a variety of physical activities.

1. Moves using concepts of body awareness, space awareness, effort, and relationships.
2. Demonstrates competence in a variety of manipulative, locomotor, and nonlocomotor skills.
3. Demonstrates competence in combinations of manipulative, locomotor, and nonlocomotor skills performed individually and with others.
4. Demonstrates competence in many different forms of physical activity.
5. Demonstrates proficiency in a few forms of physical activity.
6. Has learned how to learn new skills.

IS physically fit.

7. Assesses, achieves, and maintains physical fitness.
8. Designs safe personal fitness programs in accordance with principles of training and conditioning.

DOES participate regularly in physical activity.

9. Participates in health enhancing physical activity at least three times a week.
10. Selects and regularly participates in lifetime physical activities.

KNOWS the implications of and the benefits from involvement in physical activities.

11. Identifies the benefits, costs, and obligations associated with regular participation in physical activity.
12. Recognizes the risk and safety factors associated with regular participation in physical activity.
13. Applies concepts and principles to the development of motor skills.
14. Understands that wellness involves more than being physically fit.
15. Knows the rules, strategies, and appropriate behaviors for selected physical activities.
16. Recognizes that participation in physical activity can lead to multicultural and international understanding.
17. Understands that physical activity provides the opportunity for enjoyment, self-expression, and communication.

VALUES physical activity and its contributions to a healthful lifestyle.

18. Appreciates the relationships with others that result from participation in physical activity.
19. Respects the role that regular physical activity plays in the pursuit of lifelong health and well-being.
20. Cherishes the feelings that result from regular participation in physical activity.

▌ **Figure 2.1** Definition of a physically educated person and corresponding outcomes.

Reprinted from *Outcomes of Quality Physical Education Programs* (1992) with permission from the National Association for Sport and Physical Education (NASPE), 1900 Association Drive, Reston, VA 20191-1599.

mathematics, science, history and social science, and computer technology. The physical education standards of learning (Virginia Department of Education, 2001) identify concepts, processes, and skills in kindergarten through grade 10 for Virginia's public schools.

The physical education standards of learning are a guide for creating aligned curriculum and

Table 2.3 NASPE Content Standards and Sample K-12 Benchmarks

Content standards	Grade level sample benchmarks
Kindergarten	
1. Demonstrates competency in many movement forms and proficiency in a few movement forms	1. Travels in forward and sideways directions using a variety of locomotor (non-locomotor) patterns and changes direction quickly in response to a signal. 2. Demonstrates clear contrasts between slow and fast movement while traveling. 3. Walks and runs using mature form. 4. Rolls sideways without hesitating or stopping. 5. Tosses a ball and catches it before it bounces twice. 6. Kicks a stationary ball using a smooth continuous running step. 7. Maintains momentary stillness bearing weight on a variety of body parts.
2. Applies movement concepts and principles to the learning and development of motor skills	1. Walks, runs, hops, and skips, in forward and sideways directions, and changes direction quickly in response to a signal. 2. Identifies and uses a variety of relationships with objects (e.g., over/under, behind, alongside, through). 3. Identifies and begins to utilize the technique employed (leg flexion) to soften the landing in jumping.
3. Exhibits a physically active lifestyle	1. Participates regularly in vigorous physical activity. 2. Recognizes that physical activity is good for personal well-being. 3. Identifies feelings that result from participation in physical activities.
4. Achieves and maintains a health-enhancing level of physical fitness	1. Sustains moderate to vigorous physical activity. 2. Is aware of his or her heart beating fast during physical activity.
5. Demonstrates responsible personal and social behavior in physical activity settings	1. Knows the rules for participating in the gymnasium and on the playground. 2. Works in a group setting without interfering with others. 3. Responds to teacher signals for attention. 4. Responds to rule infractions when reminded once. 5. Follows directions given to the class for an all-class activity. 6. Handles equipment safely by putting it away when not in use. 7. Takes turns using a piece of equipment. 8. Transfers rules of the gym to "rules of the playground."
6. Demonstrates understanding and respect for differences among people in physical activity settings	1. Enjoys participation alone and with others. 2. Chooses playmates without regard to personal differences (e.g., race, gender, disability).
7. Understands that physical activity provides the opportunity for enjoyment, challenge, self-expression, and social interaction	1. Enjoys participation alone and with others. 2. Identifies feelings that result from participation in physical activities. 3. Looks forward to physical education classes.
Second grade	
1. Demonstrates competency in many movement forms and proficiency in a few movement forms	1. Demonstrates skills of chasing, fleeing, and dodging to avoid others. 2. Combines locomotor patterns in time to music. 3. Balances, demonstrating momentary stillness, in symmetrical and nonsymmetrical shapes on a variety of body parts. 4. Receives and sends an object in a continuous motion. 5. Strikes a ball repeatedly with a paddle.

(continued)

Table 2.3 *(continued)*

Content standards	Grade level sample benchmarks
Second grade	
2. Applies movement concepts and principles to the learning and development of motor skills	1. Identifies four characteristics of a mature throw. 2. Uses concepts of space awareness and movement control to run, hop, and skip in different ways in a large group without bumping into others or falling. 3. Identifies and demonstrates the major characteristics of mature walking, running, hopping, and skipping.
3. Exhibits a physically active lifestyle	1. Seeks participation in gross motor activity of a moderate to vigorous nature. 2. Participates in a wide variety of activities that involve locomotion, nonlocomotion, and manipulation of objects outside of physical education class. 3. Willingly completes physical education activity "homework" assignments.
4. Achieves and maintains a health-enhancing level of physical fitness	1. Sustains activity for longer periods of time while participating in chasing or fleeing, traveling activities in physical education, and/or on the playground. 2. Identifies changes in the body during vigorous physical activity. 3. Supports body weight for climbing, hanging, and momentarily taking weight on hands. 4. Moves each joint through a full range of motion.
5. Demonstrates responsible personal and social behavior in physical activity settings	1. Uses equipment and space safely and properly. 2. Responds positively to an occasional reminder about rule infraction. 3. Practices specific skills as assigned until the teacher signals the end of practice. 4. Stops activity immediately at the signal to do so. 5. Honestly reports the results of work. 6. Invites a peer to take his or her turn at a piece of apparatus before repeating a turn. 7. Assists partner by sharing observations about skill performance during practice.
6. Demonstrates understanding and respect for differences among people in physical activity settings	1. Appreciates the benefits that accompany cooperation and sharing. 2. Displays consideration of others in physical activity settings. 3. Demonstrates the elements of socially acceptable conflict resolution.
7. Understands that physical activity provides the opportunity for enjoyment, challenge, self-expression, and social interaction	1. Appreciates the benefits that accompany cooperation and sharing. 2. Accepts the feelings resulting from challenges, successes, and failures in physical activity. 3. Willingly tries new activities.
Fourth grade	
1. Demonstrates competency in many movement forms and proficiency in a few movement forms	1. Throws, catches, and kicks using mature form. 2. Dribbles and passes a basketball to a moving receiver. 3. Balances with control on a variety of objects (balance board, large apparatus, skates). 4. Develops and refines a gymnastics sequence demonstrating smooth transitions. 5. Develops and refines a creative dance sequence into a repeatable pattern. 6. Jumps and lands for height/distance using mature form.
2. Applies movement concepts and principles to the learning and development of motor skills	1. Transfers weight from feet to hands at fast and slow speeds using large extensions (e.g., mule kick, handstand, cartwheel). 2. Accurately recognizes the critical elements of a throw made by a fellow student and provides feedback to that student. 3. Consistently strikes a softly thrown ball with a bat or paddle demonstrating an appropriate grip. 4. Understands that appropriate practice improves performance.

Content standards	Grade level sample benchmarks
3. Exhibits a physically active lifestyle	1. Regularly participates in physical activity for the purpose of developing a healthy lifestyle. 2. Describes healthful benefits that result from regular and appropriate participation in physical activity. 3. Identifies at least one activity that they participate in on a regular basis (formal or informal). 4. Is beginning to be aware of opportunities for more formal participation in physical activities in the community.
4. Achieves and maintains a health-enhancing level of physical fitness	1. Engages in appropriate activity that results in the development of muscular strength. 2. Maintains continuous aerobic activity for a specified time and/or activity. 3. Supports, lifts, and controls body weight in a variety of activities. 4. Regularly participates in physical activity for the purpose of improving physical fitness.
5. Demonstrates responsible personal and social behavior in physical activity settings	1. When given the opportunity, arranges gymnastics equipment safely in a manner appropriate to the task. 2. Takes seriously their role to teach an activity or skill to two other classmates. 3. Works productively with a partner to improve the overhand throw pattern for distance by using the critical elements of the process. 4. Accepts the teacher's decision regarding a personal rule infraction without displaying negative reactions toward others. 5. Assesses their own performance problems without blaming others.
6. Demonstrates understanding and respect for differences among people in physical activity settings	1. Recognizes differences and similarities in others' physical activity. 2. Indicates respect for persons from different backgrounds and the cultural significance they attribute to various games, dances, and physical activities. 3. Demonstrates acceptance of the skills and abilities of others through verbal and nonverbal behavior.
7. Understands that physical activity provides the opportunity for enjoyment, challenge, self-expression, and social interaction	1. Experiences positive feelings as a result of involvement in physical activities. 2. Designs games, gymnastics, and dance sequences that are personally interesting. 3. Celebrates personal successes and achievement as well as those of others.
Sixth grade	
1. Demonstrates competency in many movement forms and proficiency in a few movement forms	1. Throws a variety of objects demonstrating both accuracy and force (e.g., basketballs, footballs, frisbees). 2. Hand dribbles and foot dribbles while preventing an opponent from stealing the ball. 3. Designs and performs gymnastics and dance sequences that combine traveling, rolling, balancing, and weight transfer into smooth flowing sequences with intentional changes in direction, speed, and flow. 4. Keeps an object going continuously with a partner using a striking pattern. 5. Places the ball away from an opponent in a racket sport activity.
2. Applies movement concepts and principles to the learning and development of motor skills	1. Detects, analyzes, and corrects errors in personal movement patterns. 2. Identifies proper warm-up and cool-down techniques and the reasons for using them. 3. Identifies basic practice and conditioning principles that enhance performance.
3. Exhibits a physically active lifestyle	1. Chooses to exercise at home for personal enjoyment and benefit. 2. Participates in games, sports, dance, and outdoor pursuits both in and out of school based on individual interests and capabilities. 3. Identifies opportunities close to home for participation in different kinds of activities.

(continued)

Table 2.3 *(continued)*

Content standards	Grade level sample benchmarks
Sixth grade	
4. Achieves and maintains a health-enhancing level of physical fitness	1. Keeps a record of heart rate before, during, and after vigorous physical activity. 2. Participates in fitness-enhancing organized physical activities outside of school (e.g., gymnastic clubs, community sponsored youth sports). 3. Engages in physical activity at the target heart rate for a minimum of 20 minutes. 4. Correctly demonstrates activities designed to improve and maintain muscular strength and endurance, flexibility, cardiorespiratory functioning, and proper body composition.
5. Demonstrates responsible personal and social behavior in physical activity settings	1. Makes responsible decisions about using time, applying rules, and following through with the decisions made. 2. Uses time wisely when given the opportunity to practice and improve performance. 3. Makes suggestions for modification in a game or activity that can improve the game. 4. Remains on-task in a group activity without close teacher monitoring. 5. Chooses a partner that he or she can work with productively. 6. Distinguishes between acts of "courage" and reckless acts. 7. Includes concerns for safety in self-designed activities.
6. Demonstrates understanding and respect for differences among people in physical activity settings	1. Recognizes the role of games, sports, and dance in getting to know and understand others of like and different backgrounds. 2. Through verbal and nonverbal behavior demonstrates cooperation with peers of different gender, race, and ethnicity in a physical activity setting. 3. Seeks out, participates with, and shows respect for persons of like and different skill levels. 4. Recognizes the importance of one's personal heritage.
7. Understands that physical activity provides the opportunity for enjoyment, challenge, self-expression, and social interaction	1. Recognizes the role of games, sports, and dance in getting to know and understand self and others. 2. Identifies benefits resulting from participation in different forms of physical activities. 3. Describes ways to use the body and movement activities to communicate ideas and feelings. 4. Seeks physical activity in informal settings that utilize skills and knowledge gained in physical education classes.
Eighth grade	
1. Demonstrates competency in many movement forms and proficiency in a few movement forms	1. Uses basic offensive and defensive strategies in a modified version of a team sport and individual sport. 2. Performs a variety of simple folk and square dances. 3. Displays the basic skills and safety procedures to participate in an outdoor pursuit.
2. Applies movement concepts and principles to the learning and development of motor skills	1. Explains and demonstrates some game strategies involved in playing tennis doubles. 2. Describes the critical elements of a racing start in freestyle swimming. 3. Having observed a team of elite volleyball players, describes the characteristics that enable success in serving, passing, and spiking. 4. Describes principles of training and conditioning for specific physical activities.

Content standards	Grade level sample benchmarks
3. Exhibits a physically active lifestyle	1. Participates in an individualized physical activity program designed with the help of the teacher. 2. Lists long-term physiological, psychological, and cultural benefits that may result from regular participation in physical activity.
4. Achieves and maintains a health-enhancing level of physical fitness	1. Maintains a record of moderate to vigorous physical activity. 2. Correctly demonstrates various weight training techniques. 3. Plans a circuit weight training program designed to meet physical fitness goals. 4. Participates in fitness-enhancing physical activities outside of school (e.g., gymnastic clubs, community sponsored youth sports). 5. Engages in physical activity at the target heart rate for a minimum of 20 minutes.
5. Demonstrates responsible personal and social behavior in physical activity settings	1. Identifies positive and negative peer influence. 2. Plays within the rules of a game or activity. 3. Considers the consequences when confronted with a behavior choice. 4. Resolves interpersonal conflicts with a sensitivity to rights and feelings of others. 5. Handles conflicts that arise with others without confrontation. 6. Finds positive ways to exert independence. 7. Tempers the desire to "belong" to a peer group with a growing awareness of independent thought. 8. Makes choices based on the safety of self and others. 9. Accepts a controversial decision of an official.
6. Demonstrates understanding and respect for differences among people in physical activity settings	1. Demonstrates an understanding of the ways sport and dance influence American culture. 2. Displays sensitivity to the feelings of others during interpersonal interactions. 3. Respects the physical and performance limitations of self and others.
7. Understands that physical activity provides the opportunity for enjoyment, challenge, self-expression, and social interaction	1. Feels satisfaction when engaging in physical activity. 2. Enjoys the aesthetic and creative aspects of performance. 3. Enjoys learning new activities. 4. Becomes more skilled (e.g., learning strategy, additional skills) in a favorite activity.
Tenth grade	
1. Demonstrates competency in many movement forms and proficiency in a few movement forms	1. Demonstrates a variety of proficient swimming strokes. 2. Uses a variety of clubs competently to play a round of golf. 3. Is competent with a variety of social dance forms. 4. Keeps a ball going with an opponent several times over the net in a game of tennis. 5. Plays a game of volleyball using all the basic skills and strategies of the sport.
2. Applies movement concepts and principles to the learning and development of motor skills	1. Performs a variety of dance forms (e.g., folk, country, social, and creative) with fluency and in time to accompaniment. 2. Applies biomechanical concepts and principles to analyze and improve performance of self and others. 3. Devises and performs a gymnastics routine after explaining the significance of some biomechanical principles to the skills involved. 4. Describes and demonstrates the significance of some basic physiological principles to the development of a personal fitness program.

(continued)

Table 2.3 *(continued)*

Content standards	Grade level sample benchmarks
Tenth grade	
3. Exhibits a physically active lifestyle	1. Participates in health-enhancing activities that can be pursued in the community. 2. Analyzes and evaluates personal fitness profile. 3. Identifies personal behavior that supports and does not support a healthy lifestyle. 4. Analyzes and compares health and fitness benefits derived from various physical activities.
4. Achieves and maintains a health-enhancing level of physical fitness	1. Assesses personal fitness status in terms of cardiovascular endurance, muscular strength and endurance, flexibility, and body composition. 2. Designs and implements a personal fitness program. 3. Participates in a variety of physical activities appropriate for enhancing physical fitness. 4. Evaluates personal fitness profile. 5. Meets personal fitness goals after a period of training.
5. Demonstrates responsible personal and social behavior in physical activity settings	1. Slides into a base in a manner that avoids injury to the defensive player. 2. Chooses an activity because they enjoy it and not because all their friends are in it. 3. Volunteers to replay a contested shot in tennis. 4. Walks away from verbal confrontation. 5. Acknowledges good play from an opponent during competition. 6. Listens to all sides before taking action in conflict situations.
6. Demonstrates understanding and respect for differences among people in physical activity settings	1. Discusses the historical roles of games, sports, and dance in the cultural life of a population. 2. Enjoys the satisfaction of meeting and cooperating with others of diverse backgrounds during physical activity.
7. Understands that physical activity provides the opportunity for enjoyment, challenge, self-expression, and social interaction	1. Identifies participation factors that contribute to enjoyment and self-expression. 2. Contributes meaningfully to the achievement of a team.
Twelfth grade	
1. Demonstrates competency in many movement forms and proficiency in a few movement forms	1. Participates in a tennis match using all of the basic skills, rules, and strategies with some consistency. 2. Passes the Red Cross intermediate swimming requirements. 3. Can get 9 out of 10 arrows on the target from 40 feet. 4. Navigates a kayak skillfully and safely through whitewater. 5. Uses advanced offensive and defensive shots successfully in a racquetball game against an opponent of similar skill. 6. Has the skills for a black belt in karate.
2. Applies movement concepts and principles to the learning and development of motor skills	1. Explains the overload principle and designs a personal fitness program where this principle is in operation. 2. Demonstrates several skills in gymnastics before explaining some biomechanical principles that govern the movement. 3. Designs a long-term plan for self-improvement in a movement activity and explains the relationship of physical, emotional, and cognitive factors that influence the rate of improvement. 4. Uses internal and external information to modify movement during performance.

Content standards	Grade level sample benchmarks
3. Exhibits a physically active lifestyle	1. Participates regularly in physical activities that contribute to the attainment of and maintenance of personal physical activity goals. 2. Willingly participates in games, sports, dance, outdoor pursuits, and other physical activities that contribute to the attainment of personal goals and the maintenance of wellness. 3. Identifies the effects of age, gender, race, ethnicity, socioeconomic status, and culture upon physical activity preferences and participation. 4. Understands the ways in which personal characteristics, performance styles, and activity preferences will change over the life span. 5. Feels empowered to maintain and improve physical fitness, motor skills, and knowledge about physical activity.
4. Achieves and maintains a health-enhancing level of physical fitness	1. Monitors exercise and other behaviors related to health-related fitness. 2. Maintains appropriate levels of cardiovascular and respiratory efficiency, muscular strength and endurance, flexibility, and body composition necessary for a healthful lifestyle. 3. Uses the results of fitness assessments to guide changes in his or her personal program of physical activity.
5. Demonstrates responsible personal and social behavior in physical activity settings	1. Sets personal goals for activity and works toward their achievement. 2. Encourages others to apply appropriate etiquette in all physical activity settings. 3. Responds to inflammatory situations with mature personal control. 4. Defuses potential conflicts by communicating with other participants. 5. Creates a safe environment for their own skill practice. 6. Takes a supportive role in an activity. 7. Cheers outstanding performances of opponents as well as the "favored" team.
6. Demonstrates understanding and respect for differences among people in physical activity settings	1. Identifies the effects of age, gender, race, ethnicity, socioeconomic status, and culture upon physical activity preferences and participation. 2. Displays a willingness to experiment with the sport and activity of other cultures. 3. Develops strategies for including persons of diverse backgrounds and abilities in physical activity.
7. Understands that physical activity provides the opportunity for enjoyment, challenge, self-expression, and social interaction	1. Derives genuine pleasure from participating in physical activity. 2. Enters competition or activity voluntarily.

Reprinted from Moving Into the Future: National Standards for Physical Education (1995) with permission from the National Association for Sport and Physical Education (NASPE), 1900 Association Drive, Reston, VA 20191-1599.

learning experiences. The five strands (goals) are skilled movement, movement principles and concepts, personal fitness, responsible behaviors, and physically active lifestyle. Standards of learning in each strand (goal) are sequenced and progress in complexity from grade level to grade level. They focus on the knowledge, processes, and skills needed for students to become physically educated, physically fit, and responsible in their physical activity choices and behaviors for a lifetime. Each school board is responsible for incorporating these standards into its curriculum in an instructional sequence that best serves its own students. The goals are as follows:

1. Demonstrate proficiency in all fundamental movement skills and patterns and competence in several specialized movement forms (skilled movement).

2. Apply movement principles and concepts to learning and developing motor skills and specialized movement forms (movement principles and concepts).

3. Achieve and maintain a health-enhancing level of personal fitness (personal fitness).

4. Demonstrate responsible personal and social behaviors in physical activity settings (responsible behaviors).

5. Demonstrate a physically active lifestyle, including activity within and outside of the physical education setting (physically active lifestyle).

District-Level Standards

National standards drive state standards, which in turn drive district standards. Ultimately, district-level standards serve as a framework for designing the school's curriculum. These sets of standards provide global intents and, possibly, grade-level benchmarks. They serve as the point of departure for designing the curriculum. In no way, however, do they remove the need to follow the recommended achievement-based approach. You may find that the full sets of national and state standards are unobtainable given the available resources and the amount of time for physical education. For illustrative purposes, however, we will describe a set of district-level standards.

The Long Beach Unified School District (2000) defined what all students in kindergarten through grade 12 should know and be able to do in physical education. Their mission, as defined by the California State Framework for Physical Education, is to develop a physically educated person who has mastered the necessary movement skills to participate confidently in many different forms of physical activity, values physical fitness, and understands that both are intimately related to health and well-being. Three strands are supported by nine standards that represent the knowledge base of physical education, guiding what is taught and when. Four levels of benchmarks are included (grades K-2, grades 3-5, grades 6-8, and grades 9-10). The strands and content standards are as follows (reprinted, by permission, from Long Beach Unified School District, 2000, Physical education content standards):

Movement Skills and Movement Knowledge

- Standard 1: Students will develop effective movement skills (motor learning).

- Standard 2: Students will demonstrate an understanding of the fundamentals of movement (biomechanics).

- Standard 3: Students will achieve and maintain a health-enhancing level of physical fitness (exercise physiology).

- Standard 4: Students will develop the skills, knowledge, and interest to independently maintain an active lifestyle (exercise physiology).

Self-Image and Personal Development

- Standard 5: Students will demonstrate an understanding of the stages of growth and development and their effect on performance (human growth and development).

- Standard 6: Students will demonstrate knowledge of, acceptance of, and appreciation for differences between themselves and others in regard to abilities and achievements (psychology).

- Standard 7: Students will develop a sense of appreciation and aesthetic pleasure of movement both as performers and as observers (aesthetics).

Social Development

- Standard 8: Students will demonstrate appropriate social behaviors by respecting others, appreciating diversity, and recognizing the importance of understanding other cultures (sociology).

- Standard 9: Students will demonstrate an understanding of the various influences on the evolution of a movement-related activity (historical perspectives).

Summary

Society in general, and education in particular, is extremely complex. This chapter revealed how complex schools have become as a result of education mandates (e.g., Title IX, IDEA), state-level curriculum models, performance testing, and student diversity (i.e., gender, race, culture, social class, physical and cognitive ability, gifted and talented, at-risk, and learning style preferences). One fact should be clear: There are many contexts—political, legal, social, and cultural—within which the curriculum is designed. Schools are affected from all sides through public demands for accountability, local initiatives, state-level requirements, national standards, and legal mandates. Beyond these kinds of considerations, federal involvement offers yet another level of influence. The No Child Left Behind framework, for example, articulates how to improve the performance of elementary and secondary schools based on accountability, choice, and flexibility.

Obviously, the physical education curriculum can neither be developed nor implemented in isolation. Fortunately, there is some help. First, you have available the definition of the physically educated person that includes a set of content standards and corresponding grade-level benchmarks (Rink et al., 1995). Second, you will be guided through the achievement-based curriculum process that addresses the educational imperatives discussed in this chapter. The remaining chapters are designed to give you the needed competencies to develop a responsive, results-oriented physical education curriculum.

Making It Work

Have you achieved the expected outcomes (see page 32) for this chapter? You should be able to recognize educational mandates and standards affecting the physical education curriculum. Still, you may have some practical questions that need answers, such as the following:

■ *Given all of the legal and state-level requirements, what flexibility do I have in designing my own curriculum?* There is plenty of room to plan a curriculum that meets the particular needs of your students. In reality, the legal mandates requiring equal opportunity for all students should not even be necessary. Educators have a professional and moral obligation to do what's best for all students regardless of gender, race, ethnicity, disability, socioeconomic status, ability level, English proficiency, or preferred learning style. Just look at the educational imperative underlying the No Child Left Behind Act of 2001 (www.ed.gov/offices/OESE/esea/) (http://www.NoChildLeftBehind.gov/). Because the makeup of your school is different from that of any other school, your curriculum should be customized. State-level requirements are generally in the form of global frameworks that guide the curriculum design process. The intent is not to be intrusive or prescriptive, but rather suggestive and helpful in establishing consistent goals that can serve as a basis for accountability. This is quite natural and fits the role of curriculum designer in an achievement-based process of curriculum design. You still need to establish your own goals and policies, develop a scope and sequence, develop functional assessments, evaluate and grade students, develop units and lessons, create learning experiences, and plan and carry out effective teaching.

■ *Is it possible to meet the needs of culturally diverse, at-risk, and gifted students if they're all in the same class?* Many of the approaches that have been found effective with these groups are good for all students. Your attitude toward these "special" students makes a difference. Varying the patterns of learning experiences while keeping in mind the particular needs of these students should improve student performance. Remember, think of student differences as strengths, not weaknesses. Capitalize on diversity rather than viewing differences as an obstacle to reaching learning potential. Let students help decide how differences will be handled, both for their benefit and for yours. The idea is to develop proactive experiences. You can build a sense of community right away through cooperative, noncompetitive games. However, you should be prepared to deal with racial or cultural remarks and disrespectful behavior. For example, you could talk to students one-on-one or in small conferences; use student mediators to handle disputes; and strictly enforce consequences for language, behavior, or clothing that is offensive for any reason (e.g., insulting to anyone's gender, race, socioeconomic status, cultural background, or ability level, whether limited or gifted).

■ *Should there be a standards-based national curriculum?* Some believe that physical education is in trouble because we lack a common understanding of what it is and what students should achieve. Proponents suggest that a national curriculum would provide a badly needed foundation for skills, understandings, and personal and social behaviors. Opponents fear that local needs and interests would be ignored, innovative programs would be stifled, and sports and games would dominate. Probably the best solution to this debate is to seek agreement on several curriculum frameworks and go about the business of designing a physical education curriculum that responds to local needs and interests. In many respects, that is the intent of NASPE's content standards, grade-level benchmarks, and assessment guidelines (Rink et al., 1995). You will learn in chapters 5 and 6 that local constraints would probably make a national curriculum impossible. Also, because there is no national policy about daily physical education and time, it would be difficult to operationalize a common curriculum.

■ *How do you sort out all the standards that are supposed to be considered?* It's tough. The documentation describing what students should know and be able to do is enormous when you consider all of the standards documents that have been produced at the national, state, and district levels. However, attempts have been made to synthesize the information in the national and state standards documents. For example, the Mid-continent Research for Education and Learning (McREL) has compiled these documents into a database containing standards organized into subject matter categories, including physical education (www.mcrel.org/compendium/browse.asp). Also, the Council for Basic Education has developed a similar database (www.c-b-e.org/). Finally, all states have compiled education standards across subject areas (www.statestandards.com). We strongly suggest that you use one of these inventories to help construct district-level standards or to augment the standards identified in your current state document. When you actually review any of these, look at them with a purpose. What are the trends or common aspects?

three

Physical Education Curriculum Models

B efore the start of each school year, the district organizes two half-day inservice programs for teachers. The rest of the day is used to get ready for the return of students on the third day. Usually, the inservice program consists of optional miniworkshops covering various topics, some of which are led by district teachers and some by outside professionals. This year, however, all of the district physical education teachers are required to attend a special session facilitated by the assistant superintendent for instruction. The purpose is to begin the process of developing a comprehensive K-12 physical education curriculum.

As a third-year middle school teacher, it's your first time to meet all of the elementary and high school physical education teachers. After welcoming the six elementary, four middle school, and five high school physical education teachers, the assistant superintendent leads an open discussion about what's happening in each of the buildings. You soon realize that the districtwide physical education curriculum is all over the place. Two of the elementary schools emphasize games and challenge activities, and the others seem to focus more on developmental movement but use different approaches to learning movement principles and concepts. Your middle school program looks like a traditional individual and team sports curriculum, although one of your teachers is into alternative sports such as cycling, in-line skating, rock climbing, and outdoor pursuits. At the high school, it's even more scattered. Ninth- and tenth-grade students are required to select two activities (courses) each year along with a half semester of health. The activities offered seem to be based on the teachers' preferences. One of the teachers has

been trying to focus the curriculum on personal fitness, and another teacher has been pushing something similar to sport education. The current K-12 physical education program clearly mixes several competing curriculum "models." At one point you turn to one of your colleagues and ask, "How can we possibly resolve this dilemma?" How common is this situation in school districts today? Can more than one focus exist for the K-12 physical education curriculum, or should there be agreement across grade levels? Are there limitations that you should consider before deciding the nature of the physical education curriculum? What process should you use to reach the intended outcome—a coherent, progressive K-12 physical education program? Is this situation really a problem?

EXPECTED OUTCOMES

This chapter will help you differentiate among various physical education curriculum models. After reading this chapter, you will be able to do the following:

1. Identify the underlying beliefs and primary purpose of each curriculum model
2. Recognize how the curriculum models use physical and motor skills as their medium, regardless of desired outcome
3. Analyze the degree and nature of students' involvement across the curriculum models
4. Accept the achievement-based curriculum model as the most appropriate model for curriculum decision making

Historically, the goals of physical education have reflected the popular culture. During the early 20th century, the primary goal was health and hygiene. The dominant goal of the 1920s emphasized social and recreational objectives. This was followed by the war years, during which physical fitness was almost the sole purpose because of its contribution to basic military training. The goal of total fitness was evident during the 1950s. Throughout the 1970s, human rights, individual social freedom, equality, and independence defined the social scene. Individualized needs were reflected through the goals of movement education at the elementary school level and lifetime pursuits at the secondary school level. More recently, the concept of wellness focuses on disease prevention rather than the treatment of sickness. Disease prevention measures include personal health regimens and lifestyles that emphasize fitness.

Throughout this history, various models of the physical education curriculum evolved, some as a direct extension of the dominant values at the time. Entire models or elements from different models can serve as a context for your own curriculum design. The models can help you make curriculum decisions because they represent a general set of beliefs. You will see how many of these models reflect the philosophical viewpoints described in chapter 1.

Eclectic models that contain components from several of the known models exist in most schools today. In fact, many beginning teachers have a tendency, after reviewing a number of curriculum models, to want their physical education curriculum to accomplish the goals of all of the models. Although this is understandable, the reality is that only so much time can be devoted to physical education in the overall school curriculum. Because the available time will not allow all of these approaches and outcomes to be addressed, difficult decisions must be made regarding which ones to include in the program. Failure to make these difficult decisions during the curriculum designing phase frequently undermines many curriculum development efforts. It also produces a curriculum planned from the bottom up, a concept described in chapter 4. Although many of the eclectic curricula in use in schools today are theoretically based and developmentally sound, they cannot be implemented as designed because they do not account for the actual amount of time available for instruction in physical education.

The various physical education curriculum models differ on what they emphasize and hope to produce. These differences are based on what each model assumes is the primary purpose of physical education and the role physical education should play in preparing individuals for life and their future role in society. Analysis of the various trends and models, however, does reveal a few common threads. First, to some extent, all of the models are designed to prepare students for later life and to become productive members of society. For example, the fitness education model evolved in response to the changing health profile in U.S. society that indicated a need for increased physical activity. Based on this perceived need, the model was designed to provide future members of society (today's children) with the knowledge and skills needed to develop and maintain a healthy lifestyle.

A second common thread is that all of the models use physical and motor skills as their medium, although they can differ markedly in their desired outcomes. For example, the sport education model is designed to produce skilled performers that possess an understanding and appreciation of the sport culture, whereas the focus of the personally meaningful model is to help students develop their own individual ways of finding and expressing themselves through movement.

A final thread that the various models have in common is the emphasis on student involvement, even though the nature and degree of involvement differs. For example, the sport education and activity-based models tend to be prescriptive in nature. The learning sequence and outcomes are defined, and students are expected to progress through these sequences and acquire the desired outcomes. In other models, such as movement education, the goal is still to produce proficient movers, but students are more actively involved in the process via movement exploration and problem-solving activities.

Allowing for overlap and duplication, we will discuss nine curriculum models that were derived from various sources (Harrison, Blakemore, & Buck, 2001; Hellison & Templin, 1991; Jewett, Bain, & Ennis, 1995; Lawson & Placek, 1981; Siedentop, Mand, & Taggart, 1986). Each model includes a rationale, description, and framework for design. Determine what aspects you like and dislike . . . and why! The tenth model is referred to as eclectic and is the model found in most schools. Finally, we present the achievement-based curriculum model separately from all of the other models for reasons that will be explained.

Movement Education

In searching for how to structure physical education subject matter, answers to two fundamental questions provide the content of the basic movement model: How do humans move? and, Why do humans move? Basic sequential units introduce fundamentals of movement, particularly at the elementary level. Themes involving the body and its relationship with space, time, force, and flow are used to structure the curriculum. Emphasis is placed on exploring (through guided discovery and problem solving) various movement skills in areas such as dance, games, and gymnastics. Students create ways of using their bodies to achieve certain outcomes. The curriculum could be structured around the following questions:

- Where can you move? (space)
- What can you move? (body awareness)
- How do you move? (force, balance, weight transfer)
- How can you move better? (time, flow)

Exploring movement skills in dance is part of the movement education model.

Fitness Education

Increasingly, children are inclined to sedentary lifestyles. Society and the environment make remaining active difficult. Physical fitness is essential to wellness, an enhanced dimension of health. An active lifestyle can help eliminate health risk factors that cause degenerative diseases and chronic ailments such as arteriosclerosis, high blood pressure, obesity, and low back problems. Emphasis is placed on the development of a healthy lifestyle. Fitness goals include knowledge of the effects of exercise, design of personal programs based on fitness principles, activities that develop fitness, and a commitment to maintaining physical fitness. The curriculum could be designed around the following subject matter:

- Health-related components (flexibility, cardio-respiratory endurance, muscular strength and endurance, and body composition)
- Motor-related components (balance, coordination, speed, agility, and power)
- Assessment methods for diagnosis and activity prescription across all components
- Application of principles of training and conditioning
- Nutrition, diet, and weight control
- Stress management
- Lifestyle management including the design and use of a personalized fitness program

Developmental Education

Educators have an obligation to create a learning environment that recognizes and fosters individual potential. Because students follow developmental stages and growth patterns, education should enhance cognitive, affective, and psychomotor learning. The contribution of physical education to these developmental patterns is the essence of "education through the physical." It often means that basic skills are taught at the elementary level, followed by varied activity or theme units, including lifetime sports, at the secondary level. The assumption is that participation in a wide range of activities will result in cognitive, affective, and psychomotor development, regardless of individual variation. The curriculum could be designed around the following developmental objectives (Annarino, 1978):

Organic Development

- Strength (static, dynamic)
- Endurance (muscle, cardiovascular)
- Flexibility (extent, dynamic)

Neuromuscular Development

- Perceptual motor abilities (balance, kinesthesis, visual discrimination, auditory discrimination, visual motor coordination, tactile sensitivity)
- Fundamental movement skills (body manipulative, object manipulative, sport)

Intellectual Development

- Knowledge (rules, safety, etiquette, terms, body functions)
- Intellectual skills and abilities (strategies, movement judgments, solving movement problems, understanding relationships, understanding immediate and long-range effects)

Social-Personal-Emotional Development

- Healthy response (positive reactions to success and failure, appreciation of aesthetics, tension release, fun, spectator appreciation)
- Self-actualization (awareness of capability, capacity, potential, and level of aspiration)
- Self-esteem (individual perception)

Activity-Based Education

Given the changing needs of learners, a wide variety of activities offers an opportunity to facilitate growth. Exposure to various activities enhances self-testing, exploration, and new interests. Usually, the program is organized around a series of activity units, whether required, elective, or in some combination. Typical categories of activities include team sports, individual and dual activities, outdoor and recreational pursuits, rhythms and dance, games, and popular local activities. In selecting activities, consideration is often given to teacher interest, teacher ability, student choice, facilities and equipment, seasonality, and the local culture. The curriculum could be designed around the categories and activities listed in table 3.1.

Table 3.1 Content Areas for Activity-Based Model

Individual and dual		
Aquatics • Diving • Scuba diving • Skin diving • Swimming • Synchronized swimming • Water polo Archery Badminton Bowling Conditioning • Aerobic dance • Calisthenics • Circuit training • Jogging • Rope jumping	Fencing Golf Gymnastics Handball Low-organization games Martial arts • Aikido • Judo • Karate • Taekwondo Mimetics • Sport actions • Story plays Movement exploration • Expressive • Fundamental	Racquetball Self-defense Skiing • Snow • Water Table tennis Tennis Track and field Trampoline Weight training Wrestling Yoga

Team sports	Rhythms and dance	Outdoor and recreational
Baseball Basketball Football • Flag • Touch Hockey • Field • Floor Lacrosse Soccer Speedball Team handball Volleyball	African American Ballet Creative rhythms Folk Modern Singing games Social Square Tap	Adventure tasks Angling Backpacking Camping Canoeing Cycling In-line skating New games Orienteering Rappelling Rock climbing Sailing Surfing

Humanistic and Social Development

The anxiety and insecurity produced by a rapidly changing society warrant an emphasis on humanistic and social development. Many believe that children exhibit more and more disruptive behavior as uncertainty builds. Whereas developmental education stresses total well-being, humanistic and social development emphasizes self-awareness and choice as a basis for personal growth. Physical activities are used to help students understand their personal identity. Focus is placed on both emotional concepts such as self-esteem, self-actualization, personal meaning, and self-understanding and social concepts such as interpersonal relations, sharing,

cooperation, and tolerance. A genuine, caring teacher is required who facilitates and counsels rather than one who prescribes and directs. As self-discipline emerges, students are allowed to develop and implement personal activity programs. They maintain a record of their goals, feelings, and behaviors. The curriculum could be designed around the following stages of social awareness and development (Hellison, 1995):

Irresponsibility

▪ Refuses to participate

▪ Blames others, makes excuses, ridicules others

▪ Is difficult to manage

Self-Control

■ Does not disrupt others

■ Begins to participate and learn

■ Displays fundamental self-discipline

■ Begins to accept responsibility for own actions

Involvement

■ Participates willingly in physical activity

■ Accepts challenges when participating

■ Shows enthusiasm without prompting

Self-Responsibility

■ Makes some decisions

■ Takes responsibility for consequences of actions

Caring

■ Exhibits behaviors beyond self

■ Cooperates and expresses concern for others

■ Demonstrates a willingness to help

■ Provides support for others

Sport Education

Some people think that the health and vitality of our culture is determined by the role of sport. Because sport is a higher form of competitive motor play,

it should be central to physical education. In sport education, learners are taught to be *players* in ways similar to athletic participation. Emphasis is placed on skills, rules, strategies, appreciation for play in our society, and ethical principles that define "good" sport.

Sport education may occur within individual classes, across classes within a class period, and during time outside of class previously used for drop-in or intramurals. To maximize participation, the forms of sports can be changed. Examples of modified sports are six-on-a-team soccer, three-person volleyball, "team" tennis, and three-person basketball. The curriculum could be designed around the six primary features of institutionalized sport (Siedentop, 1994; Siedentop, Mand, & Taggart, 1986):

■ *Seasons:* Sports are organized by seasons, not units; participation includes both practice and competition, and often ends with a culminating event.

■ *Affiliation:* Students quickly become members of teams or clubs; membership is usually retained throughout the season.

■ *Formal competition:* Sport seasons include formal schedules of competition interspersed with practice sessions.

■ *Culminating event:* A competitive event highlights the season and provides goals for players to work toward.

■ The sport education model maximizes student participation by modifying games, such as three-person volleyball.

- *Keeping records:* Records are publicized that provide feedback, define standards, and establish goals for players and teams.
- *Festivity:* The festive atmosphere of sport enhances its meaning and adds an important social element for participants.

Wilderness Sports and Adventure Education

Experiential learning is lacking in schools, particularly in relation to natural phenomena. Abstraction is substituted for sensory learning. Physical education offers unlimited potential when it comes to group involvement, leisure skills, personal commitment, risk, unique environments, and social relationships. Wilderness sports promote physically challenging outdoor activities such as camping, backpacking, canoeing, hiking, orienteering, cross-country skiing, snowshoeing, and cycling. Adventure education, although related to wilderness sports, is different. It involves activities in which obstacles are contrived or environments are created that challenge students to solve individual or group problems while under stress. Examples of activities include indoor and outdoor wall climbing, trust falls, cooperation games, high-ropes courses, and group initiative activities (Hammersley, 1992). Obviously, most of these activities are conducted away from school, at special times, and by special arrangements. The curriculum could be designed around the following general goals (Siedentop, Mand, & Taggart, 1986):

- Develop outdoor sports skills; enjoy the satisfaction of competence.
- Live within the limits of personal ability in relation to the environment and physical activities.
- Derive pleasure in accepting the challenge and risk of stressful physical activity.
- Develop awareness of mutual dependency of self and the natural world.
- Share experiences and learning in cooperation with others.

Conceptually Based Education

Students are always asking "why" and "how" kinds of questions. A curriculum based on concepts emphasizes knowledge and understanding. Typically, a problem-solving approach is used in laboratory and activity settings. It is expected that concepts (e.g., follow-through, receiving force) transfer to new skills and situations, and that they are learned better when taught *explicitly*. That is, the concepts are dealt with clearly and directly rather than implicitly (i.e., learning is assumed and often left to chance). Subject matter is organized around key ideas or principles, progressing from simple to more complex understanding. Concepts can be applied to all appropriate sport and movement skills. For example, students can learn the concept of "zone defense" (i.e., defending an area as opposed to a player) and its underlying meaning and then apply it to various sports (e.g., basketball, football, soccer, floor hockey, volleyball). The curriculum could be designed around the following biomechanics concepts:

- Center of gravity
- Balance factors
- Application of force
- Action on objects
- Laws of motion
- Performance analysis and adjustment

Personally Meaningful Education

The search for meaning is central to the mission of education. Personal meaning can be derived either intrinsically or extrinsically. For example, feelings of joy, pleasure, and satisfaction may be inherent to a movement experience (e.g., gymnastics routine, kicking a ball into a goal). The movement activity could also be used to reach some extrinsic goal (e.g., cardiovascular efficiency, object manipulation). This curriculum model responds to learners' individual and collective search for meaning. Concepts such as personal involvement with sports, self-directed learning, and individual human goals are associated with finding or extending personal meaning through movement activities. In other words, what meaning does movement bring to students? What purposes are served? The curriculum could be designed around the following purposes (Jewett & Mullan, 1977):

I. Individual development
   A. Physiological efficiency
      1. Circulorespiratory efficiency
      2. Mechanical efficiency
      3. Neuromuscular efficiency

The adventure education model creates environments to challenge students.

    B. Psychological equilibrium
        1. Joy of movement
        2. Self-knowledge
        3. Catharsis
        4. Challenge

II. Environmental coping

    A. Spatial orientation
        1. Awareness
        2. Relocation
        3. Relationships

    B. Object manipulation
        1. Maneuvering weight
        2. Object projection
        3. Object reception

III. Social interaction

    A. Communication
        1. Expression
        2. Clarification
        3. Simulation

    B. Group interaction
        1. Teamwork
        2. Competition
        3. Leadership

    C. Cultural involvement
        1. Participation
        2. Movement appreciation
        3. Cultural understanding

Eclectic Model

Although the nine curriculum models described in this chapter may seem sharply distinct from each other, they overlap in some ways. There is congruence, for example, given that each model treats selected dimensions of the cognitive, affective, and psychomotor domains of learning. Motor development (physical performance) is the means for seeking the intended outcomes of each model.

Schools rarely adopt one model. More frequently, they create and implement a curriculum that is more eclectic in nature with features of several models. At the high school level, this mixture often appears as units within a required program of physical education (e.g., fitness, lifetime sports, sport education) or as elective courses. Various content categories are used for courses such as (1) individual sports (golf, tennis, archery, self-defense), (2) team sports (soccer, basketball, volleyball), (3) dance (modern, folk, social), (4) outdoor pursuits (cycling, in-line skating, backpacking), (5) social development (new games, cooperative games, risk activities). Any of these options could include elements from the developmental, humanistic and social development, conceptually based, or personally meaningful curriculum models.

Elementary and middle schools generally have more standard programs. Even at this level, though, it is common to find programs that focus on movement education, fitness, social development, responsibility, beginning sports, and adventure. These programs look like the multi-activity program at the high school level, except that they use different activities. However, a large quantity of activities—however eclectic in nature—does not ensure quality (Siedentop, 2004).

Achievement-Based Curriculum

In chapter 1 we asserted that achievement-based education—high-quality programming that produces superior results for all students—is the professional imperative. Achievement-based education is not really a *curriculum* model. Instead, it's a *process* model that can be applied to any existing and future curriculum models. Achievement remains central regardless of the philosophy underlying the model. For example, the achievement-based curriculum process is useful when designing and implementing the sport education model. It would start with the question, What are you trying to achieve through sport education? Answers would include the development of sport skills, an understanding of and an ability to apply rules and strategies, an appreciation for sport in society, and the demonstration of ethical principles of sport. These goals become the organizing centers for the curriculum.

The achievement-based curriculum is a systematic process to sequentially plan, implement, adapt, and evaluate an instructional program based on essential educational goals and objectives. This process can be used for any length of instructional time (one lesson, one unit, one year, or multiple years) and for a school, an entire class, or an individual student. The process has a way of focusing teachers' efforts to improve the program. In this context, the term *curriculum* refers to that portion of the program that meets two criteria: essentiality and structure. Essential objectives are core learning for all students. Structured learning requires careful planning, sequencing, and articulation if students are to master the essential skills. Integrating these criteria along with the concepts, principles, mandates, and standards outlined in chapters 1 and 2

to form a coherent curriculum may seem difficult. However, you will discover how the achievement-based curriculum (ABC) process will help you synthesize these considerations.

Summary

In this chapter we described several curriculum models that reflect different philosophical and value orientations. Some of the models focus on physical parameters (e.g., fitness education, wilderness sports and adventure education), and others emphasize psychosocial themes (e.g., developmental education, humanistic and social development, personally meaningful education) or cognitive aspects (e.g., movement education, conceptually based education). In many physical education settings, the predominant curriculum model seems to be activity based (e.g., individual activities, team sports, games) or a combination of features from several models (eclectic). Because these models represent a general set of beliefs, they are potentially useful for making curriculum decisions.

By now you should understand that a curriculum is the combined philosophy of the teacher, the school, and the community. You should recognize how different perspectives can be represented in the physical education curriculum. However, these differences need to be meshed together in some way. ABC provides the "how to" process for doing this. Chapter 4 is devoted to the detailed examination of the ABC approach to curriculum designing.

Making It Work

Have you achieved the expected outcomes (see page 56) for this chapter? You should be able to differentiate among various physical education curriculum models. Still, you may have some practical questions that need answers, such as the following:

▌ *With so many curriculum models to choose from, which one is best?* There is no single best model. They all may be equally valuable. Your challenge is to develop your own preference, however similar it might be to one or more of the known models. Whatever it is, establish a solid rationale for its structure. That is, consider various contexts, such as student preferences, parent or guardian preferences, administrative feasibility, school district and state guidelines and standards, and developmental appropriateness. You should then develop the remaining curriculum components based on your own preference. In all likelihood, the curriculum that you deliver will be a synthesis of two or more models.

▌ *Are any of these models actually being implemented in real schools?* The majority of models are probably not being implemented. It really depends on the model and the extent to which the *pure* model is approximated during implementation. The movement education model, for example, is quite prevalent at the elementary level and is probably carried out in full in some schools. Fitness education is another model that is commonly advanced as the central theme for the physical education curriculum. The same could be said for the more traditional activity-based model that is often found at the secondary level in the form of seasonal individual and team sports. Some of the other more complex models (e.g., developmental education, humanistic and social development, conceptually based education, and personally meaningful education) are not usually found as distinct models. More often, the principles and concepts that define these models are represented explicitly or implicitly within program offerings. They are treated as part of the overall purpose of the physical education curriculum design. The other models, sport education and wilderness sports and adventure education, can be easily identified in practice because of their unique characteristics and subject matter. Both are gaining in popularity because of their relevance to students in today's society. However, the most common situation is a combination—the eclectic model.

▮ *Is the achievement-based curriculum model really the way to design curriculum?* Yes, absolutely! Although you may have established a philosophy or set of convictions, values, and beliefs that may be consistent with a known curriculum model, you will need to integrate it with the perspectives of other teachers. And, you still need to design, assess, implement, and continually improve the model. That's where the achievement-based approach comes in. It is a generic process for developing the physical education curriculum that focuses on the goals and outcomes you are seeking and how you can accomplish them within your given time period and contexts (setting). In theory, each physical education teacher has a unique combination of time and contexts that requires a unique curriculum design. That's why the achievement-based model is essential. Of course, the underlying assumption is that we are all seeking the same thing—superior results (achievement) for all students!

four

The Achievement-Based Physical Education Curriculum

You have just been hired as the new elementary physical education teacher for Chesterhill Elementary School. Prior to the first day of school, you meet with your school principal, who is also a new hire and is trying to get on top of her new job. She tells you that she cannot find a curriculum for physical education and would like you to supply her with some basic information as soon as possible. She is particularly interested in the following:

- What content you will be teaching your students for each grade this year
- How you plan to assess and evaluate your instructional objectives
- How much time you will be spending on each objective
- Your procedures for evaluating and making placement decisions for students with disabilities
- Your student evaluation plan and grading criteria

She notes that she knows you are new and probably need a few days to gather this information and asks that you give it to her by the end of the week. She also mentions that she believes physical education is very important for elementary students and will be looking forward to your first quarterly evaluation report.

Many teachers expect that when they get their first job, they will be told this information, not asked these questions. Other teachers are just handed a copy of the school district's physical education curriculum, shown the gymnasium, and expected to know these answers or to be able to figure them out for themselves. This is not the case for you, however. How are you going to respond to your principal's requests? Where will you go to look for these answers?

EXPECTED OUTCOMES

This chapter will provide you with an introduction to the achievement-based curriculum (ABC) model and explain how it can be used to develop and implement a functional physical education curriculum. After reading this chapter, you will be able to do the following:

1. Recognize that the ABC is a process and understand how it can be used to develop a physical education curriculum

2. Identify the five components of the ABC model and how they are interdependent

3. Differentiate between the concepts of planning-down/implementing-up and bottom-up curriculum development

4. Justify the role of assessment in the ABC model and why it is such a critical component of the model

5. Explain why implementation planning is required for effective delivery and evaluation of instruction

6. Describe the role of the teacher in implementing instruction and managing student learning in the ABC model

7. Distinguish the roles that student and program evaluation play in guiding the implementation of instruction and the refinement of a physical education curriculum

The achievement-based curriculum (ABC) model (Wessel & Kelly, 1986) is a process for addressing questions such as those posed in the preceding scenario. This chapter provides an overview, and the subsequent chapters will guide you through the five components of the model in detail using common questions and illustrative answers.

The ABC model was created to integrate the program planning, assessing, implementation planning, teaching, and evaluating components of physical education instruction. Teachers commonly acquire their knowledge base from unique, unrelated units of content presented in various courses taken during their formal preparation. For example, curriculum design and development may be taught in a curriculum course; assessment, in a test and measurements course; learning principles, in a motor learning course; pedagogy, in methods and skill courses; and knowledge of the unique needs of learners, in an adapted physical education course.

Teachers are then expected to synthesize and apply all of this information when they do their student teaching and in their first teaching job. The ABC model provides a process for teachers to organize all of this information in a systematic way to optimize instruction as well as to address the questions and problems they encounter during teaching.

The ABC model has five components: program planning, assessing, implementation planning, teaching, and evaluating as shown in figure 4.1. Although these components are introduced as discrete components, remember that they are interdependent. For example, you cannot assess until you know what the students are targeted to learn, and you cannot plan appropriate learning experiences until you know the performance levels of the students (assessment) on the content to be taught. This is all based on the premise that to be an effective teacher you must follow a specified program plan; continually assess your students; use your assess-

The Achievement-Based Curriculum Model

▌ Figure 4.1   The ABC model is made up of five interdependent components.

ment data to plan your instruction; and use your evaluation data (reassessment) to determine student progress, the effectiveness of your teaching, and the appropriateness of your program plan.

The remainder of this chapter illustrates each of the ABC components to show how the model can be used to address various problems encountered by teachers. The purpose of these examples is to provide an overview of the model and how the components are integrated. The subsequent chapters on each of the components will show you how to use the ABC model when addressing questions you encounter in your work as a physical educator.

It is important at this point to stress that the ABC model is a *process*. The ABC model does not dictate what philosophy should underlie your program, what content you should teach, or how you should teach it. What this model provides is a systematic process to guide you as you develop your curriculum. Each program plan developed using the ABC model is unique because it is designed around the unique needs of the students, teachers, school district, and community.

Program Planning

Program planning, or curriculum development, is the process of deciding what you should teach and why from day to day and year to year in physical education. The program plan should reflect the values of the school district and the community

as well as the unique characteristics of the school (e.g., space, equipment, budget, time, class sizes, and student characteristics).

Bottom-Up Curriculum Planning

Unfortunately, many physical education program plans are designed based on ideal conditions that do not exist in reality. Figure 4.2 illustrates the traditional bottom-up curriculum design commonly used to develop physical education program plans. The logic of the bottom-up design is that students must first know their body parts and actions and have sufficient strength and range of motion in their joints (the bottom tier of the pyramid) before they can learn more complex motor skills. Students then apply these body management concepts to learn object control (e.g., throwing, catching, kicking) and locomotor skills (e.g., running, hopping, skipping). These fundamental skills are then combined and practiced in low-organization games that provide the foundation for learning the traditional societal team sports. Finally, toward the end of the school years (the top tier of the pyramid), the students focus on learning lifetime leisure sports that will allow them to maintain their health and fitness throughout their lifetime.

Program plans using the bottom-up model are typically developed by getting the physical education staff together to decide what content should be taught in the physical education program. Figure 4.3 illustrates an example of a bottom-up curriculum

Figure 4.2 Illustration of the bottom-up curriculum development model.

Number of Objectives Targeted for Instruction by Grade and Goal Area in the State of Virginia Standards of Learning for Physical Education

Grade	Fit	M/E	R/D	S/T/G	G/S	I/S	T/S	Total
K	3	8	3	5	4			23
1	3	7	3	4	6			23
2	4	3	4	7	6			24
3	4	3	3	9	6			25
4	5		6	8	10			29
5	5		5	5	9			24
6	4		6	4	9			23
7	4		4	5	9			22
8	2		4	5		5	9	25
9	3		3	2		7	4	19
10	3		3	3		9	2	20
11-12	3		1	1		4	2	11
Totals:	43	21	45	58	59	25	17	268

Fit = Physical fitness   S/T/G/ = Stunts, tumbling, and gymnastics   I/S = Individual sports

M/E = Movement education   G/S = Games and sports   T/S = Team sports

R/D = Rhythm and dance

Figure 4.3 Example of a bottom-up curriculum from the Virginia standards of learning.

Reprinted with permission from *The Journal of Physical Education, Recreation & Dance,* August 1989, 30. JOPERD is a publication of the American Alliance for Health, Physical Education, Recreation and Dance, 1900 Association Drive, Reston, VA 20191-1599.

developed by the Virginia Department of Education (Kelly, 1988). In this case, the state department brought together groups of teachers at the various grade levels and asked them to delineate what content should be taught at each grade level. In this curriculum body awareness objectives (e.g., movement education, stunts, and tumbling) are emphasized in the early grades. During the upper elementary years, game and sport skills are emphasized, and in the middle school and high school years, team sports and individual sports are emphasized, respectively.

The problem with the bottom-up approach to curriculum planning is that it depends on the following assumptions that are not true of many schools:

- There is enough time to teach all students all of the objectives in the curriculum.

- Movement up the pyramid would be based on mastery of the specified content.

- Teachers at all levels (elementary, middle, and high school) and in all schools will follow the plan.

- Students given the opportunity to acquire a broad base of skills will in fact master them and therefore will have the potential to pursue the greatest number of recreational activities after the school years to maintain their health and fitness.

Let's examine what happens when one or more of these assumptions are false. What happens when instructional time has not been accounted for when designing the program? Will a school that has physical education twice a week for 30 minutes be able to cover as many of the objectives as a school that has physical education five times a week for 45 minutes? What happens when physical education specialists are used in one school to provide all of the instruction, and in another school the physical education specialists teach the students only once a week and the classroom teachers teach physical education on the other days? What happens if one school has a physical education specialist who has to teach two classes at a time (50 to 60 students), and another school has a physical education specialist who teaches a single class (25 to 30 students) at a time? Clearly, factors such as the competency of the teacher providing the physical education instruction, the number of students in the class, and the amount of instructional time available affect how much

content can be taught and how much learning can be expected of the students.

What is not clear in a bottom-up curriculum is how to make adjustments for these factors. If students have physical education only twice a week for 30 minutes (36 hours of instruction during the year), they probably cannot master 23 objectives in kindergarten (see figure 4.3). This leaves the teachers in a dilemma. They can try to teach all 23 objectives, spending approximately 1.5 hours on each. This probably will result in none of the objectives being mastered by all of the students. Another option would be to select a subset of the 23 objectives and spend more time on fewer objectives to ensure that at least some objectives are mastered by all students. Unfortunately, what frequently happens at this juncture is that teachers begin to use the bottom-up curriculum like a menu. They look at the 23 objectives targeted for a given year and select from this list the ones they want to teach. Because each teacher is picking different items off the menu each year for each grade level, the objectives do not build on each other. Over time, instead of ascending the pyramid, the students develop an array of assorted skills that do not culminate into any functional lifetime sport skills.

The second assumption of the bottom-up curriculum is that students would only be advanced to the next grade (stage of the pyramid) when they have mastered the objectives specified for the current grade. Unfortunately, most schools, particularly at the elementary level, promote and place students in physical education not based on their performance levels, but on their age and grade level. Combining this practice with the reality that many students have received instruction on only a subset of the objectives targeted for the previous year makes the implementation of most bottom-up plans impossible after a few years. It is not uncommon to find middle school sport skill units (e.g., gymnastics) in which some students have had four or more years of prior instruction on the foundations skills and others have never had any instruction on these skills.

Although the bottom-up model may be theoretically sound, it cannot be practically implemented and therefore does not produce the desired end result—providing students with a sound foundation of physical and motor skills that will allow them to maintain their health and fitness after the school years. Lacking a functional curriculum results in the common dual curriculum system found in many schools. There is the official bottom-up curriculum that is outlined in a big notebook and takes up space on a shelf, and then there is the curriculum actually being used that resides in the heads of the physical education teachers. One problem with the "in the head" curriculum is that after years of trial and error developing this curriculum, it leaves when the teacher leaves. When the replacement teacher is hired, all he or she gets is the copy of the official curriculum that was left on the desk. The new teacher then begins the trial-and-error process of reinventing the curriculum.

Planning Down/Implementing Up

Given the limitations of the bottom-up model, the ABC uses a planning-down/implementing-up approach to curriculum development (see chapter 1). Figure 4.4 illustrates the planning-down model. The major differences between the planning-down and the bottom-up models are the direction from which the content is delineated and the amount of content that is included in the plan. Once a planning-down program is defined, it is implemented up developmentally from the bottom.

Defining the Philosophy of the Program

Planning down begins by defining the philosophy of the physical education program and identifying specifically what teachers and others (see chapter 5) want the students to leave the program being able to do. These are called the program goals. An example of a program goal might be: All students will be able to play a functional game of tennis demonstrating successful use, on two out of three tries, of the overhead serve, forehand stroke, backhand stroke, and rules and strategies of the game while playing a set of tennis.

Breaking Down the Goals Into Learning Objectives

Once the program goals are determined (see chapter 5 for the actual procedures), the next step is to break down each goal developmentally into its skill components or learning objectives. Using the tennis example, what body awareness, fitness, locomotor, and object control skills are necessary to achieve the complex skills needed to play a game of tennis? For example, students would need to know their body parts and the actions of these parts to understand and benefit from instruction. In terms of locomotor skills, they would need to be able to move forward, backward, and laterally using both the run and slide patterns. Students would have to have sufficient strength to hold and swing a racket as well as leg, arm, and shoulder strength and cardiorespiratory endurance to play a set of tennis. Further, they would need to master the fundamental swinging patterns (overhead, forehand, and backhand) without implements and then follow a developmental progression of implements in terms of size, length, and weight leading to the use of a regulation tennis

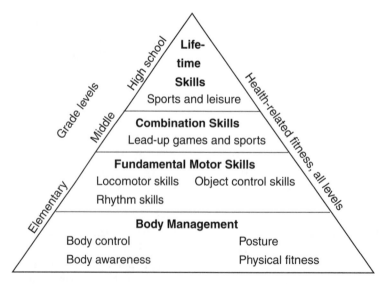

❙ Figure 4.4 Illustration of the planning-down/implementing-up curriculum development model.

racket. This process would be repeated for each program goal, resulting in a developmental list of objectives needed to achieve each of the program goals.

Calculating How Much Content Can Be Included

A unique aspect of ABC planning down is calculating how much content (goals and objectives) can actually be included in a given program plan (Kelly, 1989). Remember that not calculating how much content could be covered in the program was one of the major limitations of bottom-up planning. Because each school district has unique characteristics (e.g., time allocated to physical education, teacher-to-student ratios, teacher competencies, equipment, and facilities), each one will need to calculate its own time values.

Using the procedures outline in chapter 5, you can calculate how much time is available for physical education instruction and how long it will take to teach an average objective in your instructional settings. With these values, you can then estimate how many goals and objectives your students can learn and master.

If your school provides physical education twice a week for 30 minutes for grades 1 through 10, that would result in a total of 360 hours of instruction for the entire program (1 hour per week × 36 weeks a year × 10 years = 360 hours). Given the projected goals and objectives and the unique characteristics of your school, you determine that on the average you would need 6 hours to teach all students mastery of a typical objective. This means that you can then teach and achieve a total of 60 objectives (360 total hours / 6 hours per objective = 60 objectives) in your program.

You can now use this information to fine-tune the breadth and depth of the actual goals and objectives included in the program. For example, you may have started with 10 goals that required a total of 120 objectives. You now realize that, given the unique characteristics of your school, you will have time to achieve only 60 objectives over the 10 years of your physical education program. You must decide whether to delimit your program to fewer goals (less program breadth) with each goal containing more objectives (greater depth), or to keep the original number of goals (greater program breadth) and reduce the number of objectives achieved within each goal (less depth). For example, if you reduced your program breadth to five goals, you could include an average of 12 objectives per goal (60 total objectives for the program / 5 goals = 12). On

Class sizes, facilities, amd equipment must be considered when designing a curriculum.

the other hand, if you wanted to work on 10 goals, you would have to reduce the depth to an average of six objectives per goal (60 total objectives for the program / 10 goals = 6).

Developmentally Sequencing the Objectives

After you have selected the program goals and objectives based on the time available, the next step is to developmentally sequence the objectives across the grades of the curriculum. Once again, it is important to stress that in the ABC planning-down/implementing-up concept the goals and objectives are delineated from the top down and then implemented up developmentally from the bottom.

The planning-down/implementing-up concept also has some assumptions:

- All students are expected to achieve mastery of the specified objectives.

- The program plan is followed sequentially and developmentally rather than by grade levels.

- The amount of content included is a function of the amount of instructional time, teacher competency, equipment and facilities, and student needs and qualities.

- Teachers are expected to follow the plan and be held accountable for their students' learning.

Defining the Content

The last major differences between the planning-down/implementing-up and the bottom-up concepts are the detail in which the content is defined and the focus of instruction. Because the planning-down/implementing-up concept expects both student mastery and teacher accountability, the content (goals and objectives) must be defined operationally. For example, what does it mean if the curriculum states that students will be able to catch by the end of second grade or serve in volleyball by the end of eighth grade? How can consistency and accuracy be controlled so that one teacher does not accept trapping a beach ball two out of three times as acceptable catching and another teacher accepts catching a tennis ball with the hands only eight out of ten times? Inherent in the definition of each objective is the need for a balance between how the skill should be performed and the desired results of the performance (e.g., number of catches). The objective definition should also include the instructions for

eliciting the behavior from the student and the criteria for acceptance. Figure 4.5 illustrates a sample definition of catching.

The definition of the catch objective illustrates the value of measuring both how the skill is performed (process) and the results of the performance (product, or whether the student caught the ball). Defining the objectives in the program plan in terms of both the desired process and product informs both the students and anyone else who reviews the plan what exactly will be taught in the program and what the students are expected to learn.

Comparing the Bottom-Up and Planning-Down/ Implementing-Up Models

In the bottom-up model, the students are exposed to a wide variety of physical education skills with the hope that they will acquire the foundation needed to pursue lifetime sports of interest after the school years to maintain their health and fitness. In the bottom-up model, the teacher is responsible for exposing the students to the skills and giving them opportunities to learn, but the students are more or less responsible for deciding which ones are important for them and which ones they will try to master. In the planning-down model, the content to be mastered is determined in the planning process. The teacher is responsible for providing appropriate instruction so that all students achieve the objectives and the ultimate goals.

Although the bottom-up approach may initially appear to be the more humanistic approach, the fact that it cannot be implemented as designed results in the majority of students leaving the program without any functional lifetime skills. The planning-down model, on the other hand, may initially appear more rigid and less sensitive to the individual needs of students. However, because its design ensures that it can be implemented, all of the students leave with a specific number of functional lifetime skills.

Theoretically, the planning-down/implementing-up curriculum is independent of grade levels. That is, once the content is delineated and developmentally sequenced, the most important thing is that the students progress from the beginning to the end of the sequence. Students are assessed when they enter the program and placed developmentally in the program plan based on the assessment profile. For example, if students are starting third grade,

I CAN

Performance Objective: To demonstrate a functional catch

Skill levels	Focal points for activity
1. To catch with assistance	Given a verbal request, a demonstration, and physical assistance, the student can catch or trap, with hands or arms and chest, an 8- to 12-inch ball lofted directly into the arms from a distance of 3 to 5 feet. The student can maintain control of the ball two out of three times without resistance.
2. To catch without assistance	Given a verbal request, a demonstration, and the ability to catch with assistance, the student can catch (grasp or trap with hands or arms and chest) an 8- to 12-inch ball lofted softly to the middle of the chest from a 6-foot distance. The student can do this two out of three times in this manner: a. Eyes focused on ball, adjusting the arm position to receive the ball on cue from watching the ball's path b. Trap or catch ball with hands or arms and chest
3. To demonstrate a mature catch	Given a verbal request, a demonstration, and the ability to catch without assistance, the student can catch a 6-inch playground ball tossed to chest height from a 15-foot distance two out of three times in this manner: a. Hands in front of the body, knees slightly flexed, elbows flexed near sides in preparatory position b. Extension of the arms in preparation for ball contact c. Contact the ball with hands only (fingers spread and sightly flexed with palms facing) d. Elbows bend as arms absorb the force of the ball e. Smooth (*not* mechanical or jerky) integration of four previous points
4. To move into position and catch	Given a verbal request, a mature catching pattern, and a demonstration, the student can catch two out of three times a 4- to 6-inch ball projected at least 10 feet high from a distance of at least 20 feet to a point within 5 feet of the student. Student moves into position to receive the ball on cue from watching the ball's path.

▌**Figure 4.5** Example of an objective definition: catching.

they do not automatically start working on the third grade objectives. The students are assessed, and if they have not achieved some of the second grade objectives they continue to work on these until they are achieved and they are ready to learn the third grade objectives. The content taught is based on students' degree of mastery. Instruction is then designed around what the students need to learn next in the progression.

Unfortunately, most schools still use an age or grade organization structure. Table 4.1 illustrates a school district's developmentally sequenced objectives for the elementary grades derived from the planning-down process. Note that for each objective there are indications as to when instruction will commence and when mastery is expected. These marks are estimates based on when the average student should be ready to learn and master these objectives and are useful for communicating the scope and sequence of the curriculum to others.

Program Planning Summary

The ABC program planning process results in the following products:

- Functional goals that will be achieved by all students who participate in the program and that reflect the philosophy of the school and community

- Specific measurable objectives needed to achieve each of the program goals

Table 4.1 **Example of a K-5 Elementary Planning-Down/Implementing-Up Program Plan**

K-5 program plan		K	1	2	3	4	5	Curriculum page #
Locomotor patterns	1.1 Run	**						16
	1.2 Gallop	**						19
	1.3 Horizontal jump	- -	- -	**				58
	1.4 Vertical jump		- -	**				61
	1.5 Hop (right-left)	- -	**					37
	1.6 Slide	- -	**					40
	1.7 Skip		- -	- -	**			82
	1.8 Leap			- -	- -	**		107
Object control	2.1 Underhand roll	**						22
	2.2 Bounce/dribble		- -	**				64
	2.3 Underhand throw	- -	**					43
	2.4 Overhand throw		- -	- -	- -	**		110
	2.5 Kick		- -	- -	**			85
	2.6 Punt				- -	- -	**	130
	2.7 Two-handed sidearm strike (baseball)		- -	- -	**			88
	2.8 Catch/fielding			- -	- -	- -	**	138
	2.9 Underhand strike (volleyball serve)			- -	**			113
	2.10 Chest pass (basketball)		- -	**				67
	2.11 Bounce pass (basketball)		- -	- -	**			91
Physical fitness	3.1 Knowledge				- -	- -	**	139
	3.2 Training concepts				- -	- -	**	144
	3.3 Terminology			- -	- -	**		116
	3.4 Leg strength		- -	**				70
	3.5 Flexibility		- -	**				73

K-5 program plan								
		K	1	2	3	4	5	Curriculum page #
Physical fitness	3.6 Abdominal strength		- -	- -	**			94
	3.7 Endurance		- -	- -	- -	**		120
	3.8 Arm and shoulder strength				- -	- -	**	149
	3.9 Agility			- -	- -	**		123
	3.10 Speed				- -	- -	**	153
Social	4.1 Self-discipline (control)	- -	**					46
	4.2 Cooperation	- -	**					48
	4.3 Fair play	- -	- -	- -	**			97
	4.4 Winning and losing	- -	- -	**				76
	4.5 Respecting equipment and property	**						25
Body management	5.1 Nonlocomotor	**						27
	5.2 Body awareness	**						30
	5.3 Spatial awareness	**						32
	5.4 Use of space		- -	**				51
	5.5 Quality of movement	- -	- -	**				79
	5.6 Relationship of body to other objects	- -	- -	- -	**			100
	5.7 Basic dance patterns				- -	**		126
	5.8 Forward roll					- -	**	156
	5.9 Rope jumping		- -	- -	**			103
Game and sport skills	6.1 Following directions	**						34
	6.2 Knowledge of safety and rules	- -	**					54
	6.3 Member of team			- -	- -	**		129
	6.4 Participating in games and sports	- -	- -	- -	- -	- -	**	159

** indicates when the objective is to be mastered.

- - indicates when instruction will begin.

■ Calculations of the amount of instructional time available and the amount of time needed to teach objectives based on the unique characteristics of the school

■ Developmental sequences of objectives with indications of when instruction will begin and when mastery is expected

■ Operational definitions of all objectives in terms of both process and product measures

The program planning process provides the starting point for instruction and a reference point for ongoing program evaluation. Although we have discussed the ABC process in terms of the entire

K-12 physical education program, the same process can also be applied to designing individual programs for students with disabilities.

Assessing

Assessing is the process of collecting information to make informed decisions. The decisions that need to be made determine what to assess and the type of assessment instruments to use. The range of assessment-based decisions addressed in physical education is discussed in detail in chapter 7. The purpose of this section is to illustrate the interrelationship between assessing and the other components of the ABC model (program planning, implementation planning, teaching, and evaluating).

The most common assessment decision that physical educators make every day is, What do my students need to learn next on the objectives targeted for instruction in the program plan? The ABC model uses a curriculum-embedded assessment process to address this type of question. You start the assessment process by reviewing the program plan (see table 4.1 as an example) to ascertain what objectives are targeted for instruction for the students in question. After identifying the objectives, your next step is to review the objective definitions (see figure 4.5 for an example). The objective definitions then serve as the basis for evaluating the students in the class to determine what they already know and what components of the skill they still need to work on. Figure 4.6 shows preassessment data for a sample class of students on the catch objective. The preassessment data are the basis for planning the next lesson.

Accurate and continual assessment is the key to successfully implementing the ABC model and is an absolute necessity to be an effective teacher. Unfortunately, many teachers view assessing as a time-consuming task that is unrelated to teaching. This perception is usually the result of a mismatch between what they are assessing and the decisions they need to make for daily instruction. For example, let's say a teacher named Mr. Jones is planning to begin work on the overhand throw. Mr. Jones decides to assess the students in his class to find out where they are on this skill prior to instruction. Mr. Jones decides to use the softball throw for distance test because it is relatively easy to administer and the test provides age and gender norms. Figure 4.7 shows the results of Mr. Jones's assessment. What can you interpret from these data? What do you

think Mr. Jones should focus on first in his instruction?

One problem with Mr. Jones' assessment is that the data are not really relevant to the decision he wants to make. The fact that many of the students are performing below the 50th percentile for their age or gender norms may indicate that they need work on this objective. However, the test provides no insight into what the students did that was correct or incorrect when throwing. Knowing that a given student is in the 90th or 10th percentile provides little information on what the student is doing right or wrong. It could even be the case that two students are making the same mistakes, but one student's throw is going farther than the other's because the first student is big for her age and the other student is small for his age.

Given that this form of assessing did not provide Mr. Jones with any meaningful information, it is easy to understand why he would be less than motivated to continue to give up instructional time for assessing. However, the conclusion that he should draw from this experience is not that assessing is a useless procedure and a waste of time, but rather that the type of assessment he selected was inappropriate for the decision he wanted to make. Because Mr. Jones wanted information on where the students were on the overhand throw objective, a more appropriate assessment would have been a curriculum-embedded instrument for throwing, such as the example shown in figure 4.8. A curriculum-embedded assessment item has two parts: the objective definition created via the process of task analysis and a score sheet that lists the key components and provides space to record the student's performance.

Task analysis is the breaking down of a skill into its component parts. Figure 4.8 breaks a motor skill down first into skill levels and within by components (focal points). The task-analyzed components of a motor skill are then used as the assessment criteria. One of the advantages of the ABC planning process is that it includes the creation of these items as part of the overall planning process. Therefore, when teachers are ready to begin work on an objective, all they need to do is refer to their program plan. Another advantage of curriculum-embedded assessment instruments is that they can be further task analyzed into smaller learning components to accommodate students who learn at slower rates.

Some teachers view assessing as a task unrelated to teaching that they must do to meet school requirements. In the ABC model, assessing is the key to

I CAN

Class Performance Score Sheet
Performance objective: Catch

SCORING

Assessment:

X = Achieved

O = Not achieved

Reassessment:

⊗ = Achieved

∅ = Not achieved

Student name	1	2	3	4	5	Comments (student response)
	Preparatory position	Arm extension	Hands contact ball	Arms absorb force	Smooth integration	
1. Brandon	X	O	O	O	O	Arms slow to move.
2. Lisa	X	X	X	O	O	Ball bounces out of hands easily. Work on holding onto ball.
3. Morris	O	O	O	O	O	Needs to start with positioning. Appears nervous.
4. Chad	X	O	O	O	O	
5. Simon	X	X	X	X	X	Catches smoothly. Try running and catching.
6. Gemma	X	O	O	O	O	
7. Bruce	O	O	O	O	O	Needs to work on starting position.
8. Erin	X	O	O	O	O	
9. Karen	X	X	O	O	O	Gets into position well. Hands slow to position.
10. Brent	X	X	X	O	O	
11. Rebecca	X	O	O	O	O	Fails to meet the ball with arms/hands.
12. Jason	X	X	X	X	O	Body moves quicker than arms.
13. Courtney	X	X	X	X	O	
14. Linda	X	X	O	O	O	Hands not moving together.
15. Marcus	X	X	X	O	O	

Figure 4.6 Example score sheet with preassessment data recorded for the catching objective.

Babylon Public Schools Softball Throw for Distance Score Sheet

Class: Mrs. Kowalski's   Grade: Third   Date: Sept. 15

Student name	Trials 1	2	3	Best throw	Percentile norm	Comments
1. Morris	75	77	74	77	66	
2. Bruce	86	86	89	89	75	
3. Jennifer	45	32	40	45	39	
4. Karen	92	97	94	97	85	
5. David	108	101	107	108	95	
6. Katie	60	63	63	63	55	
7. Alyssa	32	34	36	36	25	
8. Brian	65	68	66	68	59	
9. Marty	115	118	126	126	100	
10. Mindy	40	40	41	41	35	
11. Art	76	71	77	77	66	
12. Jim	65	64	65	65	56	
13. Linda	15	17	12	17	5	
14. Denise	18	18	18	18	6	
15. Tim	51	49	54	54	47	

▌ **Figure 4.7**   Example of class results on a softball throw for distance test.

effective instruction and essential for student learning to occur. Assessment is not only a process for collecting information on student performance, but also a means of communicating to students where they are on the content being taught and what they need to learn next. Let's examine the role of assessment in the following example.

Mr. Kamide has reviewed the school curriculum and identified the overhand throw as the next objective targeted for instruction. Because time is limited and Mr. Kamide already knows from previously working with his students that they need work on this objective, he decides to forgo assessing the students and to save all of the time available for instruction. During the first class of the throwing unit, Mr. Kamide demonstrates what the correct overhand throw pattern should look like and explains why it is important to learn the correct pattern. He then involves the class in a number of highly motivating drills and games that involve throwing. There is a small behavioral problem at the end of class, but overall Mr. Kamide is pleased with the lesson. At the start of the second class Mr. Kamide reviews the class rules in an attempt to avoid any future behavior problems. Several days into the unit Mr. Kamide notes that some students appear to be throwing quite well. Mr. Kamide tries to reinforce the behavior of these students by using them as models at the start of the drills. However, a few students seem to be spending more time fooling around than practicing their throwing. Mr. Kamide lets these students know that they are not going to get better unless they practice. After a few more days Mr. Kamide notices that the students are beginning to get bored with working on this objective, so he decides to move on to another objective and to come back to this objective later in

I CAN

Performance Objective:
To demonstrate a functional overhand throw

Skill levels	Focal points for activity
1. To demonstrate an overhand throw with assistance	Given a verbal request, a demonstration, and physical assistance, a student with the ability to grasp a ball can throw a 3- to 4-inch ball a distance of at least 10 feet, two out of three times, without resistance in this manner: a. Overhand motion in the direction of the throw (hand passes above shoulder) b. Release the ball in the anticipated direction of the throw
2. To demonstrate an overhand throw without assistance	Given a verbal request and a demonstration of the mature overhand throw, a student with the ability to perform the overhand throw with assistance can throw a 3- to 4-inch ball to a 20-inch-wide target placed 15 feet away, two out of three times in this manner: a. Eyes focused on the target b. Throwing arm motion includes the hand passing above the shoulder
3. To demonstrate a mature overhand throw	Given a verbal request and a demonstration, a student with the ability to perform the overhand throw can throw a 3- to 4-inch ball, two out of three times in this manner: a. Almost complete extension of the throwing arm to initiate windup for the throwing action (assuming a side orientation prior to the throw) b. Weight transfer to the foot opposite the throwing arm c. Hip and spine rotation (1/4 rotation) in preparation for and during the throwing action d. Follow-through well beyond ball release and toward the desired direction of travel e. Smooth (*not* mechanical or jerky) integration of four previous points
4. To demonstrate a mature overhand throw for distance	Given a verbal request and a demonstration, a student with the mature throwing pattern and sufficient arm strength can throw a 3- to 4-inch ball a distance of at least the minimum performance criteria for age and gender (see table below) two out of three times with angle of release at 45° (±5°). Distance* (in feet) boys and girls 8 to 15 years old should be able to throw a 3- to 4-inch ball
	Age in years	8-9	10-12	13-15
	Girls	46	71	84
	Boys	73	114	159
	*These are the minimum acceptable distance criteria. Source: *Special Olympics Instructional Manual* (Washington, D.C., American Association for Health, Physical Education and Recreation and *The Joseph P. Kennedy, Jr. Foundation*, 1972).
5. To demonstrate a mature overhand throw for accuracy	Given a verbal request and a demonstration, the student can throw a 3- to 4-inch ball with a mature pattern two out of three times, hitting an 8-foot-square target placed 1 foot off the ground from a distance of 50 feet.

■ Figure 4.8 Example task analysis of the overhand throw objective.

Assessment instruments like the one shown in figure 4.8 are readily available for most skills taught in physical education and can be easily developed and modified using the process of task analysis (see chapter 7). Most physical education methods books and motor development textbooks include assessment instruments. Another comprehensive source for these items is the I CAN program (Wessel, 1976).

the year. Mr. Kamide decides not to spend any class time posttesting the students because he believes he has a pretty good idea of where they all are from observing them during class. Overall, Mr. Kamide is quite pleased with the progress of the students and believes that the unit went very well.

Now let's examine the experiences of two of Mr. Kamide's students during this throwing unit. The first student is Denise, who likes physical education, is one of the better-skilled students in the class, and is the best pitcher on her baseball team. Denise is excited at the beginning of the throwing unit. Denise enjoys the drills and games and perceives that she is doing really well. In fact, Denise frequently tries to position herself so that Mr. Kamide can see her throwing and on several occasions asks him for feedback. Mr. Kamide in turn frequently gives Denise praise on her throwing and on several occasions uses Denise as a model to demonstrate good throwing. At the end of the unit Denise feels very good about her throwing ability and is looking forward to the next skill they will be learning.

David is our second student. David is one of the lower-skilled students in class and generally dislikes physical education. David has been known in the past to act out in the classroom immediately before physical education time in the hope that he will be sent to the office and not have to participate in physical education. Unfortunately for David, the principal has figured out this pattern and now routinely sends him back to the gym.

At the start of the unit David is cautiously optimistic about throwing. David knows that he does not throw as well as the other kids, but has watched the kids in the neighborhood playing baseball in the street and thinks he would like to try playing some day. During Mr. Kamide's demonstration, David watches carefully and observes that Mr. Kamide can throw the ball really far and hard. When given an opportunity to practice during the drills, David attempts to throw like Mr. Kamide but is unaware that he is stepping forward on the wrong foot. After several attempts David notices that all of the other kids are throwing considerably farther than he is, and a few are watching him and making fun of him. David decides that he does not like this, so he throws one of his balls at this group of students. They in turn throw their balls back at him. Because they are better skilled and more accurate, a few of the balls hit David. David in turn starts to cry and complains to Mr. Kamide. Mr. Kamide asks the other students what happened and they inform him that David started it. David gets frustrated and curses at

the other students. Mr. Kamide reprimands David and sends him to the office.

By the second day of the unit, David is no longer interested in learning to throw. At the beginning of class Mr. Kamide reminds David of the problem he had last class and that he does not want that to happen again. David decides just to hang out during class. David keeps his eye on Mr. Kamide and tries to stay as far away from him as possible. During the drills he lets the other kids cut ahead of him on line and during the game he stays in the back and rolls the balls up to the other kids and lets them throw. At the end of class, Mr. Kamide realizes that David did not cause any problems and makes a point of letting David know that he did a good job. David decides that it is better to just hang out and put up with physical education than get sent to the office. David continues to hang out and avoid Mr. Kamide during class for the rest of the unit. David gets caught a few times by Mr. Kamide skipping turns, but is not involved in any major behavior problems for the rest of the unit.

Now let's examine how Mr. Kamide could have used assessing to improve his instruction and the experiences of the two students we have observed. Mr. Kamide could have started the first class with a throwing game or drill. While the students were participating in the game, he could have assessed and recorded what components of the throw each student did correctly and which ones still needed work. If Mr. Kamide had assessed both Denise and David, he would have known at the start of the unit that Denise had already mastered all of the process components and needed to work on her accuracy and that David was not demonstrating any of the components and was noticeably stepping with the wrong foot. With this information, Mr. Kamide would have been able to let all of the students know what specifically they needed to work on during the drills. For example, he could have told Denise to focus on her accuracy during the drills and given her specific goals to attempt to achieve (e.g., hit a smaller target three out of five times). David, on the other hand, could have been shown the difference between stepping with the unilateral foot and the contralateral foot and the effect it has on his throwing. Mr. Kamide could have given David feedback after each throw to let him know if he had stepped with the correct foot. With this additional information, David would likely now be interpreting his success or failure with this activity in terms of whether he was stepping with the correct foot and not simply in terms of the distance of his throws. Because he has been provided with a way to evaluate his performance, he would be less likely to experience failure and regress to the avoidance behaviors he exhibited in the original story.

If during the unit Mr. Kamide had continually assessed the students, he would have been able to detect that David was not practicing his throwing and subsequently not improving. With this information, Mr. Kamide could have then planned appropriate strategies to redirect David and make him more successful such as using an enrichment loop (see figure 8.1 on page 183). Unfortunately, without the continual assessment, David was able to avoid the teacher most of the time and made it through the entire unit without any improvement to his immature throwing pattern.

Finally, even if Mr. Kamide had posttested the class, he would have had no way of knowing whether the results he received were a result of his instruction or just a reflection of what the students could already do at the start of the unit. The fact that Mr. Kamide did not posttest the class means that neither he nor the students know what the students learned and what they still needed to learn on this skill. Odds are that because the students were given very little specific instruction during the unit, very little learning actually occurred. However, without any assessment data to interpret, Mr. Kamide is totally unaware that the students did not learn and in fact thinks the unit went well. Therefore, it is probably safe to assume that Mr. Kamide will teach throwing the same way next time.

Several points can be drawn from this scenario:

1. Assessment lets the teacher know where each student is on the skill targeted for instruction at the beginning of the unit.

2. Curriculum-embedded assessment also informs the students of the key components of the skill, which of the components they have already mastered, and which of the components they still need to work on.

3. With assessment data, the teacher can plan activities that focus on the specific components the students need the most work on.

4. Preassessment data provides a basis for ongoing evaluation of the effectiveness of instruction. If the teacher continually assesses and notices that the method of instruction and drills are not producing the desired changes in performance, then the instruction and activities can be modified.

5. Ongoing assessment allows the teacher to give instructionally relevant feedback to the students, which can then be used to correct their performances.

6. Postassessment data provide students with feedback on how much they learned during the unit and how much they still need to master.

7. Postassessment data provide teachers with feedback regarding the effectiveness of their instruction, the amount of time needed to obtain a given degree of improvement, as well as the amount of time needed to get all of the students to mastery.

In summary, continual assessment is integral to planning appropriate lessons, providing students with meaningful feedback, evaluating student progress, and evaluating the effectiveness of instruction. Chapter 7 contains a more complete discussion of assessment-based decisions and explains how to make assessment accommodations for students.

Implementation Planning

Implementation planning, like assessing, is frequently viewed as a process only student teachers and beginning teachers are required to do. After teachers have a few years of experience, they know how to control the students and have developed a sufficient supply of games and activities so that they no longer need to write out their plans. When there is no assessment data to work from, this may in fact be a logical argument. However, in the ABC model the implementation planning starts with interpreting the student preassessment data. In the ABC model implementation planning actually involves two processes: developing teaching templates and developing student learning formats (see chapter 10). Teaching templates define what the teacher does during instruction, and student learning formats define how the students engage with the content to be learned. For the purpose of this overview of the ABC model, the term *implementation planning* will be used to represent both of these processes.

Figure 4.9 shows a teaching template, which is part of an ABC implementation plan. In this example, the lesson is divided into three parts: introduction, body, and closure. During the introduction, the class works on fitness objectives. While the students are exercising, the teacher continually reassesses the students and gives them feedback regarding what

ABC School District Teaching Template

Teacher: D. Wilson   **Grade:** Second   **Class:** Ms. Williams   **Start time:** 10:15

Block: Third   **Start date:** 10/07/02   **End date:** 11/21/02

Standard managerial procedures: *See teacher workbook for standard class procedures. Students have assigned spots on the floor and know to go to their spots when they enter the gym. When the teacher raises her arms over her head, the students know to go to their spots. Bruce has special needs and should be kept close to the teacher so that he attends and stays on task.*

Format	Objectives (time)	Instructional focus	Instructional cue	Learning experiences	Organization	Equipment	Transition
Introduction	Hop (4) Gallop (4)	Rhythm	"Move to the beat"	Teacher directed, students move around the gym. Teacher plays music with a strong, even beat. Teacher reviews components of hop and gallop, observes, and gives feedback.	Cones placed in corners of gym. Students move around outside edge of gym.	4 cones	To start, teacher gives "go" signal. At end, teacher raises arms; students go to their spots.
Body	Catch (4)	Preparatory position	"Flex" to be ready to catch	Teacher demonstrates all catch components and emphasizes the preparatory position.	On spots in front of teacher	One 8-inch playground ball	NA
Body	Catch (10)	Preparatory position Arm extended Hand contact Arms absorb Smooth integration	"Flex" "Reach" "Fingers" "Retract" "Fluid"	Students get task cards on teacher's signal. Cards indicate who the students work with and what each student should focus on at each station. Teacher moves around assessing and giving feedback.	Gym divided in advance into 5 stations—one for each component. Signs are posted and equipment is set up. Students signaled to change stations every 2 minutes.	Balls are at each station: one for every 2 students.	At end of 10 minutes teacher raises arms—students return to their spaces.
Closure	Catch and personal space (8)	Review catch components	"Flex" "Reach" "Fingers" "Retract" "Fluid"	Play game Catching Hot Potatoes (see teaching notebook for game description). Teacher reviews and stresses respect for personal space.	Scattered formation around the gym	More balls than there are students	Arms-up signal at end. Students line up to leave from their spaces.

Reflections: _____

Figure 4.9 Sample implementation plan—teaching template.

they are doing correctly and incorrectly on the various exercises. At the start of the body section, the teacher reviews the components of the objective being worked on and informs the students that the components they each need to work on have been marked on their task cards. (A task card is an example of a student learning format, which is the other component of an implementation plan in the ABC model. Implementation planning is addressed in detail in part III of this book.)

The teacher then briefly explains the activities to be performed at each station and which students are in which group. The students are then told to get their task cards and report to their stations. As the students work at the stations, the teacher systematically observes them to make sure they are all working on their objectives and gives them appropriate feedback. At the beginning of the closure section, the teacher again demonstrates the components of the skill and points out how students can practice these components in the closure game. The teacher then introduces the game, and the students play. At the end of class the teacher concludes with some ideas on how the students can continue to practice the skill at home and during recess at school.

The first step in developing an implementation plan with the ABC model is to review the student preassessment data to determine where the students are on the objective targeted for instruction (see figure 4.6 on page 77). The teacher then decides what component each student needs to learn first and the total number of components each student is projected to learn during instruction. How these decisions are made is addressed in chapter 7. Using the data in figure 4.6 as an example, Morris and Bruce both appear to need to work on getting in the correct preparatory position, whereas Karen and Linda need to work on their hand position when catching the ball. The teacher can now use this information to make logical instructional groupings and to select appropriate learning experiences to meet the needs of each group. The teacher must also consider the learning needs of the students; for example, which students work well together or which students are going to need the most or least feedback during practice. Can some students just be shown what needs to be done, or will they need to be physically manipulated so that they can get a feel for the correct movement?

Once teachers have identified what each student needs to learn and the unique learning needs of the students, they are ready to review their reference library of drills and games to find appropriate activities to meet these needs. They must then integrate the selected activities into the normal structure of the class and connect them by appropriate transitions.

A common misconception regarding the ABC model is that the instructor stands in front of the class and recites the components of the skill while the students, all standing on a line, robotically perform the components. This is not the case; the purpose of implementation planning is to ensure that students know specifically what they are trying to correct, how to make the correction, and how they will know if they have in fact succeeded in making the correction. Once the students know what to work on, the second objective of the implementation plan is to ensure that the students are given sufficient practice trials to learn the desired pattern. Obviously, the best way to achieve this objective is to actively involve the students in drills and games that they perceive as fun and that involve the use of the skill they need to practice. Ideally, if a lesson is planned well, the teacher should be able to get the students to practice the correct pattern without the students ever perceiving that they are working!

Chapter 10 contains a more complete discussion of the ABC procedures for implementation planning and how to design teaching templates and student learning formats. Examples are provided to demonstrate how to address situations in which there are great differences in the skill levels of the students and how to accommodate students with disabilities who may need to work on different objectives in the same setting.

Teaching

Teaching in the ABC model is defined as managing a class and instruction so that all students achieve mastery of the objectives targeted for instruction. Effective teachers understand the learning requirements of their students and can manage the instructional environment to create optimal learning conditions. The teacher's job is to manage the environment so that all students' learning needs are addressed. The elements of success for learning motor skills are as follows:

▮ The student knows when to attend and what to attend to.

▮ The student knows specifically what he is expected to learn.

▮ The student values the content being taught.

▮ The student believes she can learn the content.

▪ The student knows when he is performing the content correctly so that he can repeat it.

▪ The student perceives that she is being successful in her attempts to learn the content.

▪ The student is motivated enough to repeat the correct performance as many times as needed for it to become automatic.

The ABC model also stresses the following nine essential teacher behaviors that maximize the probability that students will be both successful during physical education and achieve the objectives targeted for instruction:

1. The ability to create a positive learning environment

2. The ability to control and efficiently manage the students and the learning environment

3. The ability to communicate clear expectations of what students are to learn

4. The ability to provide explicit, relevant, and timely feedback

5. The ability to task analyze skills into achievable components

6. The ability to engage students in learning and achieve high on-task time on the objectives being taught

7. The ability to control the balance between success and failure on learning tasks

8. The ability to use appropriate cues to meet the learning needs of the students

9. The ability to motivate the students to want to learn the skills being taught and to continue to practice them outside of class

Teacher behaviors interact with students' learning needs in a variety of ways. For a complete discussion of the keys for maximum learning and teaching effectively, see chapter 8.

Many physical education teachers teach motor skills by demonstration. With this method, the teacher frequently demonstrates the desired performance of the skill while the students observe. After several demonstrations, the teacher divides the students up into a drill or an activity and gives them an opportunity to practice the skill. If during the drill the teacher observes that several students are throwing incorrectly, the teacher will stop the class, highlight the error students are making, and then repeat the demonstration of the correct pattern. For skilled students who can replicate the desired

pattern after just observing the teacher, the demonstration method is appropriate and very efficient. However, for students who do not know what to watch, the demonstration method has no effect on their performance. In fact, when asked to watch the teacher throw, most students watch where the ball goes and not how the teacher actually performed the throw. These students don't learn how to throw; they just learn that the teacher can throw far.

Let's examine why learning from a demonstration may be difficult for some students. To begin with, the students must know what to be looking for during the demonstration. If they are not instructed to look at the direction the teacher is facing before the throw or which foot the teacher steps with, they are likely to watch something else, such as the ball. Because the overhand throw takes only a second to perform and is a complex skill composed of several key movements, students probably also need guidance regarding what one thing they should concentrate on observing during the demonstration.

Assuming that the students have been able to deduce a few of the key components of the skill from the demonstration, they now have to assess themselves to determine which of the components they are already doing correctly and which they need to correct. Once they know which components they should work on, they then need to figure out which one they should try to correct first. Now they just have to figure out how to correct their problem and to practice this correction when the teacher gives them an opportunity, and they are all set. This example may seem slightly exaggerated, but it illustrates how many students can watch a demonstration and then perform a throw that looks totally different. In fact, it is not uncommon to find students throwing from the wrong orientation (e.g., facing the intended direction of throw rather than being in a side orientation) or stepping with the wrong foot who are convinced they are throwing just like the teacher. In these cases, the students either did not observe these aspects of the skill when the teacher performed it, or they did not detect these errors in their self-assessment. However, because they think they are doing it correctly, they continue to practice their inappropriate pattern during the learning drills and activities the teacher organizes.

The problem with the demonstration method of instruction is that it puts too much responsibility on students who cannot automatically replicate what they see. It is unrealistic to expect students to be able to task analyze the skill into its component parts, create a mental image of these components from the teacher's demonstration, assess which of the components they are performing correctly and which ones they need to work on, decide which error to correct first, and figure out how to correct the error, and to do all this from the few demonstrations the teacher provides.

The reality is that the majority of these tasks are the responsibility of the teacher. It is the teacher's job to first teach the students the key components of the skill so that they know what to observe during the demonstrations. The teacher then should assess the students and let each student know which components they already do correctly and which components they need to work on. Finally, the teacher should instruct the students as to how they can correct their performance during the practice drills and activities and how the students will know if they are doing the skill correctly during practice. For example, the teacher could put footprints on the floor that indicate the correct orientation of the feet in relation to the target at each throwing station. When students who are working on this component come to a throwing station, they can check to see if they are in the correct orientation by looking down and checking the position of their feet in relation to the footprints.

Successful student learning with the ABC model is a product of applying the appropriate teaching methods to match the learning needs of the students. The culmination of the teaching process is to provide a secure environment in which learning is fun and students feel comfortable taking chances and trying new behaviors and believe that they can learn what the teacher is teaching. Chapters 8 and 9 discuss the other essential teaching behaviors and their applications for addressing the needs of students with and without disabilities in the regular physical education setting.

Evaluation

Evaluation is commonly equated with determining physical education grades for report cards. Because grading in physical education has regressed to pass/fail and satisfactory/unsatisfactory systems in many schools, little attention is paid to this topic. Although grading is a by-product of evaluation, it is only one piece of the total evaluation process. Evaluation is the process of interpreting student assessment data to make decisions regarding student achievement and program merit.

Evaluation in the ABC model refers to both student evaluation and program evaluation. Student evaluation focuses on interpreting the degree to which individual students have achieved the content they were taught and overall how they are progressing toward achieving the goals of the program. The results of student evaluations allow teachers to communicate to students, parents, and any others the progress the students have made during the recent unit/year and their progress to date on achieving the overall goals of the program. Program evaluation focuses on the degree to which all students are achieving the program goals and identifies the factors that are both facilitating and inhibiting this progress. Teachers can use program evaluation results to document the effectiveness of their programs as well as to document the need for such things as more equipment, smaller class sizes, or increases in instructional time.

The ABC program plan and the student pre- and postassessment data provide the foundation for making both student and program evaluation decisions. The program plan provides the framework in which objectives should be examined. The student pre- and postassessment scores on the objectives provide the actual data to be analyzed. Figure 4.10 illustrates a completed score sheet containing student pre- and postassessment scores for the catch objective. Although only pre- and postassessment scores need to be recorded to perform the summative evaluation tasks outlined in this section and in chapters 11 and 12, teachers need to be continually reassessing their students on a daily basis to provide appropriate feedback, plan appropriate lessons, and evaluate the effectiveness of their lessons.

The columns at the far right of the score sheet in figure 4.10 illustrate some of the ways teachers can summarize student performance data. For a more complete discussion of how to compute these values, see chapter 11. For example, column A indicates how many components of the objective each student in the class had at the start of the unit prior to instruction (preperformance). Column B indicates the number of components the teacher projected the students would achieve by the end of the unit (target performance). Column C indicates the number of components the students had mastered by the end of the unit (exit performance). Column D indicates the difference between the students' preperformances and exit performances (change in performance). Summing the data in each column and dividing these values by the number of students in the class provides the teacher with class

I CAN

Class Performance Score Sheet
Performance objective: Catch

SCORING

Assessment:

X = Achieved

O = Not achieved

Reassessment:

⊗ = Achieved

∅ = Not achieved

Preparatory position

Arm extension

Hands contact ball

Arms absorb force

Smooth integration

Student name	1	2	3	4	5	Comments (student response)	(A) Pre	(B) Target	(C) Exit	(D) Change
1. Brandon	X	⊗	⊗	∅	∅	Arms slow to move.	1	1	3	2
2. Lisa	X	X	X	⊗	∅	Ball bounces out of hands easily. Work on holding onto ball.	3	1	4	1
3. Morris	⊗	⊗	∅	∅	∅	Needs to start with positioning. Appears nervous.	0	1	2	2
4. Chad	X	⊗	∅	∅	∅		1	1	2	1
5. Simon	X	X	X	X	X	Catches smoothly. Try running and catching.	5	0	5	0
6. Gemma	X	⊗	⊗	∅	∅		1	1	3	2
7. Bruce	⊗	⊗	∅	∅	∅	Needs to work on starting position.	0	2	2	2
8. Erin	X	⊗	∅	∅	∅		1	1	2	1
9. Karen	X	X	⊗	⊗	∅	Gets into position well. Hands slow to position.	2	2	4	2
10. Brent	X	X	X	⊗	∅		3	1	4	1
11. Rebecca	X	⊗	⊗	∅	∅	Fails to meet the ball with arms/hands.	1	2	3	2
12. Jason	X	X	X	X	⊗	Body moves quicker than arms.	4	1	5	1
13. Courtney	X	X	X	X	⊗		4	1	5	1
14. Linda	X	X	⊗	⊗	∅	Hands not moving together.	2	2	3	1
15. Marcus	X	X	X	⊗	∅		3	1	4	1
						Sum	31	18	51	20
						Average	2.1	1.2	3.4	1.3

■ **Figure 4.10** Sample score sheet with pre- and postassessment data recorded.

mean performance (e.g., summing the preassessment scores [31/15] reveals that on the average the students in the class had 2.1 components of this skill at the start of the unit). Review of the class target mean indicates that the class was targeted to achieve 1.2 components during the unit. By the end of the unit, the class had mastered an average of 3.4 components for an average gain of 1.3 components.

Obviously, one of the concerns teachers have about evaluation is the time required to perform all of these calculations. This is a valid concern; many physical educators serve three hundred to five hundred students and may need to perform these calculations four to six times a year for each student depending on the number of marking periods. The solution to this dilemma is to use computer technology. Figure 4.11 shows an example of a student progress report generated by a computer program. To generate reports like this, the teacher needs to enter the students' names, the objectives they will be working on, and the mastery criteria for each objective at the start of the year. Then throughout the year, prior to any reporting period, the teacher must enter pre, target, and exit values for each student. Although the time required to enter three scores per student is not insignificant for a teacher with four hundred students, the ability to produce professional reports that communicate both the content of the program and student progress should justify this investment.

As mentioned earlier, student evaluation is commonly equated with assigning grades. Clearly, with the information presented in figure 4.11, teachers could calculate and justify grades (see chapter 11 for more information on how to calculate grades). The important point, however, is the limitation of a grade compared to an individualized student progress report. What does a B grade or a grade of 82 communicate to the student and the parents? Does this mean the student mastered 82% of the content taught during this period? Do these grades communicate to the parents what content was taught or how much progress the student made? Grades are clearly limited in terms of what they communicate. We therefore recommend in the ABC model that progress reports be used in conjunction with student grades to address the progress students are making in the context of the program plan.

The second aspect of evaluation is program evaluation. The purpose of program evaluation is to examine the appropriateness of the overall program and how well the teachers are doing on implementing the program. Program evaluation uses the same pre- and postassessment scores that were used for the student evaluation except that the units for program evaluation are the class and the grade level rather than individual students. Figure 4.12 (page 89) shows a summary report for a class of 32 students working on nine objectives. With this information, teachers can make decisions regarding how well they are doing in achieving their goal of getting all of the students to mastery of the objectives specified for a given year. If a significant percentage of the class is not achieving mastery by the end of each year, then the teacher must determine what the problems are and develop strategies to address them.

Addressing program evaluation questions starts with teaching and works backward to planning. For example, if students do not achieve what was projected in a unit, teachers should first examine their teaching. If they did not have the class under control, they may have lost a significant amount of time addressing class management issues that should have been used teaching and practicing. In this case, the solution is to come up with a better class management strategy for the next unit. In another situation, it may be that the problem was related to activities the teacher selected. If the activities produced low on-task time, were perceived as boring by the students, or did not elicit the desired response, then the solution would be to select better activities for the next unit. Finally, the evaluation process may reveal that the students are not developmentally ready to learn one or more of the skills. In this case, the solution would be to move these skills to more appropriate times in the program plan.

Summary

The purpose of this chapter was to introduce the components of the achievement-based curriculum (ABC) model and to illustrate the interrelationship among the components in providing appropriate physical education to meet the needs of all students placed in regular physical education programs. The subsequent chapters of the book will provide you with how-to information on each of the ABC components so that you will have the skills to address the needs of all of your students and make accommodations for students with special needs.

ABC School District Physical Education Class Evaluation Report

Student name: Brian McElroy

Grade level: 8

Number of students in class: 24

Report date: 06/10/03

Teacher: Luke Kelly

Objectives	Entry level	Target exit	Actual exit	Net change	Target met	Mastery criteria	% mastered	Class average	Teacher comments
Abdominal strength	25	35	37	12	Yes	40	92.00	31.25	Good progress—maintain program
Leg strength	8.20	7.80	7.70	0.50	Yes	7.80	100.00	8.52	Excellent
Cardiorespiratory endurance	629.00	607.00	548.00	81	Yes	600.00	100.00	713.45	Excellent
Forehand stroke	8	13	16	8	Yes	15	100.00	14.66	Excellent
Backhand stroke	6	12	12	6	Yes	15	80.00	14.41	Focus on racket preparation
Tennis serve	4	10	9	5	No	15	60.00	13.12	Focus on ball toss and slowing down
Knowledge of rules test	61.00	85.00	100.00	39.00	Yes	85.00	100.00	87.04	Excellent
Cooperative behavior	12	16	16	4	Yes	20	80.00	16.53	Good improvement
Tennis etiquette	8	18	20	12	Yes	20	100.00	17.65	Excellent

Figure 4.11 Sample computer-generated student progress report.

ABC School District Physical Education Class Evaluation Report

Teacher: E. Dunn

Number of students in class: 32

Grade level: 8

Class: Third period—gold days

Report date: 6/10/03

Objectives	Class mean entry	Class mean target	Class mean exit	Class mean gain	% class meeting target	Mastery criteria	% class meeting mastery	Class average % mastery
Abdominal strength	25.20	35.42	37.56	12.36	90.25	40.00	75.00	93.90
Leg strength	8.20	7.91	7.80	0.40	80.36	7.60	100.00	97.40
Cardiorespiratory endurance	629.00	609.00	604.66	24.34	98.60	600.00	95.71	99.23
Forehand stroke	8.10	13.77	14.29	6.19	92.83	15.00	100.00	95.26
Backhand stroke	6.88	12.13	12.91	6.03	84.41	15.00	80.00	40.20
Tennis serve	4.79	10.32	9.98	5.19	78.26	15.00	60.00	66.53
Knowledge and rules test	61.00	85.00	100.00	39.00	100.00	85.00	100.00	100.00
Cooperative behavior	11.20	15.60	16.53	5.33	96.23	20.00	83.22	82.65
Tennis etiquette	9.12	14.02	17.65	8.53	96.71	20.00	85.69	88.26

■ **Figure 4.12** Sample computer-generated class evaluation report.

Making It Work

Have you achieved the expected outcomes (see page 66) for this chapter? You should now understand the ABC process, its five key components, and how this model differs from traditional models used in physical education. Still, you may have some practical questions that need answers, such as the following:

- *Is planning down really a new concept? It seems so logical.* The concept is not new, but its application to the design of physical education curricula is new. In fact, the two unique features of ABC planning are planning down and delimiting what is included in the curriculum to the time available for instruction. As discussed in this chapter, nothing was theoretically wrong with most bottom-up curricula other than the fact that they could not be implemented as designed because they included too much content for the time allocated for physical education. The planning-down process produces curricula that can actually be implemented and achieved in the time allocated for physical education in the overall school curriculum.

- *If my school only gives pass/fail grades in physical education, then is continual assessment as proposed in the ABC model really necessary?* Yes, because calculating grades for students is only one use of assessment data in the ABC model. In the ABC model assessment data are the key for planning instruction, providing students feedback, and evaluating both the students and the program. Without continual assessment, teachers will not know what to teach to address the unique needs of their students and students will not know specifically what they need to attend to during instruction and practice. If you walk into a physical education class in progress and ask a student what she is focusing on learning that day and she tells you soccer, what does this communicate to you? This response could be telling you a lot about both the curriculum and the teacher's quality of instruction. If all the student knows during a learning experience is that she should be working on her soccer skills, how is she going to improve? In other words, to improve their performances, students need to know at least what specific soccer skill they should be concentrating on and then what component of that skill they need to improve. You could deduce from this student's statement then that the teacher has probably not explained to the students the components of each soccer skill. You could also deduce that the teacher has probably not assessed the students and shared this information with them. In the absence of assessment data, you could also conclude that the lesson was not designed to address the unique learning needs of the students in this class. In the ABC model, we would expect a much more detailed response from a student, such as, "I am working on my instep kick and specifically on the placement of my nonkicking foot next to the ball when I kick." This response communicates that the student knows exactly what component she needs to work on for the skill being taught. For the student to know this information, the teacher must have already taught the components of the skill, assessed this student's performance, and provided this student with feedback.

- *Isn't program evaluation the job of the school administration?* The answer is yes and no. All school administrators are responsible for monitoring the curricula in their school. The differences are the goal or purpose of this evaluation and the expertise of the personnel performing the evaluation. In most cases, administrative evaluations focus on compliance and address questions such as, Is there a curriculum in place? and, Is it being implemented? As a general rule, administrative evaluations tend to be reactive. If there are complaints about the curriculum, then inquiries are made to evaluate these issues. If no complaints are voiced about the curriculum, then it is usually judged to be appropriate. Administrators are also not generally trained in the area of physical education curricula and therefore are limited in the degree to which they can evaluate the curriculum. For example, an administrator can check to see if the curriculum has goals and objectives, but would probably lack the expertise to judge whether the objectives listed for a given goal were developmentally appropriate. In the ABC model, the focus of program evaluation is on whether the program is producing the products it was designed to produce. In other words, are the students leaving the program having achieved the goals stated in the curriculum? ABC evaluation assumes that a curriculum and its implementation are never perfect and that both can always be improved. ABC program evaluation is also proactive in that it anticipates that there will be problems and establishes ways to collect student performance data to identify and correct these problems. Because ABC program evaluation is far more comprehensive than the typical administrative curriculum evaluation, most administrators would welcome this information about their physical education curriculum.

PART II

Planning the Physical Education Curriculum

This section is designed to answer two important questions: Where are you going? and, When will you know you've arrived? The achievement-based curriculum model deals explicitly with the planning decisions that will help you answer these two questions. If you're not sure where you're going, you may end up someplace else and not even know it! Therefore, chapter 5 helps you establish your program philosophy, goals, objectives, and policies. Chapter 6, on program planning, is composed of several practical considerations including scope and sequence, "unit" construction, scheduling, equipment, and facilities. Chapter 7 focuses on the development of functional assessments, an essential part of the physical education curriculum. A brief description of each chapter follows.

Chapter 5

Establishing the Philosophy, Goals, Objectives, and Policies

The task of defining a functional physical education program begins with determining its underlying philosophy. Why do students need this program, and how will they benefit from it? This chapter explores the sources from which to derive a program philosophy. In practice, mission or vision statements often reflect the program's philosophical tenets. Program goals, which represent broad learning outcomes, evolve from the philosophy. The goals, in turn, are broken down into developmental objectives that are sequenced across various grade levels; these are referred to as benchmarks. These objectives should reveal what students should know and understand, be able to do (skills), and believe and value (dispositions). Once determined, the program philosophy, goals, and objectives should be integrated into a set of program policies that support the overall program. Processes for establishing each of these elements are presented and illustrated.

Chapter 6

Program Planning

Philosophy, goals, objectives, and policies are the global organizing elements that support the next phase of decision making—planning the program itself, the next step in planning down. Planning at the program level begins with the scope and sequence of the content that will be taught. This process involves (1) delineating objectives for each goal, (2) establishing program goal emphasis (weighting), (3) calculating available instructional time, (4) calculating average objective mastery time, (5) calculating the total number of objectives in the program, and (6) sequencing the objectives developmentally throughout the program (grade-level benchmarks). This leads to constructing traditional units of instruction that consider factors such as scheduling, equipment, and facilities. All of these aspects are explored in this chapter.

Chapter 7

Developing Functional Assessments

In the achievement-based curriculum, assessment is paramount because it provides the basis for implementation and evaluation. Assessment is a dynamic, ongoing process that is linked to planned objectives and allows teachers to make informed decisions about learning and teaching. Assessment is broken down into four steps: (1) determining the type of decision needed, (2) selecting or creating an appropriate instrument, (3) administering the instrument in an accurate and valid manner, and (4) interpreting assessment data and making appropriate decisions. This chapter also addresses how to select and develop appropriate instruments to measure various kinds of curriculum objectives.

five

Establishing the Philosophy, Goals, Objectives, and Policies

You have just been hired as a middle school physical education teacher. You have been assigned to the sixth-grade classes, and your first unit is soccer. You review the school curriculum and note that the basic soccer skills (e.g., dribbling, shooting, trapping, heading) have been taught at the elementary level and you are now responsible for teaching more advanced objectives such as offensive and defensive strategies. You prepare and teach your first lesson, incorporating a review of many of the basic skills into your warm-up. You then explain and demonstrate a basic 3-4 offensive set highlighting the strengths of this formation and the responsibilities of the strikers and midfielders. You then break the class into groups and have them practice this formation in a number of short field drills.

At the end of your first day, you are totally exasperated. Every one of your classes was a total disaster. You knew you were in trouble during the warm-ups when the majority of the students demonstrated little to no ball control skills even though a few students appeared to be exceptionally skilled. When you started to explain the offensive strategy, it was clear that many of the students had no idea what you were talking about when you referred to strikers and midfielders.

At the start of your next class you ask the students about their soccer experience and learn that the students from one of the three elementary schools that feed into your middle school apparently had never worked on soccer. Students from one of the other elementary schools explain that they had played soccer occasionally but had never really worked on the specific skills. The students from the third school,

who appear to be most of the skilled, report that they had worked on soccer every year. Finding this hard to believe, you contact the elementary physical education teachers.

The first teacher informs you that there is so little time at the elementary level that he had had to choose between football and soccer and chose to focus on football. The second teacher informs you that he does a soccer unit each fall with all of his classes, but that his focus is on participation and the students having fun. To this end, he downplays drills and any emphasis on specific skills, which he believes only embarrasses the low-skilled kids. Finally, the third physical education teacher informs you that she works on soccer skills throughout the curriculum and she is confident that the majority of her students leave her program with competency levels specified in the curriculum.

Where did you go wrong? What assumptions did you make? Did you erroneously assume that the students would have the skills specified in the curriculum and that the students' previous physical educators had taught the prerequisite skills necessary to allow you to teach your content? This situation, unfortunately, is not uncommon. This scenario highlights a number of common curricular problems. When more content is specified in the curriculum than the teachers can cover, teachers often delimit the amount of content to cover. Unfortunately, each teacher elects to teach different objectives. When faced with too much content, teachers also often try to cover the content but change the focus from skill achievement to another goal such as exposure or participation. This scenario illustrates what happens to most bottom-up curricula as students progress up the program levels.

EXPECTED OUTCOMES

This chapter will introduce you to the ABC planning process and guide you through the first three steps in developing an achievement-based curriculum. After reading this chapter, you will be able to do the following:

1. Develop a philosophy statement that is representative of the values and beliefs of the physical education staff, administrations, parents, students, and community

2. Generate and rank a series of goals that define what competencies the students will achieve by the end of the physical education program

3. Identify the key policies and essential resources needed to implement an achievement-based physical education curriculum in your district

4. Describe how to use the consensus-building technique to resolve problems and arrive at consensus on issues of disagreement

5. Recognize the group dynamics involved in the curriculum planning process and the importance of involving all constituents in the process

The previous scenario highlights a number of the issues this chapter is designed to address. In this chapter we will present a step-by-step process for defining a functional physical education curriculum that all the students served by the program can achieve. Keep in mind that this chapter presents a *process*. The ABC planning process does not dictate the philosophy of the curriculum, nor does it stipulate what content should or should not be taught in the curriculum. Those decisions are made by the teachers and the consumers who will be creating and using the curriculum. The ABC planning process guides teachers through a systematic decision-making process designed to create a curriculum that produces the outcomes they desire and accounts for their unique constraints. We also want to emphasize that, although the ABC planning process was designed to create comprehensive school district K-12 programs, it can be used to design programs of any size such as a K-5 program for an individual school or an individualized education plan (IEP) for an individual student requiring a specially designed physical education program.

In part I of this book (chapters 1 through 4) you learned about the foundation for the curriculum, why curricula are needed, different curriculum models that guide what content is addressed in physical education, and the ABC model. The focus of this chapter is on how to assimilate all of this information into a functional curriculum.

Table 5.1 illustrates the 11 steps involved in the ABC planning process. The first three steps of the process are presented in this chapter. The purpose of these steps is simply to organize the content into manageable units. Depending on the size of the group developing the program, these steps can easily be combined or broken down into smaller steps. Although various products are produced in the individual steps, all of these products must be integrated into one seamless document at the end of the planning process.

Finally, you should recognize that learning about the ABC planning process and actually using the ABC planning process to develop a physical education curriculum are two different experiences. Understanding and applying the ABC process is analogous to learning to swim. Although a certain amount of valuable information can be obtained from reading and observing examples about how to prone float, flutter kick, rhythmically breathe, and perform the appropriate arm action for the crawl stroke, nothing compares to jumping into the water and trying to integrate this knowledge so that it produces a swimming action that moves you through the water. As in learning to swim, there is a learning curve when using the ABC model. The more you practice using and applying the model, the more competent you will become. Fortunately, you do not have to worry about drowning or swallowing water when learning to use the ABC model.

An ABC program planning case study is provided in appendix A at the end of the book. This hypothetical example is intended to show you the products of the ABC planning steps; it is not intended to be a model plan. Because of space limitations, we intentionally delimited the scope and depth of the plan to the minimum needed to illustrate each planning step. You are encouraged to read the text about each step in the planning process

first and then to try to apply it before looking at the example in the appendix.

When using the ABC model to actually develop a physical education curriculum, you must have a leader. This individual ideally should be well versed in the ABC planning process and have some past experience actually working with a group of teachers on developing an ABC plan. The primary role of the leader is to keep the group focused and on task. Like any new experience, the ABC planning process can be threatening to many teachers. Therefore, the leader must constantly monitor the anxiety level of the teachers and intervene when and where necessary to reduce tension before it begins to disrupt the process. The most challenging role for leaders is to separate themselves from their personal views and biases and focus solely on guiding the group to developing the group's curriculum. When learning about the ABC planning process, teachers should work in small groups and actually apply what is presented. When performing these group activities, different teachers should assume the leadership role so that they can experience the challenges of this position in the planning process.

Before actually beginning the curriculum planning process, you need to put the planning process in perspective. Curriculum planning can be viewed from a number of different perspectives, each of which plays a significant role in the final curriculum. You can view the planning process in terms of

1. the relationship between the overall school curriculum and the physical education curriculum,

2. the underlying curriculum models that shape the curriculum,

3. the curriculum philosophies of the individual teachers, and

4. the processes used to integrate these various perspectives into a unified curriculum.

Overall School Curriculum

When reviewing curriculum models, remember that the physical education curriculum is part of the overall school curriculum and should be integrated and coordinated with it to maximize student benefits and the use of the talents of the instructional staff. Clearly, some objectives such as self-discipline and respect transcend all content areas and should be addressed across the overall school curriculum by all teachers. Other goals and objectives in the

Table 5.1   Overview of the ABC Curriculum Planning Steps

Step	Chapter	Key processes	Products
1	5	Developing the curriculum philosophy statement: Form a curriculum committee; conduct a needs assessment; align the curriculum with national, state, and local recommendations and needs; and integrate with the school philosophy and curriculum.	A written philosophy statement that includes links to the overall school mission and philosophy, a statement of the underlying values and beliefs that serve as the foundation for the physical education curriculum, and a summary of the processes used to develop the curriculum as well as the members of the curriculum development committee
2	5	Defining the curriculum goals: incorporating the planning-down concept, identifying program outcomes, justifying curriculum outcomes, building consensus	A rank-ordered list of curriculum goals that indicate what students will achieve by the end of the program. Each goal is supported by a series of justification statements.
3	5	Determining policies and resources: reviewing the resources and school policies needed to implement the curriculum successfully	A written statement of the resources and polices needed to implement the curriculum
4	6	Delineating objectives for each goal: incorporating the planning-down concept, task analyzing goals, defining preliminary objectives, building consensus, rank-ordering objectives	A rank-ordered list of objectives for each goal based on their significance to the goal
5	6	Establishing program goal emphasis: determining the emphasis each goal should receive by program level, interaction of planning down and implementing up, building consensus	A table that illustrates the time that will be devoted to each curriculum goal by grade and program level across the curriculum
6	6	Calculating available instructional time: identifying the amount of instructional time available by program level, identifying the amount of lost instructional time	A table that illustrates the actual amount of instructional time available by program level and the total number of hours available for the entire program
7	6	Calculating an average objective mastery time: estimating mastery times for each goal, building consensus, reviewing objective definitions and the concept of mastery, calculating weighted estimates for each goal	A single time estimate that represents the amount of time needed to teach and achieve mastery of an average objective in the curriculum
8	6	Calculating the total number of objectives in the curriculum: using the results of steps 6 and 7 to determine the total number of objectives that can be included in the curriculum, using the program emphasis table to determine the number of objectives for each goal	A table that illustrates the number of objectives that will be included in the curriculum for each curriculum goal
9	6	Sequencing the objectives across the curriculum: using the ranked lists of objectives for each goal to determine the specific objectives that will be included, using developmental principles and the implementing-up concept, determining when instruction will be initiated and when mastery is expected	A program plan that indicates at what grade levels all of the objectives in the curriculum will be initiated and mastered to achieve the stated curriculum goals at the end of the program
10	6	Developing yearly and block teaching and learning maps for each grade and class based on scheduling, facility, and equipment availability	Yearly and block teaching and learning maps that indicate what objectives will be taught and how much emphasis each objective will receive during each class
11	6	Deciding how to organize the curriculum materials developed through the ABC processes so they can be used by both consumers and teachers	Two documents are created: a consumer curriculum guide and working teacher notebooks.

When learning about the ABC planning process, teachers should work in small groups and apply what is presented.

curriculum are more content specific and typically are emphasized in a specific content area (e.g., teaching throwing is taught in physical education).

This is not to imply, however, that content-specific objectives should be taught in isolation. All teachers working with a given group of students should be aware of all of the objectives that are being worked on so that they can complement and reinforce these objectives as opportunities present themselves. This process is commonly referred to as curriculum mapping or curriculum integration. All of the teachers working with a given group of students (e.g., third grade) meet and review the objectives targeted for the year and plan ways in which they can integrate their instruction. For example, a geography objective may be to study a given region and explore the impact that the physical geography of the area has had on the culture of the people that reside there. English could complement this objective by focusing on reading stories that relate to this culture. History could complement the objective by focusing on the history of this culture. Physical education could complement the study of this objective by focusing on a game, sport, or dance that is related to this culture.

The key here is that the teachers of each content area are still working on their own objectives, but they are capitalizing on a curriculum theme, which provides greater relevance of all the content to the students. In physical education, for example, the teacher's primary objective would be to develop a specific motor skill. However, the teacher could increase the relevance of the unit by picking a game or activity that relates to the overall school curriculum theme. That would also be true for the

other content areas. The reading objectives would be driven by the reading curriculum and the needs of the students, but the teacher could select the content the students will read so that it relates to the overall school curriculum theme.

When embedding objectives into an integrated curriculum or curriculum mapping, the goals and objectives of one content area must not supplant others. Rather, the teachers of each content area should retain their goals and objectives but try to coordinate them with the school curriculum theme to maximize the relevance and benefit to the students. Physical education teachers, for example, would not add objectives to their curriculum to complement the curriculum theme. Instead they would use an objective targeted for instruction in the physical education curriculum and then select a game, activity, or sport that complements the curriculum theme and allows the students to work on this objective.

Curriculum Models

The traditional approach to studying curricula in physical education is to review and analyze the curriculum trends and models (see chapters 1 and 3) that have evolved over the years in terms of their focus, orientation, and underlying values. From this review process teachers are then encouraged to develop their own personal curriculum philosophies presumably from which they will work when they are employed as teachers. This logic would imply that teachers either pursue jobs in which they get to define their own curriculum to match their philosophy or are hired because their curriculum view matches that of the school that hired them. The reality for most beginning teachers, however, is that their first priority is to get a job, and most are willing to work within the existing curriculum. Once hired, the second goal of most beginning teachers is to survive and succeed.

Beginning teachers pursue success and survival on several fronts simultaneously. For example, most teachers focus on things such as establishing instructional control over their classes, being accepted as a credible peer by the other teachers, earning the respect and appreciation from their students and the parents of their students, and last but not least, being evaluated as competent by the appropriate administrators. Once teachers pass these obstacles, they then typically begin to have the time and energy to start examining curriculum issues. This usually occurs after they have earned tenure.

Once tenured, teachers can be confronted with any number of issues. They may find that the curriculum they and most of the other physical education teachers are implementing has few similarities to the school's written physical education curriculum. They may find little or no coordination of what the physical education teachers are teaching at the same grades or program levels, or discrepancies between the stated focus of the curriculum and what their principal or other principals appear to value about physical education. Many physical education teachers realize that multiple curriculum systems are in place. There is the official curriculum that is outlined in a notebook and presented whenever someone asks about the curriculum, and then there is the "in the head" curriculum, which is the curriculum that the teachers believe they are implementing. Finally, there is the actual curriculum experienced by the students in the program (Goodlad, 1979). At this point teachers are usually becoming aware of the need for a revised district-wide curriculum development effort, but many are now hesitant to become involved because they think they do not have the skills necessary to define a district-wide curriculum, or they are self-conscious about how their curriculum views will stack up with those of the other physical education teachers.

From this brief scenario, we can draw four conclusions. First, discrepancies are common between the formal curriculum (i.e., what is in writing) and the actual curriculum being implemented (e.g., "in the head"). Second, the majority of the physical education staff eventually recognizes the need for a curriculum change, but most are not sure how to address this issue. Third, the members of the physi-

cal education staff will believe in a number of different curriculum models. Fourth, a new curriculum will not reflect one traditional model but will most likely be a composite that addresses the needs and interests of many groups.

The goal then in studying curricula is to understand the various curriculum trends and models so that you can appreciate the views and values of others and work cooperatively toward developing a collective curriculum. In chapter 3 we reviewed the common curriculum models employed in physical education. Analysis of the various trends and models reveals a few common threads. First and foremost, all of the models are designed to prepare the students for later life and to become productive members of society, although they emphasize different things. These differences are based on the underlying beliefs about the primary purpose of physical education and the role physical education should play in preparing individuals for life and their future role in society. For example, the fitness education model evolved in response to the changing health profile in U.S. society that indicated a need for increased physical activity. Based on this perceived need, the model was then designed to provide future members of society (today's children) with the knowledge and skills needed to develop and maintain a healthy lifestyle.

A second thread common to all of the models is that they all use physical and motor skills as their medium, although they can differ markedly in their desired outcomes. For example, the sport education model is designed to produce skilled performers with an understanding and appreciation of the value of being a member of a team, whereas the focus of the personally meaningful model would be more on helping students develop their own individual ways of finding and expressing themselves through movement.

A third thread common to all of the models is the involvement of the learner. What differs between the models is the type of involvement and the amount of control the learner has. For example, the sport education and activity-based models tend to be prescriptive in nature. The learning sequence and outcomes are defined, and the learners are expected to progress through these sequences and acquire the desired outcomes. In other models, such as movement education, the goal is still to produce proficient movers, but the learners are more actively involved in the process via movement exploration and problem-solving activities.

Curriculum models have evolved over time to respond to different needs and to expand the role and impact of physical education in the overall school curriculum. Most schools today feature eclectic models that contain components from several of the traditional models. After reviewing a number of curriculum models, many beginning teachers have a tendency to want their physical education curricula to accomplish the goals of all of the models. Although this is understandable, the reality is that only so much time can be devoted to physical education in the overall school curriculum. Because the amount of time available will not allow you to address all of these approaches and outcomes, you must make some difficult decisions regarding which ones to include in your program.

The failure to make these difficult decisions during the curriculum development process undermines many curriculum development efforts and results in bottom-up curricula as described in chapter 4. Although many of these bottom-up curricula are theoretically based and developmentally sound, they are impossible to implement because they do not account for the actual amount of time available for instruction in physical education.

Keep in mind that your own personal views on curriculum tend to reflect the programs you have participated in or in which you have been trained. For example, if you were taught and succeeded in a sport skills curriculum when you were a kid, you will tend to pursue a sport science physical education teacher preparation program and have a bias toward physical education programs that emphasis sport skills and physical fitness. Given this tendency, we recommend that you intentionally force yourself to explore the curriculum models that seem most foreign to you. A good exercise is to form groups with teachers or fellow students who support several different models. Another good exercise is to organize mini debates in which you have to research and then argue the merits of one of the models you know little about.

The final reality is that the needs of the students, school, community, and society in general are constantly changing. Both the school and the physical education curriculum need to be continually evaluated so that they can respond to these changes. Hence, the most important skill you can have as a teacher relative to curricula is an understanding of the curriculum development and evaluation processes.

Now that you understand the relationship between the overall school curriculum and the physical education curriculum (and the reality that the physical education staff will hold multiple curriculum views), you are ready to begin the program planning process.

Step 1: Developing the Program Philosophy

The first step in defining a functional physical education program is developing a program philosophy. In simple terms, the program philosophy answers the questions, Why do students need this program? and, How will they benefit from it? The underlying philosophy for the program is informed from a number of sources such as the beliefs and values of the physical educators, students, community, and school administration.

The ideal scenario for developing a program philosophy statement would be to form a committee with representatives from all interested parties. This group would then develop and implement a needs assessment survey that would solicit input from all relevant parties regarding what they value and desire as outputs from the physical education program. The committee would then use the results of the needs assessment to develop a program philosophy statement. For a district-wide curriculum the committee would include as many of the physical education staff as possible, principal representatives, central office representatives, student representatives, school board representatives, community representatives, and any others deemed relevant by the physical education staff. The reality, however, is that getting a large group like this together and conducting a community-wide needs assessment is difficult.

Depending on the scope of the program plan and the diversity of the views held by different parties, developing a philosophy statement can require from one to several lengthy meetings. To be as efficient as possible, the physical education staff generally meets and identifies the appropriate groups and representatives that should be involved in the process. Figure 5.1 contains a sample worksheet the program planning committee can use to solicit the information needed to write a philosophy statement. See appendix B, page 320, for the reproducible form. These committee members then contact individuals in the target groups, explain what they are working on, and solicit input. The needs assessment process can take many forms from surveying small samples of each target group, conducting focus groups, holding public forums, or simply asking the representatives of each group on the committee to solicit input and feedback from their constituents before each meeting. The committee then meets and reviews the input received and develops a draft philosophy statement. Time permitting, individuals on the committee would then review the draft, solicit

---

Achievement-Based Curriculum Philosophy Worksheet

This worksheet is designed to help you identify major points that may be included in a curriculum philosophy statement. These prompts are provided as guidelines. You may want to emphasize some points more or less than others, depending on the local needs and interests.

State why all students need physical education.

State the benefits gained from physical education.

State how the physical education curriculum is linked to the school curriculum or mission.

State how the physical education curriculum is linked to community interests and values.

State the time required to effectively implement the physical education curriculum.

State the teacher qualifications needed to implement the curriculum.

State the class size and instructional space the curriculum was designed to accommodate.

State the policies and resources (in general terms) needed to effectively implement the curriculum.

List those who were involved in the physical education curriculum development process.

State the process used by the curriculum committee to develop the curriculum.

State the goals the students will have achieved when they complete the curriculum.

State the rationale and benefits for students achieving these goals.

Figure 5.1   Philosophy worksheet.

---

additional input, and make revisions where appropriate. Then a meeting would be held with all of the representatives to formally review and approve the final philosophy statement.

Figure 5.2 contains a sample school philosophy statement. This sample is an example and not an ideal model statement. The amount of detail and emphasis included in the program philosophy statement will vary and should relate to the current status of physical education in the district. In districts in which physical education is valued and in relatively good shape, the philosophy statements tend to be shorter and to cite local references that support their status such as in the district's mission statement or quotes of support from the school board and community members. In districts in which physical education is under attack, the philosophy statements tend to be more detailed. In these cases, the statements may include references such as the CDC or the surgeon general's report on the health and fitness needs of today's youth as well as references that support the need for daily physical education taught by physical education specialists.

You may be thinking that this seems to be a rather elaborate process to simply state the underlying beliefs and values of the physical education

program, but it accomplishes a number of important objectives. First, it provides the physical education staff with an important opportunity to educate key decision makers who may play a role in future decisions regarding the program. Second, it establishes a working relationship between these groups and the physical education staff. Third, it establishes a level of ownership between these key groups and the physical education program; this is the first step in gaining support for the total program now and later on down the road. Finally, it provides a unified base for the physical education staff to work from during the planning process. When conflicts arise later in the planning process (and yes, they do arise), the philosophy statement provides a point of common ground for resolving them.

Involving the entire physical education staff that will ultimately be responsible for implementing the program is extremely important. This said, a few teachers are generally either unable or unwilling to participate in the planning process. In these cases, every effort should be made to communicate regularly with these individuals about the planning process and to solicit their input and feedback. One technique to link these teachers to the process is to pair them up with one of the teachers in the group.

Sample School Physical Education Philosophy Statement

We, the members of the SAMPLE school district physical education staff in collaboration with representatives from the student body, the community, the school board, and the central administration, have developed this statement as an indication of our belief in the benefits to be derived by our students from participation in physical education.

We believe that each student should be provided daily physical education instruction by a qualified physical education specialist. This belief is supported by the American Alliance for Health, Physical Education, Recreation and Dance, which recommends that all students receive a minimum of 30 minutes of daily physical education. The need for physical education and activity is greater today than in the past, as evidenced by this quote regarding physical activity and health from the surgeon general: "Nearly half of young people 12-21 years of age are not vigorously active; moreover, physical activity sharply declines during adolescence. Childhood and adolescence may thus be pivotal times for preventing sedentary behavior among adults by maintaining the habit of physical activity throughout the school years. School-based interventions have been shown to be successful in increasing physical activity levels."

In light of these findings, we believe that students must acquire the cognitive knowledge, physical skills, and fitness needed to develop and maintain an active and healthy lifestyle that will enable them to be gainfully employed, free from sickness, and able to participate actively in individual lifetime sport activities. To meet these goals, all students must achieve the developmental sequence of objectives delineated in the physical education curriculum. As a direct result of mastering the objectives in the physical education curriculum, students will leave the program with the following:

(List program goals here)

▌ **Figure 5.2**   Sample physical education philosophy statement.

The teachers in the group are then responsible for contacting the uninvolved teachers after each meeting to explain what happened and to solicit input. The program planning leader should also periodically touch base with the uninvolved teachers to confirm that they are being kept up to speed on the group's progress and to encourage their participation. Involving uninterested teachers in the planning process may seem like a lot of work, but it is time well spent. When the time comes for these teachers to implement the curriculum that has been developed, they will be much more likely to buy in.

Some physical educators are frequently in a hurry to get to the nuts and bolts of defining a functional physical education curriculum and are tempted to skip the program philosophy step or to perform this step quickly with a small group of like-minded individuals (i.e., a few of their peer physical educators). Once they define the actual program, they figure, they will then come back and use it to involve the other physical education staff, decision makers, and consumers. Experience suggests that this approach usually results in failure. The uninvolved physical education teachers are frequently both offended that they were not included in the development process and threatened by what the other teachers have produced. Instead of focusing their time and energy on buying into the program, they typically get defensive and spend their time and energy attacking it. Instead of rallying behind this new approach, the staff divides into factions. The original developers frequently end up feeling unvalued and unappreciated by their peers. From their perspective, they were acting in good faith and did all the hard work to develop the curriculum. They were expecting to be praised by their peers, but instead the uninvolved group has rejected their efforts and criticized their work. When this divided physical education staff ultimately meets with the other representatives, instead of presenting a unified message, they appear at odds with each other and in disagreement. Instead of impressing these representatives, they leave them with a negative impression of both the staff and the program, which could have negative consequences for them later.

This is not to imply that some of the work cannot be performed by small groups and then brought back to the entire group for review and approval. Ideally, it would be desirable for the full committee to participate in all of the planning steps. In reality, this is usually not practical particularly for many of the nonphysical education representatives on the committee. After the program philosophy is developed and adopted by the committee, the physical education staff typically does a lot of the detailed work related to the other steps. After the detail work is done for each step, it is shared and reviewed by the total committee and then approved.

Step 2: Defining Program Goals

The uniqueness of the ABC planning process is its emphasis on "planning down." When planning down, you start with goal statements that define specifically what students will be able to do when they complete the program. These goal statements are then broken down into developmental lists of objectives that are sequenced across the various grade levels in the program. Although the ABC planning process can be applied to curriculum development at any level (i.e., elementary, middle, secondary), it is ideally designed to be used in comprehensive K-12 programs. In contrast, many physical education curricula are developed using a bottom-up approach (see chapter 4). In this approach, physical educators get together by program levels (e.g., elementary, middle, high school), and each group independently delineates what content they will teach in their programs. They then organize the content around themes and units and compile it into a document called a curriculum. In most cases, you have three independent curricula that are linked only by coincidence and chance.

It is important to recognize that this change from the bottom-up model to the planning-down model represents a major change in the way many physical educators think about curriculum development. To avoid confusion and resistance to change, make a concerted effort to introduce the model clearly and to illustrate why it is preferred.

Program goals are broad statements of what the students will be able to do when they have completed the program. The program goals translate the needs and values outlined in the philosophy statement into observable outcomes. They are not a wish list, but actual outcomes *all* students are expected to leave the program with. Program goals should not just be pulled out of the air. They should be anchored to national or state standards for physical education. They must also be consistent with the program philosophy and reflect what the physical educators and other members of the program planning committee value and see as the needs for the program to address.

Although many similarities may exist among the goals developed by different schools, each needs to be developed around the unique attributes of that particular school or district. You cannot simply adopt another school's goals. Figure 5.3 illustrates the relationship between a sample school's physical education goals and the NASPE standards for physical education. Most states that have state standards for physical education have adopted the NASPE standards (Rink et al., 1995; see chapter 2, table 2.3). You should, however, check to see whether your state has standards for physical education, and, if they do, link your program goals to their standards as well.

You may be thinking about simply using the NASPE standards as your goals. This is not a good idea because the standards are too broad to serve as program goals. Program goals are more specific and indicate what students will be able to do at the end of the program that will indicate that they have met a standard. For example, the first NASPE standard states that students should "Demonstrate competency in many movement forms and proficiency in a few movement forms." A program goal related to this standard could be: Students will be able to play a functional game of tennis using appropriate strokes, rules, and strategies.

Getting a group of physical educators to agree on a common set of program goals can be a very challenging task. Typically, teachers have a variety of different views on what students should achieve as outcomes from the program. If some process is not used to guide the discussion, a number of heated arguments may result or a small group of teachers may dominate the discussion while other teachers just withdraw. To avoid these problems, agree on a systematic process such as the consensus-building technique outlined in the following section and use it whenever you need to make decisions in the curriculum development process.

NASPE National Standards for Physical Education

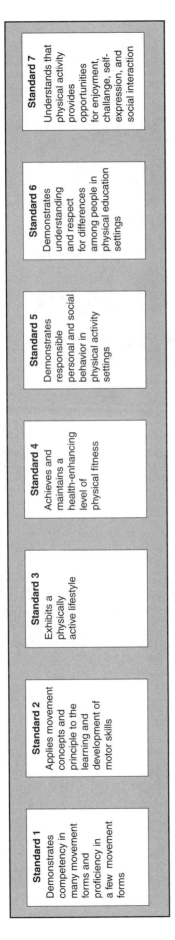

School Curriculum Goals

1. Play a functional game of golf
2. Play a functional game of bowling
3. Play a functional game of tennis

4. Play a functional game of badminton
5. Functionally participate in rock climbing
6. Play a functional game of volleyball

7. Play a functional game of softball
8. Play a functional game of basketball
9. Play a functional game of soccer

10. Play a functional game of football
11. Develop and maintain a functional level of fitness
12. Be responsible and display appropriate social behavior in sport settings

Standard 1
Demonstrates competency in many movement forms and proficiency in a few movement forms

Standard 2
Applies movement concepts and principle to the learning and development of motor skills

Standard 3
Exhibits a physically active lifestyle

Standard 4
Achieves and maintains a health-enhancing level of physical fitness

Standard 5
Demonstrates responsible personal and social behavior in physical activity settings

Standard 6
Demonstrates understanding and respect for differences among people in physical education settings

Standard 7
Understands that physical activity provides opportunities for enjoyment, challenge, self-expression, and social interaction

Program Instructional Objectives

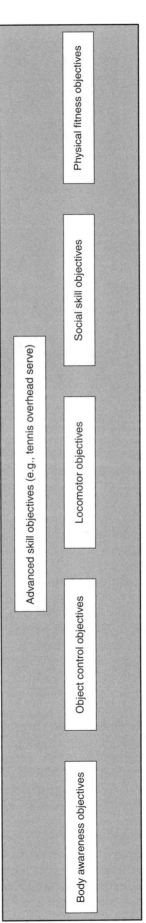

Body awareness objectives

Object control objectives

Advanced skill objectives (e.g., tennis overhead serve)

Locomotor objectives

Social skill objectives

Physical fitness objectives

■ **Figure 5.3** Relationship between program goals and NASPE standards.

The consensus-building technique gives all paricipants equal weight and influence in decision making.

Consensus-Building Technique

When working with a group of teachers on program planning, you will often need to get the teachers to agree on a set of conditions or on an issue before proceeding. The consensus-building technique is a way to establish agreement on a variety of different types of issues when there are competing views. Establish at the start of the planning process that this will be the procedure you will use to establish a consensus when issues are encountered during the planning process. The consensus-building technique will give all participants equal weight and influence in decision making. The steps of the technique are illustrated in figure 5.4 (see appendix B, page 322, for the reproducible form).

The process of defining program goals is an excellent place to introduce the consensus-building technique. First all of the physical educators should individually develop a list of the goals they believe should be included in the program. (See the goal development worksheet in figure 5.5. See appendix B, page 323, for the blank form.) Because of the time involved, this step is usually performed by just the physical education staff. If the other members of the curriculum committee (e.g., principals, school board members, etc.) are involved, they should be paired up with physical educators for this step.

After all of the physical educators have outlined their goals, ask them to write three reasons why each goal they have listed should be included in the curriculum. The general rule is that if teachers cannot think of three good reasons to justify a goal, then it is probably not a high-priority goal. These rationale statements can also be integrated into the program philosophy statement after the goals are finalized. When everyone is ready, collect and compile the lists. Compiling the lists can be performed in a number of ways depending on the size of the group and the resources available. A common process is to give the group a small break and then have the leader list the goals on the blackboard. Any obvious duplications can be removed as the goals are listed. Any questionable duplications should be listed so the group can review and discuss them. When the group reconvenes, members should review and remove any remaining possible duplications where appropriate.

Once the duplications have been removed, each goal on the board should be assigned a unique number. Now the curriculum committee members are asked to individually rank the goals from most important (rank = 1) to least important. Figure 5.6 (page 108) shows a sample form that can be used for ranking program goals. See appendix B, page 324, for the blank form. The goals are listed down the left side of the form in the same order for all teachers, and each is assigned a unique number. The committee members then independently rank the goals. After the members have ranked the items, the leader

Consensus-Building Technique

1. List the competing items or issues and assign each a unique number from 1 to x (where x is the number of the last item in the list).

2. Have each member independently rate, or rank, the items from highest priority (1) to lowest priority (x). All items must be ranked, and all items must be assigned a unique rank—no ties.

3. Collect the individual rankings, compute the average ranks for each item, and then relist the items in rank order from 1 to x based on the calculated average ranks.

4. Provide members a timed individual opportunity to address why they believe any item should either be moved farther up or down the list. All comments must be directed to the content in question; no personal references to the comments of other members should be allowed. Depending on the complexity of the issue, a time limit should be placed on the individual comments ranging from 1 to 3 minutes. Each member should systematically be provided with an opportunity to speak to the rankings. This process is specifically designed to rein in the domineering, overly verbal members and to encourage the quiet, less verbal members to participate.

5. After the comment period, all members again rank the items. This process allows individuals to reflect on the insights, new information, and comments that have been made and to indicate the impact on their ranking of the items.

6. Compute average ranks for each item and then relist the items in rank order from 1 to x based on the calculated average ranks.

7. Repeat steps 4 through 6 until the relative rankings stabilize. Although the actual average ranks (values) will vary after each reranking, as soon as the items stay in the same order for two rankings, consensus has been reached. Once a consensus is reached, the issue is closed to further discussion during the planning process.

▌Figure 5.4   Steps in the consensus-building technique.

Program Goals and Supporting Rationales

Goal statement: All students will be able to play a functional game of tennis using appropriate strokes, rules, and strategies.

Rationale statements:

1. Tennis is a lifetime sport that can be played throughout the life span.
2. Tennis involves minimal equipment and can be played on courts that are generally available to the public at little or no cost.
3. Tennis is a good activity for maintaining health and fitness.

▌Figure 5.5   A sample portion of a goal development worksheet.

Goal Ranking Worksheet

Goals	Ranking Rounds				
	1	2	3	4	Final
1. Tennis	1.75(1)*	2.50(3)	2.00(2)	2.00(2)	(2)
2. Volleyball	2.50(3)	2.25(2)	2.50(3)	2.50(3)	(3)
3. Fitness	2.25(2)	1.50(1)	1.50(1)	1.50(1)	(1)
4. Social responsibility	4.00(4)	4.25(4)	4.50(4)	4.50(4)	(4)
5. Basketball	5.00(5)	5.00(5)	5.00(5)	5.00(5)	(5)
6. Golf	5.50(6)	5.50(6)	5.50(6)	5.50(6)	(6)

*The first value is the average of the teachers' ratings for that goal in that round. The value in parentheses is the relative rank of that goal in relation to the other goals for that round. For example, the average rating of the teachers for tennis in the first round was 1.75. This rating was the lowest compared to the other goals so its relative ranking is (1).

▌ **Figure 5.6** Sample goal ranking form.

should collect them and compute average ranks for each item. The leader should relist the items in rank order based on their average rank, and then call on each member to comment on the rankings. During the comment period the members can argue why a given goal should be ranked higher or lower. Having the members record three reasons for each of their original goals ensures that all members have some rationale they can present. After each member has an opportunity to comment on the rankings, they are again asked to individually rank the goals based on the new information they have received. This process is repeated until the goals stay in the same relative rank order.

To facilitate the ranking calculations and save time, the curriculum committee can use a simple spreadsheet to perform the calculations. Figure 5.7 shows an example of the basic format of a spreadsheet that could be used to average the ranks for goals. Note that the last two columns of this sheet contain formulas that automatically average and rank the data. Figure 5.8 shows an example of the summary rankings for a set of goals. Note that even though the actual averages changed in the last two rankings (i.e., columns), the relative rank order of the objectives did not change. When this occurs, you have reached consensus. If you use spreadsheets like the one in figure 5.7 to calculate the ranks for each round, you can link them to a spreadsheet like the one in figure 5.8; the data will automatically be

transferred and updated in the figure 5.8 sheet each time changes are made in the figure 5.7 sheets.

Never throw out any goals during the ranking process. At this point in the planning process it is too early to determine exactly how many goals the final program can address. All of the goals should be recorded in their final rank order and then held for future reference in the planning process.

Step 3: Policies and Resources

Designing a program that is achievement based and accountable involves more than just identifying the content and deciding when to teach it. School policies should be in place that define expectations for such things as scheduling of classes, grading, attendance, and waivers of participation. In addition, the staff must know what resources (e.g., facilities and equipment) they will have access to and when.

Policies

The goal of this section is not to identify and develop every little policy that needs to exist to conduct a physical education program. Rather, the goal is to highlight policies that have a direct impact on student achievement of the program goals. The policies chosen to be highlighted will be a function of the needs and issues in each school district. A common issue is scheduling of physical education.

Round 1							Final	
		Teacher Goal Ranks						
Goals	T1	T2	T3	T4	T5	T6	Average	Rank
G1	1	2	2	2	1	2	1.67	1
G2	2	1	3	4	3	4	2.83	2
G3	3	4	10	6	2	6	5.17	4
G4	4	3	9	8	4	1	4.83	3
G5	5	6	4	10	5	3	5.50	6
G6	6	5	5	1	7	8	5.33	5
G7	7	8	8	3	6	7	6.50	7
G8	8	7	7	5	8	5	6.67	8
G9	9	10	6	7	9	10	8.50	10
G10	10	9	1	9	10	9	8.00	9

- The goals are listed down the left side. Each goal is represented by a unique number, such as G1, G2, and so on.
- Each teacher is represented by a unique number (e.g., T1, T2, and so on) and their ranks for each goal are listed below their number.
- The second to last column on the right in the spreadsheet is defined to calculate the average for each row.
- The last column on the right is defined to rank the averages.
- This spreadsheet can easily be modified to accommodate more goals or more teachers by simply inserting more rows or columns into the sheet.

▮ **Figure 5.7**   Sample spreadsheet for averaging ranks.

	Ranking Rounds							
	Round 1		Round 2		Round 3		Round 4	
Goals	Average	Rank	Average	Rank	Average	Rank	Average	Rank
G1	1.67	1	2.00	1	1.33	1	1.33	1
G2	2.83	2	3.00	2	2.67	2	2.67	2
G3	5.17	4	4.33	4	4.83	4	4.67	4
G4	4.83	3	5.67	6	5.33	6	5.67	6
G5	5.50	6	4.00	3	4.00	3	4.33	3
G6	5.33	5	5.00	5	5.00	5	5.00	5
G7	6.50	7	8.00	10	7.67	9	7.33	9
G8	6.67	8	7.00	8	7.00	8	7.00	8
G9	8.50	10	6.00	7	6.67	7	6.87	7
G10	8.00	9	7.33	9	8.00	10	7.87	10

▮ **Figure 5.8**   Sample summary ranking for a set of goals.

That is, how much time is allocated for physical education and how it is distributed in terms of its duration and frequency. Related issues are who makes these decisions, how the physical education staff is involved, how big the classes are, and who provides the instruction.

Some states require that elementary students received physical education for a minimum of 60 minutes each week. If not carefully defined, this requirement could be interpreted and implemented in several different ways by school principals. One school could decide to have physical education once a week for 60 minutes for each of its classes to simplify the scheduling. Another school, less concerned with simplifying scheduling and more concerned with student development, may decide to have physical education three times a week for 20 minutes each period, but decide that it should be taught by the classroom teachers and not by a physical education specialist. Another school could decide to allocate 90 minutes for physical education (three times a week for 30 minutes), but decide to double up the classes so that the classroom teachers could have a common planning period. These are only some examples to illustrate the complexity of this issue. To avoid these problems, the duration and frequency of physical education classes, class size, and who should provide the instruction should be defined in the curriculum and justified in terms of what is needed to teach and have the students achieve the goals of the program.

Scheduling of instructional time is usually just one of the common policy issues addressed in the curriculum. Some of the other common issues are as follows:

■ *Waivers for physical education.* Can participation in athletics, the school marching band, or after-school youth sports be used as substitutes for attending physical education? Who makes these decisions, and how are these students graded? What happens when these students return to physical education and now lack the prerequisite skills for the content being taught?

■ *Grading.* How is physical education graded, and how are these grades used in the students' grade point averages (GPA)? Typically, if pass/fail or satisfactory/unsatisfactory dichotomous grading systems are used, these grades are not counted in the GPA. The issue here is that if physical education grades do not count, why should the students be motivated to get good grades?

■ *Consequences for student attendance and preparedness for class.* These issues are related to grading. If students do not attend, do not come dressed to participate, or choose not to participate, what are the consequences, and how is this time made up?

■ *Student placement in physical education.* Ideally, students should be placed in physical education based on their developmental and instructional needs. Unfortunately, most physical education placement is done by grade level. The issue here is that physical educators should be involved in this decision-making process. A related issue is addressing the needs of students with disabilities. If a student with a severe disability is included in a regular physical education class, what adjustments are made to class size so that the teacher can attend to this student's needs? Is this student's aide required to attend physical education with the student? Again, the issue is, How are the physical educators involved in this decision process?

■ *Physical education pullout.* Who can remove students from physical education? Can a classroom teacher not allow a student to go to physical education as a punishment for a classroom infraction? Can students be removed from physical education for a block of time to make up missed work or for extra help when they are having trouble academically?

Resources

The two primary resources needed to implement the program are facilities and equipment. Clearly, you must have the necessary facilities and equipment to teach the goals identified in the curriculum. The bigger issues are usually control over the facilities and a budget for maintenance and equipment replacement. Strategies for enhancing your control of your facilities and increasing your equipment resources are discussed in more detail in chapter 6. The curriculum would address any known problem areas. The goal would be to have predictable and appropriate teaching facilities so that all teachers can teach the program goals equally. For example, an elementary school may have two physical educators who teach two classes each period. One teacher is assigned to the gym, and the other to the outside blacktop area. When it rains, the outside teacher is reassigned to the cafeteria, except for during the lunch periods; then both teachers must share the gym. This combining of classes into one instructional setting for three or four periods every time the weather is inclement will have an adverse effect on the achievement of the students in both classes. A solution might be to install a divider in the gym so that both classes can share the space. Having a statement in the curriculum that the school must provide an appropriate teaching environment could be used as the basis for ensuring that such a divider is installed when a gym must be used for two instructional settings.

The second major resource issue is equipment. Each teacher needs to have the appropriate type and amount of equipment to implement the curriculum. The issue is usually inequities in how schools are budgeted for equipment. As a result, some schools have everything they need and other schools have inadequate or insufficient amounts of equipment. Again, the purpose of adding a statement or policy on equipment to the curriculum would be to establish that the equipment specified in the curriculum must be provided by the schools so that the curriculum can achieve its stated goals. When equipment inequities or problems arise, this statement could be used to leverage support for getting the needed equipment. However, as a general rule these statements should be used to justify the maintenance of existing resources and policies and not as a backdoor way to make changes.

Summary

You have now learned the first three steps in the ABC planning process. At this point you should know how to create a program philosophy, establish and rank-order program goals, and identify any district-wide policies that are needed to implement the curriculum. Once you have identified the program philosophy, goals, and policies, you must integrate these into a written statement that both justifies the curriculum and links them to the common elements in the overall school curriculum. This introduction to the curriculum document should also outline the process that was used and who was involved in the process. The next task is to present the program goals using a rationale for each goal that cites relevant research literature.

Finally, this section should conclude with a list of the resources and policies needed to support the program so that these goals can be achieved. In most cases, this narrative is developed by a subcommittee of physical educators and then reviewed and approved by the entire curriculum committee. This extremely important component of the curriculum should be carefully developed. The length and detail included in these statements is usually a function of the physical education program being developed. In districts in which physical education is in good shape and well supported by the community, these statements tend to be shorter and to have less documentation. In districts in which physical education is in trouble or targeted for reductions, these statements tend to be more detailed and heavily referenced. In addition, you should understand the issues involved in working with a group of teachers on developing a curriculum and how to use the consensus-building technique to avoid problems and resolve conflicts.

Making It Work

Have you achieved the expected outcomes (see page 96) for this chapter? You should now understand the first three steps in the ABC planning process and how to implement them to develop the program philosophy, goals, and policies. Still, you may have some practical questions that need answers, such as the following:

▌ *If the principal and physical education teachers in my school are interested in creating an achievement-based curriculum, but physical educators in the other schools are not interested, is it OK to create a curriculum just for our school?* Yes, you definitely should create your own curriculum, but you must understand the limitations of the curriculum you create. Depending on the level of your school (i.e., elementary, middle, high school) you will have no control over the content covered before or after your curriculum. Because your final curriculum will only represent the needs, values, and resources of your school, you should not expect it to generalize and be accepted by the other schools in your district. Remember that one of the most important elements in developing a curriculum is involvement and ownership in what is created. For this to occur, everyone involved with the curriculum should be involved in its creation. All this said, once your curriculum is defined and up and working, it could be used as a model to encourage the other teachers and schools to come together and create a district curriculum. You and your staff then could serve as the leaders for this district-wide process, and you could use your curriculum as an example for how to perform each step in the planning process.

▌ *Assuming that all of the physical educators in my school know and trust each other, is all the ranking and computing averages really necessary to identify and select the goals for the program?* In reality, even when teachers know and respect each other, there will always be differences of opinion on what is important and should be included in the curriculum. It is best to establish a process like the consensus-building technique at the beginning and use it to guide the decision-making process. If after the first round of rankings everyone is in agreement, then there is no need to repeat the ranking process. However, if after the first round of rankings there is not agreement, you now have a means to control and guide the discussion to a resolution. One of the major advantages of the consensus-building technique is that it prevents a few very persuasive or powerful teachers from having more than their share of influence on curriculum decisions. They can make their arguments, but in the end they get only one vote (i.e., rank) just like all of the other members of the staff.

∎ *No one really cares about physical education in some districts, and it is difficult to generate interest among the physical educators. Is it really necessary to involve administrators, parents, and school board members?* Yes, it is essential to have these other groups involved in your curriculum development process. One of the reasons no one cares about physical education in your district may be that they do not understand what it is and the benefits it has to offer to the students and society. A functional ABC for physical education is not only a means of ensuring that students receive an appropriate program, but also a tool for educating others about the values and benefits of physical education (see chapter 13 for more on how to promote your program). One way to educate others about physical education is to involve them in the curriculum development process. Take care in selecting these representatives and decide when you want to involve them in the process. For example, the physical educators may want to meet first on some issues and build consensus so that they can present a unified view when meeting with the other representatives.

∎ *Physical education has been woefully undersupported in many districts to the point that the facilities and equipment needed to run a quality program are not available. Shouldn't we demand that the district supply each school with a gym and the appropriate equipment before wasting our time creating a curriculum we can't implement?* Although this sounds like the right thing to do, in reality it rarely works. The fact that physical education is not currently well supported suggests that it is not well understood and subsequently not highly valued by the key decision makers who control the resources. If you expect to get more resources from these groups, the first thing you will need to do is to educate them and change their current opinions of physical education. You could use the ABC process as a means to this end. Once your curriculum is up and running, you could use your program evaluation data (see chapter 12) to justify your requests for facility improvements and more equipment.

six

Program Planning

You have been recruited to teach a young man the basic skills of tennis based on your reputation as an outstanding physical education teacher. The young man you will be teaching is in excellent physical condition, is highly motivated, and possesses average cognitive functioning. He has recently moved to the United States where he has just seen the sport of tennis for the first time. In his home country there are no racket sports, so he has no prior experience in this area.

Your assignment is to teach this young man three basic tennis skills: the forehand stroke, the backhand stroke, and the overhead serve. To determine whether you have been successful in your assignment, the young man must be able to (1) return in bounds three out of five tennis balls hit moderately fast to his forehand side (within 8 feet of his racket); (b) return in bounds three out of five tennis balls hit moderately fast to his backhand side (within 8 feet of his racket); and (3) hit three out of five overhead serves into the opposing service box. If your student can meet these criteria, you will be paid $10,000. If your student does not, you will not be paid anything.

1. How much time in hours would you require to teach this student so he could meet the stated criteria? Note that your time estimate should include time for practice because this student will only have access to the court and equipment during your lessons. Number of hours = _____

Now there is an option to make an additional $5,000. It turns out that this young man has 18 friends with similar attributes and no experience with tennis who are also interested in learning to play tennis. These individuals must meet the same performance criteria established for the original young man. Each student will be provided with a tennis racket and three tennis balls, and you will have access to a tennis court for every two students.

2. How much additional time would you need to add to your original estimate to get these 18 friends to the same competency level? Additional number of hours = _____

There is one final option. There is a young lady who lives near where you will be teaching. She has completed 12 years of public school physical education and now lives in a group home for individuals with mild mental retardation. She works in a local factory and is very interested in learning tennis so she can play with some of the other workers at the factory. If you can teach this young lady along with the other students to the same competency level criteria described, you will receive an additional $5,000.

3. How much additional time would you need to add to your other estimates to get this young lady to the same competency level? Additional number of hours = _____

4. Sum your answers for questions 1 through 3. Total hours needed = _____

5. Divide the sum you calculated in question 4 by 3. Time needed to teach an average tennis objective = _____

This exercise was designed to guide you through a process of estimating how much time you perceive you need to teach a typical motor skill. This critical step in designing a functional physical education program plan is frequently omitted when physical education curricula are defined. There are no right or wrong answers to this exercise. Compare your estimates with those of other students in your class or other teachers. What were some of the lowest and highest estimates? Record these estimates and keep them with your estimates so that you can refer to them later in this chapter.

EXPECTED OUTCOMES

This chapter will provide you with the step-by-step procedures for developing an achievement-based physical education curriculum. After reading this chapter, you will be able to do the following:

1. Delineate the content you must teach to achieve each of your program goals

2. Establish the percent emphasis each program goal should receive throughout the program

3. Calculate the amount of time available for instruction as well as the amount of time needed to teach mastery of an average objective

4. Determine what and how much content to include and how to distribute that content across the program for implementation

5. Develop teaching and learning maps for each year of your program that indicate what content you will teach when

6. Create a functional ABC guide that consumers can use to understand your physical education curriculum

In chapter 5 you completed the first three steps in the planning process and learned how to develop your program philosophy and goals. This chapter continues the planning process and guides you through the procedures of developing the scope and sequence of the content that will be actually taught in the curriculum to achieve these goals. It is important to reiterate that what we are presenting in this chapter is a *process*. The ABC planning process does not dictate what content should or should not be taught in the curriculum. These decisions are made by the teachers and consumers that will be using the curriculum. What the ABC planning process does is guide teachers through a systematic decision-making process that will produce the outcomes they desire and that accounts for their unique constraints. The process of developing the scope and sequence of the curriculum is continued in this chapter with the following eight steps:

Step 4: Delineating objectives for each program goal

Step 5: Establishing program goal emphasis

Step 6: Calculating available instructional time

Step 7: Calculating average objective mastery times

Step 8: Calculating how much content to include in the curriculum

Step 9: Sequencing the content across the curriculum

Step 10: Developing teaching and learning maps

Step 11: Creating a functional ABC guide

Steps 1 through 3 were addressed in chapter 5. This chapter focuses on steps 4 through 11. Again, there is nothing sacred about the number of steps. What is important, however, is the sequence of the steps. We strongly recommend that you do each step as presented. If possible, do each step with a small group of classmates or teachers. If you are not currently teaching, feel free to make up hypothetical values as you complete each step.

Step 4: Delineating Objectives for Each Goal

The aim of this step is to operationalize the *planning-down* concept by breaking down the goals, which define what the students should leave the program with, into smaller learning objectives. These objectives are then sequenced developmentally throughout the curriculum. The number of objectives listed for each goal will vary depending on the nature of the goal and the depth that the staff wants the students to achieve.

Remember that the planning-down process can be applied to any size program from a single student's program to a program level such as elementary or to the entire K-12 program. The process is the same regardless of the program size; however, the complexity of the task increases with the size of the program. Typically, elementary programs teach the foundational skills such as body awareness, locomotor skills, object control skills, fitness, and social and cognitive skills. At the middle school level these foundation skills may be combined to teach various activities and sports. At the high school level the foundation skills may be combined to teach various lifetime sport skills.

Table 6.1 shows the relationship between the foundation skills and two common sport skill goals. Each goal is divided into a set of subskills (i.e., objectives) a student would need to master to be able to play these sports functionally. Note that the objectives are divided into sport-specific skills and prerequisite skills. The sport-specific skills are the new objectives that are introduced and taught at the upper grade levels, whereas the prerequisite skills are the objectives taught at the lower grade levels. The prerequisite skills are further subdivided into five categories: body awareness, locomotor, object control, fitness, and social and cognitive, which parallel common goal areas for elementary physical education programs.

The key here is to see the relationship between the desired program outcomes (i.e., goals) and the content of the program. All of the objectives taught in the elementary program should be directly linked with the content taught in the upper levels and with the goals the students eventually achieve and leave the program with.

For the initial phase of objective identification, short labels or phrases should be used to describe the objectives. Later in the planning process, once the final objectives for each goal have been determined, each objective will be operationally defined in detail. Figure 6.1 (page 117) shows an example of a detailed objective description for the object control skill of the overhand throw. Note that the objective is stated in observable and measurable terms so that anyone can determine if the student has achieved it. Figure 6.2 (page 117) contains an example of a cognitive objective for learning the rules and scoring of badminton. Note that this objective not only specifies the facts and concepts students should know but also stipulates how to measure this knowledge.

Table 6.1 Relationship Between Foundation Skills and Two Sport Skill Goals

	Tennis	Volleyball
Body awareness	Body parts	Body parts
	Body actions	Body actions
	Spatial awareness	Spatial awareness
	Directionality	Directionality
Locomotor skills	Running forward	Running forward
	Running backward	Running backward
	Lateral movement	Lateral movement
	Changing directions	Changing directions
		Vertical jump
Object control skills	Underhand toss	Underhand toss
	Catch	Catch
	Overhand throw	Overhand throw
	Forehand strike	Underhand strike
	Backhand strike	Overhand strike
	Overhand strike	
Fitness	Aerobic endurance	Aerobic endurance
	Arm and shoulder strength	Arm and shoulder strength
	Leg strength	Leg strength
	Arm and shoulder flexibility	Arm and shoulder flexibility
	Leg and trunk flexibility	Leg and trunk flexibility
Social and cognitive	Etiquette	Etiquette
	Honor system	Honor system
	Rules of tennis	Rules of volleyball
	Tennis strategy	Volleyball strategy
	Doubles play	6-3-2 play
Advanced skills	Forehand strike with racket	Volleyball set
	Backhand strike with racket	Volleyball bump (two-arm pass)
	Overhead serve with racket	Spike
	Forehand slice with racket	Underhand serve
	Backhand slice with racket	Overhead serve
	Volley with racket	
	Top spin serve with racket	

Goal: The student will demonstrate mature object control skills.

Objective: Given a verbal request to throw a ball in an overhand pattern using the preferred hand, the student will throw a 3-inch (e.g., tennis ball) at least 50 feet*, on two out of three trials, while demonstrating the following performance standards:

1. *Eyes focused* on target or *direction of throw.*
2. *Side orientation* parallel to the direction of the throw, shift of the body weight to the rear leg during windup.
3. Near complete *extension* of the throwing arm as the *throwing arm* passes above the shoulder.
4. *Weight transfer* to the foot *opposite the throwing arm* as the throwing arm passes above the shoulder.
5. Marked sequential *hip to shoulder rotation* during the throwing motion.
6. A *follow-through* well beyond the ball release and toward the direction of travel.

* Distance should be downplayed. More emphasis should be put on the mechanics of the skill according to the criteria.

▌**Figure 6.1** Overhand throw objective definition.

Cognitive learning objective: To apply the rules of badminton, the student will identify correct scoring and serving decisions with at least 80% accuracy, given a variety of badminton situations.

Criterion-referenced item: The student refers to the badminton court diagram in answering the questions on scoring and serving.

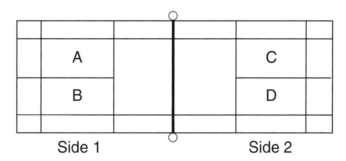

1. At the beginning of the game, side 2 wins the toss and decides to receive. Who is the first server? _____
2. The server wins two points, making the score 2 (serving) to 0. The server loses the next serve. Who serves next? _____
3. From what side of the court (as server looks toward net) does the second server begin to serve? _____
4. The second server loses the serve. No points are scored. Who is the third server? _____
5. The third server scores one point and then loses the serve. Who serves next? _____
6. The fourth server wins three points and then loses the serve. What is the score at this point? _____

▌**Figure 6.2** Badminton rules objective definition.
Reprinted, by permission, from V.J. Melograno, 1996, *Designing the physical education curriculum* (Champaign, IL; Human Kinetics), 156.

Teachers must understand that in addition to teaching all objectives in the curriculum, they must also ensure that all students in the program master them. As illustrated in figure 6.1, the objective definition defines what mastery means for a given objective. For the curriculum to achieve its goals, all teachers must employ the same standards for the objectives delineated in the curriculum.

Depending on the size of the program being designed and the size of the physical education staff working on the process, it is sometimes more time efficient to divide the members into small groups and allow them to develop the objectives for the goals in areas in which they feel most knowledgeable. Teachers also do not need to start with a blank piece of paper when developing their goal delineations. Many bottom-up curricula that teachers already have may contain detailed lists of objectives. Also, many published sources contain lists of objectives for various goal areas.

When developing multilevel programs (i.e., K-12), groups working on each goal should have members from each program level. Using the goals proposed at the end of chapter 5, each group would be given a goal and a worksheet like the completed example in figure 6.3 (see appendix B, page 325, for the blank worksheet). The full worksheet would be used with motor skills that have prerequisite objectives in the traditional foundation areas. Just the top portion of the form would be used for nonsport skill goals such as social or cognitive goals. At the end of this process, the staff would have 12 of these sheets, one for each goal.

Figure 6.3 shows a sample completed worksheet for one goal—tennis. Note the ranking columns on the right side of the worksheet. After a subcommittee has delineated the objectives for each goal, the next step is to rank-order the objectives within each goal. If subcommittees created the objective delineations for the goals, then the entire committee should perform the ranking. All of the committee members should independently rank the objectives within each goal area based on the contribution that each objective makes to achieving the overall goal. If subgroups developed the initial objective lists for each goal, then the entire committee should have the option to add or delete objectives from the list during the first ranking.

Because for most sport skill goals the prerequisites are needed to perform the higher-order skills, these should be given higher ranks than the more advanced skills that build on them. The sport-specific objectives within each goal should be ranked in terms of the importance for allowing students to perform a functional game of tennis. In the example shown in figure 6.3 all of the basic strokes were ranked higher than the more advanced skills such as the topspin serve and volley. If time is available to teach all these objectives, great; however, if time is limited, the students should leave with the basic skills needed to play a functional game of tennis.

The ranking and consensus-building processes need to be completed for each goal. For many goals with only a small number of objectives, a consensus can be reached after one round of ranking. For goals with many objectives, several ranking rounds may be necessary. At the end of the ranking and consensus-building processes, the committee should have a completed goal and objective worksheet like the example shown in figure 6.3 for each goal.

A review of the sheets will probably reveal that several objectives, particularly in the foundation areas, are repeated across two or more goals. For example, running or the overhand throw could be a prerequisite skill for several goals. You should remove these duplications in a systematic manner. The goal is to have each objective appear only once and for the objectives to be equally distributed across the goals. Lay the objective lists for each goal out on a table. Using color highlighters, mark all the duplicate objectives, each in a unique color across the lists. Then systematically decide within which goal each objective will be retained and then cross out the duplicates. Repeat this process until all of the duplicates are removed and the primary objectives that remain are approximately equally distributed across the goals.

Step 5: Establishing Program Goal Emphasis

Once you have delineated the goals and objectives, the next step in the planning process is to determine what emphasis each goal should receive across the various levels of the program. For example, a goal such as physical fitness may start out with a relatively low emphasis during the lower elementary grades and then gradually increase in emphasis as the students get older. Other goals such as locomotor skills may receive a high emphasis during the lower elementary grades and no emphasis later in the program, whereas goals related to team and lifetime sports may receive emphasis only in the upper grades. The point is to determine the emphasis each goal should receive so it will actually occur when the program is implemented. In other words, the time allocated and spent on each goal area should be

Goal and Objective Worksheet

Program goal: Tennis

Summative ratings and relative (ranks)*

| | Rounds | | |
	1	2	3
Sport-specific objectives			
Forehand strike with racket	13.4(14)	13.3(14)	13.4(14)
Volley with racket	18.1(17)	18.3(17)	18.2(17)
Overhead serve	16.2(16)	16.4(16)	16.6(16)
Backhand strike with racket	14.6(15)	13.9(15)	14.0(15)
Top spin serve	19.2(20)	19.4(20)	19.4(20)
Forehand slice with racket	18.9(19)	18.6(19)	18.6(19)
Backhand slice with racket	18.7(18)	18.6(18)	18.4(18)
Prerequisite objectives			
Body awareness			
Body parts	1.8(1)	1.8(1)	1.8(1)
Body actions	2.3(2)	2.5(2)	2.4(2)
Spatial awareness	5.8(7)	5.6(7)	5.7(7)
Directionality	8.5(10)	8.2(9)	8.3(9)
Locomotor skills			
Running forward	2.4(3)	2.5(3)	2.5(3)
Running backward	6.7(8)	6.5(8)	6.3(8)
Moving laterally	10.3(11)	8.5(11)	8.6(11)
Changing directions	7.6(9)	8.3(10)	8.5(10)
Object control skills			
Underhand toss	4.4(6)	4.2(6)	4.2(6)
Catch	3.9(5)	4.1(5)	4.0(5)
Overhand throw	3.6(4)	3.7(4)	3.6(4)
Forehand strike with hand	12.2(12)	12.5(13)	12.3(13)
Backhand strike with hand	12.4(13)	11.9(12)	12.0(12)

*Initially, each teacher would complete this form individually. The teachers would rank each objective in the list from 1 to 20 with 1 being assigned to the most important objective and 20 to the least important. The individual teacher ratings would be averaged to produce a summative rating for each objective. These average ratings are shown in the three columns for each of the three rounds. For example, 13.4 is the average ranking for the forehand strike objective received in the first round. These ratings would then be rank-ordered to produce a relative ranking for the objectives. The relative rank is shown in parentheses next to the average ranking. For example, the relative rank for the forehand strike was (14). This means of the 20 objectives, this objective was the 14th most important. When the relative rankings stay the same between rounds, consensus has been reached.

■ **Figure 6.3** Sample completed goal and objective worksheet for tennis with final rankings.

consistent with the intent. All too often curriculum designers select the appropriate emphasis for each goal, but when they select the objectives (content) for inclusion in the curriculum, the actual weighting based on those objectives does not reflect the original intent for the weighting of the goals. For example, the committee might want equal emphasis on fitness, team sports, and lifetime sports across the curriculum; however, when they start selecting the objectives for each goal and sequencing them in the curriculum, the balanced emphasis is lost. Instead of being 33/33/33 they may select more team sport objectives and end up with something like 20/50/30.

Establishing the percentage of emphasis for the program goals across the program is a relatively straightforward process. Prior to this step, teachers should have applied their knowledge and experience related to motor learning, growth, maturation, and motor development. A brief review of these topics at the beginning of this step will frequently reduce the number of iterations required to achieve consensus at the end.

Using a worksheet like the completed one in figure 6.4 (see appendix B, page 326, for the blank form), members of the staff independently indicate what emphasis they believe each goal should receive across the various grades. For this process to work, each column (grade or year) must sum to 100%. We recommend that the percentages be assigned in either 2% or 5% increments to facilitate compiling the data. After all the teachers have made their initial ratings, the rating should be compiled and a composite chart developed like the example shown in figure 6.4. The consensus-building technique should be used to obtain the final ratings. If while compiling the data, there appears to be general agreement, the chart can be fine-tuned via group discussion, using the consensus-building technique only in areas of major discrepancy. Note that in figure 6.4 the emphasis for the sport skill goals has been divided into two categories: prerequisite, which is subdivided into foundation areas of body awareness, locomotor skills, and object control skills; and advanced skills for each sport. This is necessary to get the appropriate emphasis for the elementary grades.

Advanced skills *(a)* require mastery of prerequisite skills *(b and c)* to be achieved.

Goal	K	1	2	3	4	5	6	7	8	9	10	11	12	Program weight
Fitness	5	10	10	10	15	20	20	25	25	25	25	25	25	18.5
Social	15	15	15	15	10	10	10	10	10	5	5	5	5	10.0
Prerequisite														
Body awareness	40	30	20	20	10									9.2
Locomotor	20	25	25	25	30	25	15							12.7
Object control	20	20	30	30	35	25	20							13.8
Advanced skill														
Rock climbing											15	20	15	3.9
Tennis								10	15	15	20	15	15	6.9
Golf										15	20	20	25	6.1
Bowling										5	5	5	5	1.5
Badminton										5	5	10	10	2.3
Soccer						10	10	15	10	10				4.2
Volleyball							5	10	10	10	5			3.1
Softball							5	10	10					1.9
Football							5	10	10					1.9
Basketball						10	10	10	10	10				3.8
Sum = 100%	100	100	100	100	100	100	100	100	100	100	100	100	100	100

* Each value in the chart represents the average of all teachers' ratings.

▌ **Figure 6.4**   Sample completed percentage goal emphasis worksheet.

While completing the percentage goal emphasis worksheet, many teachers begin to see the inverse relationship between the number of goals they have in their program and the amount of time available. Obviously, the more goals the program contains, the less time teachers will have to work on each one. This relationship will become even more apparent in step 6, when the percentage of time is converted into actual hours and minutes.

Step 6: Calculating Available Instructional Time

Calculating the amount of available instructional time for physical education is a fairly simple procedure. Multiply the number of weeks in the school year by the number of times physical education is offered each week by the length of each instructional period in minutes. Figure 6.5 contains a completed worksheet for calculating available instructional time.

Note that for middle and high school programs only the time allocated for physical education should be included in the time calculation. If students alternate between physical education and health every 6 weeks during ninth grade, then 18 weeks should be used instead of 36 weeks for that year. Take a few moments and review a few examples. How much time is available in a school in which students receive 30 minutes of daily physical education across 36 weeks? How does this compare to another school that provides physical education only 20 minutes twice a week for 36 weeks?

Annual time available in physical education by number of days of instruction per week for a 36-week school year

Days of instruction per week	1	2	3	4	5
Total instructional days available per year	36	72	108	144	180
Minutes per class	30	30	30	30	30
Total time scheduled per year in minutes	1,080	2,160	3,240	4,320	5,400
Uncontrolled lost instructional time	108	216	324	432	540
Available instructional time per year in hours	16.2	32.4	48.6	64.6	81.0

▌**Figure 6.5**   Instructional time worksheet.

One of the unique qualities of the ABC planning process is that it is designed around the time actually available for instruction. For this reason the calculation of available instructional time must be as accurate as possible. Note in figure 6.5 that 10% of the instructional time was removed for lost instructional days. Based on past experience working with schools on ABC planning, we have found that on average about 10% of the scheduled instructional time is lost each year because of uncontrollable events such as holidays, teacher workdays, assemblies, and teacher absences. If teachers have accurate calendars of how many days of instruction were lost in the previous year, these values should be used. If no past data are available, the 10% value should be used as a starting point. If for some reason the curriculum committee knows at the outset that more than 10% of the time will be lost, the actual amount of time removed should be adjusted accordingly. The goal is to have as accurate an estimate as possible.

Teachers are better off overestimating the amount of lost instructional time; this will result in a more conservative estimate of the time available. If it turns out that they have more time than anticipated, they will have more time to achieve their target objectives. If a lot of time is lost because the gym is being used for other school activities, teachers should communicate the impact of these lost instructional days to the school administration, the school board, or both.

Figure 6.6 shows that using a conservative estimate of 10% results in 4,738 minutes of lost instructional time across a K-12 program. This is equivalent to almost 2.5 years of elementary physical education (4,738 minutes [total time lost in the program] /

1,944 minutes [average number of minutes of time per year during elementary] = 2.44 years of lost instruction).

The time estimates calculated in figure 6.5 may be a little surprising. Many physical educators are unaware of the limited amount of time they actually have with their students in a year and across the total program. Figure 6.6 shows an example of the time available by program level for a typical school district. Note that although the length of the instructional periods and the frequency per week tend to increase as the students advance through the program, large chunks of physical educational time are also lost in the upper grades to other content (e.g., health). See appendix B, page 327, for the blank form.

Step 7: Calculating Average Objective Mastery Times

One of the major differences between ABC planning-down and the traditional bottom-up curriculum development is that the ABC model expects students to master all of the stipulated objectives. To determine how much content to include in the overall program plan, curriculum designers must know how long it takes to teach the average student each of the objectives. Unfortunately, there is little published data on how long it typically takes physical educators to teach various motor skills. This is partly because of the uniqueness of most physical education settings (i.e., number of students, facilities, equipment, range of student abilities) and partly because time to mastery is rarely evaluated. Lacking established values, teachers must draw on their experience and make estimates.

Level	# grades	Weeks per year	# min per class	# classes per week	Total minutes	Minus 10%	Total hours available	Hours per year
Elementary	6	36	30	2	12,960	−1,296	194.4	32.4
Middle school	3	27	45	5	18,225	−1,822	273.4	91.1
High school	2	18	90	5	16,200	−1,620	243.0	121.5
Totals					47,385	−4,738	710.8	64.6

❚ **Figure 6.6**   Instruction time by program level.

At this time, take out your answers to the five questions posed in the scenario at the beginning of this chapter. If you skipped the scenario, please go back and review it now and respond to the five questions. If possible, get together with a group of teachers or classmates and list your estimates. The purpose of listing the values for each question is not to criticize any of them, but to illustrate the amount of variance that is normally found when teachers estimate the time needed to master a motor skill. The answers to question 5 (the time needed to teach an average tennis objective to this group of 20 individuals), for example, can range from 2 to 100 hours. This variance can partly be explained by differences in expectations and interpretations of the information presented in the scenario and partly by differences in teacher expertise in teaching these specific tennis skills. A major part of the variance is also due to the fact that most teachers are unaware of how long it actually takes them to teach various skills, and therefore their estimates are just guesses.

Accepting these as limitations, the current estimates can still be used as a starting point. Given that there will usually be extremes (i.e., very high and low estimates), the best option is to use the group mean or the median. Because the mean can be skewed by an extremely high or low estimate, the median is usually the best choice. To find the median, list the values from smallest to the largest and then find the value that is in the middle of the distribution (see figure 6.7).

Different types of objectives require different amounts of time (e.g., cognitive objectives tend to require less time than motor skill objectives). Because it would be time prohibitive to have a large group of teachers make time estimates and reach consensus on every objective in the curriculum, a useful technique (see figure 6.8) is to group the objectives into logical categories and then have the teachers

Teacher 1	2 hours
Teacher 2	8 hours
Teacher 3	10 hours
Teacher 4	14 hours
Teacher 5	46 hours

Sum = 80 hours

Mean = 16 hours

Median = 10 hours

❚ **Figure 6.7**   Calculating the median estimate.

estimate how much time would be needed to teach an average objective in each category. Students may be able to learn some objectives in a certain amount of time, but may require additional time to maintain those objectives (e.g., fitness objectives). If students need maintenance time for a given objective, teachers should build it into the estimate. Repeat this procedure for each category. Then multiply the average estimates by the number of the objectives in the category to create a weighted estimate for each category. To get the overall objective mastery time for the curriculum, you would sum the weighted averages for each category and divide by the total number of objectives. See appendix B, page 328, for the blank, form.

Mastery times can be influenced by many factors, such as teacher competency, class size, equipment ratio, or student age. Prior to making their estimates, teachers should discuss these factors. They should be encouraged to analyze and share their teaching settings during this discussion. This is also very informative for the non-physical educators on the curriculum development team.

A. Review the objectives listed in your goal and objective delineations and identify three to five categories that you can use to group all of the objectives (e.g., fitness, social, cognitive, and motor skill).

B. Pick one representative objective from each category and list it in the following table. Now have all the teachers individually estimate how long it would take to teach all of the students in one of their classes mastery of this objective and put their values in the table. Values should be in 10-minute intervals.

Category	Sample objective	Teacher ratings					Average
		1	2	3	4	5	
Fitness	Develop abdominal strength	520	600	240	360	495	443
Social	Learn to work cooperatively with a partner	320	300	90	300	410	284
Cognitive	Learn the strategies involved in tennis singles	195	240	60	180	290	193
Motor skill	Perform a mature overhand throw	660	580	230	320	400	438

C. Now you need to weight the average you have calculated for each category by the number of objectives in each category. To do this, you need to multiply the number of objectives in each category by the average estimate calculated for each category in step 6.

Category	(a) Estimated average from step 2	(b) Number of objectives in this category	(c) Weighted average (the product of column a × column b)
Fitness	443	10	4,430
Social	284	12	3,408
Cognitive	193	22	4,246
Motor skill	438	70	30,660
Sum		114	42,744

D. Divide the sum at the bottom of column (c) in step C by the sum at the bottom of column (b) in step C. The quotient is the overall mastery time for your curriculum: sum of column (c) (42,744) / sum of column (b) (114) = 375 minutes or 6.25 hours

▌ **Figure 6.8**   Using weighted estimates to calculate an overall mastery estimate.

As a general rule, the amount of time needed to teach an average objective will decrease as the students get older because their cognitive abilities will increase, which should facilitate more efficient learning. When in doubt, teachers should overestimate rather than underestimate the time they will need.

Calculating average objective mastery times with a group of people for a specific group of students is important. Sometimes doing just one motor skill objective with a group of teachers can be very informative.

When you get your average value, compare it to the values you wrote down for the tennis example at the beginning of this chapter. How do they compare? Teachers tend to underestimate the time they need to teach mastery of objectives. As a general rule, the estimates you make for your actual teach-

Classes with a low student-to-teacher ratio can help to decrease the overall time needed for mastering an objective.

ing setting should be greater than the estimates you made for the tennis example. The estimates for the tennis example were based on an ideal teaching situation. The teacher had a small class of 20 students, all of whom were highly motivated and interested in learning tennis. The teacher also had adequate facilities and ample equipment for each student. Odds are good that your actual teaching setting will be less than ideal, which means that you will require more time to achieve mastery.

Step 8: Calculating How Much Content Can Be Included in the Curriculum

Having estimated how long it takes to teach and master a typical objective in the curriculum (step 7), you are now ready to calculate how much content you can teach in each year, at each program level, and in the total program. Look back at figure 6.5 (instructional time available) on page 122. If a given school had a total of 81 hours of instruction in a given year, they theoretically could teach 13 objectives a year if 6.25 hours was used as the average objective mastery time. In another school (using

figure 6.5), they have only 32.4 hours of instruction each year, so they would only be able to master approximately five objectives each year. Many teachers are surprised when they see these numbers. Most teachers expect that they should be teaching more objectives than these calculations suggest. The unfortunate facts are that we do not have much time in physical education, and we typically try to cover too much content in this small amount of time.

To calculate how much content you can address in the overall curriculum, you have to organize the results of your various calculations from steps 4 through 7 in this chapter. From step 4 you should now have a rank-ordered list of curriculum goals. For each goal you have a rank-ordered list of objectives (see figure 6.3 on page 119). From step 5 you should have a worksheet that indicates the percentage emphasis of the total time each goal should receive across each year and each level of the program (see figure 6.4 on page 121). From step 6 you should have a worksheet that indicates the amount of time available during each year and the total time available for the program (see figures 6.5 and 6.6 on pages 122 and 123, respectively). Finally, from step 7 you should have an estimate of how long it will take to teach mastery of an average objective in your curriculum (see figure 6.8).

Working backward through your calculations, here is how you determine what objectives (content) to include in your curriculum (see figure 6.9). See appendix B, page 329, for the blank form. First, take the total time available for instruction in your curriculum (e.g., 710 hours) and divide it by the overall estimate of how long it takes to teach an average objective (e.g., 6.25 hours). Using the values from figures 6.6 and 6.8, there is a total of 710 hours of instructional time in the program divided by 6.25 hours, which was the overall estimate of how long it would take to teach mastery of an average objective. The quotient of this division reveals that a total of 114 objectives can be addressed in this curriculum. This value indicates that a total of 114 objectives can be taught in the entire K-12 grade curriculum.

Now that you know how many objectives can be taught in the time available, the next decision is to determine how many objectives to allocate to each goal in the program. To calculate these values, you need the percentage goal emphasis values from step 5 (see figure 6.4). The average percentage goal

A. Calculate the number of objectives to include in the curriculum based on the instructional time available (step 6) and the average objective mastery time (step 7).

Total instructional time / average objective mastery time = total number of objectives

710 hours / 6.25 hours = 114 objectives

B. Calculate how many objectives to teach in each goal area by multiplying the percentage goal emphasis for each goal (calculated in step 5) by the total number of objectives in the program (calculated in part A).

Goal	% goal weight	Total # of program objectives	# of objectives for this goal
Fitness	18.5	114	21.0
Social	10.0	114	11.0
Body awareness	9.2	114	10.0
Locomotor	12.7	114	14.0
Object control	13.8	114	16.0
Rock climbing	3.9	114	4.0
Tennis	6.9	114	8.0
Golf	6.1	114	7.0
Bowling	1.5	114	2.0
Badminton	2.3	114	3.0
Soccer	4.2	114	5.0
Volleyball	3.1	114	4.0
Softball	1.9	114	2.0
Football	1.9	114	2.0
Basketball	3.8	114	4.0

C. Select the top-ranked objectives for each goal using the values calculated in part B.

❚ Figure 6.9 Calculating how much content can be included in the curriculum.

emphasis for each goal is multiplied by the total number of objectives in the curriculum (see figure 6.9). The product of these multiplications indicates the number of objectives that can be worked on for each goal. For example, fitness had a goal emphasis of 18.5%. Multiply this value by 114 ($0.185 \times 114 = 21.09$) and you will see that you can work on a total of 21 objectives in the curriculum for this goal area. Repeat this procedure for each goal.

Now that you know the number of objectives for each goal, the last step is to select the predetermined number of objectives for each goal. To do this, go back to your rank-ordered lists of objectives for each goal area produced in step 4 (see figure 6.3). Starting with the top-ranked objective (i.e., the one ranked number 1), select the predetermined number of objectives for each goal. For fitness, 25 objectives were ranked from 1 to 25. Based on the previous calculations, you would select the top 21 objectives.

Following the rankings is very important. The purpose of ranking was to ensure that the most appropriate objectives were included in the curriculum so that the program goals can be achieved. At this point many teachers realize that their favorite objective or goal is not going to make the cut. If you do not follow these procedures, these special interest groups will try to undermine the process to get their objectives added.

The results of step 8, part B (figure 6.9) illustrate the relationship between breadth and depth in the program. If the teachers elected to have a large number of goals (i.e., greater breadth), the result is that they have only a small number of objectives within each goal (less depth). Conversely, if they elected to have fewer goals, they would have more objectives per goal. The most common tendency for teachers is to select too many goals. After they complete the process, they realized that they have time to work on only a few objectives for each goal, and in many cases this is not sufficient time for students to develop enough competency in each goal area to be functional.

Many teachers are shocked when they see the discrepancy between the amount of content they formerly taught and the amount they can actually teach given the time available. This shock is frequently amplified by the realization that some of their favorite content did not make the cut when the final objectives were selected according to the rankings. They should understand at this point that with the ABC model they are now responsible for teaching and getting all of their students to master these objectives as opposed to just exposing the students to the content. What they are looking at is the school's core curriculum, for which all teachers

are responsible. If they can teach and achieve all of the objectives targeted for each year, then they can use any remaining time to work on elective objectives that did not make the curriculum but that they believe are important for their students.

Curricula developed with the ABC process represent just a starting point in an ongoing and dynamic developmental process. At several points during this process the curriculum committee members made decisions based on their best estimates. Once they have implemented the curriculum and collected evaluation data, they can choose to slowly refine the curriculum to accurately reflect the realities in their school district. Three to four years are generally needed to refine the curriculum to the point at which it reflects what the teachers are implementing and the students are achieving. Be sure to keep the goal and objective delineations that you developed in step 4 for future reference. If after implementing the curriculum for a period of time you find that you can add more content in a given goal area, these delineations will help you identify the next most important objectives to add.

Step 9: Sequencing the Content Across the Curriculum From the Bottom Up Developmentally

Now that you know what content is to be included in the overall curriculum, the next step is to distribute the content across the various grades in the program. This part of the process is like putting a puzzle together. The goal is to produce a chart that indicates how many objectives should be included for each goal at each program level and within each program level for each grade. To create this chart you need the time estimates for the various objectives at the different program levels, the program goal emphasis worksheet developed in step 5 (see figure 6.4), and the time available for each grade level.

Figure 6.10 illustrates an example of how to calculate the number of objectives to include for each grade within each program level (see appendix B, page 330, for the blank form). The values in the chart were taken from the previous worksheets used in this chapter. Looking at the elementary level, there are 32.4 hours of available instruction time during each year (taken from figure 6.6). This value was divided by 6.25 hours (taken from figure 6.8), which is the average mastery time for an objective in the curriculum, to reveal that students can work on

Program level	Time per year (hours)	Average mastery time (hours)	# of objectives per year (time / mastery)*	# of years in program level	Total # of objectives per level
Elementary	32.4	6.25	5	6	30
Middle	91.1	6.25	15	3	45
Secondary	121.5	6.25	19	2	38

*This value is calculated by dividing the time per year (column 2) by the average mastery time (column 3). Note that the quotient from this calculation will usually be a whole number plus a fraction (e.g., 5.18). Because it is preferable to use whole numbers, these numbers should be rounded up or down systematically so that you end up with the correct number of objectives at the end of your calculations. In this example, the elementary and secondary values were each rounded down and the middle school level was rounded up. The resulting sum of all the objectives by level equals 113, which is one short of the total 114. In this case, one additional objective would be added in one of the secondary years to make up for the rounding error.

Figure 6.10 Calculating the number of objectives by grade and program level.

five objectives during each year at the elementary level. Multiplying this value by 6, the number of grades in the elementary level, shows that a total of 30 objectives can be taught and mastered during the elementary years.

Once you know how many objectives students need to master during each year of the program, the final process is to identify exactly which objectives those should be. At this point you must look across the objectives identified for all of the goals and apply what you know about student physical, social, and cognitive development.

To complete this step, teachers are typically divided into subgroups by program level. First, they identify all of the objectives that are appropriate for their program level. They then sequence them developmentally within each goal area. For example, learning to run would precede learning to hop, which would precede learning to skip. Once the objectives are sequenced developmentally, the next step would be to identify the first five (the lowest developmentally) and assign them to the first grade level in the program—kindergarten. This process is repeated until all of the objectives have been assigned to a grade.

Once you have determined the grade during which students will achieve mastery for each objective, the final decision is to indicate when you should begin instruction on each objective. This is a critical decision. Although a given objective such as kicking may be targeted to be achieved by the end of fourth grade, work would probably start on this objective a few years earlier, perhaps in second grade. What this means is that you have 6.25 hours to bring your students to mastery of this objective by the end of fourth grade. The next decision is how

to distribute this time to achieve this end. In this example, you could decide to start working on kicking in second grade with the goal of your students achieving mastery by the end of fourth grade. You could allocate two hours to kicking during second and third grade and the final two and a quarter hours to fourth grade. At this point you do not have to decide how to divide up the time, but simply when to begin instruction. Keep in mind that the average allocation of time for each objective (6.25 hours in our current example) is not all used in one year for most objectives. For most objectives the time will be distributed across multiple years.

Table 6.2 shows an example distribution of objectives for an elementary program (see appendix B, page 331, for the blank form). Note that there are two codes for each objective. The ** code indicates when the objective is targeted to be mastered. The - - code indicates the grades during which each objective will be introduced and developed. The R code is used for those objectives for which time is needed in the curriculum to review or maintain proficiency.

Once you have targeted and coded the objectives for a given grade level, the last step is to indicate how much time you will spend on each objective during each year. For the examples used in this chapter, we have been using the estimate of 6.25 hours, or 375 minutes, as the amount of time to teach the average objective to the point of mastery. The question is, How should these 375 minutes be divided across the years you have indicated that the objective will be worked on? Table 6.3 (page 130) shows an alternative form of table 6.2 that includes estimates of how much time will be spent on each objective during each year.

In the example given in the chapter, skipping is introduced in first grade with mastery targeted for third grade.

Table 6.2 Sample Elementary Objectives Scope and Sequence

Goal area	Objective	Grades					
		K	1	2	3	4	5
Locomotor	Run	**					
	Hop	- -	**				
	Gallop	- -	- -	**			
	Skip		- -	- -	**		
	Leap		- -	- -	**		
	Horizontal jump			- -	- -	**	
Object control	Catch	- -	- -	**			
	Underhand throw	**					
	Bounce	- -	**				
	Overhand throw			- -	- -	**	
	Kick		- -	- -	**		
	Strike			- -	- -	**	
Fitness	Flexibility			- -	**	R	R
	Abdominal strength			- -	- -	**	R
	Arm strength				- -	- -	**

**= Mastery expected by the end of this grade
- - = Objective is introduced or worked on during this grade
R = Objective is reviewed or time is allocated for maintenance

Table 6.3   Sample Elementary Objectives Scope and Sequence With Time Estimates

Goal area	Objective	Grades					
		K	1	2	3	4	5
Locomotor	Run	** 375					
	Hop	- - 100	** 275				
	Gallop	- - 100	- - 100	** 175			
	Skip		- - 100	- - 100	** 175		
	Leap		- - 100	- - 100	** 175		
	Horizontal jump			- - 100	- - 100	** 175	
Object control	Catch	- - 100	- - 100	** 175			
	Underhand throw	** 375					
	Bounce	- - 150	** 225				
	Overhand throw			- - 100	- - 100	** 175	
	Kick		- - 100	- - 100	** 175		
	Strike			- - 100	- - 100	** 175	
Fitness	Flexibility			- - 150	** 150	R 15	R 15
	Abdominal strength			- - 100	- - 100	** 100	R 15
	Arm strength				- - 100	- - 100	** 100

**= Mastery expected by the end of this grade
- - = Objective is introduced or worked on during this grade
R = Objective is reviewed or time is allocated for maintenance
# = actual number of minutes allocated during this year

Teachers who were previously concerned when only four or five objectives were identified for mastery during each year now realize that they will actually be working on two or three times this many in any given year. Although five objectives may be targeted to be mastered during any given year, four or five other objectives will most likely be introduced and another four or five will require continued instruction. In reality they will probably be teaching 12 to 15 objectives in any given year.

Step 10: Developing Teaching and Learning Maps (TLMs)

You now know what content is scheduled to be introduced, worked on, mastered, and reviewed for each year in your curriculum. The next step is to organize this content into logical groupings for instruction. In the ABC model this is referred to as developing teaching and learning maps (TLMs).

Traditionally, this phase of planning has been referred to as unit planning. The problem with unit planning approaches is that the objectives are frequently grouped around one sport theme and then taught in one block during the year. For example, kicking might be addressed only during a unit on soccer in the fall and dribbling during a basketball unit in the winter. The problem with this approach is that most motor skills require instruction and practice over a prolonged period of time to be learned. If the instruction and practice is confined to one condensed unit, many students will not master the objectives. Also, if students are absent during a significant amount of time during this one unit, they have no opportunity to learn this objective later in the year.

The concept behind a TLM is to plan a learning sequence in which students work on objectives repeatedly over an entire year. Let's assume that 100 minutes is allocated in the curriculum for catching

during third grade. Which of the following options do you believe would result in the greatest amount of learning for a class of students: working on catching for 20 minutes a class for five consecutive classes in one unit, or reviewing the components of catching at the beginning of the year via two 15-minute lessons and then working on and reviewing catching once every other week for 5 minutes throughout the entire year?

Of course the nature of the objectives must be considered when determining the best way to distribute the instructional time. Many cognitive and social objectives can be taught in a concentrated amount of time, but then require small intervals of time over the course of the year for review and application to other situations. Fitness objectives frequently can be taught in short instructional blocks but require short regular time intervals throughout the year to be maintained.

The ABC model does not prescribe how all teachers must teach the objectives in the curriculum. Clearly, objectives can be taught and mastery achieved by the established grades in many different ways. Therefore this step should be performed individually by each teacher. If you are working with a group of teachers, we recommend that you create a model TLM to illustrate the process. Teachers can then use this model to develop their own TLMs. The model is also a good starting point for new

Reviewing catching frequently throughout the year will help students to master the skill.

teachers who lack experience in making TLMs. The critical point is that each teacher must have a written TLM. Keep in mind that these maps are starting points; you will need to adjust them during the first few years of implementation. The TLM is also the starting point for program evaluation. Once a TLM is defined, it can be evaluated and revised until it produces the desired results. If the plan is only in your head, then there is nothing to evaluate.

Although teachers need to develop their own TLMs for the grades they teach, it is usually most efficient and productive to have teachers work on their maps in small groups. The group format promotes the exchange of ideas and usually results in the creation of better TLMs than those created by teachers in isolation. Initially many teachers fear that this is going to be an overwhelming task. In reality teachers need to develop only a small number of TLMs for each grade level they teach.

To start creating a TLM, review the chart created at the end of step 9 (see table 6.3 on page 130). In this section, you are going to learn how to make two types of TLMs. The first will organize the objectives identified for a given grade level into instructional blocks for the year. These are called yearly teaching and learning maps, or YTLMs. After you have created your YTLMs, you will then create block teaching and learning maps (BTLMs). The BTLMs will identify what content you will work on during each class of an instructional block.

Developing Yearly Teaching and Learning Maps (YTLMs)

Although no hard and fast rules exist for creating YTLMs, we do have some recommendations:

1. Review your objective scope and sequence chart (see step 9, table 6.3) and identify all of the objectives that need to be addressed for a given grade. This includes the objectives targeted for mastery as well as any objectives that need to be introduced, worked on, or reviewed.

2. Review the objectives for instructional compatibility. Objectives that require the same equipment such as balls and targets could be grouped together, or objectives that require the same type of instructional space such as locomotor skills could be grouped together. Another possibility is combining fitness objectives in the warm-up of the lesson when they are compatible with the activity and muscles to be used during the instructional part of the lesson.

3. Consider any limitations imposed by access to facilities and equipment during certain times of the year. If you share equipment with another school, this would influence how often and when you could rotate back to certain objectives. If you have to rotate and use different facilities such as a gym, cafeteria, or outside area, your YTLMs should reflect the limitations imposed by these settings.

4. Do not limit your YTLMs to certain sport or seasonal events. Students may be excited about working on kicking during soccer season or dribbling during basketball season, but instruction should not be limited to just these seasons.

5. Develop titles or themes for each block in your YTLM, and be creative. The goal of the block titles is to create interest and excitement in the students. The themes can parallel school events, holidays, or local events. The names need not be etched in stone. You can change them as needed to increase student motivation. For example, if there is a lot of attention in the news on an upcoming space mission, a theme for an elementary program could be astronaut training, which could include work on any combination of fitness, body awareness, social, or motor skills.

6. Vary the lengths of the theme blocks. There is nothing wrong with having blocks that vary in length from two to six weeks. Remember to align the end of theme blocks with the school traditional grading periods so that you can provide students and parents with accurate progress information on all of the content you have been teaching.

A YTLM is an outline of when you will work on each objective during a year. Instead of just saying that you are going to teach certain objectives sometime during this year, the YTLM indicates exactly when you will work on each objective and for how long. This is a marked departure from what is typically done in unit planning and takes a little while for teachers to adjust to. Taking a trip across country is a good analogy. If your time is short and you have to drive from New York to California, which would be the better plan: to just hop in the car and start driving and figure out the rest while you're on the road, or to preplan, such as plotting the quickest route, going to the bank and getting money, and making reservations so that you have places to stay along the way? Although the first option will get you started more quickly, there is a good chance you will never make it to your destination, and if you do, it will probably take you much longer than if you had used the second option. A YTLM is an example of the latter approach.

A YTLM is composed of blocks and cells. A block is composed of a number of cells that constitute a theme. A cell is a class period. The first decision you must make when creating a YTLM is the number of blocks. Blocks typically range from two to six weeks in length depending on the nature of the objectives and the theme. The sum of the weeks in the blocks, however, cannot exceed the available instructional time. If an elementary grade has physical education twice a week for 30 minutes, they have a total of 32 weeks or 64 classes of instruction (36 weeks × 2 days a week = 72 total days – 10% lost time = 64 days or 32 weeks).

A simple way to outline the theme blocks for YTLM is to make a matrix like the one shown in figure 6.11 (see appendix B, page 332, for the blank form). In the matrix the themes are listed down the left side and the objectives are abbreviated across the top. The example in figure 6.11 has rows for eight 4-week blocks. Again, you can adjust the number of blocks and their length as needed to match the objectives you are teaching and the nature of the themes. After creating the matrix, indicate the blocks for each objective by entering the amount of time into the appropriate square. Some teachers find calculating and distributing the time for each objective in minutes a little overwhelming. You can minimize this by using standard intervals such as two, three, four, or five minutes or by using computerized spreadsheets, which can be set up and defined to do all the math (see the example in figure 6.12 on page 135).

Many teachers also initially fear that they will be unable to manage their instruction around all of these little time estimates. The fact of the matter is that if you do not plan for something to occur, it is not likely to occur. For example, if you want to spend 10% of each class on fitness, then you need to know that is three minutes and what exactly you plan to do during those three minutes each class. Although we do not expect you to time your lessons with a stopwatch, you should at least define a plan and implement it to the best of your ability Clearly, you will lose some time, and not every class is going to work out so that you are on task 100% of the time. That is why we have already made an adjustment for a 10% loss in instructional time.

Developing Block Teaching and Learning Maps (BTLMs)

The last task is to translate each row in the YTLM matrix, which represents a block, into a BTLM for each theme. This is the final step in which the time allocated for each objective in the block is divided into the amount of time you will spend on each objective during each class of the block. To develop a TLM for a theme block, refer to the example in figure 6.13 (page 136) and perform the following steps:

1. Review the YTLM matrix and identify the row for the theme block to be developed. Read across this row and identify the objectives to be worked on during this block. Record the name of the objective and the corresponding amount of time for this objective during this block on the top of the form in parentheses. You can abbreviate objective names to save space.

2. Make a row down the left side of the matrix for each class period in this block.

3. Distribute the number of minutes each objective will be worked on for each class period in the cell that intersects the objective with the class period. Remember that for all objectives you will need time to preassess them before instruction and time to postassess them all at least once during the year. After allocating all of the time for each objective in the matrix, sum the columns and rows and make sure the sum at the end of each column matches the time allocated for that objective for this block and that the sum of each row matches the time allocated for each theme block. Again, you can define a spreadsheet to do this math.

There is nothing sacred about the actual format for the BTLM. Any format that is functional for the teachers and contains the requisite information is fine. The key is that at the end of this step you have a written plan for each grade, each block, and each class that explicitly states the following:

1. When you will work on each objective

2. How you will group the objectives for instruction

3. How much time you will spend on each objective during instruction

Scheduling, Facilities, and Equipment

Throughout the planning process issues will arise related to scheduling and access, use, and control of facilities and equipment. In many school districts these can be complicated issues that are usually further compounded by politics and past practices. The bottom line is that you need to know what facilities and equipment you definitely have access to and when you can use them and then base your planning on this information. Once these baseline conditions are established, you can then begin to work on plans to improve your access for future years.

Teacher: Mr. Kamide   **Program level:** Elementary   **Grade:** Third

Objectives for This Year

Mastery (minutes)	Work on (minutes)	Review (minutes)
Skip (175)	Horizontal jump (100)	Following directions (55)
Leap (175)	Overhand throw (100)	Class rules (55)
Kick (175)	Strike (100)	Working as partners (90)
Flexibility (150)	Abdominal strength (100)	
Spatial relationships (90)	Arm strength (100)	
	Cardiorespiratory endurance (150)	
	Respecting personal space (90)	
	Respecting equipment (90)	
	Self-advocacy (125)	

Theme blocks	Skip 175	Leap 175	Kick 175	Flexibility 150	Spatial relationships 90	Horizontal jump 100	Overhand throw 100	Strike 100	Abdominal strength 100	Arm strength 100	Cardiorespiratory endurance 150	Respecting personal space 90	Respecting equipment 90	Self-advocacy 125	Following directions 55	Class rules 55	Working as partners 90
Good will games (4 wk, 240 min)	60	40				40			20	20		20	20		10	10	
All-American obstacle course (4 wk, 240 min)					30	40	40	36	12	12		20	20		10	10	10
Astronaut training (3 wk, 180 min)	30	30		30					18	18				24	10	5	15
Himalayan mountain climbing (5 wk, 300 min)	10	35	84	30					10	10	30	10	10	36	5	5	25
American gladiators (4 wk, 240 min)	30	30		30	20	20			10	10	30	10	10	20	5	5	10
African safari (4 wk, 240 min)	10	20	40	20			35		10	10	30	10	10	20	5	10	10
Australian survival (4 wk, 240 min)	35	20		20			25	35	10	10	30	10	10	15	5	5	10
Olympic training camp (4 wk, 240 min)			51	20	40			29	10	10	30	10	10	10	5	5	10
Sums = 1,920	175	175	175	150	90	100	100	100	100	100	150	90	90	125	55	55	90

Figure 6.11 TLM matrix of block themes by objectives.

Objectives	Skipping	Leaping	Kicking	Flexibility	Spatial relationships	High jump	Overhand throw	Striking	Ab. strength	Arm strength	Cardio-respiratory endurance	Respect personal space	Respect equipment	Self-advocacy	Follow directions	Class rules	Working as partners	Block summary
Time available	175	175	175	150	90	100	100	100	100	100	150	90	90	125	55	55	90	1920
Blocks																		
240	60	40				40			20	20		20	20		10	10		0
240					30	40	40	36	12	12		20	20		10	10	10	0
180	30	30		30					18	18		0	0	24	10	5	15	0
300	10	35	84	30					10	10	30	10	10	36	5	5	25	0
240	30	30		30	20	20			10	10	30	10	10	20	5	5	10	0
240	10	20	40	20			35		10	10	30	10	10	20	5	10	10	0
240	35	20		20			25	35	10	10	30	10	10	15	5	5	10	0
240			51	20	40			29	10	10	30	10	10	10	5	5	10	0
Time used	175	175	175	150	90	100	100	100	100	100	150	90	90	125	55	55	90	

■ **Figure 6.12** Sample spreadsheet format for TLM matrix calculations.

Teacher: Mr. Kamide   **Program level:** Elementary   **Grade:** Third

Theme block title: Astronaut training   **Theme block #:** 3

Theme block length: 3 weeks for a total of 6 classes for a total of 180 minutes

Objectives for this block: Skip, leap, abdominal strength, flexibility, arm strength

	Skip (30)	Leap (30)	Flexibility (30)	Abdominal strength (18)	Arm strength (18)	Self-advocacy (24)	Following directions (10)	Class rules (5)	Working as partners (15)
Class 1 (30)	5	5	5	3	3	4	3	2	0
Class 2 (30)	5	5	5	3	3	4	3	2	0
Class 3 (30)	5	5	5	3	3	4	2	1	2
Class 4 (30)	5	5	5	3	3	4	2	0	3
Class 5 (30)	5	5	5	3	3	4	0	0	5
Class 6 (30)	5	5	5	3	3	4	0	0	5
Total	30	30	30	18	18	24	10	5	15

*Note: To avoid needing to do all the math related to monitoring how much time is used for each objective, all of these forms can be made into linked sheets in a program such as Excel.

∎ **Figure 6.13** Sample block teaching and learning map.

Scheduling

Knowing how scheduling is done in your school and school district is essential if you are going to be a successful negotiator. You will need to consider a number of scheduling issues. First and most important is how students are grouped and scheduled for physical education. You need to know when these decisions are made and by whom. At the elementary level this is typically done by the principal or an assistant principal with input from the teachers during the summer. At the middle school and high school levels this is typically done by the guidance department with input from the principals and teachers. Make sure you are involved in these processes and decisions.

Too often physical education is the primary content area that is manipulated to solve a school's scheduling problems. This frequently happens when physical educators are not involved in the scheduling process. To be effective, you must know what your scheduling needs are, you must be able to explain them to the decision makers, and you must know what the competing issues are that are negatively affecting your scheduling requests.

What are your scheduling needs? First, you must know what facilities you have access to and control over. If other instructional spaces are used in addition to the gym, such as the cafeteria, athletic fields, and blacktop areas, when do you have access to these spaces, and what happens when these spaces are not available or are unusable? For example, if the grass is too wet to use the athletic fields for three or four months each year for the first few periods each day, then this is not a viable instructional station. What happens to the classes in the outside spaces when it rains? If you do not anticipate and plan for these issues, your classes will need to be moved inside and doubled up whenever there is a problem with the outside space. This negatively affects both the instruction and student learning in all the classes.

After you know what facilities you have access to for instruction, your next consideration should be the needs of the students. Would some groups of students benefit more or less from receiving physical education at certain times during the day? How will you make such decisions? Are some days or some time slots more subject to conflicts and potential missed instruction? You must know the answers to these questions and be able to communicate them effectively. For example, would it be better for kindergarten children to receive physical education early in the day or later? For most kindergarten students 6.5 hours is a long day. Most come to school excited and raring to go and are exhausted at the end of day. As a result, having physical education at the end of the day would not be the ideal learning time for this group. A better time would probably be midmorning.

If some students at the elementary level could receive a little more instruction in physical education each week, how should you decide this? Should you base it on which classroom teachers are willing to give their students up for a little more instruction, or on the developmental needs of the students? Research would support giving this time to the students in the lower elementary grades who are at a significant developmental stage for acquiring motor skills.

At the secondary level most schools are now using some form of block scheduling in which the majority of students meet less frequently for longer periods ranging from 90 to 120 minutes. A few groups may meet daily for shorter instructional blocks. Secondary physical education teachers should carefully consider the implications of these different scheduling blocks and their effect on both the content taught and which groups of students are scheduled into the various instructional blocks.

Finally, you should also consider which classes are scheduled on certain days and time slots. If Mondays or Fridays are commonly missed because of national holidays or school-scheduled holidays to provide long weekends, then this pattern may adversely affect the amount of instructional time a given group of students receive in physical education if they receive physical education only a couple of times a week.

The point of these examples is to stress that you need to know and be able to communicate these issues and their impact on student learning in physical education. This is not to imply that you will prevail in all of these discussions, but you

should at least be at the table participating in the decisions that affect your program and your students' learning.

Two other issues that can have adverse effects on instructional time and should be considered during scheduling are transitions between classes and time for equipment management. Although pertinent at all levels, these problems are usually more common at the elementary level. The issue is whether to build time into the schedule for transitions between classes and to take down or set up equipment between classes. Without careful planning, these transitions end up using physical education instructional time.

In some elementary schools physical education is scheduled in 30-minute blocks with classes starting on the hour and half hour. At the end of a physical education class, one classroom teacher is expected to pick up her class, and the other classroom teacher is expected to have her class waiting to enter the gym. The problem occurs if one or both of the classroom teachers are late. In these situations the next class does not receive their allotted 30 minutes of instructional time. In some extreme cases, the physical educators are actually asked to drop off and pick up their classes from their homerooms.

A concurrent problem when classes are scheduled back to back is that teachers have no time to set up equipment for the next class. As a result they must use instructional time to both set up and take down the equipment for each class. This can be minimized to some degree by scheduling the same grade levels in sequence, thereby reducing the set-up and take-down time to transition between grade levels.

Obviously, the ideal solution is to schedule a transition time interval of 5 to 10 minutes between classes. However, if this has not been the practice in the past, you should anticipate some initial resistance. You should emphasize that your curriculum is based on 30 minutes of instruction, which is already very limited (refer to your program planning time calculations to illustrate this point).

Once the master schedule is set for the year, the next thing you need to know is how it can be modified and by whom. Nothing is worse than going into the last week of an instructional block in which you are planning to postassess the students on several objectives only to find out that the gym has been reassigned to the fifth grade for the last two periods for the final rehearsals of their school play. Not only are you losing the gym completely for the last two periods, but you now have to work around their sets and other props in all of your other classes. The issue here is not to prevent others from using your space, but to minimize the negative impact these conflicts have on your instructional program. During the year numerous events will conflict with the physical education schedule and facilities. What is needed is a well-established procedure that is followed by everyone for requesting changes in the physical education schedule or the use of the physical education facilities. With sufficient warning you should be able to make adjustments to reduce the negative impact these conflicts have on your instructional program. The key is *sufficient warning*.

Facilities

Some events occur annually and should be anticipated such as concerts, school plays, graduation, and election day. In addition to the time associated with the actual event, you should also anticipate the time lost to set up and take down equipment. For example, some areas use school gyms on election day as polling places. Time is not lost only on election day, however. Frequently the equipment is delivered on the Friday before and may not be picked up until Wednesday or Thursday after election day. This could result is the loss of the gym for an entire week if you have not planned for the situation. Other events such as assemblies and class field trips are less predictable but still are planned well enough in advance that you should be given adequate notice so you can plan accordingly.

Because your schedule and facilities are affected the most by these events, you need to play an active role in making sure there are established procedures for requesting and approving requests that affect your program. A common practice is to have a notebook in the main office that contains all approved requests to use the school's facilities during the day, including the physical education spaces. These would include the gym and any other instructional spaces such as athletic fields, blacktop areas, or the cafeteria. Anyone wanting to use the school's facilities would need to complete a facility request form and have it signed by all the staff that use that facility on the days in question and then ultimately by the school principal. In addition to the dates and times the facility would be used, the form would also require information on the following:

1. The nature of the event
2. Who will be involved in the event
3. What will be set up in the facility (e.g., tables and chairs, voting machines, and so on)
4. Anything else the group planned to use in addition to the facility (e.g., locker rooms, equipment, and so on)
5. When access is desired for setup

6. When the space will be available for use after the event
7. Who is responsible for cleaning the space
8. A refundable cleaning deposit sufficient to motivate the group to clean the facility when they are done

A number of computer network and Web-compatible calendar and scheduling programs can be used to manage the scheduling of facilities. These programs incorporate online request forms and have functions that will automatically send requests for approvals to the appropriate parties by e-mail. As a general rule, the easier you can make it for people to comply with procedures, the more likely they will be to follow them.

An additional advantage, regardless of whether you use a traditional notebook system or a computer-based system, is that at the end of the year you have a written record of all of the events that interfered with the implementation of your program. If these events are adversely affecting your program, you can meet with your school administrator and use these data to document the problem.

In the long run having good procedures for scheduling the use of facilities is good for everyone and will avoid most conflicts. What you want to facilitate is good planning and advance communication. Whenever possible, you should try to avoid creating conflicts in which someone has to lose. This may mean that you have to occasionally make some compromises to accommodate the needs of other teachers who have not followed the established procedures but have legitimate requests that would be beneficial to the students. In these cases, you should compromise but also take advantage of these situations to explain to these teachers and the administration the adverse effects these conflicts have on your instructional program.

Equipment

The last factor that you must consider both in scheduling and in planning TLMs is the availability and access to appropriate types and amounts of equipment. As a general rule, lack of equipment should never be an acceptable reason for not teaching an objective in the curriculum. In most communities there is always a way to get the equipment. The real issue is usually planning to make sure you have the right amount and the right type of equipment to meet the needs of your students. The ideal situation would be to have all of the equipment needed to implement the curriculum in each school. If this is not the case, this should be a long-term goal of the physical education staff. Once the curriculum is designed, it can be used as a lobbying tool with the central administration and the school board. In the interim, you can pursue the following three strategies to ensure that all of your programs have the equipment they need:

1. *Share equipment between schools.* This can be the ideal and most cost-effective solution for handling most equipment problems. In theory a database could be created that identified the type, quantity, and location of all the equipment available in the district. Teachers could use this same program to reserve the equipment they needed around their TLMs. Unfortunately, this solution is not always as simple as it may seem. Most school districts use site-based management systems in which budgets are passed down and administered at the school level for the purchase of local items. The school budget for equipment is usually also supplemented by the school's Parent–Teacher Organization (PTO). The majority of the equipment needed for physical education (e.g., balls, rackets, markers, nets, and so on) would qualify as local items that would be funded from these sources. Physical educators therefore need to compete within their school with the other instructional needs for these funds. As a result physical education may be well supported in one school and poorly supported in another. When the equipment is purchased, it is perceived as belonging to the school and in most cases to the physical education department of that school. Schools are subsequently reticent to lend their equipment because they know if it is lost or damaged, the other school will probably not have the resources to pay for replacement. Although these are real issues that must be addressed, they should be pursued so that all students have access to the appropriate equipment. In reality the majority of the physical education equipment spends more time in storage in the various schools in the district than it does being used by students.

2. *Share equipment with other programs that use your facilities such as after-school programs, intramurals, or community-based youth sport programs.* Although this option for sharing equipment may seem logical, it is complicated by similar budget and ownership issues as discussed earlier. The key to being successful at this level of sharing is to be involved when the deal is being negotiated. For example, if the local youth soccer league wants to use the school athletic fields after school for practices, what is the school getting in return? Maybe the local soccer league would be willing to supply goals and nets

that the school could use. The critical point here is that you need to know who makes these deals for your school and how you can become involved in these negotiations.

3. *Tap professional organizations and local businesses that can provide short-term use of equipment for free or at reduced costs.* Many professional sport organizations, such as the Professional Golf Association (PGA), Professional Tennis Association (PTA), or the Professional Bowling Association (PBA), have programs designed to promote their sport at the grassroots level. Many of these organizations will supply not only the equipment but also instructional materials and in some cases professional instructors. The key to taking advantage of these resources is planning. Initial contacts can be made via the Web to find out whom you should contact in your local area. To get involved initially, you should plan four to six months in advance of when you would actually like to use these materials in your program. Another option for tapping local resources is to contact commercial businesses in your community that have equipment you need. Let's assume that you want to teach cross-country skiing as part of your secondary program, but you do not have the resources to buy skis, poles, and boots for all of your students. Odds are good that you could work out a mutually beneficial deal with a local ski shop. Most ski shops rent skis, and most of the rental business is on the weekends. During the week the rental skis just sit in the shop. You could propose a deal in which your school could either rent the ski equipment you need during the week at a greatly reduced rate or even for nothing in return for providing free publicity and advertising for the ski shop. The ski shop could use the donated rental fees as a tax write-off and would also benefit from the increase in business by being associated with your program. Presumably, if you taught the students how to ski, they would be inclined to rent or even buy their own equipment in the future from this ski shop. Similar deals can be negotiated with other local business such as health clubs and sporting goods stores.

Step 11: Creating a Functional ABC Guide

Now that you have completed the first 10 steps in ABC program planning, the last step is to organize your materials into a functional curriculum guide. The emphasis here is on the word *functional*. The goal is to have a guide that accurately communicates both the intent and what is actually taught in the curriculum. It is important to consider who the target audiences are for this document and how the document will be used. The two target audiences are the consumers and the users of the curriculum.

Consumers are those who participate in, benefit from, and pay for the curriculum. They include administrators, parents, teachers, students, and members of the community. For consumers the curriculum is an educational tool. It defines what physical education is, how the program is implemented, and what students are expected to learn and have achieved by completing the program. Although it is important for this group to understand the process that was used to develop the curriculum and the key components that are involved, they should not be overwhelmed with details.

The second target audience is users—current and future members of the physical education staff. This audience needs enough detail so that they understand how the curriculum was created and, most important, what they are responsible for in terms of its implementation and ongoing evaluation. Users will always have access to other members of the physical education staff who can provided more detail on the procedures and processes involved in designing and implementing the curriculum.

Given that consumers are the primary audience for the curriculum guide, the guide should be organized around their needs, concerns, and biases. Figure 6.14 shows a typical outline for the curriculum guide. Although this is a reasonable format, you should feel free to modify it to meet the needs of your consumers. If physical education is under attack in your district, you may choose to expand and add more emphasis to the philosophy section or the rationales for your program goals.

Consumer Curriculum Guide

The example in figure 6.14 is divided into four sections. The first section is the executive summary, which should be a short one- to two-page overview of the curriculum. This is an extremely important part of the guide. This may be the only section many consumers read. It should be carefully crafted and designed to ensure that the reader understands not only what physical education is, but how and why the program was designed the way it was, and what students are expected to learn and to achieve by completing the program. This section also usually acknowledges who was involved in the development of the curriculum and recognizes the authorities that have reviewed and approved the document such as the school board and the

superintendent. Finally, this section typically ends with an overview of how the remainder of the guide has been organized.

The second section of the document focuses on how the content for the curriculum was selected. This section starts with the philosophy statement that was the end product of step 1 in chapter 5. Integrated into the philosophy statement are any policies or resources the physical education staff believes are needed to implement the curriculum. These were identified in step 3 in chapter 5. This statement should be designed to focus attention on any particular issues that the physical education staff wants to draw attention to. For example, if the staff believes it is extremely important that all students receive daily physical education taught by a physical education specialist, then this would be embedded in the philosophy statement. This statement must be clear and concise and link directly to the next section on program goals.

The program goals and rationales are the end results of step 2 in chapter 5. The goals state what competencies the students will leave the program with, and the rationales explain why these goals are important. Typically, a short description of the process and procedures that were used to develop the program philosophy and the goals and rationales appears at the end of this section. The intent of this brief summary is to communicate that these statements were developed by and represent the collective beliefs and values of the entire staff.

The program scope and sequence by grade section typically begins with a chart similar to the one produced in step 9 in this chapter. This chart indicates what content is to be taught and when across all grades in the program. Following this chart should be a brief overview of steps 1 through 8 in chapters 5 and 6, which were used to create the scope and sequence by grade chart. The end products of each step should be presented with brief explanations. Again, the goal is not to train the reader how to perform these steps but rather to communicate that a series of steps were followed to determine what content should be included in the curriculum.

The third section of the curriculum guide is the grade section. This section outlines the materials and procedures that will be used to implement the curriculum and is typically organized by grades. Each grade segment starts with the yearly teaching and learning map for that grade followed by the block teaching and learning maps from step 10 in this chapter. Following the TLMs are the objective definitions, assessment procedures, score sheets, and objective evaluation forms for each objective

Section I: Executive summary

    Purpose

    Process used

    How the guide is organized

Section II: Curriculum design

    Philosophy statement

        Policies and resources

    Program goals and rationales

        Summary of procedures used

    Program scope and sequence by grade

        Summary of development steps

        Objective delineations for each goal

            Program goal emphasis

            Available instructional time

            Average objective mastery times

            How much content can be included in the curriculum

Section III: Grade section

    Yearly teaching and learning maps (YTLMs) for the grade

    Block teaching and learning maps (BTLMs) for each block

    Objective information

        Definitions

        Assessment procedures

        Assessment and reassessment score sheets

        Objective evaluation forms

Section IV: Evaluation

    Overview of what student and program evaluations are

    Sample student evaluation reports (covered in chapter 11)

    Sample program evaluation reports (covered in chapter 12)

    Consumer feedback form

▌ **Figure 6.14**   Sample outline for a functional ABC guide.

taught within that grade (these are developed in chapter 7).

The final section focuses on evaluation, which is addressed in chapters 11 and 12. This section starts with a brief overview of what student and program evaluations are and how this information is used to refine and improve the curriculum.

Sample evaluation reports are then presented with explanations of how to interpret the values in the reports and how this information is used. The last page of this section should be a feedback form. Anyone who takes the time to review the physical education curriculum should be asked to provide feedback so that the curriculum document can be revised to best meet their needs. The feedback form should be relatively simple and easy to complete. Typically the form starts with a rating section in which the readers are asked to rate features such as readability, clarity, and completeness. Then there is an open response section in which readers are asked to respond to questions such as, What do you see as this document's strengths? What do you see as this document's weaknesses? What could be done to improve this document? and, Did you find any sections of this document confusing or hard to understand?

Teacher Workbooks

All teachers should start with the functional curriculum guide as described earlier. However, this guide is usually modified into a teacher workbook for everyday use. The teacher workbook is usually organized around a grade with tabs for each class. To keep the workbook manageable, a different workbook is created for each grade. Teachers can modify the actual format of the workbook to meet their needs. The goal is to have a functional medium to store, record, and manage both what the teacher has implemented and what the students have learned of the objectives targeted for instruction during each year of the program.

Figure 6.15 illustrates a sample teacher workbook outline organized by class within each grade. This means that within each grade section there would be tabs for each class (e.g., Ms. Jones', Ms. Smith's, Ms. Predmore's) and for each class there would be a TLM, SLF, and the score sheets for the objectives being worked on. The first document in the workbook is the scope and sequence for all the objectives in the program. This provides an easy reference to when objectives are to be worked on and mastered throughout the curriculum as well as the relationship between objectives that contribute to the same goals. It also identifies the specific objectives targeted to be worked on, reviewed, and mastered for this grade level. The grade-specific information can either be read from the program scope and sequence chart or listed on a separate sheet for clarity.

The next section of the workbook contains all of the relevant information about the objectives that will be taught to this grade level for the year. These documents are discussed in detail in chapter 7 and include objective definitions, assessment procedures for each objective, and a master score sheet for each objective that is used to make working copies for each class. In addition an activity list for each objective contains instructional cues and learning experiences coded to the key components of each

---

Curriculum scope and sequence by grade

Objective information for each objective to be worked on during this grade

- Objective definitions (see chapter 7)

- Assessment procedures for each objective (see chapter 7)

- Master score sheet for each objective

- Objective evaluation form (see chapters 11 and 12)

- Instructional cues and activity lists for each objective (see chapter 10)

Teaching and learning maps for this grade

- Yearly

- Block

Tabs for each class

- Teaching and learning templates for each block (see chapter 10)

- Student learning formats (SLFs) for each class (see chapter 10)

- Score sheets with student assessment and reassessment data for each objective
(see chapter 7)

▌ **Figure 6.15** Sample workbook contents by class within each grade.

objective. These lists are created in chapter 10. At the end of this section is an objective evaluation form that is completed by the teacher at the end of the year as part of the program evaluation procedures. This form is explained in chapters 11 and 12.

The third section of the workbook contains the yearly and block teaching and learning maps for this grade level. As discussed earlier, these maps outline how the objectives will be grouped for instruction and when they will be worked on during the year. The final sections of the teacher workbook are tabs for each of the teacher's classes for this grade level. Within each tabbed section are the teaching and student learning templates for each. These templates are covered in chapter 10. These sections also include a working objective score sheet for recording student assessment and reassessment data for each objective they work on. The assessment score sheets are discussed in chapter 7.

Summary

You should now understand the procedures for designing an achievement-based curriculum. This chapter guided you through the processes of delineating the objectives for each goal, establishing the program percentage emphasis for each goal, calculating instructional time, estimating average objective mastery time, and finally how to use these calculations to determine how much content can be included in your curriculum. Once your content was identified and delimited, procedures were presented to guide you through sequencing the content across the curriculum and then organizing it into teaching and learning maps for each year. Finally, recommendations were provided on how to organize your curricula material so that it could be used both to promote the program and on a daily basis by teachers to implement the program.

Making It Work

Have you achieved the expected outcomes (see page 114) for this chapter? You should now understand the process and procedures for developing an ABC program plan. Still, you may have some practical questions that need answers, such as the following:

- *Does identifying what content should be included in the curriculum really have to be this complicated?* No! It does not have to be complicated, but it must be comprehensive and systematic. The keys are that first you must have a process that involves, solicits, and incorporates the needs, values, and interests of all of the teachers in the curriculum development process. The second key is that you have to ensure that what you create can actually be accomplished within the unique constraints of the district. This is where the concept of planning down and all of the procedures related to time calculations come in. Many of these procedures initially appear complicated because they are new and different from what teachers have traditionally done when planning their curricula. In reality these procedures are straightforward. Once you have done them a few times, they are easy to implement.

- *What happens if the teachers do not like to be told what to teach?* This is an important question and a common misconception regarding the ABC process. The ABC process does not tell teachers what to teach or what content to include in their curriculum. The ABC process is just that—a process. It guides teachers through the decision-making procedures so that they can decide what content to include and teach in their curriculum. What the ABC process does assume is that teachers will be held responsible for teaching the curriculum they develop. The demand for more accountability in our schools is arising from many sources such as the federal mandate for "No Child Left Behind," state mandates for benchmarks, and statewide testing programs. Instead of perceiving the ABC process as a threat, teachers should view it as a way to respond to these needs and ensure that their curricula are both effective and accountable.

- *If you find out that your school district has not allotted enough time for physical education to achieve any functional goals, shouldn't this problem be addressed first?* The underlying issue here is which battle to fight first. Given tight economic times and ever increasing demands for accountability, you should not request more resources (e.g., time, staff, space, and so on) before you can design and implement an effective physical education curriculum. This argument may cost you your program instead of getting you the additional resources you desire. The reality is that you have to start with the resources you have and show what you can do with them. If you can document that you can effectively teach and achieve a small number of goals with your current resources, you can then make data-based arguments of what you could produce with more resources. The ABC model will give you a process and products that sell better than emotional arguments.

▎ *The ABC process appears to prescribe how everything must be taught down to the minute. What happens if the teachers cannot agree on how the objectives should be grouped for instruction or how the time should be distributed?* The intent of the ABC model and the use of teaching and learning maps is not to have all teachers teaching the same content in the same way like robots. In fact, the intent is just the opposite. Teachers should be encouraged to be creative and innovative in how they teach their content. What the ABC process does is guide the teachers through a decision-making process to determine what content (which the teachers determined during the planning process) should be taught when and how much emphasis it should receive. Yearly and block teaching and learning maps are intended to be developed individually by each teacher and to reflect their interests and talents. The number and length of the instruction blocks, how teachers group their objectives, and how teachers distribute their time for each objective are all determined by the individual teachers. These maps are not expected to look alike, but they are expected to produce the same results. The key is that teachers need to record this information so that they know what they intended to do and then can evaluate whether they effectively did it. What makes this process initially challenging for teachers is that they are not accustomed to thinking and planning at this level.

Developing Functional Assessments

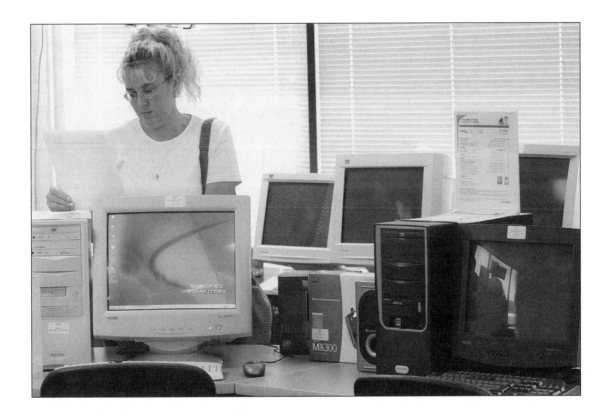

U nderstanding that as the physical education teacher you work with more students than any other teacher in the school, your principal has given you $1,000 to buy the most powerful computer you can to assist you in managing all of your student performance data. Unfortunately, budget rules in the district require that you spend this money today, so you have to buy it from a local merchant who will accept a purchase order from the school district. How would you go about making sure you buy the most powerful computer you could with this $1,000? You could just go to the closest computer store and ask them for the best computer they have for $1,000, but how would you know if they are giving you a good deal or the power you need? What would happen if you went to several different stores, and they all recommended different computers?

Logic might suggest that before you go out and start looking at computers, you first identify the key components you need in your computer. To help you here, you call the computer expert in your district. She asks you how you want to use the computer. You tell her you want to manage a large database of student performance information on all objectives in your curriculum and to produce professional-looking reports every four to six weeks. Based on this information, she recommends that you buy a name brand computer with the fastest processor available, at least a megabyte of RAM memory, at least a 100-gigabyte hard drive, and a built-in CD-ROM burner so that you can back up your data. Now you go to all of the local stores and collect information on these components on the computers offered for $1,000. Once you have collected this information, you can then compare the computers and select the one that gives you the most power for your money.

EXPECTED OUTCOMES

This chapter is designed to guide you through the process of developing functional assessments that are linked to your planned objectives. After reading this chapter, you will be able to do the following:

1. Define assessment and explain why it is a critical component of the ABC model
2. Identify the role of assessment in teacher decision making
3. List and describe the four steps in the assessment process
4. Design assessment items for the objectives in your curriculum
5. Collect and record, in an efficient manner, valid and reliable assessment data on your students

---

What does buying a computer have to do with curriculum development and this chapter on assessment? The scenario illustrates the basic decision-making process used to solve problems. The basic process is: (1) identify the goal or problem, (2) define the objective or decision, (3) collect relevant information, (4) interpret the information, and (5) make a decision. Table 7.1 illustrates the decision-making process as it applies to the computer problem and a typical teaching situation: how do you know what

students need to learn on the next objective in the curriculum?

The key to the decision-making process is assessment. Of course, first you need to define the problem or question, but in our case we have already done that in our curriculum planning. We now know what content is to be taught and when. The next question is, What do students need to learn to master the content targeted for instruction? To answer this question, you have to understand the assessment process.

Table 7.1   Comparing Decision-Making Processes

Decision-making process	Computer	Teaching
A. Identify the problem or question.	Which powerful computer should I buy for $1,000?	What do students need to learn to be able to throw?
B. Define the decision or objective.	What are the key components of a powerful computer?	What are the essential components of the overhand throw?
C. Collect relevant information.	Collect data on various computers.	Assess students to see what components they know and are able to do.
D. Interpret information.	Compare computers on key components.	Look at student assessment data and identify common needs.
E. Make a decision.	Buy the most powerful computer available.	Plan a lesson designed to meet the needs of the students.

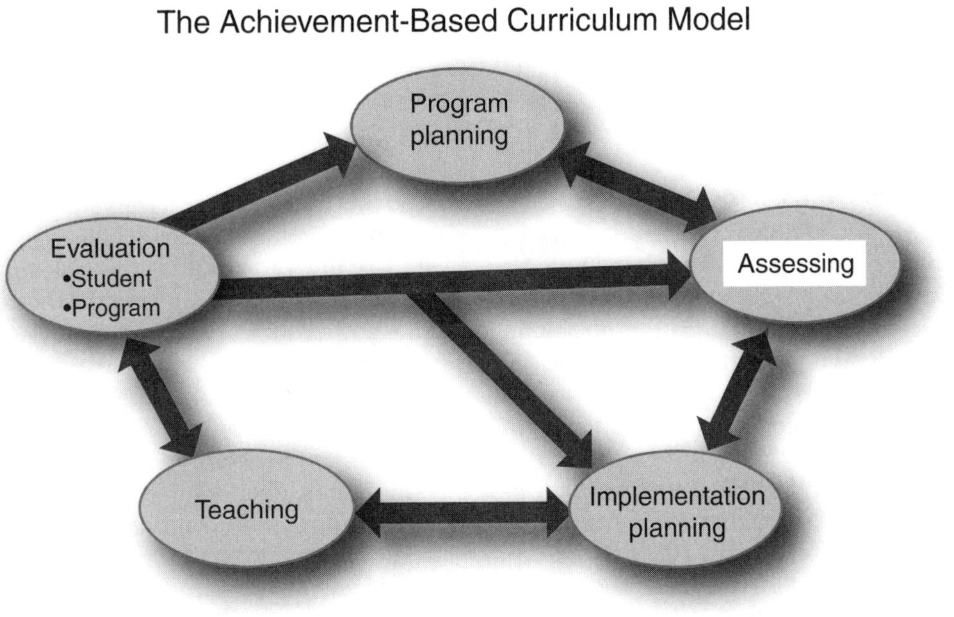

The Achievement-Based Curriculum Model

Figure 7.1 Assessing is an integral part of the ABC model.

As illustrated in figure 7.1, assessment is the second component in the ABC model. Keep in mind that although each component of the ABC model is introduced discretely for the sake of clarity, all of the components are in fact mutually dependent. For example, you do not know what to assess without the curriculum, and you do not know what specifically you should teach on a given objective without ongoing assessment data. All of the ABC components are essential, but the assessment component is paramount because it provides the basis for the implementation and evaluation components.

A critical dimension of assessment in the ABC model is that it is a dynamic, ongoing process. Many people view assessment as a rather static process to perform periodically at some established intervals such as the beginning and end of the year. In the ABC model, assessment is an integral part of everything a teacher does. In essence, you cannot plan instruction, teach, or evaluate without continually assessing.

Many misconceptions exist regarding assessment because the term is used to describe many different things. When discussing student performance, the terms *testing, assessing, evaluating,* and *measuring* are often used interchangeably. For the purposes of this book, we will use the umbrella term *assessment* to describe the process teachers use to make informed decisions. The term *instruments* will refer to the methods and procedures teachers use to actually collect information, which they will then use to make their decisions. We chose the term *instruments*

instead of *tests* to avoid any negative connotations that may be associated with the term *test. Measurement* will refer to the type of information or data the instruments are designed to collect. For example, some instruments may be designed to collect ratings on a scale from high to low, whereas other instruments are designed to collect quantities such as the number of curl-ups performed in a minute or the time needed to run a specific distance. Finally, *evaluation* will be defined as the process of comparing initial assessment data with reassessment data to make informed decisions. More detailed information on issues such as formative and summative evaluation will be addressed in chapters 11 and 12.

The first part of this chapter will review the four steps in the assessment process. The second part will focus on how to select or develop appropriate assessment instruments to measure each of the objectives included in your curriculum. This section will also discuss common issues and concerns regarding assessment such as how to find the time to assess or how to practically record assessment data on three hundred students.

Assessment Process

As defined earlier, assessment is the process through which teachers make informed decisions. The assessment process can be broken down into four steps. First, teachers need to understand the type of decision they need to make. Second, they need to know how to either select or create an appropriate assessment instrument to match this decision. Third, they need to be able to administer the instrument so that they collect accurate and valid data. Finally, they need to interpret the assessment data collected and make an appropriate decision.

Step 1: Assessment Decisions

The types of assessment-based decisions teachers are commonly called on to make can be broadly grouped into three categories: identification, placement, and instructional. Identification decisions, which are sometimes referred to as eligibility decisions, are most commonly associated with whether students' abilities warrant special attention. For example, students can qualify for a Presidential Physical Fitness award if their performance levels are at the 85th percentile or higher on select physical fitness measures. Students with special needs can qualify for special education services if their needs are great enough. The key to these decisions is to determine the magnitude of the difference between a student or group of students and an established reference group. To qualify for special education services, for example, a difference of two standard deviations from the mean is a common criterion.

The second type of decisions teachers frequently have to make are placement decisions. Placement decisions can involve determining how students are placed in classes to control for variations in ability. The term *placement* should not be taken negatively. It does not mean that students are segregated or somehow made to feel inferior. In physical education, students are "placed" on teams of similar or mixed abilities, assigned to a particular station, or given a task card based on identified needs. For special education students, placement decisions involve determining what is the most appropriate and least restrictive environment in which their IEP objectives can be addressed. In both of these cases, assessment information is needed about the student being placed and the performance attributes of the students in the target placement.

How would you decide whether to place a new student in an advanced tennis class in your secondary physical education program? To address this question, you would need to know what objectives the other students have already mastered to enter the unit and what objectives are targeted for instruction in this unit. You could then assess the new student to determine if she has the prerequisite skills to be successful in this unit.

A similar scenario applies to determining appropriate placements for students with disabilities. How would you determine whether a student with spina bifida who uses a wheelchair should be in regular physical education or in an alternative placement for a volleyball unit? To make this decision, you would have to determine what skills the student currently has and what skills he would need to be successful in this unit. With this information, and maybe with consultation with an adapted physical educator, you could make an informed decision about whether this would be the most appropriate placement for this student.

The third and most common type of decisions teachers make are instructional decisions. Although the curriculum indicates what objectives to address at any given grade within the program, teachers still need to make a host of decisions regarding what they should actually teach. For example, the curricu-

How do you determine the most appropriate and least restrictive physical education placement for a student with a disability?

lum indicates that catching should be taught during the third grade. What are some of the decisions you need to make? To start, you need to know how good the students are at catching already. Once you have identified a component of catching that needs work, such as retracting the arms to absorb the force of the ball, how are you going to address this need? What teaching method will you use? What drills can your students use to work on this component? What games can they play that emphasize this component? How will your students get feedback during instruction and class activities to know if they are doing this component correctly?

Finally, but equally as important, is how you will know which of your decisions were good ones that you should repeat and which ones were poor ones that you should change. The key to instructional decisions is having a clear definition of the objective to be taught. In most cases you can translate the objective definition into an assessment instrument that clearly identifies in observable and measurable terms what the students are expected to demonstrate to show mastery.

Step 2: Matching Assessment Instruments With Assessment Decisions

The next step in the assessment process is to match the appropriate assessment instrument with the type of assessment decision being made. Although hundreds of assessment instruments are available to physical educators, these can be generally grouped into one of two categories: norm-referenced instruments and criterion-referenced instruments. Norm-referenced instruments (NRIs) generally are standardized instruments designed to collect *product measures* (scores), which in turn are compared to reference standards provided with the instrument. Criterion-referenced instruments (CRIs) can be standardized or nonstandardized instruments designed primarily to collect *process measures*, which are then compared to established reference standards.

To fully understand these definitions, we must further define some of the terms. In relation to instruments, the term *standardized* means that there are established procedures that must be followed when administering the instrument. These procedures can specify the type of equipment to be used, the space needed for a test item, the number of practice trials allowed, or the specific instructions that must be read to the student. These standardized procedures are designed to ensure that students taking the test are measured under the same conditions as the students used in the normative sample. Because NRIs by definition are designed

to allow teachers to compare the scores they collect with the norms provided by the instrument, these instruments tend to be highly standardized. CRIs, on the other hand, tend to be slightly more adaptable in their administrative standards. Because CRIs are more concerned with getting an accurate measurement of what the students can and cannot do or what they know in relation to performing a given behavior, they tend to provide teachers with more flexibility. For example, a CRI would probably operationally define the components that the teacher should observe, but might allow the teacher to determine how many practice trials a student could have or to choose an appropriate activity to involve the students in to facilitate observation of their performance.

Product and *process measures* refer to the aspect of the performance that the instrument actually measures. Generally, items tend to focus on either the outcomes, or products, of performance or on the process of performance. For example, teachers could assess students' throwing performance by measuring how far they can throw a ball or by how many times they can hit a target. These would be product measures because they focus on the outcomes of the throwing performance. Teachers could also assess how the students actually throw the ball. For example, did they start with a side orientation, did they transfer their weight, and did they follow through when they threw?

Although NRIs can be designed to measure both the process and products of performance, most NRIs tend to focus exclusively on product measures because they are more objective and easier to measure accurately and reliably. Common product measures focus on the products or outcomes of performance such as the number of repetitions, the time needed to complete a task, or the number of times a target was hit out of so many trials. Note that these measurements are very objective and require little training or skill to be accurate. Process measures, on the other hand, measure how a skill is performed. These measures are less concerned with the end result and more concerned with measuring what happens during the process of the performance of a skill. Process measures generally require more knowledge and skill to administer. In the throwing example described earlier, teachers must not only know the key components of the skill they are assessing, but also possess prior training and practice so that they can accurately and reliably judge these components as students perform them.

Finally, *reference standards* refer to how the data collected during testing is interpreted. In the case of NRIs, norms are the most common reference standard. Norms are typically provided by gender in either percentiles or age equivalency tables. Figure 7.2 shows a sample normative chart. To use the chart, the teacher administers the standardized instrument to the student and then looks up the score obtained in the appropriate normative chart. Using the normative data in figure 7.2, you can

NCYFS* II Norms by Age for the Distance Walk/Run (in minutes and seconds)

	Age							
	Boys				Girls			
	Half mile		Mile		Half mile		Mile	
Percentile	6	7	8	9	6	7	8	9
99	3:53	3:34	7:42	7:31	4:05	4:03	8:18	8:06
95	4:15	3:56	8:18	7:54	4:29	4:18	9:14	8:41
90	4:27	4:11	8:46	8:10	4:46	4:32	9:39	9:08
85	4:35	4:22	9:02	8:33	4:57	4:38	9:55	9:26
80	4:45	4:28	9:19	8:48	5:07	4:46	10:08	9:40
75	4:52	4:33	9:29	9:00	5:13	4:54	10:23	9:50
70	4:59	4:40	9:40	9:13	5:20	5:00	10:35	10:15
65	5:04	4:46	9:52	9:29	5:25	5:06	10:46	10:31
60	5:10	4:50	10:04	9:44	5:31	5:11	10:59	10:41
55	5:17	4:54	10:16	9:58	5:39	5:18	11:14	10:56
50	5:23	5:00	10:39	10:10	5:44	5:25	11:32	11:13
45	5:28	5:05	11:00	10:27	5:49	5:32	11:46	11:30
40	5:33	5:11	11:14	10:41	5:55	5:39	12:03	11:46
35	5:41	5:17	11:30	10:59	6:00	5:46	12:14	12:09
30	5:50	5:28	11:51	11:16	6:07	5:55	12:37	12:26
25	5:58	5:35	12:14	11:44	6:14	6:01	12:59	12:45
20	6:09	5:46	12:39	12:02	6:27	6:10	13:26	13:13
15	6:21	6:06	13:16	12:46	6:39	6:20	14:18	13:44
10	6:40	6:20	14:05	13:37	6:51	6:38	14:48	14:31
5	7:15	6:50	15:24	15:15	7:16	7:09	16:35	15:40

*National Children and Youth Fitness Study

▌ Figure 7.2 Sample normative chart with age and gender norms.

Reprinted with permission from *The Journal of Physical Education, Recreation & Dance,* November/December 1987, 70. *JOPERD* is a publication of the American Alliance for Health, Physical Education, Recreation, and Dance, 1900 Association Drive, Reston, VA 20191.

see that an 8-year-old female student who ran the mile in 10:46 would fall in the 65th percentile. This means that this student's performance was as good or better than 65% of the students in the normative sample. As a general rule, the larger and more representative the sample used by the instrument developers to create the norms, the greater the validity, and the greater the confidence teachers can have in the instrument's norms.

The reference standard for CRIs is typically one or more performance criteria that the students' performances are compared against. Figure 7.3 contains a typical CRI for the overhand throw. Following the instructions provided with the instrument, the teacher administers the item and observes the student's performance and records whether the student has demonstrated each performance criterion. If, for example, a student is observed to demonstrate only two of the five criteria three out of five times, then the teacher would indicate which two components were mastered. CRIs can also occasionally have age and gender norms for the various performance criteria for an objective. Figure 7.4 (page 153) shows sample age norms for when 60% and 80% of children normally demonstrate the components of five common object control skills.

Table 7.2 summarizes the major differences between NRIs and CRIs. We present this table as a simple dichotomy for purposes of highlighting the differences; some tests do not fit neatly in one of these two categories. The TGMD is an example of a CRI that also has norms. In fact, the ideal test would include the positive attributes of both NRIs and CRIs.

Step 3: Collecting Accurate and Valid Data

By definition an instrument is *valid* if it measures what it declares to measure. It is *reliable* if it produces the same results on repeated administrations; that is, the results are consistent and stable. Although these may initially appear to be rather obvious criteria that all instruments would clearly meet, in reality they can sometimes be difficult to interpret. Many instruments in physical education rely heavily on "face validity," which means there is a direct and observable connection between what the instrument assesses and what it measures. For example, a scale would be considered to have face validity as a measure of a student's weight because that is what a scale measures. This, of course, could also be evaluated statistically by comparing the measurements of known weights with the values generated by the scale.

The problem with many physical education instruments is that validity can be confounded by the complexity of the items. For example, the softball throw for distance was once used as a measure of arm strength. This item was shown to correlate highly (good validity) with other arm strength measures when college physical education majors were used as subjects. One of the problems with the validity of this item was that it was dependent on a prerequisite skill—the ability to throw. For this to be a valid measure, the students first needed to have a mature throwing pattern. When the validity was generalized to school-aged populations, it was no longer clear what was being measured. For example, some students could have excellent arm strength but a poor or immature throwing pattern. These students would score poorly on this item, falsely suggesting that they had poor arm strength when in fact their arm strength was good but their throwing skill was poor.

Another factor that threatens the validity of many instruments used in physical education is the administration instructions. If the instructions are too complicated, the instruments may actually be measuring the students' ability to understand the task and not their ability to perform the task. This is a particularly critical factor to consider when using many instruments with students with disabilities in regular physical education.

As stated previously, reliability refers to the ability of an instrument to produce the same results on repeated administrations. When you are interested in whether the same teacher gets the same results on repeated administrations, this is referred to as *intrarater reliability*. When the issue is whether different teachers are reliably measuring the same thing, this is referred to as *interrater reliability*. Using a scale as an example, if we weighed the same student three times, a reliable scale would produce the same measurement each time. As a general rule, the more objective the measurement is, the easier it is to achieve high reliability. For example, measures that involve the number of repetitions, distances, or time tend to be relatively objective and subsequently are usually very reliable.

Unfortunately, many of the assessments commonly performed in physical education are more subjective in nature and depend on the ability of the teacher to make complex judgments. For example, when assessing whether students have a mature throwing pattern, teachers must know the key components of the skill and be able to observe whether they are being performed correctly when a student

I CAN

Performance Objective:
To demonstrate a functional overhand throw

Skill levels	Focal points for activity
1. To demonstrate an overhand throw with assistance	Given a verbal request, a demonstration, and physical assistance, a student with the ability to grasp a ball can throw a 3- to 4-inch ball a distance of at least 10 feet, two out of three times, without resistance in this manner: a. Overhand motion in the direction of the throw (hand passes above shoulder) b. Release the ball in the anticipated direction of the throw
2. To demonstrate an overhand throw without assistance 	Given a verbal request and a demonstration of the mature overhand throw, a student with the ability to perform the overhand throw with assistance can throw a 3- to 4-inch ball to a 20-inch-wide target placed 15 feet away, two out of three times in this manner: a. Eyes focused on the target b. Throwing arm motion includes the hand passing above the shoulder
3. To demonstrate a mature overhand throw	Given a verbal request and a demonstration, a student with the ability to perform the overhand throw can throw a 3- to 4-inch ball, two out of three times in this manner: a. Almost complete extension of the throwing arm to initiate windup for the throwing action (assuming a side orientation prior to the throw) b. Weight transfer to the foot opposite the throwing arm c. Hip and spine rotation (1/4 rotation) in preparation for and during the throwing action d. Follow-through well beyond ball release and toward the desired direction of travel e. Smooth (not mechanical or jerky) integration of four previous points
4. To demonstrate a mature overhand throw for distance	Given a verbal request and a demonstration, a student with the mature throwing pattern and sufficient arm strength can throw a 3- to 4-inch ball a distance of at least the minimum performance criteria for age and gender (see table below) two out of three times with angle of release at 45° (±5°). Distance* (in feet) boys and girls 8 to 15 years old should be able to throw a 3- to 4-inch ball | Age in years	8-9	10-12	13-15
---	---	---	---
Girls	46	71	84
Boys	73	114	159	 *These are the minimum acceptable distance criteria. *Source: Special Olympics Instructional Manual (Washington, D.C., American Association for Health, Physical Education and Recreation and The Joseph P. Kennedy, Jr. Foundation, 1972).*
5. To demonstrate a mature overhand throw for accuracy	Given a verbal request and a demonstration, the student can throw a 3- to 4-inch ball with a mature pattern two out of three times, hitting an 8-foot-square target placed 1 foot off the ground from a distance of 50 feet.

Figure 7.3 I CAN overhand throw.

Age at Which 60% and 80% of the Standardization Sample Achieved the Specific Performance Criteria for the Object Control Skills

Skill	Performance criteria	60%	80%
Two-hand strike	1. Dominant hand grips bat above nondominant hand	3	5
	2. Nondominant side of body faces the tosser	5	7
	3. Hip and spine rotation	8	9
	4. Weight is transferred by stepping with front foot	8	10
Stationary bounce	1. Contacts ball with one hand at about hip height	7	8
	2. Pushes ball with fingers (not a slap)	6	8
	3. Ball contacts floor in front of (or to the outside of) foot on the side of the hand being used	7	8
Catch	1. Preparation phase in which elbows are flexed and hands are in front of body	4	5
	2. Arms extend in preparation for ball contact	4	6
	3. Ball is caught and controlled by hands only	7	8
	4. Elbows bend to absorb force	7	8
Kick	1. Rapid continuous approach to the ball	4	4
	2. The trunk is inclined backward during ball contact	8	9
	3. Forward swing of the arm opposite kicking leg	8	9
	4. Follow-through by hopping on the nonkicking foot	10	NA[1]
Overhand throw	1. A downward arc of the throwing arm initiates the windup	6	7
	2. Rotation of hip and shoulder to a point where the nondominant side faces an imaginary target	7	8
	3. Weight is transferred by stepping with the foot opposite the throwing hand	6	8
	4. Follow-through beyond ball release diagonally across body toward side opposite throwing arm	8	10

[1]This performance criterion was not achieved by 80% of the standardization sample at any age between 3 and 10 years.

▌ **Figure 7.4** Ulrich TGMDII norms for object control.

Ulrich, D.A. (2000). *Test of gross motor development – Examiner's manual* (2nd ed.). Austin, TX: PRO-ED.

Table 7.2 Differences Between NRIs and CRIs

Type	Reference	Source	Procedures	Measures	Decision	Examples
NRIs	Normative data	Commercial	Standardized	Primarily product	Identification and placement	AAHPERD physical best
CRIs	Performance criteria	Commercial/ teacher made	Standardized/ informal	Primarily process	Placement and instructional	TGMD I CAN tests

throws, which takes less than a second. These judgments are further complicated by student variability (i.e., students do not perform in exactly the same way from trial to trial). Because of these factors, most motor skill instruments involve repeated measures. The criterion may be that the student demonstrate the appropriate components on three out of four trials, or that the student demonstrate a social behavior such as fair play consistently over several days.

In most cases, reliability is a function of the experience and competency of the individual using the instrument. Judges in a high-level diving, gymnastics, or skating competition illustrate how highly sophisticated movement patterns can be reliably measured with practice.

Teachers are responsible for making sure that the instruments they use for assessment are both valid and reliable. An instrument's validity is usually a function of its design. Threats to validity increase when an instrument is used for purposes or on populations for which it was not intended. Reliability of an instrument in most cases is a function of the teacher's knowledge and experience with the instrument. Most concerns related to reliability can be addressed through training and practice.

The teacher is responsible for making sure that the validity and reliability data provided with the instrument apply to how the teacher plans to use the instrument. Just because an instrument is commercially marketed does not mean that it is valid or reliable. Physical educators must carefully evaluate the intended purpose of the test and how it must be administered in comparison with what information they need to collect to make the decision at hand.

Another factor commonly discussed in conjunction with validity and reliability is *administrative feasibility*. Administrative feasibility refers to a number of factors such as cost, time, training, and specialized equipment required to use an assessment instrument accurately and reliably. In most cases, compromises need to be made between the ideal instruments and practicality. For example, a measurement of percent body fat may be desirable at the start of a fitness unit. The ideal choice may be to administer one-on-one assessments using a body pod. The reality, however, is that most physical educators could not afford to spend $10,000 of their equipment budget on one device to measure body fat or to spend several classes getting this measurement when an accurate estimate could be obtained using a $50 skin-fold caliper in a fraction of the time. The ideal instrument is one that requires no specialized equipment, can be administered to a group of students quickly, is cheap (or better yet, free), and requires no specialized skills or practice to administer. Because few instruments meet these criteria, teachers often develop their own assessment instruments to match their curriculum objectives. In so doing, they are well advised to remember the importance of administrative feasibility.

Another issue related to administrative feasibility is the setting required for using the instrument. Again, the ideal setting may be a distraction-free space in which all of the appropriate equipment can be set up in advance and where each student can be assessed individually. The reality is that most teachers have 30 to 40 minutes to assess 25 to 35 students in a less-than-adequate space full of distractions. Again, teachers must address these factors when designing their own assessment instruments.

General Assessment Guidelines

The final factor of administrative feasibility to consider is the training and preparation required to administer the instrument. Regardless of whether you are using a standardized NRI or a teacher-made CRI, you must attend to both preparation and the actual administration of the instrument. For most NRIs these procedures will be clearly defined in the manual and must be followed exactly to use the interpretative data provided. Most CRIs give teachers a little more latitude; nevertheless, they must follow certain guidelines and rules to ensure that the data they collect is both valid and reliable. Following is a general set of guidelines that can be applied to most assessment situations:

1. Select the appropriate type of instrument to match the decision you need to make. Table 7.2 (page 150) summarizes the major decision categories teachers face and the types of instruments that apply. Because the majority of the decisions you make will apply to instruction, most of the instruments you use will probably be CRIs.

2. Review and know how to administer the instrument well enough so that you can focus your attention on the student you are assessing and not on the mechanics of administering the items (e.g., reading the instructions).

3. Whenever possible, set up any necessary equipment in advance and anticipate any potential problems. Be prepared with backup equipment such as stopwatches and targets that are critical to administering a given item.

4. When using an instrument for the first time, plan for a few practice trials. These will help you internalize the procedures and will most likely identify other potential administration problems.

5. When using instruments that focus on the process of a skill (e.g., throwing), identify where you need to stand (how far away and at what angle) so that you can see the components students need to perform.

6. Choose an appropriate assessing activity or organizational format so that the students are actively engaged and you are free to move as needed to conduct the assessment.

7. Develop an efficient method to accurately record the assessment data you need to collect.

Remember that the primary reason for conducting assessments is to obtain valid information so that you can make accurate decisions. Although the focus of assessment is on evaluating where students are on a given physical education objective, you must also consider the total student when conducting and interpreting performance. This means that in addition to focusing on the content being assessed, you must also assess how the student responds during the assessment. Student responses can be grouped according to the ACE factors: attention, comprehension, and effort. The following scenario illustrates why these factors need to be considered.

John's teacher asks John to perform an overhand throw so she can assess his throwing pattern. Instead of throwing, John takes the ball and kicks it. What has just been assessed? What does the teacher know? Did John kick the ball because he did not understand the instructions? Did John kick the ball because he understood the instructions but knew he could kick better than he could throw? Did John kick the ball to avoid throwing because he knows this behavior will make the other kids laugh and distract the teacher from looking at his throw? Can you think of other possible reasons?

What John's teacher learned from this assessment was that she had made a mistake. As soon as she saw John's behavior, she remembered that he had an auditory processing learning disability that makes it hard for John to process complex auditory instructions. Realizing her mistake, John's teacher repeats her request using short instructional prompts, makes sure she has eye contact with John, and concurrently demonstrates the skill.

What does this scenario tell us about the ACE factors of attention, comprehension, and effort during assessing? First, for a student's assessment data to be valid, you must be certain that the student has actually attended to the instructions. This may appear an obvious consideration, but there is frequently a difference between what teachers expect

students to attend to and what they actually attend to. When you demonstrate the overhand throw to show students the correct form, the logical assumption is that they will watch how you extend your arm, transfer your weight, and follow through—correct? In fact, what most kids do is watch the ball. They can tell you how far it went or whether you hit the target you were throwing at, but most have no idea about what your throw actually looked like. In the previous scenario John's failure to perform the assessment task correctly was a result of his inability to attend to the instructions. Once the teacher recognized this problem and communicated the instructions in a way that facilitated John's attention, he had no problem responding to the task and she then was able to get an accurate assessment of his throwing pattern.

Once you are sure that your students are attending to your instructions, the next factor you must consider when assessing is whether the students comprehend or understand the instructions. Again, this may appear obvious, but a gap sometimes exists between what teachers think they have communicated and what the students comprehend. Consider the following scenario:

Mr. Britton wants to assess the throwing patterns of his students. He uses a station organization so that he can be at one of the stations to assess the throwing patterns. Because space is limited in the gym, he sets up the throwing station facing a wall about 25 feet away and puts a small 12-inch yellow circle target on the wall to give the students something to aim at. Before each student throws, he reminds them to throw as hard as they can. During the assessment Mr. Britton finds that many of the students are not fully extending their throwing arms, not transferring their weight appropriately, and not following through. Is it that these students still need more work on these components, or is possible that they did not understand what they were supposed to be focusing on during this assessment? Careful observation during the assessment reveals that many of the students are really focusing on trying to hit the target and are comparing their results when they finish. Given that the target is only 25 feet away, Mr. Britton wonders whether the students are not performing all of the appropriate components because they do not need them to reach the target.

In this scenario the problem is actually related to how Mr. Britton designed the assessment task. The fact that the students are too close to the wall and have been given a target to focus on distracts the students from the real goal of the assessment. The conflict is that Mr. Britton has asked them to do one thing, and the task seems to suggest that they do another. The problem is that the students do not understand what exactly they should be focusing on. So what is being assessed in this situation—their ability to perform the overhand throw correctly or their ability to interpret what they should do on this assessment task? When in doubt, a simple way to check whether the students understand the focus of the assessment is to ask them.

Another issue when assessing is whether students are trying their hardest. Consider the following scenario:

> Ms. Dunn wants to assess her students' cardiorespiratory endurance so that she can design a fitness unit to meet their needs. She decides to use the 12-minute walk/run test to assess her students because she has read that performance on this test is highly correlated with maximum oxygen uptake. During the assessment she notes that several groups of students are walking together and talking. She prompts them to run, but after a few running steps they resume walking.

What has Ms. Dunn measured with this assessment? Does she have an accurate measurement of her students' cardiorespiratory endurance, or does she have an indication of their willingness to do this task? Most assessments assume that when the students are being assessed they are trying as hard as they can to do their best. This is not always true. It is the teachers' responsibility to concurrently assess students' effort while they are being assessed. Many middle school and high school students, if they do not anticipate that they can do well on the assessment, decide that it is better to act as though they just don't care. Some just go through the motions; others make a joke out of their performance. They would rather be perceived by their peers as not caring about the assessment than to actually try and not perform well.

The bottom line is that you need to know what you have assessed: performance or willingness to perform. When effort becomes a concern, you must then design assessment items that allow you to evaluate effort as well. For example, you could require that students perform the 12-minute walk/run test with a heart monitor that records the percentage of time their heart rates are at or above their target training rate during the assessment.

Basic Assessment Rules

In summary, there is no substitute for good planning and preparation when assessing. Although being aware of the students' attention, comprehension, and effort during assessment will improve the validity of the data collected, you must also use common sense. Following are a few simple rules to follow when assessing:

1. Make sure the students know what you are asking them to do. When using NRIs, you usually do not have much flexibility in how you administer the instrument. However, if while administering the instrument you observe that the students appear confused by the instructions, you should question the validity of the data you collect. With most CRIs you have a little more flexibility in how you administer the items. If a student appears confused, you should ask the student if she understands what you are requesting.

2. Be aware of any potential audience effects. Because most assessments in physical education must be administered in a public setting, there is always a threat that one or more environmental factor(s) may negatively affect performance. Students who know they are going to perform worse than other students often just blow off the assessment and act as though they don't care. Unfortunately, if students do not give their best effort, you do not get an accurate assessment of their ability. Therefore it is critical that you conduct assessments in such a fashion that students do not think they are being "tested." One of the best ways to deal with test avoidance is to make assessment an ongoing process and to integrate it into natural activities in the class.

3. Do not teach while formally assessing. Periodically, at least at the beginning and end of units of instruction, formally assess students to determine where they are on the objectives being taught. One of the toughest things to do while formally assessing students is to not immediately use the assessment information to give instructional feedback. Again, one of the best ways to conduct this form of assessment is to observe the students in a naturalistic setting such as a game in which they are applying the skills being assessed and can be observed without the expectation of immediate feedback.

4. Give general positive feedback. Sometimes you will not be able to avoid the fact that students know they are being evaluated. In these situations they are going to naturally look to you after each

performance for feedback. If you just say nothing, they may interpret this as negative feedback and try to alter their performance. In these instances, it is probably best to give a general positive statement such as, "Good job."

5.   Devise and use a method that allows you to record student performance data as soon as possible. Probably the single greatest complaint teachers have about assessment relates to the time involved in collecting and recording assessment data. To this end, you must be creative in developing innovative ways to record student assessment data quickly and accurately (see chapter 11 for more information on this topic).

6.   When in doubt, do not give students credit. Given the complexity and subjective nature of many of the behaviors assessed in physical education, ambiguity as to whether a student is consistently demonstrating a given motor skill or behavior pattern is common. Whenever you have any doubt, the rule to follow is not to give the student credit for mastery of the behavior in question. If you err in this direction, the worst that can happen is that you will continue to work on this behavior. If the students actually have mastered the behavior in question, the worst they can experience is success and maybe a little boredom until you reassess. On the other hand, if you err in the direction of giving them credit for the behavior, you will not focus any additional instruction on this behavior. If they in fact have not mastered this behavior, they now will potentially fail or at a minimum practice the incorrect pattern until you reassess them and catch your error.

7.   Make sure the testing conditions do not compete with or confound the performance. If you want to assess a student's qualitative throwing performance, then the assessment task should require that the student throw the ball hard. Because of space and motivation considerations, teachers often assign a throwing task that involves students throwing at a small target that is relatively close. If students misinterpret the task, they may decide that it is more important to hit the target than to throw hard. In this case, they may modify their throwing pattern to maximize accuracy at the expense of correct form. The end result would be that the teacher gets an assessment of how well the students could modify their throwing pattern to do well on an accuracy task and not an accurate assessment of their throwing pattern.

8.   Be prepared. All assessments require some amount of practice to administer efficiently. To be effective, you must internalize the components of

the skills you are going to observe. If you need to refer to your checklist while assessing to review the components of a skill, you are not ready. You will typically need about an hour of practice to memorize the components of most motor skills and to see them accurately. After several hours of practice you will begin to see the skill in terms of the components. At that point, instead of looking at the skill and mentally comparing the performance to the checklist, you will just see the performance in terms of which components the students are performing correctly and incorrectly.

Step 4: Interpreting Assessment Data and Making Appropriate Decisions

The last step in the assessment process is interpreting the data and making a decision. For an identification decision, this typically involves looking up raw scores or a composite score in the normative tables provided with the instrument and obtaining a percentile or age equivalency score. You then compare this value to the established eligibility criteria. If the value meets or exceeds this standard, the student would be deemed eligible. For students with special needs, this type of decision will determine whether they qualify for special education services. Students are typically assessed on a number of factors such as motor skills, IQ, and adaptive behavior and must be found to have delays greater than two standard deviations below the mean for their age and gender.

For placement decisions, the process is similar to the procedures described for identification decisions. The major difference is that for placement decisions you may need to use either an NRI or a CRI test depending on the nature of the decision. Reiterating the example used earlier in this chapter, a placement decision could involve needing to determine whether a new student should be placed in an intermediate or advanced tennis class. To address this question, you would need to know the prerequisite objectives for the intermediate and advanced classes as well as what objectives are targeted for instruction in each. You could then assess the new student on these prerequisite and target skills and compare the results to the performance levels of the students in the intermediate and advanced classes.

A second common type of placement decision you may need to make is the most appropriate and least restrictive physical education setting for a student with a disability. The law requires that students with disabilities be placed in the regular educational setting to the maximum degree possible as long as their instructional needs can be met and they can be successful. To make this decision, you would need to know what skills the students in the regular physical education class already possess and what skills they are targeted to learn. You would then assess the student with the disability on these objectives and determine his present abilities. The next step would be to compare the results and make a judgment as to whether this student's needs could be accommodated in this setting.

Interpreting assessment data for instructional decisions has several dimensions. At the start of the unit, initial assessment data are used to determine where the students are on the content targeted for instruction. This information is in turn used to guide a variety of decisions such as the focus of instruction for the next class; how students will be grouped for instruction; and what games, drills, and activities you will use (this is discussed in greater detail in chapters 8, 9, and 10). During instruction you should use assessment data every time you observe students and give them feedback. Finally, use reassessment and postassessment data to evaluate and make decisions regarding student progress, your effectiveness, the appropriateness of your instructional methods, and the overall merit of the program.

Selecting or Developing Assessment Instruments for the Curriculum Objectives

You should now have a basic understanding of assessment, the role of assessment in teacher decision making, and the common types of assessment instruments used in physical education. It should also be clear that the majority of the assessment-based decisions teachers make on a daily basis (e.g., placement and instruction) are based on the objectives in their curriculum. To make these decisions, you need valid and reliable assessment instruments. The purpose of this section of the chapter is to highlight how you can develop your own assessment instruments.

Although presented here under assessment, the creation of assessment instruments for each of the objectives in the curriculum is actually a continuation of the curriculum development process. In chapter 6 we determined what objectives would be included in the curriculum and when instruction would begin on each objective. Once the curriculum committee has identified the objectives, they must then find or create assessment instruments for each objective. Because the objectives have already been developmentally sequenced across the grades

in the program, a common practice is to divide the teachers into a number of small groups of two or three by program levels (elementary, middle, and high school). Each group is then assigned a subset of the objectives for their program level and asked to develop assessment instruments for each of these objectives. The small groups then bring their items back and share them with the total group where they are reviewed, revised, and finalized.

With the increased attention being devoted to state performance standards and demands for more accountability in schools, much has been written about assessment. One of the prevailing themes in the recent assessment literature has been that assessments must be instructionally relevant and authentic (Doolittle & Fay, 2000; Melograno, 1994, 1997). In other words, assessments should focus on measuring what was taught and should be conducted in naturalistic rather than artificial or contrived environments. This may seem rather obvious, but it is a marked departure from how assessments were commonly conducted in the past.

If the goal of instruction were to teach students to perform a forehand tennis stroke so that they could play a functional game of tennis, a traditional approach might be to assess the students on a tennis wall volley test. For this test the students would be scored on the number of times they could volley a tennis ball against a wall from a specified distance in a specified time interval (e.g., 30 seconds). This test was probably selected because it was relatively easy to administer and score and was believed to correlate highly with tennis performance. That is, good tennis players performed better on the test than did poor tennis players. What was not immediately apparent was that this assessment item actually misdirected the focus of the learners. If the students wanted to do well in tennis as measured by this test, what they needed to practice was volleying a tennis ball against a wall as quickly as possible. Although practicing this skill would result in a better score on the test, it would not likely have much carryover to being able to play tennis on a tennis court. Conversely, if the instruction and practice occurred in applied tennis situations and then the students were tested by volleying a ball against a wall, the scores obtained would probably not be an accurate measure of what the students had learned.

An authentic assessment would focus on the degree to which the students performed each of the essential components of the forehand tennis stroke, for example, while playing a game of tennis. This instrument would probably be a CRI similar to the example in figure 7.5. This is not to imply that all of the instruction must occur on tennis courts and in

Theme: Leisure pursuits
Sport: Tennis
Task: Execute the forehand drive in returning a real serve
Learning dimensions: Physical, emotional
Level: Grades 7–8
Type of assessment (circle one):   Teacher   Peer   Self (videotape)

Criteria/elements (circle the letter of elements that need work)	Scale			
	① All silence	② Scattered applause	③ Round of applause	④ Standing ovation

1. Criterion: **Grip**
  a. Base knuckle of thumb centered on top of grip
  b. Palm is behind handle
  c. Thumb overlaps and is next to middle finger with index finger spread
  d. Fingers evenly spread
  e. Butt end just protrudes from hand
	①
	Comments:
		②	③	④

2. Criterion: **Backswing**
  a. Move as quickly as possible into position after opponent hits ball
  b. Turn both shoulders and pivot hips so forward shoulder points in direction of ball flight
  c. Racket drawn back approximately parallel to body between waist and knee height (below intended point of contact)
  d. Straight-back technique with racket
  e. Racket at comfortable length from body; grip hand hidden from opponent
	①
	Comments:
		②	③	④

3. Criterion: **Forward swing**
  a. Dictate body and racket position at impact by "going after" ball
  b. As forward foot hits the ground, front knee is bent so that eyes are closer to line of flight of ball
  c. Arm and racket move forward as a unit with racket head trailing wrist before contact; racket moves forward and upward
  d. At impact, racket is laid back (hyperextended); ball struck in line with or slightly in front of lead foot
  e. Wrist kept firm; not changed from original position during forward swing; vertical racket head in line with wrist at impact.
	①
	Comments:
		②	③	④

4. Criterion: **Follow-through**
  a. Wrist and racket stay together as a unit for short time during early follow-through
  b. Watch spot where contact was made to avoid pulling eyes off ball
  c. Head remains in precisely the same position as when ball was contacted
  d. Stroke completed with full sweep of arm close to chin with body balanced to move to next shot
	①
	Comments:
		②	③	④

▌**Figure 7.5**   Sample tennis criterion-referenced instrument.

Reprinted, by permission, from V.J. Melograno, 1996, *Designing the physical education curriculum* (Champaign, IL: Human Kinetics), 112.

Is this a form of authentic assessment?

the context of a tennis game. It would be appropriate to practice drills and activities that focus on specific components of the forehand stroke. However, these drills would then need to be integrated and applied to actually playing tennis if that is the ultimate goal of the instruction.

To be an effective teacher, you must continually assess with assessment instruments that are instructionally relevant and authentic. To be instructionally relevant, instruments must be specifically designed around the content delineated in the physical education curriculum. This is sometimes referred to as curriculum-embedded assessment. Although the thought of creating assessment items for all of the objectives in your curriculum may initially seem overwhelming, the task can be efficiently managed by following a few simple procedures:

1. Define the objective.
2. Determine the conditions for administering the assessment.
3. Determine how the assessment will be scored.
4. Create an efficient method for recording assessment data.

Defining the Objective

What are students expected to demonstrate to show mastery of this objective? What are the key components of this skill or behavior that students must learn to achieve mastery? These are the key questions you must answer when defining an objective. Examples of definitions of a motor skill objec-

tive, cognitive objective, and affective objective are shown in figures 7.6, 7.7 (page 162), and 7.8 (page 163), respectively. Definitions like these are created using a process called task analysis, in which the essential components of a skill are identified and listed either developmentally as they are normally acquired or sequentially as they occur over time when the skill is performed.

Fortunately, most objectives taught in physical education have already been task analyzed and are readily available in motor development and physical education methods textbooks, so there is no need to reinvent the wheel. The recommended procedure is to collect a few existing definitions and then modify these to meet your needs.

One factor to consider carefully is the number of components to include in the definition. The goal is to have enough components to cover the key elements of the objective and to detect progress over time. Many task analyses of physical education objectives found in the literature have been developed by researchers who analyze motor skills using high-speed video, which they then analyze in slow motion. These analyses may contain 15 to 20 components. This large number of components is excellent for detecting small performance errors and for documenting progress, but in most cases this number is not practical to observe and record in a typical physical education setting. Given that most motor skills occur very quickly, we recommend that you limit the number of components to a practical number (usually four or five) that you can realistically observe.

A second factor to consider is matching the components of the objective to the developmental level of the students. For example, the catching definition for sixth grade may require the student to move to a tennis ball thrown within a certain area and then catch it, whereas the definition for third grade may not require the student to move and would use a larger, softer ball.

You should follow a similar process when developing assessment definitions for nonmotor skill objectives such as cognitive and social objectives (O'Sullivan & Henniger, 2000). You could measure cognitive objectives, for example, by having the students take a 20-question exam. In this case the exam you use should be part of the definition. In other words, the definition for this objective would state that the student would be able to answer at least 17 out of 20 of the following questions correctly and then would list the 20 exam items. Another way to measure cognitive objectives is to use instruments that evaluate whether students can use the knowledge or content correctly. For example, can the student design a weight training program that correctly uses the overload principle? Occasionally, you will identify a novel objective for which there are no existing definitions to modify. In these cases we recommended that you find an existing objective that is similar and then use this objective as a model for creating the definition for the novel objective.

Determining the Conditions for Administering the Assessment

Although presented here as a separate procedure, many of the administration conditions are embed-

ded in the objective definition. For example, in figure 7.6 the definition of the catch includes information regarding how the item should be presented, the size of the ball that should be used, and how the ball should be thrown to the student. The goal here is to clearly define the conditions under which the assessment is administered so that repeated assessments are conducted under similar conditions and results can be compared. In other words, when you make repeated assessments of students' performances, you want to be sure that any changes you observe are a function of student learning and

Performance Objective: To demonstrate a functional catch

Skill levels	Focal points for activity
1. To catch with assistance	Given a verbal request, a demonstration, and physical assistance, the student can catch (grasp or trap with hands or arms and chest) an 8- to 12-inch ball lofted directly into the arms from a distance of 3 to 5 feet. The student can maintain control of the ball two out of three times without resistance.
2. To catch without assistance	Given a verbal request, a demonstration, and the ability to catch with assistance, the student can catch (grasp or trap with hands or arms and chest) an 8- to 12-inch ball lofted softly to the middle of the chest from a 6-foot distance. The student can do this two out of three times in this manner: a. Eyes focused on ball, adjusting the arm position to receive the ball on cue from watching the ball's path b. Trap or catch ball with hands or arms and chest
3. To demonstrate a mature catch	Given a verbal request, a demonstration, and the ability to catch without assistance, the student can catch a 6-inch playground ball tossed to chest height from a 15-foot distance two out of three times in this manner: a. Hands in front of the body, knees slightly flexed, elbows flexed near sides in preparatory position b. Extension of the arms in preparation for ball contact c. Contact the ball with hands only (fingers spread and slightly flexed with palms facing) d. Elbows bend as arms absorb the force of the ball e. Smooth (*not* mechanical or jerky) integration of four previous points
4. To move into position and catch	Given a verbal request, a mature catching pattern, and a demonstration, the student can catch two out of three times a 4- to 6-inch ball projected at least 10 feet high from a distance of at least 20 feet to a point within 5 feet of the student. Student moves into position to receive the ball on cue from watching the ball's path.

Figure 7.6 Example of a definition of a motor skill objective (catching).

Cognitive learning objective: To apply the rules of badminton, the student will identify correct scoring and serving decisions with at least 80% accuracy, given a variety of badminton situations.

Criterion-referenced item: The student refers to the badminton court diagram in answering the questions on scoring and serving.

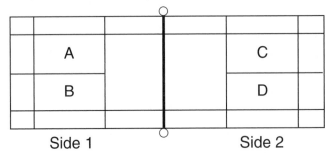

1. At the beginning of the game, side 2 wins the toss and decides to receive. Who is the first server? _____

2. The server wins two points, making the score 2 (serving) to 0. The server loses the next serve. Who serves next? _____

3. From what side of the court (as server looks toward net) does the second server begin to serve? _____

4. The second server loses the serve. No points are scored. Who is the third server? _____

5. The third server scores one point and then loses the serve. Who serves next? _____

6. The fourth server wins three points and then loses the serve. What is the score at this point?

_____

▌ **Figure 7.7** Example of a definition of a cognitive objective (badminton).

Reprinted, by permission, from V.J. Melograno, 1996, *Designing the physical education curriculum* (Champaign, IL: Human Kinetics), 156.

not just a change in the conditions of the assessment. Using the catch definition in figure 7.6, what would happen if the size of the ball were not defined? If you used an 8.5-inch ball on the pretest at the start of the unit and a tennis ball on the posttest at the end of the unit, what impact would this have on student performance?

A second concern related to administration conditions is making sure that the instructions or activity used to solicit the performance requires the correct performance. For example, if you want to assess the components of the overhand throw, your students must throw as hard as they can. If the conditions of the assessment require students to throw the ball only a short distance such as 20 feet to a wall, the students may not demonstrate the proper arm extension, weight transfer, or follow-through because they can reach the wall without these components. Another example would be using a game such as Cleaning Out the Backyard as a way to observe students' throwing patterns

in a naturalistic environment. For this activity to be appropriate, you would have to manipulate the height of the net, the size and weight of the balls, and the distance from the net so that students are required to throw balls as hard as they can to get them over the net.

One of the challenges in creating assessment items is striking a balance between control of the conditions and getting a valid measure of the students' true performances. At one end of the continuum you can standardize all of the conditions and prescribe the exact conditions for doing the assessment. In this case you have total control, but the student is put in a contrived and potentially anxiety-producing testing situation. This form of assessment also typically has to be administered individually, which can have a negative impact on instructional time. At the other end of the continuum you can embed the conditions into an activity and observe the students in applied settings such as games. In this case, you give up a certain amount of control, but your students can

Affective learning objective: To demonstrate positive interpersonal relations skills, the student will, following a unit involving reciprocal learning experiences, display behavior trends representing peer group expectancy at a frequency index rating of 3.0 or better during a group physical fitness program.

Evaluation instrument: The student is observed at least twice during the group physical fitness program. Behavior trends are rated according to the following criteria. Ratings for each behavior trend are circled and averaged. The frequency index rating is calculated as indicated.

Behavior trends	First observation					Second observation					Rating average
	Never	Seldom	Fairly often	Frequently	Regularly	Never	Seldom	Fairly often	Frequently	Regularly	
1. Limits interactions to friends; excludes others	5	4	3	2	1	5	4	3	2	1	
2. Shares equipment	1	2	3	4	5	1	2	3	4	5	
3. Takes turn at circuit stations	1	2	3	4	5	1	2	3	4	5	
4. Provides mutual assistance voluntarily	1	2	3	4	5	1	2	3	4	5	
5. Seeks seclusion from fitness group	5	4	3	2	1	5	4	3	2	1	
6. Interacts consistently with both males and females	1	2	3	4	5	1	2	3	4	5	
7. Criticizes others in fitness group	5	4	3	2	1	5	4	3	2	1	
8. Shows favoritism toward highly skilled peers	5	4	3	2	2	5	4	3	2	1	
										Total	
										Index rating (total / 8)	

▌ **Figure 7.8**   Example of a definition of an affective objective (interpersonal relationships).

Reprinted, by permission, from V.J. Melograno, 1996, *Designing the physical education curriculum* (Champaign, IL: Human Kinetics), 168.

perform in a naturalistic environment. The downside to this method is that you are responsible for making sure the game solicits the correct behavior and is standardized so that it can be repeated. You must also adapt and be creative to ensure that you can observe and assess all of your students under similar conditions. Regardless of where you decided to define your objectives along this continuum, the conditions must be described in the item in enough detail so that all teachers using the curriculum can interpret and implement the assessment in the same way.

Determining How the Assessment Will Be Scored

Now that you have defined your objective, the next step is to establish scoring criteria or a scoring rubric (Lund, 2000). Scoring criteria can range from simple yes or no ratings to sophisticated holistic rating scales. The simplest scoring systems define a dichotomy for each of the key components to be observed. Using the score sheet for the catch objective in figure 7.9, you would observe the student and then indicate

Catch Assessment

Instructions	Scoring
Given a verbal request and a demonstration, the student can catch a 4-inch ball tossed to chest height from a 15-foot distance two out of three times in the following manner: 1. Hands in front of the body, knees flexed, and elbows flexed and near sides 2. Extension of the arms in preparation for ball contact 3. Contacts the ball with hands only (fingers spread, slightly flexed, and palms facing) 4. Elbows bend as arms absorb the force of the ball being caught 5. Smooth (not mechanical or jerky) integration of the previous four standards	Skill: 0 = No evidence 1 = Occasionally 2 = Usually 3 = Always ACE: a = Above average b = Average c = Below average

Score Sheet

Student names	Components								Comments
	1	2	3	4	5	A	C	E	

Figure 7.9 Catch assessment with ACE and scoring rubric.

whether the student demonstrated each component of the skill. This could also be recorded as yes or no, *x* or *o*, check or no check, and so on. You can create more complicated scoring systems by increasing the complexity of the judgments made and the number of scoring options. For example, you could use a four-point scale to rate each component: 0 = no evidence, 1 = occasionally, 2 = usually, and 3 =

always. Objectives can also have multiple scoring systems. For example, you could use a four-point scale in conjunction with three other scoring systems designed to assess the students' attention, comprehension, and effort during the assessment as seen in figure 7.9. Clearly there is no limit to how complex you can make scoring systems. Figure 7.10 shows a rating scale for badminton game play. Note that

Badminton Rubric

Shot execution

4   Student executes all shots presented by teacher with good form using them at appropriate times.

3   Student uses most shots presented with good form, usually using them at appropriate times.

2   Student uses several of the shots presented but not always at the appropriate time. Some form breaks are apparent; however, form is mostly correct.

1   Student relies on one or two shots for the entire game. Incorrect form causes shots to be misplaced or ineffective.

Court movement

4   Student moves around covering all parts of the court and consistently attempts to return to home position. Weight is on the balls of the feet to move quickly. Is in position to play all shots. Footwork is correct. Anticipates where the opponent will place the next shot and moves into position.

3   Student covers court, generally attempting to return to home position. Weight is usually on the balls of the feet to move quickly. Is usually in position to play shots; uses correct footwork. Some anticipation of the opponent's shot.

2   Student covers court but occasionally is out of position. Weight shifts to the balls of the feet may be necessary

before student can move to the shot. Student attempts to return to home position but may not always get there. Limited attempts to anticipate opponent's return shot.

1   Student moves to play a shot (reacts) and then remains there. Parts of the court are uncovered at times. Weight is usually back on the heels, slowing the ability to respond to the shot. Tends to reach to play shots rather than moving feet to get into position.

Serving

4   Student always uses correct form to execute both long and short serves, depending on the position of the opponent; varies the use of the shots to avoid anticipation by the opponent.

3   Student usually uses correct form to execute both long and short serves; shows some variation in the use of the shots to avoid anticipation by the opponent.

2   Student demonstrates several elements of correct form to execute both long and short serves although does commit errors; student varies the use of serves, giving some attention to where the opponent is positioned.

1   Student uses predominately one serve. May have form breaks. Does not look at opponent when making serve selection.

(continued)

▌ **Figure 7.10**   Badminton play rubric.

(continued)

Rules

4 Student shows evidence of thoroughly knowing and applying rules. Serving order and rotation are correct. Uses rules to advantage (e.g., setting the score when receiving, calling an incorrect serve). Can answer any question when asked.

3 Student shows evidence of generally knowing and applying rules. Serving order and rotation are correct. Usually uses rules to advantage. Can answer most questions when asked.

2 Student shows some evidence of knowing rules. Serving order and rotation are correct. May have a few errors regarding rules. May struggle with some questions.

1 Student is unfamiliar with rules. Depends on opponents or partner for direction. Is unsure of serving order and rotation.

Strategy

4 Demonstrates much evidence of strategy to defeat an opponent. Hits shots to the open places on the court. Tries to anticipate opponent's shots, moving into position to play them. Communicates well with partner. Consistently works with partner to cover the court.

3 Demonstrates evidence of strategy to defeat an opponent. Hits shots to the open places on the court. Generally communicates with partner. Usually works with partner to cover the court.

2 Uses some strategy to defeat an opponent. Hits shots to the open places on the court. Some communication with partner. Some evidence of working with partner to cover the court.

1 Hits shots directly back to opponent so that they are easy to return. Does not talk to partner. At times, both partners go after the shuttlecock. Little evidence of teamwork.

Etiquette

4 Student consistently recognizes good play by others. Works well with partner to cover the court at all times. Shows strong evidence of cooperation and teamwork. Does not try to dominate the court. Calls shots honestly and fairly.

3 Student usually recognizes good play by others. Works with partner to cover the court most of the time. Shows evidence of cooperation and teamwork. Does not try to dominate the court. Calls shots honestly and fairly.

2 Student may recognize good play by others. Shows some evidence of working with partner to cover the court. May dominate court play from time to time. Calls shots honestly and fairly.

1 Student rarely talks with others. Is not working as a team with partner. Incorrect calls may result from incomplete knowledge of the rules or poor etiquette.

▌**Figure 7.10** *(continued)*

Reprinted from *Creating Rubrics for Physical Education* (2000) with permission from the National Association for Sport and Physical Education (NASPE), 1900 Association Drive, Reston, VA 20191-1599.

there are six factors to be judged (i.e., shot, execution, court movement, serving, rules, and strategy and etiquette), and each is scored on a four-point scale.

The key to deciding what scoring method to use is knowing how you will use the information, who is going to do the scoring, and the time and training needed to administer it. As discussed earlier, the primary purpose of most assessment information is to inform teachers so that they can make appropriate instructional decisions. Teachers need to balance the desire to collect lots of data against the time and energy needed to analyze, interpret, and use the information collected. The critical question is, How much assessment information is needed to make the decision at hand? If you want to know what component of the catch you want to emphasize in your next class, then you simply need to know which students need work on which components. If you want to know why a specific student is having trouble leaning a specific component, you probably want additional information about that student's attention, comprehension, and effort. On the other hand, if you want to know if your students use the appropriate tennis strokes while playing tennis, then you need a scoring system that allows you to judge the appropriateness of their stroke selection during the context of an actual game.

The final criterion to consider when deciding on the complexity of the scoring system is whether the scoring system is sensitive enough to detect changes in student performance and communicate progress. For example, in an attempt to save time when assessing a complex skill such as the overhand throw, you may be tempted to define this skill in terms of three compound elements as shown in figure 7.11. Again, to save time you may decide to use a simple dichotomous 0 = no and 1 = yes scoring system to make scoring fast and easy. The risk here is that a lot of learning or progress could occur during an instructional unit that would not be detected by this scoring system. Because each component includes several elements and a student must possess all of the elements within a component to get a score of yes, the student could have learned one new element in each of the three components during the past unit, but still have a score of zero for each component.

As a general rule, the more complex the scoring system is, the more time and training will be required to use it correctly. We recommend that you start with relatively simple scoring systems and then gradually increase their sophistication as your skills increase. The level of complexity of both the objectives and the scoring systems also tend to increase with grade level. During the elementary grades the majority of the emphasis is on learning discrete skills. As grade level increases, students start combining skills and using these combined skills in applied settings (i.e., games and sports). The complexity of the scoring systems will need to parallel the complexity of the objective definitions.

Assessment items discussed in this section are designed to be used by teachers. Teachers should also consider designing and using student peer and self-assessment instruments. This topic is addressed in more detail in chapter 10. Logic would suggest that student peer and self-assessment instruments would closely parallel teacher instruments, but may have simpler scoring systems.

Creating an Efficient Method for Recording Assessment Data

Although most teachers can be sold on the value of assessment, the greatest challenge is convincing them that the data must be recorded—that is, written down. Concerns regarding the time needed to record assessment data are valid and deserve considerable attention. The question, however, is not whether assessment data should be recorded. Assessment data must be recorded. The issues are how often data should be recorded, how much data should be recorded, who should collect the data, and how the data should be recorded.

How Often Should Data Be Recorded?

The first issue is how often assessment data should be recorded. The correct answer is somewhere between constantly and at least twice—at the beginning and at the end of instruction. For evaluation purposes, you should at the very least collect pre- and postmeasures on each objective taught in a given year. You need to know where the students are before you start your instruction so that you can design your instruction to meet their needs. You also need to know where the students are at the end of your instruction so that you can determine what they have learned as a result of your instruction. Consider the following scenario:

Ms. Lawson has designed a six-week volleyball unit focusing on the serve, bump, and set. She has allocated two hours for instruction and practice of each the skills. At the start of the unit she pretests all of the students and records these data. She uses the pretest data to ability group the students and to refine her teaching and learning maps for the instructional block. She then implements the unit, and at the end of the unit she posttests the students. When Ms. Lawson compares students' pre- and postperformance data on the three objectives, she notes that the class made very little progress across these three objectives. In fact, only three students improved by one component on each of the volleyball objectives. Although this is important information for Ms. Lawson, which she can use to evaluate and revise her teaching and learning map and blocks for next year, it is of little value to the students who just

Overhand Throw Assessment

Instructions	Scoring
Given a verbal request to throw a ball in an overhand pattern using the preferred hand, the student will throw a 3-inch ball (e.g., tennis ball) at least 50 feet on two out of three trials while demonstrating the following performance standards: Start: Eyes on target, side orientation, weight shifted to the rear foot Action: Arm extension to initiate the throw, weight transfer to the opposite foot, arm passes over the shoulder Stop: Follow-through well beyond ball release and in the intended direction of the throw	Y = Yes, the components are demonstrated correctly N = No, the components are not demonstrated correctly

Score Sheet

Student names	Start	Action	Stop	Comments

Figure 7.11 A simple overhand throw assessment with a dichotomous scoring system.

participated in this block. In essence, six weeks of instruction, or two hours on each of three objectives, has been lost. Worse yet, the students have just worked for six weeks on three objectives and have not seen much improvement in their skills, which probably means they have not become big fans of volleyball.

This example illustrates the problem when only pre- and postmeasures are recorded. By the time Ms. Lawson learned that her instruction did not produce the desired results, she had already used up all of her allotted instructional time for these objectives. If Ms. Lawson had reassessed the students every two weeks or, better yet, every week, she would have lost only one or two weeks of instruction and would have had four or five weeks left to make changes in her instruction.

You may be thinking that if Ms. Lawson had been continually assessing during her unit, even though she was not recording the data, she should have noticed that the students were not learning as expected. This is an excellent observation. The fact is, Ms. Lawson may have noticed her students' lack of progress if she had been systematic in her ongoing assessment. Many teachers, in fact, argue that they buy into the concept of ongoing assessment, but they just do not record the results. The problem with ongoing instructional assessment is that it is not always systematic. For example, during instruction the better-performing students usually tend to seek out the teacher's attention, and the poorer-performing students tend to avoid the teacher. Without a systematic method of ongoing assessment you are likely to have an inaccurate perception of how well the class is performing until you see the final assessment results. To avoid this problem, we recommend a combination of formal (i.e., recorded) and informal (i.e., ongoing systematic nonrecorded) assessments.

How often any given teacher can formally and informally assess is a function of many factors such as class size, the amount of instructional time, the age of the students, and the competency of the teacher. At the minimum you should formally record the performance of your students at the beginning and end of each unit in which you teach an objective. You should also informally systematically assess students at least once a week during the unit. If you have very large class sizes or very limited instructional time, you can use a modified form of systematic informal assessment. Instead of trying to informally assess all of the students, you can assess five or six randomly selected students

and use their results as indicators of the overall class performance. The important point to remember here is that this sample is representative of the range of abilities in the class.

How Much Data Should Be Recorded?

The second issue is how much data should be collected and recorded during the assessment. How much data are collected is usually a function of the scoring checklist, rating scale, or rubric designed for the objective being assessed. Again, because each measurement takes time to observe and record, the tendency is to limit the number of factors to be judged and to use a simple dichotomous rating scale (e.g., yes or no). As discussed earlier in this chapter, the limitation of using only a few factors and a simple scale is that these measures may not be sensitive enough to detect changes in students' behavior. At the other extreme are very sophisticated rubrics that can be very sensitive to complex changes in students' behavior, but require more time and skill to administer. In the end, you want to select a scoring rubric that you can administer efficiently and that provides the information you need to monitor and document your students' progress. A simple rule is to collect only data that you are going to use. These factors should have been considered when the assessment items and scoring rubrics were created. At a minimum we recommend that the data collected for each objective include pre- and postmeasures of the key components of the objectives as well as ACE responses for each student.

Who Should Collect the Data?

The third issue is who should collect the data. This may initially seem like an odd question because it is assumed that the teacher will be the person collecting the data. Although the teacher will play a major role in the formal data collection procedures, there are many other alternatives to consider. Teachers initially tend to control the assessment process and then over time slowly share some of this responsibility with their students. There is no set formula for how much of the assessment should be done by the teacher and how much should be done by the students. The bottom line is that teachers should try to be as efficient as they can so that they can maximize their instructional time.

As we will discuss in chapters 8 and 10, we highly recommend that you integrate assessment into your instruction and that you teach your students to be responsible for their own evaluation and the evaluation of others. Once students understand how and what to assess, they can play an important role in recording assessment data via mechanisms such as progress charts, journals, and portfolios (see chapter 9, page 207). Also, as students get older, they can play a greater role in evaluating not only themselves but also each other.

As with all assessments the accuracy of the data depends on the skill and integrity of the assessor. Many teachers are reluctant to allow students to play a role in the assessment process because they fear they will not be able to make accurate judgments or will cheat and not provide accurate data. These concerns are legitimate; however, they are usually based on traditional testing situations in which students feel pressure to get a "good" or the "right" score. As assessment becomes an integral part of the way students learn in physical education, they will learn that it is in their best interest to provide accurate assessment data so that they can get the feedback and instruction they need to learn.

As the teacher, you should initially plan to be the primary collector of the formal pre-, post-, and informal systematic assessment data. As you integrate assessment into the learning process, you should gradually give students more responsibility for collecting and recording their assessment data. You should then explore ways of using the student data to supplement or complement your informal data and ultimately to replace these measures when appropriate. Depending on the age of the students and the nature of the objectives, you may eventually be able to allocate some of the formal assessment measures to the students; in most cases, however, you will remain the primary recorder of these data.

Although some student-based assessment alternatives may save class time, they may require significant amounts of your time. For example, portfolios and class projects are excellent alternatives for assessing student performance on cognitive objectives and require very little class time. However, you still need to read, evaluate, and provide feedback to the students on these products, which can involve a substantial amount of your out-of-class time.

How Should the Data Be Recorded?

The last issue is how the data will actually be recorded. This, in fact, is the root of the aversion teachers have to assessment, and it is a serious problem. Physical education teachers have much higher teaching loads than the average teacher. Initially, it seems overwhelming to contemplate recording pre- and postmeasures on 300 to 400 students across several objectives each year. Although the problem is formidable, it is solvable. As discussed earlier, the magnitude of this problem is a function of how often you assess, how much data are collected, and

who does the collecting. You can establish the basic parameters by assuming that you will record pre- and postmeasures on each of the objectives using a simple scoring rubric that is sensitive enough to detect and show student progress. To this end, you should design a score sheet for each objective that allows data for pre- and postmeasures to be collected on all key components for all the students in the class. Ideally, score sheets should be one page in length for a given class.

Figure 7.12 shows a standard score sheet for a typical motor skill objective. Each score sheet should contain the following information:

- Descriptive information on the class
- Instruction start and stop dates
- Space to list the names of the students in the class
- Directions for administering the assessment
- Administrative considerations
- Key components to be observed
- Scoring rubric
- Student ACE response ratings
- Room for at least pre- and postmeasures for each component to be assessed
- Space for teacher reflection
- Space for evaluation values (to be used later)

Score sheets are intended to be teaching tools used by the teachers for planning and evaluation. They do not have to be pretty, but they must be functional so you can efficiently record and use the data when it is needed. The example in figure 7.12 contains a lot of descriptive information such as the scoring rubric and ACE ratings (see appendix B, page 334, for the blank form). Once you know the administrative considerations and scoring rubrics, you may want to remove features like these to make more room for additional students on a page or to increase the space for your comments. The point here is that these features should exist permanently in the curriculum, probably on the master or model score sheet for each objective, but they do not have to be copied on every score sheet.

Organize the information on the score sheets so that they are efficient to use. How you actually organize it is up to you. Some teachers like to list their students on the score sheet in alphabetical order, whereas others prefer to organize their classes in groups and list the students on the score sheet by these groups. We recommend that you create a management system to keep all of your assessment data organized. How to organize the actual

ABC School District Class Performance Score Sheet—Tennis Overhead Serve

Teacher: E. Dunn

Class: Third period—gold days

Start date: _____

Grade level: 8

Mastery criterion: 8

End date: _____

Scoring rubric:
- 0 = not present
- 1 = emerging, but needs work
- 2 = demonstrates correct pattern consistently

ACE ratings:
- a = above average
- b = average
- c = below average

Student names	Appropriate grip (1)	Correct orientation (2)	Toss well above head (3)	Weight transfers back during toss (4)	Racket back (5)	Weight transfer forward (6)	Ball contact above head and in front of body (7)	Follow-through (8)	Attention (A)	Comprehension (C)	Effort (E)	Comments

Evaluation Values

	A	B	C	D	E	F

Directions: Given a verbal request to serve, the student should perform an overhead serve demonstrating the correct components from behind the baseline into the service box on two out of three trials.

Administrative considerations: Stand in front and on dominant side of the student to observe.

Reflections: _____

Figure 7.12 Standard score sheet for motor skills.

materials, again, is up to you. The important point is to organize the score sheets so that you can locate and store them on a daily basis.

A common method of organizing assessment data is to place it all into one notebook that is divided into major sections with one section for each class. Within each class section, subsections are created for each of the objectives to be taught and managed that year. In each objective subsection would be two pages: the objective definition and the score sheet for that objective. This way you have ready access to the full objective definition in case you have to review something prior to an assessment. Many teachers also prefer to store the score sheets in plastic sleeves in their notebooks so that they can easily slide them in and out without damaging the holes in the paper.

Because time is the major factor to consider, you need to be efficient in how you conduct the assessment and record your assessment data. A common method is to use a clipboard that holds the score sheet for the objective you are assessing. Again, use any method that works for you. Some other common methods are using note cards, videotaping the class and then analyzing the tape, using individual student progress charts or folders, or using station charts in which student performance is recorded at each station. Regardless of what method you use, the assessment recording process is not complete until the assessment data are on the official score sheet. This should be considered when using methods that require extra steps, such as recording the data on students' progress cards, which the students keep in their gym folders. At some point you will need to go through the folders for each class and transfer the assessment data from these cards to the score sheet.

One of the most time-consuming tasks related to recording assessment data is just getting the names of the students on the score sheets. With a little planning and practice, you can do a number of things to expedite this task. The first option is to find someone else to do this task for you. Many schools have volunteers who donate their time to help. If you have your class rolls and your score sheets organized, a small group of volunteers can prepare your score sheets for the year in one afternoon.

Another option is to take advantage of your school photocopier. Some handy teachers have figured out how to standardize the location of the name column on the score sheet so that they can prepare one list of the students' names for each class and then photocopy this list onto the score sheets. This involves putting the blank score sheets for the objectives to be taught to the class in the paper tray

and then positioning the list on the photocopier so that the names are copied onto the forms.

The ultimate method is to use some form of computer manipulation. These manipulations can be as simple as cut-and-paste techniques. To use these, you must either have or create a computer file containing the class rolls and have the master version of each score sheet in a computer file. The ideal method is to have all of your data in a computerized database. The names are imported into your database from the school's central computer and organized by grade and class. You then use predefined reports in your database to generate your score sheets containing the appropriate names. The ideal situation would be to export your score sheets to a handheld computer or personal digital assistant (PDA). You could then use your PDA during class to collect student assessment data. After class you could transfer the assessment data back to your database, which would then be ready for analysis. Figure 7.13 shows a PDA with a score sheet created with Microsoft® Excel®.

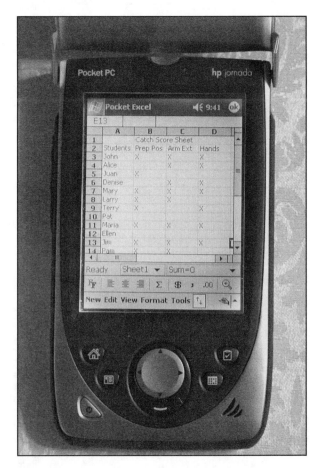

■ **Figure 7.13** PDA with a score sheet created in Microsoft® Excel®.

Summary

This chapter has explained how assessment is the key to teacher decision making and is an integral part of the ABC model. In essence, if you do not have assessment data, you do not know what you need to teach or how to teach it. What assessment instruments should be used and when were discussed as functions of the types of decisions you need to make: identification, placement, or instruction. A four-step process was presented to guide you through the assessment decision process so that you can collect valid and reliable data and make accurate decisions. Procedures were provided to guide you through the process of developing assessment items for each of the objectives targeted for instruction in your curriculum. Finally, recommendations were presented to assist you in efficiently implementing and recording your assessment data.

Assessing is a skill that you acquire through practice and experience. You can read about assessing and understand what it is and how it should be done, but that is not enough. To assess accurately and reliably, you must have both valid and reliable assessment instruments and the skill to make accurate observations and judgments of student behavior across a wide range of physical, motor, and social skills. Hopefully you will have acquired these observation and judgment skills for most of the behaviors you will need to assess. When you find you do not have these skills, you need to stop and acquire them. Being proficient at assessing is a lifelong pursuit. You can always improve the efficiency of both the instruments and your assessing skills.

Finally, assessment data are only valuable if they are recorded and organized so you can use them to make instructional decisions that result in student learning. You must not only assess student behavior but also record this information so that you can use it to guide instructional planning and as the basis for student and program evaluation.

Making It Work

Have you achieved the expected outcomes (see page 146) for this chapter? You should now understand why assessing is a critical component of the ABC model, how to match your decisions with the appropriate type of assessment, how to design your own assessment instruments, and how to implement and record assessment data that are both valid and reliable. Still, you may have some practical questions that need answers, such as the following:

▌ *What if I am a new teacher at a school and none of the other teachers are assessing?* Unfortunately, this situation could occur, particularly if the school does not have an ABC physical education program. However, with the increasing demands on schools for accountability, it is only a matter of time before the physical educators at this school will be required to assess their students and report the results. You should take advantage of this situation and develop your own assessment instruments and perfect your assessing skills. When the time comes and assessment is required, you will be all set and ready to submit your results. You could also share your assessment practices with your colleagues and explain why assessment is important. You should be careful, however, in how you present your ideas. Some veteran teachers may be threatened by a new teacher coming in and telling them what they should be doing. The best way is to teach by example. Incorporate assessment into your teaching and wait until one of the teachers asks you what you are doing. Then use that opportunity to share what you are doing and why.

▌ *How do I know exactly which objectives to assess and when?* Using the ABC model, the answer is simple. You just need to go to your program plan (developed in chapter 6) and look at the scope and sequence chart developed in step 9 (see tables 6.2 and 6.3). This chart will indicate when you should start instruction on each objective and when to expect mastery. You should then look at your yearly and block teaching and learning maps developed in step 10. These will tell you exactly when during the year to assess each objective.

▌ *What if I find that one of the assessment instruments in the curriculum is just not working?* This is possible during the first few years the curriculum is implemented. It may be that the teachers that developed the assessment instrument in question knew what they were assessing, but did not do a good job of defining it when they created the instrument. Your first course of action would be to contact a couple of the veteran teachers at your program level and ask them how they use this assessment instrument. Odds are that you will find that they are doing something that was not clearly explained in the assessment procedures. In this case, you should complete the objective evaluation form and submit it to the physical education curriculum committee so that it can be revised accordingly. This form and the function of this committee are discussed in chapters 12 and 13.

- *What happens if I do not know how to assess some of the objectives in my curriculum?* Given the breadth and depth of the content to be taught in physical education, you are very likely to find objectives during your first few years of teaching that you do not know how to assess. Fortunately, with the ABC model you will have the objective definitions, assessment procedures, and score sheets in your curriculum. What you will need to do is pair up with another teacher who is competent in assessing the objective in question. In many schools beginning teachers are assigned mentors who are experienced teachers. This would be the logical person to ask for assistance. If you do not have a mentor, then you will need to select a colleague. Most schools start the year with inservices in which you get to meet the other teachers in your area. Pick a teacher you met at one of these meetings who appeared to be knowledgeable and willing to share his or her expertise.

- *What do I do if I am just overwhelmed with the assessment process?* The first time you begin to implement an ABC program, the assessment can seem overwhelming. This is particularly true if you did not assess before. A good technique is to start small and gradually progress into assessing your objectives. Start with one objective for each class that you feel confident in assessing. Use these objectives to get a handle on administering the assessment activities and learning to efficiently record the assessment data. During the next instructional block, begin to assess two objectives. Continue this progression until you can assess all of the objectives in your instructional blocks. You should also not think that you have to figure this out all by yourself. Ask your veteran colleagues how they assess their objectives. There is no need to reinvent the wheel. If one teacher has figured out an efficient way to measure a group of objectives, find out what that technique is and adopt it.

PART III

Implementing the Physical Education Curriculum

Now that you understand the importance of goals, objectives, and assessment strategies, it's time to make decisions that will help you to "implement up." This section is organized around one primary question: How will you get there? To begin, chapter 8 summarizes what we know about organizing instruction for maximum learning and reviews the principles of effective teaching. Next, chapter 9 offers a comprehensive analysis of learning experiences including discussions of structure, criteria for selection, alternative approaches, and accommodations for special needs. The key factors from chapters 8 and 9 are synthesized in chapter 10. A plan is presented for learning and teaching that introduces a new scheme for curriculum designers—teaching templates and student learning formats. A brief description of each chapter follows.

Chapter 8

Maximizing Learning and Effective Teaching

The essentials of learning are included in the proposed curriculum development process because of the emphasis on *achievement*. Two broad topics are covered in this chapter: organizing instruction for maximum learning and principles of effective teaching. Assuring maximum learning begins by creating a positive, safe, and orderly learning environment. Other topics include expectations for achievement, student readiness and needs, management procedures, and discipline systems. The principles of effective teaching are synthesized into five teaching functions: communicating clearly and accurately, executing instruction skillfully, motivating students to achieve, engaging students to achieve, and providing feedback to students.

Chapter 9

Learning Experiences

Goals, objectives, and assessments represent the ends to be attained, and they serve as useful criteria for determining how to attain these ends. Achievement occurs when students engage in active behavior—the learning experience. In this chapter we outline a structure for learning experiences and suggest criteria for selecting learning experiences. Exemplary learning experiences are analyzed according to two broad patterns—individualization and interaction. For each pattern, we identify basic principles and qualities and provide alternative approaches for illustrative purposes. A framework for K-12 student portfolios is also presented. Finally, the chapter addresses learning experiences that seem to be effective for accommodating the needs of culturally diverse, at-risk, and talented students.

Chapter 10

Planning for Learning and Teaching

This chapter proposes a scheme to synthesize all of the components of the achievement-based process into a teaching template (to define overall parameters) and student learning formats (to address individual student needs). Student assessment data serve as the prerequisite and help you interpret student needs and set expectations. Given these data, the necessary components for templates and learning formats include factors such as objectives, time allocation, learning experiences, organization, equipment, facilities, and methods to observe and evaluate student behavior. Step-by-step procedures are provided to guide you through the implementation planning process so that you can design your instruction and student learning experiences to ensure that students learn the objectives targeted for instruction and that the curriculum is implemented as intended.

eight

Maximizing Learning and Effective Teaching

By the end of the fourth grade, students should be able to perform refined fundamental movements. Therefore, one of the expected exit outcomes in your school's curriculum guide is attainment of mature motor patterns for basic locomotor, nonlocomotor, and selected manipulative skills such as throwing, catching, and striking. When teaching motor skills, your typical approach is to demonstrate the skill while pointing out its critical elements (e.g., foot placement, body direction, arm position, follow-through). Then you have students practice the skill through individual, partner, or small group drills and activities.

On this particular day in the fall, your students are arranged in pairs to practice striking. Specifically, they are practicing the one-hand sidearm pattern from a partner toss using a paddle and a foam ball. Eventually, you hope to introduce the basics of tennis in the spring. Invariably, some students perform a totally inappropriate pattern. As you go around watching the students, you notice that Johnny is having problems. His arm initiates the striking action followed by trunk rotation instead of differentiated rotation with the hip rotation forward followed by the trunk. After you demonstrate the appropriate pattern again, you have Johnny try it a few times from a self-drop and actually help him strike the ball to get the feel of it. His response is, "I'm OK now; I know how to do this!" A little later you come back and Johnny is still using the incorrect pattern. He says, "This is just like how you did it!"

Johnny believes that his pattern is just like yours and that there is nothing wrong with his pattern. He thinks he has mastered the skill when in fact he has not. How could this happen? How can Johnny believe that he has mastered the skill? What does a student need to be able to do to learn from a demonstration? What conditions for learning are necessary? What should you do as a teacher?

EXPECTED OUTCOMES

This chapter will help you organize instruction for maximum learning and apply principles of effective teaching. After reading this chapter, you will be able to do the following:

1. Describe the features of a positive learning environment
2. Recognize why teacher expectations and students' readiness and needs have a significant impact on learning
3. Generate a set of management procedures and discipline techniques that help maximize student learning
4. Distinguish between effective and ineffective means of communicating and executing instruction
5. Develop skills in motivating and engaging students to achieve
6. Analyze the qualities of effective feedback to students

Basically, the curriculum provides the planned sequence of what students are to learn, how students acquire that learning, and how students' learning is verified. In one way or another, curriculum planning models involve decisions about content (subject matter), goals, objectives, activities, and evaluation. If the ABC model is true to its meaning, then implementation decisions are also needed. Teaching is defined as the delivery system for implementing the curriculum. It also consists of a planning phase to decide about aspects such as time allocation, organizational schemes, management and discipline strategies, equipment and space usage, learning experiences, and best teaching practices. The planning phase is followed by the interactive phase in which the range of actual teacher and student behaviors occurs. This latter phase is *not* treated in this book.

Given the emphasis on student achievement, curricula must include the essentials of learning if they are to succeed. Although this chapter is not intended to repeat content found in methods books, it does describe how you can use that content to optimally implement a physical education program. What does a student need to learn a concept, motor skill, or social behavior? What are the signs that a student's needs are not being addressed? Are there effective teaching practices to help meet these student needs? What are the principles of teaching that maximize student achievement? Do teachers have a responsibility for student learning? To answer these questions, we have divided the chapter into two broad topics—organizing instruction for maximum learning and principles of effective teaching. When these topics are viewed together, a set of teacher characteristics emerges. The successful teacher

▮ knows the subject matter;

▮ can organize and communicate the subject matter;

▮ is an extremely good manager of the environment;

▮ has positive or high expectations for student success;

▮ knows how to design learning experiences for student mastery;

▮ can relate to students in positive ways, including motivation; and

▮ uses effective discipline techniques.

Maximizing Learning

The goal of teaching is to help students achieve. That is the essence of the data-driven achievement-based curriculum model. The ultimate success of a physical education program is reflected not in what the teacher did, but in what the students did in response. Whereas teachers determine purposes, organize the setting, facilitate student engagement, collect achievement data, and make program adjustments, students produce their own learning through attention, comprehension, and effort (ACE).

Chapter 6 addressed some program planning elements that relate to implementation (e.g., scheduling, equipment, facilities). Beyond these practical and logistical concerns lies the issue of how to organize instruction for maximum learning. That is done by creating a positive, safe, and orderly learning environment. Other issues teachers must consider are expectations for achievement, student readiness and needs, management procedures, and discipline systems. Each of these factors is analyzed in this section.

Positive Learning Environment

School climate is determined by the interactions that occur in classrooms. We know that a pleasant, safe, and supportive atmosphere makes a difference. Teachers decide the characteristics of the environment. If they cannot create a positive learning environment, then this entire curriculum planning process is for naught. It's that important! Although the interactions that determine the environment are largely noninstructional, they are necessary for effective learning and teaching. In physical education, activities and tasks that establish a comfortable and respectful environment will promote a "culture for learning" and a safe place for risk-taking. The atmosphere should be business-like, with noninstructional managerial routines and procedures handled efficiently. Student behavior that is cooperative and nondisruptive should be reinforced, and the physical space should be organized to be supportive of the planned instructional outcomes. The following sections describe briefly the components of a positive learning environment (Danielson, 1996).

Creating an Atmosphere of Respect and Rapport

Teachers create an atmosphere of respect and rapport by the ways in which they interact with students and by the interactions they encourage and cultivate among students. In such an environment, all students feel valued and safe, and they know they will be treated with dignity. Respect and rapport are often characterized by friendliness, openness, and humor, although teachers maintain their role as an adult. Lack of respect and rapport is evidenced by teachers who disregard or demean students' contributions, use sarcasm and put-downs or allow students to exhibit similar behavior, show favoritism, or try to be pals with students.

Establishing a Culture for Learning

A strong culture for learning means that everyone, including the teacher, engages in activities and tasks that are highly valued and has expectations of high-quality work. Students and teachers take pride in their work and give their best energy. High expectations and a safe environment for taking risks are implied. Students do not have to fear ridicule. In classrooms lacking a culture for learning, no one cares about the content to be learned; students are lethargic or alienated and content to get by with as little effort as possible. A more detailed discussion

A culture for learning where students and teachers are equally engaged helps everyone feel safe in a high-risk environment.

of high expectations for learning and achievement appears later in the chapter (pages 180-181).

Managing Class Procedures

Teachers must develop procedures for the smooth operation of the environment and the efficient use of time. Routines are needed for the management and movement of individuals and groups, the distribution and collection of materials and equipment, the performance of noninstructional responsibilities (e.g., facilities set-up), and the supervision of personnel (e.g., teacher aides) and facilities (e.g., locker rooms). In poorly managed settings time is wasted on noninstructional episodes, students spend a lot of time waiting or are frequently off-task, materials and equipment are not ready, and confusion prevails. This component is addressed in greater detail later in this chapter in the section on management procedures (pages 183-186).

Managing Student Behavior

Agreed-on standards of conduct and clear consequences are the keys to respectful management of student behavior. These standards may cover appropriate language, attire, and various procedures (e.g., stopping, starting, being recognized to speak, entering the gym, getting equipment, or going to the rest room). The characteristics of well-run settings include (1) clearly communicated expectations, (2) standards appropriate to students' developmental levels and consistent with cultural norms, (3) standards consistently applied, (4) teachers who are aware of what is going on, (5) teachers who maintain their composure, (6) focus on a student's behavior, not on the student, and (7) students who monitor their own behavior. This component is addressed in more detail later in this chapter in the section dealing with discipline systems (pages 186-187).

Organizing Physical Space

Use of gymnasiums, activity fields and courts, and special rooms is important to the total learning environment. Organization of space reveals to students how teachers view learning—for example, the use of areas for "exploring," well-arranged stations, space for individual or group practice, markings for games, and "mat walls" (mats stood up on edge to reduce stimuli for easily distracted students). Students should feel safe in the physical environment and have access to learning resources. The space should also accommodate efficient traffic flow. Finally, physical resources (e.g., chalkboards, VCRs, digital cameras, computers, overhead projectors, flip charts) must be fully operable and used skillfully to enhance learning. Otherwise, they detract from learning.

The following general principles will help you maximize student learning and achievement (Lavay, French, & Henderson, 1997):

■ *Examine yourself.* Reflect on yourself as a teacher. You can ask yourself a series of questions that relate to a positive learning atmosphere. Are you "tuned in"? Try to know what is going on at all times and act immediately to stop misbehavior. Are you enthusiastic? Being enthusiastic about physical education will spread and help create a pleasant class climate. Are you flexible? Recognize the need, for example, to adapt behavioral standards and renegotiate performance targets. Are you personable? Learn the names of students and interact with them about their personal interests (e.g., favorite movies, books, hobbies, travel).

■ *Use positive approaches.* You can create a favorable class spirit by using positive practices such as (1) catching students being good as a way to give attention; (2) recognizing student successes; (3) expecting students to follow instructions; (4) keeping your cool and addressing problems quickly; (5) focusing on the behavior to be corrected, not on the student; (6) being consistent (i.e., making sure yes always means yes, always checking for compliance, and responding in the same way to the same behavior); and (7) using positive tools (i.e., varying tasks, playing music, relaxing students with physical activity).

■ *Avoid negative approaches.* Avoid approaches that guarantee inappropriate behavior, such as the following: (1) making comparisons, (2) making idle threats, (3) being sarcastic, (4) giving public reprimands or making fun (humiliating), and (5) overstating the situation.

Expectations for Achievement

Setting expectations for students helps them evaluate their performance and progress accurately. Unfortunately, because of personal biases they may not be aware of, some teachers set low expectations for certain students. You need to be aware of any biases (however unintended they may be) and their impact on your students' learning. The expectancy phenomenon is extremely powerful in the context of learning and teaching because students tend to produce what the teacher expects. If the teacher expects a student to be low performing, the student will perform as such because that is the belief the teacher has conveyed. Although unintentional, the sometimes subtle ways the teacher interacts with students will send a message of expected failure or success. If students know that teachers have a high regard for their abilities and their potential to learn, then their commitment to high-quality performance is strengthened. Setting high expectations for student achievement and behavior helps students internalize positive outcomes.

Teachers should form reasonable judgments about student achievement based on assessment and performance results. Effective teachers will reassess and adjust their initial impressions based on actual in-class performance. Less effective teachers will unconsciously see only those behaviors that reinforce stereotypes such as "slow learner," "lazy underachiever," or "gifted." The way teachers respond to students plays a critical role in student motivation. Less effective teachers who put students in the back where they can be safely ignored or give up on students who struggle with an answer or a movement are communicating clearly their low expectations. Students usually respond accordingly (Glatthorn, 1993). To maximize learning,

■ be careful about how you express your expectations of students;

■ avoid making judgments based on others' opinions or biases;

■ be open to new information about students' attitudes and achievement;

■ be sensitive to students' cognitive, physical, and emotional developmental levels;

■ match learning tasks with developmental levels to promote legitimate achievement and success; and

■ try to see students from their point of view and eliminate any preconceived notions of who they are or what they should be.

Readiness and Needs

Prerequisite to any attempt to maximize learning is knowledge of a student's readiness to learn. Students must be ready to learn physically, socially, emotionally, and cognitively. Students will not learn a motor skill (volleyball serve), a social behavior (tolerance), a self-concept (confidence), or an intellectual ability (problem solving) unless they are ready, regardless of the number of practice trials.

Beyond creating a positive learning environment (i.e., safe, orderly, pleasant, supportive), you should ensure that your expected outcomes are developmentally appropriate. This means that you should consider the universal, predictable sequences of growth and change (age appropriateness) and individual patterns and timing of growth, including individual personality and learning styles (individual appropriateness). Knowledge of typical development within an age span (e.g., third- and fourth-graders) offers a framework from which you can prepare the learning environment and plan appropriate learning experiences. For example, the NASPE content standards for physical education (Rink et al, 1995) are supported by grade-level performance benchmarks that describe developmentally appropriate behaviors representing progress toward achieving the standard. These standards and benchmarks were detailed in table 2.3 (pages 45-51).

In preparing to maximize learning, you should ask, What does a student need to know, be able to do, or feel in order to acquire cognitive, social, emotional, or motor learning? Needs represent the difference between the present condition of the student and the acceptable or desired behavior. Consideration for students' needs also represents a developmentally appropriate practice in physical education. Graham, Castenada, Hopple, Manross,

and Sanders (1992) offered the following description of student needs:

■ *Cognitive development.* Students need to question, integrate, analyze, communicate, and apply cognitive concepts, as well as gain a multicultural view of the world.

■ *Affective development.* Students need to (1) work together for the purpose of improving their emerging social and cooperation skills, (2) develop a positive self-concept, and (3) experience and feel the satisfaction and joy that results from regular participation in physical activity.

■ *Development of movement concepts and motor skills.* Students need to develop a functional understanding of movement concepts (body awareness, spatial awareness, effort, and relationships) and build competence and confidence in their ability to perform a variety of motor skills (locomotor, nonlocomotor, and manipulative).

■ *Concepts of fitness.* Students need to understand and value the important concepts of physical fitness and the contribution they make to a healthy lifestyle.

As a teacher, you should also recognize other kinds of needs that influence maximum learning. Students need to be receptive to learning; they need to know what they need to learn in general (e.g., kicking) and specifically (e.g., foot placement); they need to know why it is important to learn the skill (relevance); they need to know how to go about learning the skill; they need to believe they can learn the skill; and they need to make progress. On the other hand, you need to know the signs and symptoms of a student whose learning needs are not addressed. Students might avoid learning tasks, act out or disrupt the environment, perseverate on components or skills already learned, or regress to lower skills for success. Because these negative factors could be a function of teaching, these needs are also addressed later in the chapter in the section on effective teaching (pages 187-193).

This discussion of readiness and needs reinforces the importance of collecting accurate preassessment data as described in chapter 7 (pages 151-157). Student analysis in the form of entry assessment ensures that you do not waste time and energy when learning has already occurred and helps you determine an appropriate starting point. Entry appraisal is also useful in identifying students along the learning continuum—gifted students as well as those who may need special attention. In this way, you are continually diagnosing student strengths and weaknesses. Ideally, your entry appraisal will arouse students' interest and motivate them to improve, particularly if the assessment is not graded. Finally, the results of entry appraisal could clarify the need to eliminate, modify, or add goals and objective. The following two sections examine the primary outcomes of entry appraisal that should help you maximize student learning—identification and placement, and programming and intervention.

Identification and Placement

Approach the identification and placement of students with caution. There's a risk of group labeling because the corresponding stigmas are difficult to overcome, even when the problem no longer exists. Any classification scheme (e.g., distinguished, proficient, basic, novice) is relative; that is, students may be placed in a certain category for one situation, but not for another. Identification and placement will be accepted favorably as long as you use the results to maximize learning.

The typical reasons for classifying students are to (1) create an effective atmosphere for students of similar ability, (2) equalize competition, (3) motivate student participation and performance, (4) enhance program continuity, (5) meet health and safety needs, and (6) provide a basis for comparison. Although these reasons seem positive, in practice, classification often leads to loss of prestige, poor self-image, rejection, isolation, and labeling (e.g., retarded, slow, disabled).

Some approaches to identification are interests, general ability (e.g., fitness, motor ability), specific abilities (e.g., sport skills), social and emotional development (e.g., ability to interact with others), and medical status (e.g., participation may be unlimited, modified, or restricted). Because identified needs and abilities are specific and do not transfer to other needs or abilities, preassessment should be an ongoing process and students should be constantly reclassified.

Once students are identified as belonging to a certain category, you need to make placement decisions. Again, the term *placement* should not be taken negatively. It does not mean that students are segregated, isolated, or somehow made to feel inferior. In physical education, you can place students on teams of similar or mixed abilities, assign them to particular fitness stations, or give them task cards based on identified needs. For students with special needs, be sure to consider placement in the least restrictive environment.

Programming and Intervention

Entry appraisal will also help you determine appropriate programming and intervention. For the assessment results to be relevant, the data-gathering process should be based on intended goals, objectives, and learning tasks. Thus, if you understand your students' needs *before* making your final decisions about learning experiences, you enhance the probability of individual achievement.

Two related concepts describe this approach. First, *mastery learning* means that students achieve mastery at a specified level before going on to the next. Time for learning is manipulated according to individual pace. Entry assessment identifies the current performance level; what remains becomes the mastery target. For example, in swimming, skill tests for mastery could determine beginner, intermediate, and advanced categories for each stroke. Students would then receive programming and intervention (i.e., instruction, practice, feedback) until they have mastered each skill. At that point, the student moves on to the next level of difficulty.

Diagnostic–prescriptive teaching means that you view entry appraisal as a diagnostic tool for assessing individual needs. Results are useful as a baseline to determine areas of needed improvement and areas of lesser need. Your task here is to examine strengths and weaknesses continually and prescribe learning tasks accordingly (intervention). Several options are available for students experiencing difficulty or who need improvement:

- *Conduct a task analysis.* Analyze the skill to be learned in relation to the specific area of difficulty or needed improvement. Focus programming on the subskills leading to the primary skill.

- *Revise instruction.* Consider matching your teaching style and the student's learning experiences with the student's learning style preferences. A change in the teaching or learning mode may result in improvement. Chapter 9 presents various approaches to tailoring learning experiences.

- *Repeat a portion, or the entirety, of the instructional sequence.* This form of "overlearning" may lead to achievement, particularly if you provide additional feedback and encouragement.

- *Provide remediation or enrichment.* The "enrichment loop" consists of a series of small tasks leading to mastery of a skill in the regular learning sequence. This kind of intervention considers that the gap between two tasks in a sequence may be too great for some students. To reduce or bridge the gap, insert some enabling subtasks. This scheme for accommodating individual learning is illustrated in figure 8.1.

Management Procedures

Classroom management is probably the most important factor governing student learning. Classroom management is everything that a teacher does to organize students, space, time, materials, equipment, and facilities to maximize student learning. The general characteristics of a well-managed classroom are that (1) students are clearly involved in general learning activities and tasks; (2) students know what is expected of them and are generally successful; (3) there is relatively little wasted time, confusion, or disruptions; and (4) the climate is work oriented, but relaxed and pleasant (Wong & Wong, 1998).

Teachers often make two critical mistakes. First, they ignore the management function, and second, they assume students will exhibit the appropriate behavior for a positive learning environment. To avoid these errors, develop a management plan in advance of teaching that will increase learning time and decrease behavior problems. The plan should be guided by two concepts: (1) reducing the length of

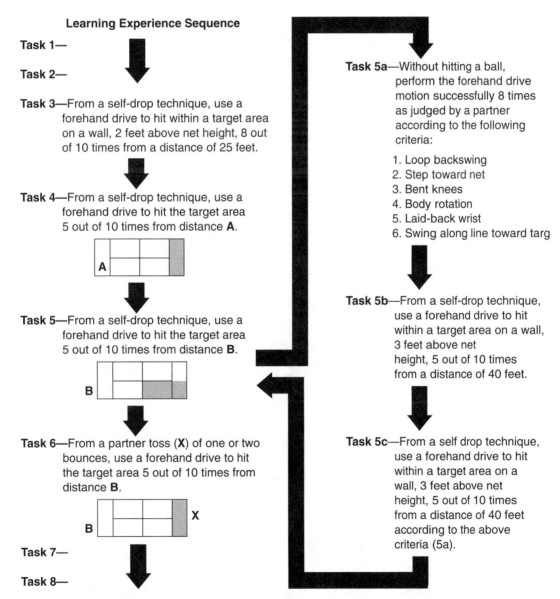

Learning Experience Sequence

Task 1—

Task 2—

Task 3—From a self-drop technique, use a forehand drive to hit within a target area on a wall, 2 feet above net height, 8 out of 10 times from a distance of 25 feet.

Task 4—From a self-drop technique, use a forehand drive to hit the target area 5 out of 10 times from distance **A**.

A

Task 5—From a self-drop technique, use a forehand drive to hit the target area 5 out of 10 times from distance **B**.

B

Task 6—From a partner toss (**X**) of one or two bounces, use a forehand drive to hit the target area 5 out of 10 times from distance **B**.

B   X

Task 7—

Task 8—

Task 5a—Without hitting a ball, perform the forehand drive motion successfully 8 times as judged by a partner according to the following criteria:

1. Loop backswing
2. Step toward net
3. Bent knees
4. Body rotation
5. Laid-back wrist
6. Swing along line toward targ

Task 5b—From a self-drop technique, use a forehand drive to hit within a target area on a wall, 3 feet above net height, 5 out of 10 times from a distance of 40 feet.

Task 5c—From a self drop technique, use a forehand drive to hit within a target area on a wall, 3 feet above net height, 5 out of 10 times from a distance of 40 feet according to the above criteria (5a).

▌ Figure 8.1   "Enrichment loop" for use when encountering difficulty in the regular sequence of learning the forehand stroke in tennis.

managerial activity (noninstructional time devoid of learning opportunities) and (2) achieving acceptable levels of appropriate student behavior. In addition, skills in classroom management will lead to the following (Siedentop, 1991):

■ Optimal efficiency in the use of class time

■ Development of self-management skills in students

■ Acceptable rate of appropriate student behavior

■ Use of positive motivational management techniques

■ Ability to cope with and remediate unexpected disruptions

The notion of "managing" the learning environment and students may sound negative, controlling, or even dehumanizing. When the environment is left unmanaged, however, think about the likely results—chaos, an unpleasant atmosphere, off-task behavior, and minimal learning. No single management strategy will yield optimum learning. Collectively, however, the management decisions you make will ultimately influence the nature and degree of student response.

You must decide on numerous management routines, all of which contribute to maximizing student learning. Keep in mind that these routines (e.g., entering the gym, getting equipment, working in pairs) need to be taught and practiced in much

the same way as motor skill patterns. For example, what are the component parts of forming a circle efficiently? Some important management routines are described briefly in the following sections (Graham, 2001; Lavay, French, & Henderson, 1997; Wong & Wong, 1998).

Time

Five kinds of time exist in schools. *Allocated time* is the total amount of time within which teaching and learning can take place (e.g., the number of minutes per week for physical education). *Instructional time* is the time used for teaching (e.g., demonstrating a series of skills). *Management time* is the time used for organizational routines (e.g., forming a small group and finding space). *Engaged time* is the time a student is involved in a task (e.g., at a learning station). Finally, *learning time* is the time that results in the student comprehending, mastering a skill, or displaying a behavior (e.g., using knowledge, skill, or behavior repeatedly). Achievement is the result of learning time.

Unfortunately, in physical education settings more time is spent on management episodes and waiting than on learning content. The range of nonlearning management routines includes organizing orientation tasks, taking attendance, giving signals or directions, establishing the initial activity, prompting students, handling unforeseen circumstances, and collecting equipment. If carried out inefficiently, these routines can consume a great deal of time at the expense of real learning time.

Management routines involve organizing students to maximize learning.

Strategies that can help you reduce management time include posting the first activity on a bulletin board, beginning class at a definite time, using a time-saving method for attendance, using high rates of feedback and positive interactions, and teaching self-management skills to students. The information in chapter 6 on calculating instructional time and skills mastery time (pages 121-125) revealed how limited time really is for actual learning.

Rules

In positive learning environments, the teacher and students have clear expectations of student behavior. Rules are reminders of those behaviors. If you invest time to teach, reinforce, and enforce rules, including establishing consequences, you will be repaid by the effective use of class time. Rules prevent or encourage behavior by clearly stating expectations. General rules, which are more encompassing and cover broad behaviors, include being supportive of others, trying your best, respecting the equipment, and following instructions. Specific rules, which are more to the point and cover one behavior, include being on time, listening to instructions without talking, waiting for the signal to start, and moving within five seconds to each activity area. The following suggestions can help you design and implement rules:

- Identify appropriate and inappropriate behaviors.
- Involve students in the development of rules when possible.
- Keep rules simple and to the point.
- Limit rules to five or six.
- State rules in positive, measurable, age-appropriate terms.
- State consequences clearly.
- Practice and review rules periodically.
- Enforce rules.
- Enforce consequences consistently.

Entering and Leaving

Establish protocols for how to enter and exit the physical education setting including locker rooms, gym, pool, playground, and playing fields. To save time, provide students with a familiar noninstructional activity (e.g., exercise routine, self-directed practice task). Post instructions for the first class activity along with the program highlights for the day. Exit protocols might include a cool-down period or a relaxation activity followed by an orderly routine for leaving the physical education setting.

Starting and Stopping

Use signals to start and stop class or to get students' attention. For starting, most teachers use *go* or a special word that means *go*. To encourage listening, students should not be allowed to start before you say the verbal cue. The words *stop* or *freeze*, a clap, a drumbeat, or a hand held up can signal the class to stop moving and be quiet. A whistle can be used outside where students may be spread out.

Transitions

Protocols for managing the flow of activities help reduce management time, thereby increasing learning time. Smooth transitions are likely when signals and directions are clear and concise (e.g., "You have 10 seconds to get to the next station when the music stops."). Establish boundaries and movement patterns with cones, flags, floor markings, and task cards. Verbal and nonverbal prompts may be necessary.

Equipment

Procedures relating to equipment, with a focus on time efficiency, involve three phases: getting equipment, deciding what to do with equipment, and putting equipment away. You can use various approaches such as spreading equipment throughout the area or calling on a few students at a time (e.g., by groups, birth month, shirt color, type of shoe). Rather than ask students to hold the equipment, provide a task for students to do once they get their equipment (e.g., finding a self-space and dribbling the ball in place). The same techniques can be used for putting equipment away. To save time, you and your students must learn and practice these procedures.

Selecting Partners, Groups, and Teams

The purpose of working in groups or with a partner is not to embarrass or damage the self-image of students. Depending on the developmental level of your students, you can allow them to find partners or form small groups themselves. You can also select groups or teams in advance and post them. Whatever technique you use (e.g., birth month, color of clothes, deck of playing cards, counting off), students need to carry out the routine quickly without hurt feelings. However, no matter how fair and objective you are, recognize that some students are very difficult to work with in pairs or in a group. Preempt such difficulty by initially placing students in the role of partner or member of a small group for simple kinds of tasks (e.g., recording data, checking off items completed). Then, proceed in small increments to more complex kinds of involvement.

Other Routines

You will need to prepare for and practice routines for many other situations that infringe on learning time, such as fire drills, accidents or injuries, student fights, or stealing. Other more mundane situations include getting a drink of water, going to the rest room, coming unprepared for class, or bringing valuables to class. Your choice of routines will depend on your students and your teaching environment.

Discipline Systems

When asked to identify the greatest concern in schools, many teachers respond, "management and discipline!" The management protocols presented in the previous section are no guarantee that all students will behave appropriately. No doubt, a well-managed, task-oriented environment in which students can learn will go a long way in preventing misbehavior. But you will still need to cope with and remediate unexpected disruptions. Following are some general techniques to consider (Glatthorn, 1993; Graham, 2001):

- *Increase the pace of class events.* Keep activities and tasks moving quickly instead of repeating information, giving instructions in too much detail, making long pauses, and talking unnecessarily.
- *Use smooth transitions.* An uninterrupted flow of learning activities helps maintain student attention and avoids fragmented teaching.
- *Develop "with-it-ness."* Be aware of all that is going on (i.e., have "eyes in the back of your

head"). Scan the environment constantly, giving special attention to where misbehavior is likely to occur (Kounin, 1970).

- *Be able to "overlap."* Deal with the direction of the class and a minor discipline problem simultaneously, rather than interrupting the flow of the class.
- *Keep students active and engaged.* High engagement rates are associated with active students.
- *Build in success.* Motivation to learn is associated with high success rates that are the result of reasonable challenges. This factor is covered in more detail later in this chapter (pages 190-191).
- *Control proximity.* Move toward off-task or potential off-task situations. This includes getting close enough so that students can see your "look."
- *Learn students' names.* It helps to know students' names when trying to prevent off-task behavior. Several techniques are available (e.g., name tags, greeting with names, class photo with names).
- *Ignore selected behavior.* Ignore students who behave outside of the "normal" pattern, but whose behavior is not really disruptive.

To maximize student learning, you need to minimize off-task and disruptive student behavior. Because this is easier said than done, an effective discipline system is essential. To begin, you need to determine what you consider to be appropriate and inappropriate. Table 8.1 gives some examples

Table 8.1   Examples of Appropriate and Inappropriate Behaviors

Appropriate behaviors	Inappropriate behaviors
Works toward completing independent tasks	Wastes time leading to incomplete tasks
Watches demonstrations	Daydreams or interacts with others during demonstrations
Follows instructions quickly	Ignores instructions or is late to follow them
Uses equipment properly	Mistreats equipment or uses wrong equipment
Complies with class rules	Breaks rules constantly
Changes activities quickly	Delays in moving to next activity
Observes rules during game play	Disrupts game play by breaking rules
Respects others' space	Uses the space of others

of appropriate and inappropriate behaviors. Develop a repertoire of strategies from which to draw for increasing appropriate student behavior and decreasing inappropriate behavior. Some alternatives to consider are described briefly in the following sections.

Increasing Appropriate Behavior

Consequences result when a student exhibits certain behaviors (e.g., abides by or breaks the rules). Thus, consequences can be positive or negative. To increase the frequency of appropriate behavior, offer positive reinforcement (something valued) after the student exhibits the desired behavior. Positive reinforcement could be (1) a social reward (e.g., a smile, approving nod, thumbs-up, approving verbal statement), (2) a tangible reward (e.g., stickers, certificates, medals, bonus points of value), (3) physical activity (e.g., using certain equipment, choosing an activity), or (4) privileges (e.g., being an exercise leader, selecting equipment, participating in special activities). Once the desired behavior is established, you should systematically eliminate the reinforcer before its effectiveness fades.

Methods of reinforcement include (1) a prompt (giving a cue to help the students perform a skill), (2) the token economy system (students can exchange tokens for something desired), (3) public posting (post names of students who display a desired behavior that all can achieve), (4) a contract (verbal or written agreements regarding behavior), and (5) group contingencies or good behavior games (presenting a highly desired reinforcer to a group based on one person or the group as a whole) (Lavay, French, & Henderson, 1997).

Once you have determined the type and method of reinforcement you will use, you will want to set up a reinforcement schedule. Reinforcement can be (1) continual (reinforcement is provided each time the behavior occurs), (2) intermittent (reinforcement is provided at specific scheduled times), (3) ratio (reinforcement depends on the number of times behavior occurs; either fixed or variable), or (4) interval (reinforcement depends on the period of time behavior occurs; either fixed or variable).

Decreasing Inappropriate Behavior

To maintain a pleasant, supportive environment, you must correct undesirable behavior with positive methods. This is particularly true of mild misbehavior (e.g., talking, fooling around, tardiness). However, for more severe misbehavior (e.g., fighting, throwing equipment, ignoring positive efforts, constant interference with others), punishment methods may be necessary to decrease the inappropriate behavior; use these only after positive methods have failed.

We have found three punishment methods to be effective. First, you can withdraw a reinforcer (take away something the student likes). This can be accomplished by (1) extinction (ignore by withholding reinforcement of inappropriate behavior), (2) response cost (take away points, privileges, free time, next turn), or (3) time-out (remove student from a reinforcing environment such as a game for a certain time period). Second, you can present an unpleasant (aversive) stimulus. Direct discussion and verbal reprimands are common approaches. Third, you can require the student to do something aversive. In this case, a student or group of students might repeatedly perform a behavior appropriately as a consequence of performing the behavior inappropriately (e.g., practice moving to assigned station several times) (Lavay, French, & Henderson, 1997). When addressing behavioral problems, make sure that the rest of the class is under control and focused on a task or activity.

Effective Teaching

Every aspect of the American educational enterprise is on trial; educators are increasingly being asked to examine their accomplishments, a task many are either unable or unwilling to undertake. In this atmosphere of high-stakes testing, data-based decision making, and standards-based programming, several patterns of accountability have been proposed, one of which is the ABC model.

In the past, certain occupations have been labeled as *ascriptive* in nature, meaning that the individual attained and maintains the job on categorical grounds rather than on the basis of achievement. Business is not an ascribed profession. Salespersons are judged by how much they sell, not by how they carry out recommended procedures for selling. Teaching has been an ascribed profession. Preparing classes, conducting classes in a democratic and controlled manner, displaying great effort in teaching, and simply going through the routines of the typical school day are the criteria on which many teachers want to be judged. They claim that these kinds of efforts are indeed related to student progress and achievement. If so, then teachers with this view should not be opposed to measuring student performance as the criterion of accountability because their teaching efforts are supposedly the cause.

Consider the situation in a large school district. Certain physical education teachers in the district had for many years been rated as outstanding. When the district finally examined the status of students in physical fitness, general motor development, and ability to perform various sport skills, they discovered that the majority of students under the instruction of highly rated teachers had not achieved well in any of these aspects. How could the teachers be judged outstanding when their students were not learning? The answer is simple: They were being judged or evaluated on categorical grounds. The extent to which an ascribed role was being followed served as the basis for judgment. Was the teacher effective in transitioning students from one area to another? Were the dress requirements enforced? Was the teacher on time? Did the teacher discipline and control students' behavior? Were the students engaged in appropriate activities? These questions were answered affirmatively in the case of teachers who were rated as outstanding. In this case, however, successful teaching did not result in student achievement and competency.

In the preceding example, teachers were judged on the extent to which they created a positive learning environment rather than on whether that environment resulted in student learning. In the present climate of accountability, attention should be focused on the results of teachers' procedures and methods. You may be free to develop your own curriculum, but you should be expected to get results. This form of accountability links teacher performance with student performance.

An effective teacher, as defined here, gets learning results. We can no longer be satisfied by merely *describing* what teachers do. Instead we need to *correlate* what teachers do with student learning and achievement. What do effective teachers do? Clearly, implementing the curriculum involves more than making preinstructional decisions for maximizing student learning. Equally important are the explicit decisions associated with the teaching function. No cookbook for effective teaching exists. Neither are there teaching acts that will invariably produce desired results. However, five principles of effective teaching are associated with student learning and achievement: communicating clearly and accurately, executing instruction skillfully, motivating students to achieve, engaging students for achievement, and providing feedback to students.

Communicating Clearly and Accurately

To become engaged in learning, students must be exposed to clear instructions and explanations.

Two factors deserve attention. The first is clarity of procedures. When students work on their own, with a partner, in a small group, or on a team, the instructions they receive must be clear and precise. They should understand clearly both their roles and your expectations. If not, valuable time is lost while students are confused, engaged in the wrong activity, pursuing the wrong outcome, or behaving inappropriately. Students need to be clear on what is being emphasized. For example, the general skill to be learned might be serving, but the specific skill to be learned is arm motion. It is not volleyball or how to serve harder. Effective teachers also anticipate possible student misunderstanding. The second consideration is the quality of verbal and written communication. The language should be audible and legible as well as developmentally appropriate. Your spoken and written language should reflect correct usage and contain expressive, well-chosen vocabulary that enriches the subject matter (Danielson, 1996).

You must also strive to communicate a sense of enthusiasm about the significance of the physical education content and the importance of learning. This will provoke the students' interest and enthusiasm. This "set induction" usually occurs at the beginning of an instructional sequence. For example, you might say, "You're going to learn two things today that will help you keep your balance for in-line skating." Make sure that you share the purpose of the lesson with students.

Along with set induction, "scaffolding" is another useful strategy to use to communicate the purpose of what students are to learn and its relation to past and future learning experiences. Because students may have difficulty connecting sequentially designed activities, they need to see how a single experience is linked to an organizing theme, program model, or curriculum framework. Some techniques include posting daily, weekly, monthly, or yearly content areas; displaying vocabulary; and maintaining notebooks, journals, or logs (Graham, 2001).

Although more complex, student portfolios can also accomplish this purpose. The types of portfolios that offer the greatest potential are thematic (relate artifacts to a particular focus), integrated (make connections between subjects), showcase (exhibit growth over time), and multiage (a collection of items from a cluster of grade levels). Whether you use these types of portfolios alone or in combination, the overall portfolio system should be standards based. Student portfolios are also described in chapter 9 (pages 207-209).

Executing Instruction Skillfully

The foundation for instruction has been laid—a positive learning environment, high expectations, a program that is readiness and needs-based, effective management procedures, effective discipline techniques, and clear communication. The ability to instruct involves many complex variables. There is no one best way of instructing. However, certain instructional skills are important to student achievement. These can be grouped into two broad categories: model or information communication, and observing and analyzing.

Model or Information Communication

Instruction usually begins with model or information communication. It consists of either the demonstration or explanation of the processes, skills, procedures, values, or attitudes to be learned, or the presentation or explanation of the facts, concepts, principles, or materials that students will learn or deal with. This process, also referred to as input, is built into the structure of learning experiences as identified in chapter 9 (page 197). You can help your students by keeping this process simple (offering one idea at a time), keeping it brief (avoiding repetitious explanations), and providing verbal cues (e.g., "lead with your elbow").

Visualizing a motor skill is far more meaningful than hearing an oral description. When demonstrating, physical education teachers often use phrases such as, "Like this" or "Watch how I'm doing it." Unfortunately, the teachers don't know what students see or if they are focused on the right elements. An effective demonstration (1) takes place in a location in which all students can see it, (2) makes appropriate use of the whole-part-whole (show an entire skill, followed by the parts that make up the skill, followed by the entire skill again) or part-part-whole presentation (show the parts of the skill separately followed by the entire skill), (3) uses normal or slow speed depending on the motor skill element, and (4) has a verbal focus to direct students' attention.

At the end of a demonstration, there are several quick techniques to use to check for understanding: (1) a recognition check (students raise their hands when they recognize correct movement), (2) a verbal check (students explain the cue or concept), (3) a comprehension check (students explain the concept), and (4) a performance check (teacher quickly scans students). You can also pinpoint two or more students (not one) who are correctly performing the skill components and have them demonstrate the skill (Graham, 2001).

Demonstrating a motor skill is more meaningful to students than an oral description.

Observing and Analyzing

The ability to observe and analyze students' performance as a function of ongoing assessment is an essential instructional skill. However, teachers tend to focus too often on what is being taught (i.e., content). If the focus is on individual student achievement rather than content, the decisions that follow observing and analyzing (i.e., change the task, offer a cue, present a challenge) are more difficult because of the variance across students. If you were teaching only one student, these decisions would be easier. Typically, however, physical education teachers must be able to observe and analyze a large number of students simultaneously. Some techniques for observing and analyzing are as follows: (1) back-to-the-wall (observing from the boundaries), (2) scanning (constantly sweeping the teaching area), and (3) one component at a time (focusing on a cue rather than on the entire movement). In practice, you should be continually looking for assurance that students are working safely, that they are on-task, and that the task is developmentally appropriate. Once assured that these factors are met, you can decide if and when to change the task for the entire class or for individual students (Graham, 2001).

Motivating Students to Achieve

Students' willingness to learn and interest in learning play an active role in shaping teacher behavior and decision making. For example, students will attempt to avoid failure and embarrassment by pressuring teachers to simplify the curriculum, assign low-demand activities, and reduce evaluation standards. Motivation or demotivation to achieve depends on contextual variables. Threat is the primary reason for demotivation (e.g., grades, meaningless tasks, punishment, mistrust). In a positive motivational climate, students grow, mature, and achieve more quickly, and they have a more lasting positive attitude about learning. A positive environment is nonthreatening, cooperative, and inviting. Effective teachers set reasonably high expectations, achieve high success rates, have positive behavioral interactions, assign developmentally appropriate learning tasks, and use sensible reward structures. The result is motivated students.

Reasonably High Expectations

When teachers believe that students are high or low achieving, their expectations tend to become self-fulfilling prophecies. Reasonable expectations serve as a motivator when the standards are clear, open, and based on the student's own unique history. For students who need additional time or support, the standard should reflect achievement *for them.*

High Success Rates

Along with high expectations, students need to experience success. Physical education programs should provide enough uncertainty, ambiguity, and frustration to challenge students, but not so much that they do not succeed. To motivate students, create and change tasks so they can reach success (e.g., adjusted target distances, percentage gains versus absolute levels, self-paced tasks, alternative learning sequences). However, keep in mind that success rates can vary. Students who are competent in motor skills can endure more failure or lower success rates when learning new skills than can students with low competency, who require high success rates given their past history of failure.

Positive Behavioral Interactions

Students are motivated toward appropriate learning behaviors if teachers respond or interact positively when those student behaviors are exhibited. Ineffective teachers typically interact with students only after inappropriate behavior. Positive behavioral interactions can be divided into general (e.g., "good," "nice job," or "well done"), nonverbal (e.g.,

a smile, nod, or thumbs-up), specific information content (e.g., "that was a great effort," "you did a good job getting organized"), and value content (e.g., "that was good so you must have paid attention"). Depending on the purpose, you can deliver positive behavior interactions in private, in public (which offers the modeling effect), or with a group or subset of the group (which strengthens group standards of behavior) (Siedentop, 1991).

Developmentally Appropriate Learning Tasks

Students will find the learning environment more motivating if learning tasks are meaningful. The tasks should be equitable, culturally sensitive, and within students' reach from a developmental standpoint. Students at different levels of ability may require different levels of praise and encouragement to remain motivated. All students should have equal access to learning tasks; past practices should not interfere with new, alternative kinds of learning opportunities; and students should not be limited by their physical, social, or intellectual development.

Sensible Reward Structures

As motivators, reward structures can be classified as competitive (e.g., who can make the most shots?), individual (e.g., can you improve your arm strength?), and cooperative (can your group solve the movement problem?). Intrinsic rewards to improve satisfaction, accomplishment, or competence are best accomplished through the individual structure. Effective teachers encourage students to succeed on their own and downplay comparisons. The competitive structure has negative consequences for student motivation, and the benefits of the cooperative structure are mixed. Extrinsic rewards are outside of and unrelated to the learning task (e.g., grades, prizes, points, choices). They can increase effort and help overcome boring and routine learning tasks, but they can also produce the long-term effect of decreasing the inner drive to achieve (Glatthorn, 1993).

Obviously, as a teacher you play a major role in motivating your students. Your attitude and approach directly influence student perceptions and response. As a role model, you should elicit joy in learning and enthusiasm for teaching. How can you expect students to be motivated if you are not? To be effective, you must believe that you can make a difference; this is commonly referred to as a sense of efficacy. Following are some motivational techniques you might find helpful (Graham, 2001):

■ *Teaching by invitation.* Allow students to decide between two or more tasks or to work alone or with a partner.

■ *Intratask variation.* Offer easier tasks for lower-skilled students or more advanced activities (e.g., games) for higher-skilled students.

■ *Task sheets.* Keep track of student progress on a continuum from simple to complex skills or abilities.

■ *Peer tutors and cooperative learning.* Factors to consider include age, maturity, communication skills, motor skill level, and willingness to be a tutor.

■ *Stations or learning centers.* Self-responsibility is built into the nature of the activity.

■ *Student-designed activities.* Have students work with peers to solve a problem or meet a challenge.

■ *Videotaping and video clips.* Allow students to view the progress of a project or a performance skill.

■ *Homework practice.* Present a series of tasks to work on outside of class.

Engaging Students for Achievement

This principle of effective teaching could be the most important. All of the planning to maximize learning and the other principles of effective teaching are directed toward student engagement. Lack of engagement is evident in students who "play around," talk constantly, skip tasks, daydream, and to a greater extent, exhibit disruptive behavior. "Time on-task" does not necessarily reflect student engagement. Students could be "on-task" by completing a task card at a fitness station, but the task card does not engage them in significant learning. The task card could require prerequisites not yet acquired or content already learned, thus producing no challenge. Mere activity and participation do not constitute engagement.

To be engaged, students need motor, cognitive, or social or emotional involvement with the content. In physical education, for example, students can work unproductively with manipulatives (e.g., wands, balloons, beanbags, balls) and learn nothing. Mental and physical engagement, however, will help them learn concepts and movements that produce trajectory, resistance, and force. As a teacher, you can facilitate student engagement by addressing representation of content, structure and pacing, the nature of the activities, and student grouping (Danielson, 1996).

Representation of Content

Engaging students usually begins with the presentation, or re-presentation, of new content. This instructional skill is similar to model or information communication (page 189). To be effective, use examples, modeling, and metaphors that illustrate the new concept, skill, or behavior. Make connections to students' knowledge, interests, and environment. For example, you might introduce the cartwheel by having students visualize the action of a Ferris wheel relative to head, arm, and leg actions.

Structure and Pacing

Learning tasks should have a well-designed structure so that students know where they are in that structure. The tasks should be logically sequenced with a recognizable beginning, middle, and end. The point at which students are able to begin the task sequence is considered a form of preassessment. Changes in behavior can be compared against this initial ability level. Students would then advance along the learning continuum (task sequence) at their own paces. Students should not feel rushed; nor should time drag. Table 8.2 shows a jump rope sequence. When the tasks are completed in order, the last task completed successfully becomes the student's entry status for the next one and beyond. When students experience difficulty, you should be prepared with enrichment loops (page 182-183).

Nature of Activities

To engage deeply with the learning content, students must be challenged to construct understanding (cognitive), perform skills habitually (motor), and act in accordance with accepted values (affective). One way to create challenge is to emphasize problem-based learning. The activity would require students to solve a problem or answer a perplexing question. For example, once your students have learned basic soccer skills, you can ask them how to create an advantage for scoring. Other examples are asking students to make a pattern moving around a beanbag using different directions, or to count how many times in a row they can gallop that look the same. Activities designed for maximum engagement permit student choice (e.g., ball size, weight, texture, and color), initiative (e.g., generate own questions and design solutions), and authentic, real-life applications (e.g., passing the ball to the setter upon receiving a floater serve in a volleyball game).

Table 8.2   Illustrative Task Sequence

	Jump rope sequence
Task 1	Hold rope so that loop is behind the ankles.
Task 2	Swing rope overhead and down under feet; raise feet enough for rope to pass under.
Task 3	Repeat task 2 successfully three times in a row.
Task 4	Swing rope overhead and, as it reaches its full height, raise both feet lightly.
Task 5	Repeat task 4 successfully three times in a row.
Task 6	Jump rope eight times without missing at "slow time" (one jump per turn).
Task 7	Jump rope eight times without missing at "double time" (one jump per turn twice as fast as in task 6).
Task 8	Jump rope eight times without missing at "fast time" (one jump per turn even faster than in task 7).
Task 9	Swing rope overhead and under both feet, landing on the ball of the right foot with left foot extending (alternating jump).

Student Grouping

You can also choose to group students to enhance their level of engagement. Possibilities include (1) a single large group led by the teacher; (2) small groups including partners, triads, or more per group working either independently or with the teacher; and (3) independent, self-directed groups. In small groups, the ability levels, maturity, and experiences can be the same or mixed depending on what you are trying to accomplish.

Grouping students in threes can enhance their level of engagement.

Providing Feedback to Students

Students should receive information about their learning progress (feedback) from the teacher, other students, or the learning materials and equipment. Even when learning tasks are common to an entire group, the process of feedback individualizes teaching. It is essential that feedback be provided equitably to *all* students.

Before looking at the qualities of effective feedback, we need to distinguish between two terms. *Knowledge of results* refers to the outcome or product (e.g., targets hit, items matched, behavior frequencies). *Knowledge of performance* refers to characteristics or process (e.g., cues or key elements of a skill). For example, after serving a volleyball, the student knows if the ball went over the net and landed in the correct area (knowledge of results). Knowledge of performance, on the other hand, reveals whether the student performed the serve correctly (i.e., ball toss, form, striking position, ball trajectory). Effective teachers focus on knowledge of performance (characteristics and process) because feedback of this nature leads to repeated successful patterns or adjustments to patterns that need correction. To be effective, feedback must have the following qualities (Danielson, 1996):

▪ *Accurate.* As a teacher, you are responsible for accurate feedback, even if that feedback comes from peers using a criteria rating sheet. Your criteria must be clear, observable, and simple. Direct feedback should correspond specifically to what you just taught and what students are practicing. For example, if you demonstrated the forehand stroke in tennis with an emphasis on the concept of "low to high" (path of racket), feedback about the grip or feet placement, although not wrong, would not match what students are supposed to focus and work on.

▪ *Specific.* Global comments such as "good," "terrific," and "way to go" are positive interactions that may help create a pleasant climate, but they do not qualify as feedback. Specific feedback about the movement cues or key elements is more valuable (e.g., "bend your knees more" or "step in the direction of the throwing target").

▪ *Constructive.* Ineffective teachers have a tendency to give corrective, negative, and sometimes harsh feedback. Positive feedback is more encouraging and leads to improved performance. A strategy to overcome constant negative feedback is to use the "compliment sandwich" approach. This technique includes three steps: (1) point out what the student did correctly, (2) identify what was incorrect and how to correct it, and (3) encourage the student by reemphasizing what the student did well.

▪ *Timely.* Feedback should be provided consistently in a timely manner. Immediate is almost always better than delayed so that students can make prompt use of feedback in their learning.

Summary

This chapter dealt with the complexities of learning and teaching. Needless to say, we only scratched the surface. Entire books are devoted to the topics of organizing instruction for maximum learning and the principles of effective teaching. However, you should benefit from an understanding of the fundamental concepts and features underlying these broad areas. If you integrate the factors and principles listed in table 8.3 into your curriculum, it will be all the stronger in producing high levels of student achievement.

Table 8.3   Maximizing Learning and Effective Teaching

Maximum learning factors	Effective teaching principles
Positive learning environment	Communicating clearly and accurately
High expectations for achievement	Executing instruction skillfully
Focus on student readiness and needs	Motivating students to achieve
Effective management procedures	Engaging students to achieve
Effective discipline systems	Providing feedback to students

Making It Work

Have you achieved the expected outcomes (see page 178) for this chapter? You should be able to organize instruction for maximum learning and apply principles of effective teaching. Still, you may have some practical questions that need answers, such as the following:

▪ *With so many management and discipline problems in physical education, can students learn anything?* You're probably thinking, why can't I just go teach? It would be easy if we had to teach only one student at a time. Instead, we are sometimes confronted with very large class sizes. Therefore, we need to spend a great deal of time and energy planning to manage the environment and discipline students, and then we have to go out and do it. No doubt, the reality for many teachers is to manage and discipline students first and deliver some kind of instruction second. The characteristics of a well-managed environment are known (i.e., high level of student involvement; clear expectations; little wasted time, confusion, or disruption; and a work-oriented, but pleasant and relaxed climate). It's a matter of initiating your "system" of management and enforcing discipline techniques (i.e., types of reinforcement, schedules of reinforcement, methods of reinforcement, and consequences). The system should be designed so that students understand and practice responsibility for their own behavior and working with others. Until this is achieved, expect a high proportion of management time and little time for learning. Students are, for the most part, responsive, adaptable, hard working, and willing to comply with the "system." Don't be frustrated by the few students for whom management procedures and discipline routines are necessary.

■ *When students are classified into different groups, isn't this the same as labeling?* No! We do this all the time whether we realize it or not. For example, trying to equalize teams for competition is indirectly saying that some students belong to an advanced skill group, some are average in ability, and others are not as skilled. Teams are formed in which these groups are distributed as equally as possible. Another common practice is to put students of similar interests together in a learning group. The fact is that there are many justifiable reasons for identifying and classifying students that don't result in labeling, embarrassment, and poor self-image.

■ *Doesn't the placement of students refer only to special education?* The term *placement* has many meanings. It is not limited to students with special needs, especially those with disabling conditions, but, that's how it's usually thought of. Instead, it can mean that students are "placed" at a learning station to work on skills that show the greatest need for improvement. Students won't view this negatively if they see it as a *genuine* attempt to help them improve their abilities, not to isolate or reject them. Sometimes students are placed in groups for safety reasons (e.g., swimming, obstacle course spotting). As long as there is flexibility and student mobility from one placement to the next, then such placements should be accepted for the right reasons.

■ *Is there really enough time to carry out some of the programming and intervention options?* Here again, you probably would use some of the suggested options, but initially on a smaller scale. For example, you can choose to have students repeat some task or drill when they experience difficulty. Or you might have them try some other subtasks when they get to a task in the regular sequence and experience difficulty. The idea is ultimately to bring the student back to the regular task. Although the process has been formally called an enrichment loop, it is done all the time out of common sense. You don't need a task card with arrows as long as you carry out the underlying purpose of providing remediation or enrichment. Ultimately, you might anticipate where students are going to have problems and have enrichment loops ready.

■ *Are bad teachers the reason middle and high school students don't seem to like physical education?* Regretfully, we've all probably had "throw out the ball" physical education teachers. Hopefully, you've also experienced effective teachers who understand and practice the principles of communication, skillful instruction, motivation, engagement, and feedback. Beyond the craft of teaching, the curriculum needs to be relevant and achievement based. It should approximate real life in which students can find success. Possibly this means that traditional sports-oriented curricula are no longer meaningful *as we know them*. There's nothing wrong with sports per se, but maybe the orientation needs to change to appeal to secondary students. The sport education model offers that potential with a focus on learning and achievement. Another possibility is to operate physical education like a commercial wellness or fitness center. Programming could be personalized based on individual diagnostic assessments.

nine

Learning Experiences

Because of a shifting school population, many teachers in your suburban school district have been reassigned to other buildings. Although your elementary school has fewer students, another elementary building was opened to accommodate the influx of new students, primarily from a large housing development. Also, the community in general has become more transient in nature. More and more families are moving into the area with school-aged children. The number of students in the two middle schools and high school has increased significantly over the past three years. The district has developed a strategic plan for recruiting new teachers and reassigning existing teachers to respond to this change.

As a result of the situation, you accept reassignment to the high school. It represents a dramatic change because your only high school experience occurred during student teaching. However, you are enthusiastic about teaching older students and the prospect of working within a fairly large physical education department. The high school curriculum consists of a required program in 9th and 10th grades that includes a half-semester of fitness followed by three half-semesters of individual and team sports that are supposed to be lifetime activities. The program for 11th- and 12th-graders is completely elective. Modest attempts have been made to offer popular courses such as aerobic dance, yoga, and weight control. For the most part, students go through a warm-up routine, complete some lead-up games or drills, and then play games.

Your attempt to use a variety of self-directed tasks, partner activities, and cooperative learning groups is laughed at behind your back by some of the other physical education teachers, and some students complain,"We didn't do it this way before!" In addition, you try to use various problem-solving techniques, a personal activity program, showcase portfolios, and computer-assisted strategies as much as possible.

The dilemma you face is whether to continue doing what you think is best or to change to the high school system—one that you believe is a "throw out the ball" approach. Should you conform to the practices of other teachers if they differ from your sense of appropriateness? How important is it to use a variety of learning experiences in the physical education setting? What criteria should be used for selecting learning experiences? Are certain kinds of learning experiences better for producing different kinds of outcomes such as cognitive, affective, and psychomotor? How can physical education teachers provide experiences that compensate for the physiological, psychological, and sociological diversity of students?

EXPECTED OUTCOMES

This chapter will help you devise learning experiences for the achievement-based physical education curriculum. After reading this chapter, you will be able to do the following:

1. Define learning experiences and their structure
2. Determine the degree to which learning experiences satisfy fundamental criteria for selection
3. Identify the qualities of individualized learning experiences and differentiate among various approaches to individualization, including portfolios
4. Identify the characteristics of interactive learning experiences and differentiate among various approaches to interaction
5. Describe learning experiences that are effective for accommodating "special" students (culturally diverse, at-risk, gifted and talented)

Students must be given the opportunity to interact with the environment if they are to acquire the intended knowledge, understanding, attitudes, values, and physical skills. In the ABC design model, developing goals, objectives, and assessments represent the ends to be attained. These goals, objectives, and assessments are used for determining how students will acquire knowledge, skills, and values. Essentially, learning occurs when students engage in active behavior (learning experiences). *Students have learning experiences; teachers have methods.*

This chapter is organized around several questions: What are learning experiences, and how are they structured? On what basis are learning experiences selected? How can learning experiences be individualized? Do portfolio systems provide valuable learning experiences? Can learning experiences foster interaction among learners? What kinds of learning experiences are effective for accommodating "special" students? Ultimately, this chapter will help you devise learning experiences for your own physical education curriculum.

Definition and Structure

In designing the curriculum to achieve intended outcomes, you must decide on the kinds of learning experiences you will offer your students. Before doing so, however, you must understand the definition and structure of learning experiences. Your choice of learning experiences should also be influenced by your desire to satisfy your students' needs. In this section we will establish a direct relationship between learning experiences and cognitive, affective, and psychomotor needs.

A learning experience is defined as the interaction between a student and the external conditions found in the environment. It should evoke the desired responses (behavioral change) in the student or exemplify some cultural or psychological value. Learning experiences are considered valid if they create the intended outcomes—knowledge, understanding, normative social behaviors, self-reliance, attitudes, values, and physical skills. The ultimate criterion for judging a learning experience is whether the opportunity, activity, or instructional intervention actually creates the desired responses (behaviors).

This definition is consistent with developmentally appropriate practices in physical education. In fact, several of these practices refer directly to the link between experience and outcome. For example, (1) *cognitive* development occurs through experiences that encourage students to question, integrate, analyze, communicate, and apply concepts; (2) *affective* development occurs through activities that allow students to work together cooperatively, develop a positive self-concept, and feel satisfaction and joy; (3) *movement concepts* and *motor skills* develop through frequent, meaningful, and age-appropriate practice of movement concepts (body awareness, spatial awareness, effort, relationships) and motor skills (locomotor, nonlocomotor, manipulative); and (4) *concepts of fitness* develop through participation in activities designed to understand and value the important concepts of physical fitness and the contribution these concepts make to a healthy lifestyle (Graham, Castenada, Hopple, Manross, & Sanders, 1992).

Because devising learning experiences can be a demanding task, you will need a framework to help you structure them. You will foster consistency if you use a common structure for evoking the desired responses (behavioral change) in students. To simplify the task, we suggest a structure that consists of input and content interaction (Hurwitz, 2002). Although various labels are given to different kinds of learning experiences (e.g., exploration, self-directed tasks, contracting), all learning experiences, regardless of what they are called, contain some form of input and content interaction.

Input

This component consists of either the demonstration or explanation of processes, skills, procedures, values, or attitudes students will learn, or the presentation or explanation of facts, concepts, principles, or materials that students will learn or deal with. The sources and types of input are shown in figure 9.1. As you look at the figure, think of how the sources and types could produce different kinds of input. Here are some examples in physical education:

- Demonstration of the soccer dribble by a student
- Task sheet with diagrams of flexibility exercises and explanations
- Teacher presentation of the characteristics of the 2-1-2 zone defense in basketball
- Demonstration of the observer role in a small group learning station for the tennis serve

Content Interaction

Content interaction describes how students are actually involved in dealing with skills, procedures, values, attitudes, facts, concepts, principles, or materials as they attempt to meet objectives. The types of content interaction and associated learning factors are shown in figure 9.2. As you can see, when the various types are combined with factors of pace or duration, organizational pattern, interaction

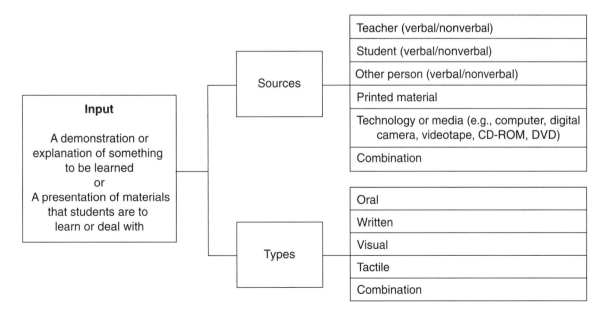

Figure 9.1 Sources and types of input.

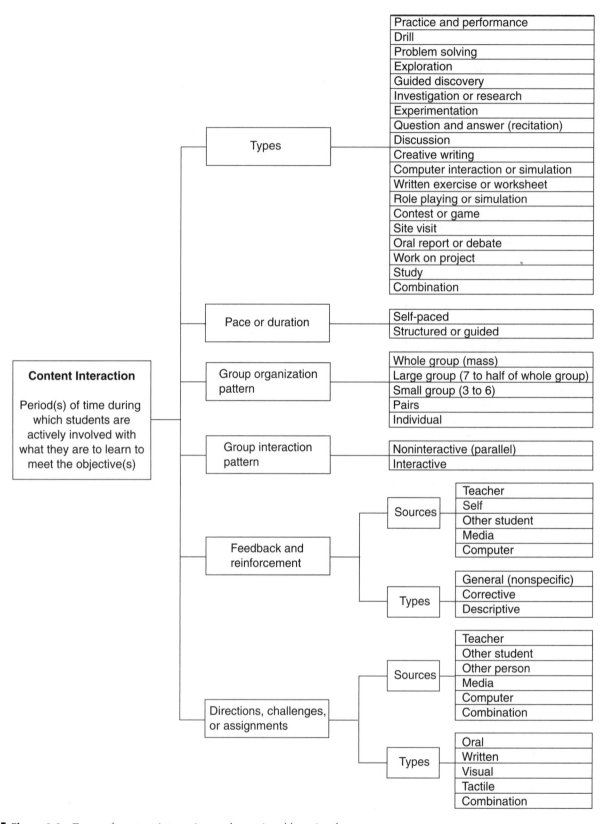

Figure 9.2 Types of content interaction and associated learning factors.

pattern, feedback or reinforcement, and directions or challenges, an unlimited number of possible content interactions exist. Here are some examples in physical education:

- Relay-type drills in which students dribble a soccer ball
- Flexibility exercises completed as described on a task sheet
- "Walk-through" 2-1-2 zone defense in basketball followed by "full-speed" practice
- Feedback from a peer based on a criteria checklist for the tennis serve

Criteria for Selection

When selecting learning experiences, you must first decide which activities would help your students attain the targeted objectives and then arrange stimulating situations that will provide the desired experiences. The underlying framework for your selection should be student centered. That is, you should emphasize the active role of your students, not your own procedures and behaviors.

Unfortunately, there are no universal learning experiences that relate best to a grade level, ability level, or kind of objective. In spite of the fact that these "perfect" learning experiences do not exist, however, fundamental criteria are suggested here that may help you. Because of the wealth of possibilities, you need to select learning experiences based on the purposes they serve, students' capability and interest, the potential for success, match with objectives, and student needs.

Purposes Served

The learning experience should foster total student development in the cognitive, affective, and psychomotor domains. You will find it useful to classify learning experiences according to these three purposes when designing your curriculum.

Useful kinds of learning experiences are also associated with specific levels of learning. For example, if you want students to acquire information about facts, terms, principles, and ideas (cognitive), experiences such as listening to a presentation, viewing a demonstration, and reading handout materials may be helpful. If you want students to develop skill in applying information, a worksheet, discussion exercise, or guided discovery activity might be desirable. When students are expected to develop social attitudes (affective), some appropriate experiences include assimilation activities, role-playing, and small group exercises. In the case of psychomotor learning, some useful experiences are mental practice exercises, self-directed tasks, and problem-solving activities. The purpose of the learning experience should always serve as a criterion for selection.

Capability and Interest

Learning experiences should be directed toward behaviors that are within the students' range of capability. Without some indication that the student has the background necessary for successful completion of the activity, failure and unfulfilled objectives result. Knowledge of the students' previous and present abilities help determine whether the intended learning experience is feasible. Assessing entry behaviors (see chapter 7) will help you determine students' capabilities.

Learning experiences that match students' developmental readiness enhance curiosity and interest in learning. For example, the degree of independence afforded in a learning activity should depend on the students. Some students may not be able to cope with much independence, whereas others could function very successfully in independent situations. Readiness was identified in chapter 8 as a factor in maximizing student learning.

Potential for Success

You should always attempt to select learning experiences in which students can be successful. Students who do not experience success may try to avoid the targeted behavior or lose their motivation to learn. For example, failure is inevitable when students are not *physically* ready to perform a particular skill movement, even though other students of similar age are mature enough to do so. However, success should not be viewed as transitory or immediate. Instead, cumulative successes in learning experiences reinforce students' feelings of improvement. Chapter 8 identified a high success rate as a factor in motivating students to achieve.

Match With Objectives

The behavioral and content aspects of objectives, when taken together, serve as a criterion for selecting learning experiences. Students must understand the relationship between the objective and the learning experience. Learning experiences should match the content referred to in the objective and offer activities at the level of behavior called for by the objective. Depending on the level of the objective, learning experiences might range from memory

With assistance from her teachers, the student has a successful learning experience.

tasks to problem-solving activities. Affective objectives might be achieved through activities in which students acquire or transform interests, attitudes, or values. On the other hand, pencil-and-paper activities would not appear to match an objective in the area of social development. Thus, the nature of the objective should be a criterion for selecting appropriate learning experiences.

Student Needs

Learning experiences suggested by the behavior and content aspects of objectives should result in explicit learning. Chapter 8 identified student needs as a factor in maximizing student learning. Because of the interdependent nature of students' needs, isolating learning experiences for this purpose is difficult, but not impossible.

One of the best-known teaching models, the spectrum of styles (Mosston & Ashworth, 2002), facilitates learning in all developmental channels

(needs)—physical responses, social interaction, emotional growth, cognitive involvement, and ethical behaviors. Through a series of learning experiences, decision making is shifted from the teacher to the student. The various styles include command, practice, reciprocal, self-check, inclusion, guided discovery, convergent discovery, divergent discovery, and student-designed individual program. The physical channel involves the exploration of movement and the identification of individual physical capacities and limitations. In the cognitive channel, the student is concerned with remembering, drawing conclusions, judging and organizing information, and thinking creatively. The social channel includes interpersonal and intergroup practices such as cooperation, communication, and courtesy. Physical self-concept and individual self-image emerge through the emotional channel. The moral, or ethical, channel consists of attributes such as respect, tolerance, honesty, and fair play. Examples of learning experiences representing these styles are presented later in this chapter.

Explicit learning experiences are formulated from the kind of behavior specified by the objective and the content to which the behavior is applied. To illustrate this relationship, table 9.1 depicts learning experiences that correspond to cognitive, affective, and psychomotor goals and objectives (needs). The descriptions include the input and content interaction components of learning experiences.

Individualization Pattern

Educators have long been concerned about the problem of compensating for the physiological, psychological, and sociological differences among students, and of providing experiences that meet diverse students' needs. Given the mission of physical education, the concept of individualization should serve as a guiding principle, allowing students to engage in experiences suited to their unique characteristics.

Individualization should not be viewed as a method of instruction. Rather, it is a way of learning in which ends and means are interwoven through the respective roles of the teacher and the student. As described in chapter 2 (page 40), students vary significantly in their needs, and they come to school with diverse backgrounds, attitudes, motivations, behavior patterns, and experiences. In recognition of this diversity, we identify the principles and qualities of individualization here and illustrate various approaches to individualization.

Table 9.1   Learning Experiences Based on Needs

Need (domain)	Objective	Learning experience	
		Input	Content interaction
Intellectual (cognitive)	To understand basic directional movements and levels of movement, students will be able to use general and personal space appropriately at least 80% of the time.	Teacher shows the difference between general and personal space and demonstrates one direction and one level of movement.	Students engage in the following activities: (1) practice running, leaping, landing, and rolling on their own mats; (2) show changes of direction and levels by moving forward, backward, and sideways using rolls, locomotor movements, and balances; and (3) make up a sequence for traveling along the mats in different directions and levels.
Social (affective)	To function in harmony with others (teamwork), students will exhibit approach and avoidance behaviors at a ratio not less than 4 to 1 by sharing responsibility for reaching common movement goals while using an elastic rope.	Teacher explains what it means to "share responsibility" and presents one sample movement goal.	Students respond to various challenges to their group (four or five students), including (1) using different body parts to stretch the rope while forming different body shapes, geometric shapes, spatial designs, numerals, and letters; (2) using different body parts as bases of support; and (3) using two students to stretch the rope into different shapes and have others leap over it, jump into it, leap into it, and jump into it, take a step, and leap out of it.
Emotional (affective)	To gain self-understanding and appreciation, students will determine their own ability to perform the volleyball forearm pass by completing all progressive levels of an individualized worksheet.	Students are used to demonstrate the forearm pass; teacher discusses and clarifies the worksheet.	Students use an individualized worksheet to evaluate their own performance in the following progressive levels: (1) partner drop, single forearm pass; (2) self-toss, single forearm pass; (3) wall rebound, single forearm pass; (4) partner underhand toss, single forearm pass; (5) self-toss, multiple forearm passes (2-5); (6) wall rebound, multiple forearm passes (2-5); (7) partner overhand throw (half force), single forearm pass; and (8) partner overhand throw (half force), multiple forearm passes (2-5). Criteria are: (1) movement starts from ready position, (2) movement results in "creating time," and (3) ball comes down within "self-space" or on target.
Values (affective)	To show a preference for maintaining physical fitness during leisure time, students will, given a variety of choices, develop and use a personalized fitness program as indicated by an overall increase of 25% of leisure time from the beginning of the 6-week program.	Teacher outlines the advantages and disadvantages of various uses of leisure time; hands out a learning activity packet that shows how to develop a personalized fitness program.	Students engage in the following sequence: (1) plot a personal physical fitness profile summarizing their ratings in the various aspects of fitness; (2) generate specific physical fitness goals based on areas of concern, needed improvement, or maintenance; (3) select individualized programs, general exercise programs, or sports or leisure activities that they enjoy in terms of their contribution to students' fitness goals; and (4) design a personal fitness program based on their fitness goals, selection of programs or activities, and schedule of programs or activities.
Skill (psychomotor)	To demonstrate compound adaptive skills in basketball, students will dribble to a one-count stop and rear pivot with at least an 80% rating for "form" on a criteria rating scale.	Students view a videotape that shows the stop and pivot; teacher reviews the task card and procedures for getting a partner.	Students complete the following tasks: (1) select a partner; (2) each partner takes two sets of 10 stops and pivot; (3) partner checks criteria on a task card for the stop (both feet hit floor at same time, wide base, knees flexed, tail dropped, on balance) and the pivot (knees flexed, ball protected, pivot foot heel raised, step with the nonpivot foot); and (4) switch roles after each set.

Underlying Principles

When designing a curriculum, you should be able to identify the presence or absence of certain principles of individualization. The four principles you should consider when devising individualized learning experiences are practice, variation, multiple outcomes, and positive feedback and reinforcement.

Practice

Individualized learning experiences allow students to practice the kind of behavior specified by objectives. This principle does not refer to the act of performing repeatedly in order to learn. Practice is defined as the use of physical acts, emotions and feelings, and knowledge to reinforce or strengthen learning. For example, if you want a student to learn how to kick a soccer ball into a goal during a game, you must provide an opportunity to practice this behavior in the appropriate setting. Kicking a soccer ball into an uncontested goal through drills and lead-up games will not achieve the objective.

A particular challenge arises when establishing a relationship between behavior and content in the affective domain. For example, suppose you want students to learn self-control (emotional need) through perseverance (behavioral aspect) in hitting a tennis ball with a backhand drive (content aspect). You may decide to set up a learning experience involving instructions from a task card or learning contract in which the sequence of tasks demands continuous and concentrated effort.

You may need to arrange additional situations that evoke a desired response in your students. For example, you may decide to help students develop their ability to function in a helping relationship (social value) through learning experiences that require giving assistance or support to another person. Partner activities, self-testing dual activities, and reciprocal learning opportunities that require peer feedback are good examples.

Finally, you should always offer practice that is at the same level of behavior defined by the objective. An understanding of the educational domains is useful for matching learning experiences to objectives because of their hierarchical nature. Learning activities often inappropriately involve the recall and identification of facts and principles when the objective calls for students to apply information in unfamiliar situations.

Variation

Varied learning experiences consider individual students' interests, competencies, and needs. You can often devise a wide range of learning experiences to bring about the same outcome. Consider the multiple interests and competencies of both you and your students. For example, assume that you want your students to know the proper techniques of passing in volleyball. You could provide alternative learning experiences based on an assessment of student competencies, interests, and learning styles. In terms of input, students might (1) read a description of the passing techniques, (2) listen to a presentation, (3) view a videotape, or (4) view a live demonstration. Content interaction could include (1) self-directed activities, (2) drills in small groups, or (3) partner feedback with a criteria checklist. Thus, several learning experiences could help your students attain the same objective.

Multiple Outcomes

Individualized learning experiences contribute to multiple outcomes such as thinking, feeling, and moving. Activities are more satisfying when they reflect the concept of confluence. This means that thinking, feeling, and moving are integrated in a single learning experience. Confluent learning experiences are economical because of their contribution to multiple outcomes. For example, the student might analyze a game situation that requires a rule interpretation and at the same time acquire information about the strategies being employed. In addition, the student may develop an appreciation for the importance of officiating as well as an interest in or dislike of officiating. You must also be cognizant of undesirable outcomes that may develop from a learning experience planned for some other purpose. Suppose that the learning experiences for developing gymnastics routines become too intense. The student may develop a proficiency in performance but a strong dislike for gymnastics.

Positive Feedback and Reinforcement

Individualized learning experiences provide positive feedback and reinforcement as a guide to learning. As students strive toward individual goals, they seek feedback on their progress as a guide to further efforts. Because many students have experienced failure throughout their lives, feedback (information of results) and positive responses from other students and the teacher can have a significant impact on their learning. When individualizing learning experiences, make sure that the mechanism for feedback is apparent to both you and your student.

Feedback or positive reinforcement is usually structured in terms of (1) a verbal response from the teacher; (2) a nonverbal response from the teacher (a touch or facial expression); (3) a written response from the teacher; (4) a verbal peer response; (5) a written peer response; (6) a verbal group response; or

(7) a combination of verbal, nonverbal, and written responses from either the teacher or peers. Here we are referring to positive feedback and reinforcement that is received directly through the learning experience. For example, the activity may require the use of a task card for receiving feedback from another student. Programmed materials such as a learning activity package would include direct feedback through self-assessment. The sources and types of feedback and reinforcement were identified in figure 9.2 (page 198) as factors of content interaction. Feedback was also described in chapter 8 (pages 192-193) as an important principle of effective teaching.

Qualities of Individualization

When designing a curriculum, you are obligated both ethically and educationally to devise learning experiences that can be matched with each student's interests, abilities, achievement level, and preferred learning style. To satisfy this obligation, you must respect individual differences when planning specific learning experiences. This quality of individualization is realized through diagnostic–prescriptive learning experiences, in which you continually examine the strengths and weaknesses of the student and prescribe learning tasks accordingly. The diagnostic data generated through entry appraisal should be transferred into relevant learning experiences that result in desired behavioral changes. This leads to the second quality of individualization—its link to intended outcomes. Individualized learning is dependent on objectives that relate to individual talents, needs, interests, and abilities.

The third quality of individualization relates to the approaches employed. Individualized approaches must include a wide variety of materials, individual student–teacher interaction, student selection of materials, self-pacing, and both individual and group opportunities. The latter aspect may be composed of interaction between the teacher and the student (one-on-one) and between the teacher and small groups. Various types of individualized learning are described and illustrated on pages 204-206.

Finally, the individualized learning experience should incorporate a method of learning that truly permits individual pursuit of a given learning objective. At least four options are available: varying the pace, providing content options, developing alternative approaches on the basis of difficulty, and creating learning style alternatives.

Pace Options

The pace option of individualization permits the student to decide how fast or slowly he learns. Student-controlled pacing often requires rigorous systems of assessment and record keeping to maintain integrity and efficiency. Self-paced programming is almost a necessity when individualizing learning experiences, such as with IEPs (individualized education plans) for students with disabilities. The IEP concept was discussed in chapter 2 (page 34).

The opportunities for self-pacing in physical education are endless. For example, you might give students a series of progressive tasks to perform. They would assume responsibility for indicating the date in the "I Have Achieved" column as they accomplish each task. At certain time intervals, student would indicate the status of each task by the date recorded in the "Working to Achieve" column. Elementary-aged students could practice developmental skills at different assigned stations without regard for the time taken by other students to move from station to station. Even warm-up exercise routines could be self-paced if students were permitted to complete the exercises at their own rate rather than in cadence with others.

Content Options

With the content individualization option, students experience different content under the same basic topic or theme. This option is similar to the principle of variation presented earlier (page 202). For example, the student may be expected to complete a task card for the basketball jump shot. Before choosing one of the distance arcs marked on the floor, the student must attain information on the jump shot by selecting one of the following content options: (1) jump shot off a dribble, (2) jump shot behind a screen, or (3) jump shot off a pass. Content options may also be illustrated for a curriculum unit organized around a lifetime sports theme. The options might include archery, bowling, golf, and tennis. Each student might be expected to select two of the four sports.

Level-of-Difficulty Options

Establishing alternative tracks according to difficulty is particularly suited to individualization. There is no reason to develop a separate curriculum or to segregate students when different mastery levels exist. Chapter 8 addressed programming and intervention options that satisfy this quality of individualization (pages 182-183). Students can fulfill objectives if the learning experience sequence is consistent with their level of ability and achievement. The implementation of this option depends on students' entry-level characteristics. Students can begin learning at different points along a learning continuum.

Learning Style Options

Another set of individualizing options emerges when we consider how each student prefers to learn. Some of these learning style options are as follows:

▌ *Medium of instruction.* Some students prefer listening and responding to the teacher or other students, whereas others prefer interacting with printed materials such as task cards, worksheets, problems to solve, and programmed learning. Films, slides, transparencies, videotapes, DVDs, and CD-ROMs with video clips provide another dimension. Adding sound to visual presentations offers still another option. As students are encouraged to select from alternative presentations (interactive, oral, visual, tactile), their motivation, attention, and perseverance toward learning may improve.

▌ *Grouping and interaction patterns.* Some students prefer to learn in large groups; others prefer small groups. Still others prefer learning through individual study or in a tutorial setting with a peer or teacher.

▌ *Structure.* Some students prefer learning in small increments with frequent feedback and reward or correction. Other students learn better when they are free to develop ideas and investigate alternatives with less supervision. They respond well to divergent or problem-solving activities that permit them to structure tasks themselves.

Approaches to Individualization

A commitment to individualization places demands of time and creative effort on the curriculum designer. This section categorizes, describes, and illustrates various approaches to individualized learning. These approaches can be as simple as giving students the chance to decide at which station to begin an obstacle course or as complex as technology-assisted instruction. Approaches to individualization will vary according to your preferences and how much you want to use them in the local setting. Table 9.2 describes various approaches and offers a sample learning experience for each approach.

A fitness class can incorporate many different learning style options.

Table 9.2   Individualized Learning Approaches

Approach	Description	Sample learning experience
1. Self-directed tasks	Students pursue their own learning tasks until their objective is reached. A range of learning tasks (task continuum) can accommodate the individual student's range of capability. Tasks will vary in the amount of self-determination and independence according to the teacher–student relationship and corresponding transactions.	Students complete the following tasks: 1. View the videotape showing the two-hand set in volleyball. 2. Take a volleyball and select one of the wall stations. 3. Stand behind the line. Throw the ball over your head. 4. Use the two-hand set technique to make the ball travel 10 to 15 feet in the air toward the wall. The ball should make an arch so that it just skims or touches the wall above the 8-foot line. 5. After doing part of the task, return to the videotape for additional information or insight. Then, return to the task. 6. Do the two-hand set 25 times.
2. Exploration	Movement tasks are broad in nature with no particular anticipated response. Students are encouraged to examine, investigate, and seek out a variety of responses. Experimentation is beneficial at any level of learning. The teacher presents a problem-solving situation with increasingly more challenging movement problems for the students to solve in their own unique ways.	Students are directed to do the following: 1. Take a beanbag to a space and hop around the beanbag. 2. Jump forward over your beanbag. Teacher says, "What other directions do you know? Show me!" 3. Make a pattern moving around your beanbag using different directions. Make up a new sequence . . . with a partner if you like. 4. Now, make a bridge with your body over the beanbag. Make a different bridge using other parts of your body. Make more than one bridge. 5. Find ways of making your beanbag travel through the arches of your bridges.
3. Guided discovery	The teacher leads the student through a carefully planned sequence of questions, clues, or tasks arranged so that the student's response is always reinforced until the correct target response is "discovered." A *convergent* thinking process is used since the discovery is directed toward a predetermined answer or movement response. The teacher's role is to guide the student from one step to the next, thus ensuring success in learning.	To discover the use of the toe kick in long and high flying soccer kicks, the student is asked the following questions, each of which is followed by the student's response and teacher feedback (acceptance or reinforcement) of the response (Mosston & Ashworth, 2002): 1. What distance kick is needed when you want to pass the ball to a player who is far from you? 2. Suppose there is a player from the opposing team between you and your teammate and there are no other teammates nearby. How can you safely kick the ball to your teammate? 3. To raise the ball off the ground, where should you apply force on the ball? 4. While you are running, which part of your foot can comfortably get to the lowest part of the ball?
4. Problem solving	The student proceeds through experimentation or logical thinking to determine answers or solutions. The problem should allow the student to choose the best of her alternative solutions. This process of *divergent* thinking promotes the creation of independent solutions. Students can learn facts, skills, concepts, relationships, preferences and validity, limits, variations, and strategies through problem solving.	Students are given the problem of designing three different sequences in balance by changing the order and the movements. Requirements (any order of elements) for the possible solutions are as follows (Mosston & Ashworth, 2002): 1. High position on one foot 2. Low position on two feet, on toes 3. A front scale 4. A jump turn, land on one foot, with bending at all joints 5. Upside-down posture

(continued)

Table 9.2 *(continued)*

Approach	Description	Sample learning experience
5. Contracting	Diagnosis is needed to establish an agreement between the teacher and the student regarding the expected quantity and quality of work, standard of performance, and time period required to complete the task. The student knows that the task is within his capability because of the diagnosis. Students are allowed to vary the time period, work at their own ability level, select many and varied learning experiences according to interests, and work independently.	Students decide when to complete various items for a particular grade. Failure to meet the required percentage means that the grade will be based on the number achieved. Students will receive a lower grade if they do not complete the items on time. For example, the tennis contract for a B might be as follows: 1. Videotape, then digitize and analyze, your performance skill for the serve, forehand drive, and backhand drive. List errors and the tasks used to correct them. 2. Chart the progress you made in the three skills from the beginning to the end of the time period. 3. Interview one tennis team player. Watch the player in a practice session or match and analyze her strengths and weaknesses. 4. Score 80% on three quizzes to determine your knowledge of skill techniques, rules, and strategy.
6. Technology-assisted learning	Learning is directed through the use of a desktop, laptop, or handheld computer along with appropriate software and other electronic technologies such as scanners, video and digital cameras, DVDs, the World Wide Web, digital pedometers, and heart rate monitors. The benefits are as follows: student responsibility is encouraged, individual goals can be set and adjusted based on performance levels, differentiated learning activities and tasks can be prescribed, and each student can progress at her own rate. The computer can also serve as an "instructor" (e.g., drill and practice, tutorial) and a "laboratory" (e.g., problem solving, simulation).	The teacher determines the student's beginning levels of fitness—cardiorespiratory endurance, muscular strength and endurance, flexibility, and body composition—through preassessment. Target standards are set for each fitness component. A fitness or wellness "center" is created that consists of a cardiorespiratory circuit (stair steppers, recumbent cycles, treadmills), strength training circuit (machines, free weights), and computer minilab (desktop computers, body composition analyzers). The student wears a heart rate monitor during the cardiorespiratory circuit and records weight training data in a handheld computer during the strength training circuit. At the computer minilab the student uploads his heart monitor and weight training data to update his electronic "Healthy Lifestyle" portfolio. The student uses a fitness planning software program to create individual workouts based on fitness data and goals. In addition, the student uses a nutrition analysis software program to calculate individual caloric output and input along with recommended food menus.
7. Independent study	With the teacher's guidance, the student pursues an area of interest and takes responsibility for completing predetermined tasks. Experiences may be organized around seminars, study periods, and outside school endeavors. Evaluation schemes include oral reports, final projects, conferences, demonstrations, and observations, in addition to traditional mastery tests. The student uses tasks to supplement teacher instruction and organizes them to facilitate the learning of a skill, concept, generalization, or significant problem; this provides substantial opportunity for learning options.	The student arranges with the teacher to complete the following badminton tasks outside of class: 1. Improve performance by at least one ability rating in six of eight skills: overhead clear, forehand drive, attack clear, defense clear, smash, overhead drop, long serve, and short serve. 2. Using mechanical principles, points of contact, and possible uses of criteria, compare and contrast the following: overhead clear vs. forehand drive, attack clear vs. defense clear, smash vs. overhead drop, and long serve vs. short serve. 3. Write a brief report (4-5 pages) on the history of badminton covering facts, people, and places connected with the sport. 4. Make up a test using badminton terms, rules, and singles and doubles strategy. Give the test to three other members of the class and grade it. There should be at least 25 items with three types of questions (e.g., true or false, multiple choice, matching, fill-in, short essay).

Portfolios

Student portfolios are usually associated with authentic assessment. However, the process and learning experiences that characterize the portfolio process truly represents a comprehensive, systematic approach to individualization. By definition, a portfolio is a purposeful, integrated collection of actual exhibits and work samples showing effort, progress, and achievement (Melograno, 1994, 1998). It presents a broad, genuine picture of student learning that allows all concerned to have input (ongoing feedback) about that learning. Portfolios are not made up of anything and everything. Selection of items, also called artifacts, is a key phase in the portfolio process. Because artifacts are collected over time, portfolios are well suited for demonstrating student growth and achievement of standards. For example, to indicate the extent to which students "understand how to monitor and maintain a health-enhancing level of physical fitness," an array of artifacts could be used (e.g., exercise logs, nutrition journals, self-check rating scales, workout schedules, and diagnosis and prescription charts of weight training routines).

Portfolios offer a dynamic, visual presentation of student abilities, strengths, and areas of needed improvement over time—a more naturalistic, authentic, and performance-based assessment of student learning. Thus, traditional teaching roles may not work with the portfolio process. Rather than inform, direct, and predetermine priorities, teachers using portfolios need to facilitate, guide, and offer choices. They need to plan for student input and involvement, provide time for decision making and reflection, model expectations, help students manage portfolios, use positive interactions, and rethink the environment. Students observe, practice, and refine behaviors associated with decision making, self-management, and self-directed learning. They make critical choices in selecting and judging the quality of their own work including self-reflection (Melograno, 1997).

Portfolios can motivate and empower individual students because responsibility for many of the learning experiences is transferred to the student in terms of self-management, self-directed tasks, self-assessment, and peer conferencing and evaluation. If students are guided toward a system of portfolios, time restrictions and high student-teacher ratios are seemingly reduced. For the purpose of this book, table 9.3 presents a framework for K-12 student portfolios. More complete suggestions for designing comprehensive portfolio systems, illustrative materials, and sample K-12 portfolio models are available in other sources (Melograno, 1998, 2000a, 2000b).

Table 9.3   Framework for K-12 Student Portfolios

Component	Description	Considerations
1. Purposes	There needs to be a reason for creating portfolios. For students, it offers a sense of empowerment, motivation to learn, and encouragement to engage in reflection and self-assessment. For teachers, it offers an opportunity to examine teaching practices. Portfolio purposes may come from district-level mission statements, goals, or outcomes and state-mandated standards; content that is important for students to learn (e.g., motor abilities, sport skills, strategies, rules); processes of learning (e.g., skill practice, problem solving, formulating attitudes); and diversity that exists among students (e.g., learning styles, multiple intelligences, ability levels, multicultural differences). Although the number of purposes is large, a manageable number should be set, particularly in the beginning. Since the purposes will govern what goes into the portfolio, think of portfolios as serving both general and specific purposes.	General purposes • Keep track of progress • Assess own accomplishments • Assist in instructional planning • Determine achievement of objectives • Help parents • Determine student placement Specific purposes • Help practice a healthy lifestyle • Communicate strengths and weaknesses in motor skills • Develop student outcomes relative to the physically educated person • Document status of content standards in physical education

(continued)

Table 9.3 *(continued)*

Component	Description	Considerations
2. Types	The wide variety of purposes suggests that portfolios may take various forms. A portfolio that emphasizes personal fitness, for example, would look much different from one that documents content standards and benchmarks. Once the purposes are clear, consideration should be given to what types of portfolio can best achieve these purposes. The different types of portfolios can be used alone, in combination, or with other types.	*Personal portfolio:* Celebrates interests, hobbies, skills; catalyst for reflection *Working portfolio:* Ongoing, systematic collection of products *Record-keeping portfolio:* Assessment data; skill checklists; rating scales *Group portfolio:* Cooperative learning group *Thematic portfolio:* Relates to a particular focus or organizing center *Integrated portfolio:* View of "whole" student across subjects *Showcase portfolio:* Limited display usually representing best work *Electronic portfolio:* Computer management of data and products *Multiyear portfolio:* Collection from a cluster of grade levels
3. Organizing framework	Since a universal construct for organizing portfolios does not exist, the purpose and type of portfolio directs its organizational scheme. For example, if the purpose is to monitor the development of locomotor skills and a showcase portfolio is used, the portfolio would likely be organized around the concepts and skills associated with the walk, run, jump, hop, gallop, slide, skip, and leap. Students might be expected to select their best work for each movement (e.g., task sheet, drawing of an exercise, matching worksheet) and to demonstrate the movements to a group of peers who provide feedback using a criteria checklist.	Content standards and benchmarks Physically educated person Mission statements of school district and physical education curriculum Learning dimensions or developmental needs Multiple intelligences Organizing centers or curriculum focus
4. Construction, storage, and management	Teacher and student expectations should be clear, including ways to handle portfolio logistics. Decisions are needed about the method of construction, how and where to store portfolios, and how to manage portfolios.	*Construction:* File folders, notebooks, hanging files, albums, large envelopes, accordion files, packet folders with spiral bindings, boxes *Storage:* File cabinets, file drawers, milk crates, shelves, large cardboard boxes, cereal boxes cut like magazine holders, pizza boxes, large notebooks with jacket folders, computer disk, CD-ROMs, media center *Management tools:* Dividers, color codes, table of contents, artifact registry, work log, index, Post-it® notes or index cards, stamps, personalize (graphics, tone)
5. Item selection	Once the purposes and types of portfolios are determined and the organizational scheme and logistics are planned, it is necessary to establish a process for selecting portfolio items. For example, an integrated portfolio organized around developmental needs would contain evidence of a student's cognitive abilities (e.g., problem solving), affective behaviors (e.g., preferences), and psychomotor abilities (e.g., manipulative skills) across several subjects including physical education. Artifacts selected in physical education might include a problem task sheet, self-report inventory, and rating scale.	*What to include:* Baseline samples, preassessment inventories, task sheets, self-assessment checklists, frequency index scales, rating scales, performance checklists, peer reviews, attitude surveys, self-reports, workbook pages, logs, journals, reflections, projects, independent contracts, videotapes, anecdotal statements, parent observations or comments, skill tests, quizzes, written tests, commercial instruments

Component	Description	Considerations
5. Item selection *(continued)*		*How to select:* Something that was hard, something that makes you feel good, best skill, work in progress, samples organized chronologically according to a theme, verify content standards and benchmarks *Who will select:* Student, peer, parent, teacher, local or state mandates *When to decide:* Weekly, monthly, end of unit, scheduled conference, exhibition, end of grading period, end of year, K-12 intervals
6. Reflection and self-assessment	Inherent to portfolios is the chance for students to think about why certain items are included and to gain personal insights throughout the entire process. Students should reflect on individual pieces and their value to the whole portfolio and on how they learn and why they fail to learn. Students should also engage in a self-assessment of their portfolio relative to growth in targeted areas, strengths and weaknesses, and short-term and long-term goals.	Strategies for reflection • Visualization • Tag, label, or stamp • Reflective stems • Bridging questions • Benchmarking • Artifact registry Self-assessment techniques • Checklists • Learning logs • Journals • Strengths and weaknesses chart • Goal setting sheet
7. Conferences	In some systems, student conferences are treated as a culminating event at the end of a portfolio cycle. However, portfolio-related conferences are also recommended during the artifact selection, reflection, and self-assessment phases. Such conferences can range from a simple, informal dialogue between the student and the teacher, a peer, or a parent to more involved, formal meetings among the same parties. Regardless of who is involved and when, conferences should be consciously planned and implemented.	Purposes • Foster goal setting • Promote communication • Satisfy standards Focus • Achievement • Goals • Learning process • Personal satisfaction • Group accomplishments • Total portfolio Audiences • Teacher • Parents • Peers • Significant others Strategies • Miniconferences • Conference station • Student-directed conferences
8. Evaluation criteria and procedures	Collecting portfolio items serves no meaningful teaching or learning function without some measure of worth. The portfolio's purpose should help define the nature of evaluation for the persons who will do the evaluating. Teachers should collaborate with students so that expectations are clearly communicated. To complete this component, teachers, students, or both must decide among several grading options. In addition, scoring rubrics have emerged as a popular evaluation tool in conjunction with portfolio systems.	Grading options • Not graded • Graded (whole portfolio, separate items, selected key items, continual tracking) Use of rubrics • Measurement scale of criteria • Descriptive levels • Anchors • Performance tasks • Overall portfolio

Interaction Pattern

Most learning experiences involve some degree of teacher-to-student, student-to-teacher, or student-to-student interaction. For example, the student is often on the receiving end of a one-way communication when the teacher tells, shows, or demonstrates subject matter followed by activities that require the student to make physical movements or to be challenged mentally. These typical forms of interaction, however, should not be confused with the interaction pattern of learning experiences.

The purpose of interaction in learning experiences is the process itself. Students seek to improve achievement while working together as partners or in small groups to discuss, question, report, and provide feedback. The interaction pattern maximizes the chance to learn social attitudes and values (e.g., respect for others, acceptance, dignity, consideration for differences).

Given the realities of our culturally pluralistic society, it follows that students should learn positive social values such as cooperation, empathy, and caring. Because of this need, devising interactive learning experiences is crucial. To help you learn to devise such experiences, we will first review some critical elements. We will then identify and describe various approaches to interaction and present sample learning experiences for each.

Critical Elements

Interactive learning experiences, as defined, are characteristically different from learning experiences that simply include exchanges between the teacher and students. They are structured for the purpose of both achievement (e.g., movement skill, cognitive ability) and social growth (e.g., responsibility, honesty, sharing, helping). Four critical elements common to interactive learning experiences, regardless of the approach taken, are social skills, grouping, interdependence, and accountability. These elements, which are similar to the characteristics of cooperative learning, are described here:

■ *Social skills.* Motor skills and cognitive abilities are often learned through types of input that involve direct explanation, demonstration, or modeling. Similarly, social skills need to be developed explicitly. You can't assume that students know how to help others or work together in a small group. You must explain, demonstrate, and model social skills as well. For example, students need to learn how to provide feedback to others, observe and rate the performance of others, engage in a discussion,

receive feedback from a partner, and assume a role in resolving a problem. Certain social skills will be inherent in any approach you use.

■ *Grouping.* In general, groups should be heterogeneous (mixed) in membership. The information presented in chapter 8 on identification and placement may help you understand some of the issues of grouping (page 182). Depending on the intended outcome, the basis for "mixing" groups could be ability (high-, middle-, and low-achieving); status (popular, less popular); gender, race, ethnic, or home background; or language proficiency. We recommend small groups of two to six students to ensure high participation. Even numbers help facilitate pairing and avoid "odd person out" situations.

■ *Interdependence.* You should try to structure experiences, as much as possible, so that the success of the pair or small group depends on the success of each individual in the group. This creates a sense of positive interdependence. Strategies for enhancing interdependence include (1) limiting materials or equipment (e.g., one copy of a worksheet must be shared), (2) using "experts" to teach component parts of task, (3) assigning roles (e.g., recorder, observer, encourager), and (4) offering group rewards (i.e., all members must succeed for the group to receive privileges or points).

■ *Accountability.* As a teacher, you are responsible for holding the expectation that each student will learn the given skill, understanding, or value. Make individual students responsible for their own learning. For example, in a partner situation, do not simply demand that students just carry out the role of partner (e.g., observer, rater, recorder). Instead, expect each partner to demonstrate learning. In group situations, hold each member accountable even if the group succeeds. You may want to use performance tests to determine individual achievement.

Approaches to Interaction

Clearly, the distinguishing feature of the interaction pattern is its focus on social outcomes through the use of physical education content. You are confronted with the task of making explicit what is usually implicit—affective learning of a social nature. Some of the content interactions presented in figure 9.2 (page 198) qualify, namely, question and answer (recitation), discussion, and oral report or debate. However, even these approaches often lack a true social element because of their emphasis on content rather than process. Three approaches to interaction that focus on the development of social skills are reciprocal learning, role-playing and simulation, and cooperative learning.

Reciprocal Learning

Intrinsic to the reciprocal approach are the social relationships among peers and the conditions for immediate feedback (Mosston & Ashworth, 2002). The student's role includes observing the peer's performance, comparing and contrasting the performance against the teacher's criteria, drawing conclusions, and communicating results to the peer. The socializing process unique to this approach—giving and receiving feedback with a peer—develops patience, tolerance, dignity, and a social bond that goes beyond the task. It offers the optimum one-to-one ratio for providing immediate feedback that is positively related to achievement. Reciprocal learning can be carried out in pairs or small groups:

■ *Pairs.* When students are organized in pairs, one student is designated as "doer," and the other as "observer." Roles are then reversed. The teacher provides the criteria for correct performance and communicates only with the observer. Performance criteria are usually identified on a checklist or scoring rubric. For example, one of the criteria on a tennis forehand task sheet could be "swing the racket back at about hip height, transfer weight to the front foot, and swing from low to high." One student (the doer) performs the skill several times using a self-drop technique. The other student (the observer) indicates "accomplished" or "needs work" on the task sheet.

■ *Small groups.* Tasks are carried out in groups of three or more. In a triad, students might be designated as "doer," "tosser," and "observer." For example, the task could be the badminton forehand overhead clear. The "tosser" would throw a high, clear service to the "doer," and the "observer" would check off the criteria met (e.g., "shuttle struck overhead but in front of body with arm fully extended").

Role-Playing and Simulation

In role-playing, students pretend they are someone else to solve a problem or act out a situation. Role-playing may be carried out in pairs, in small groups, or in front of the entire class. With simulations, learners take on lifelike roles as a simplified version of reality. Simulation usually involves a larger number of participants in a larger variety of roles than does role-playing. In both role-playing and simulation, the ultimate outcome rests with the students. An opportunity is afforded students to discuss the consequences of their actions. Role-playing allows students to re-create or act out issues in interpersonal relations such as social events, personal concerns, values, problem behaviors, or social skills. Students can explore and begin to understand the feelings, attitudes, and values of others in social situations, as well as the impact of their behavior on others. Procedures for role-playing include the following (Harrison, Blakemore, & Buck, 2001):

1. Select and define the problem situation; clarify roles. If necessary, prepare role sheets that describe the feelings or values of the characters to be played.

2. Use a real-life situation to introduce the problem, far enough removed from the students for comfort, yet close enough so that students can see parallel behavior within the class or school.

3. Select participants and observers from volunteers. Clarify setting (place, time, situation, roles) and give players time to prepare. Assign observers specific questions to answer relative to the feelings of certain players or alternative endings.

4. Have players act out the roles, several times if needed. This will bring out alternative behaviors and their consequences.

5. Review the experience by discussing behaviors and feelings. Ask players to share their feelings and observers to offer their insights. Discussion should be focused on the values, attitudes, and concerns associated with the problem situation.

Role-playing and simulation in physical education can range from a simple social skill (e.g., acting out effective listening with a partner by reflecting what has been heard) to a complex social concern (e.g., acting out the formation of a volleyball team that is integrated in ability level and gender). Other interpersonal relations issues might include

■ expressing what it feels like to be insulted or "put down" when performing a movement task,

■ showing sensitivity toward students with disabling conditions who are trying to develop motor skills, and

■ respecting the calls of a tennis opponent when the honor system for officiating is being used.

Table 9.4 Role-Playing As an Approach to Interaction

Objective

To develop sharing behaviors, the student will demonstrate a willingness to trade equipment when asked to do so by a peer while peers are working with a variety of equipment.

Step	Description
1. Introduction	Present idea of role-playing. Tell students that they are expected to participate in good faith and that they will enjoy the experience.
2. Input	Describe a situation in which two students both want to use the same ball. One student gets the ball from the box, and the other says, "I want to use that one." The two start to argue and a third student comes over to try to settle things.
3. Content interaction	Explain how the role-playing is going to work. Pick the actors for the situation. Tell the rest of the class what to observe (i.e., how real, feelings brought out, how it might be played differently). Then, actors role-play the situation for 5 minutes while the teacher and the rest of the class observe.
4. Closure	Analyze the role-playing. Discuss how real the actions were, what feelings and values were demonstrated, and how the situation might be played out differently.
5. Content interaction	With the help of the class, pick new actors. Set roles of observers again. Then repeat role-playing as in step 3.
6. Closure	Analyze the second round and summarize. Discuss conclusions as to "right" and "wrong" ways to act in the situation. Discuss the importance of sharing. Show and explain the "sharing behavioral checklist" that will be used later during class interactions.
7. Assessment	The next two times that students are using a variety of equipment to practice their soccer, archery, and badminton skills, the teacher completes the "sharing behavioral checklist" as a means of evaluation. The checklist would not be created as a step in the role-play, but the addition above in step 6 introduces its use.
8. Closure	Discuss the results of the application and evaluation. Suggest ways to improve sharing.

The problem situation presented in table 9.4 further illustrates role-playing as an approach to interactive learning experiences (Hurwitz, 1993b).

Cooperative Learning

The critical elements of interactive learning experiences presented earlier (page 210) were adapted from the cooperative learning literature. Needless to say, they are integral to this approach. The characteristics of cooperative learning are as follows (Siedentop, 1991):

- Student activities require interdependence in the achievement of group goals.

- Individual accountability is fostered.

- Groups (teams) are heterogeneous in terms of skill level, gender, race, or cultural background.

- Cooperative behaviors are treated explicitly with much feedback.

- Each group (team) is judged by its success as a group, yet the team "score" is a collection of individual scores, thus maximizing the performance of each team member.

The intent of cooperative learning is to produce social outcomes along with content mastery. A review of the research on cooperative learning suggests that it supports both achievement and social growth (Glatthorn, 1993) as follows: (1) achievement is improved when cooperative groups have both group goals and individual accountability, (2) relationships among different racial groups and across skill levels are improved when cooperative learning involves consistent contact over extended periods, (3) acceptance of learners with disabilities in regular classes is increased, (4) cooperative learning seems to have a positive impact on self-esteem and motivation to learn, and (5) over time, students display more interest in working together than in competing with each other.

Some social skills cooperative learning might emphasize include sharing materials and equipment, being tolerant of others, praising and encouraging one another, listening to others without interruption, staying on task, ensuring equal participation, and carrying out responsibility. You can use a variety of approaches for teaching these social skills including direct explanation, demonstration, guided discovery, problem solving, or role-playing. Working in cooperative groups then provides students the opportunity to practice those skills using monitoring and feedback. Following are some examples of different cooperative learning structures (Siedentop, 1991):

▌ *Pairs-check.* Students work in groups of four with two pairs in each group. Each pair pursues a learning task using the reciprocal approach. Then, the two pairs get together to compare outcomes resulting in more feedback and follow-up practice.

▌ *Jigsaw.* Students on teams become "experts" at one element or skill by working with "experts" of the same element or skill from other teams. Experts then return to their teams and teach the element or skill to their team members.

▌ *Co-op co-op.* Students work in groups to create a product; each student makes a contribution that can be evaluated. Groups present their products to the rest of the class.

The uses of cooperative learning in physical education seem unlimited for two reasons: (1) the wide variety of content areas offers an extensive knowledge base as a foundation for lessons, and (2) interactive experiences facilitate the adoption of the social values inherent to most forms of physical activity. Many physical education teachers have successfully incorporated cooperative learning strategies into their curricula. Figure 9.3 shows a cooperative learning lesson that focuses on the psychomotor domain (Dunn & Wilson, 1991).

Another popular structure is STAD, or student teams achievement divisions (Slavin, 1990). The teacher presents information on a specific topic that could involve some discussion or guided practice. Time is provided for team study of the information. Using worksheets, and working in pairs or triads, students help each other master the material. Students are tested and earn points for their team based on "gain scores" (improvement). Students are expected to make a genuine effort when establishing

Volleyball Unit

Student group activities:

- ▌ Develop offensive strategies based on group's strengths.
- ▌ Develop defensive strategies based on group's weaknesses.
- ▌ Practice and refine volleyball skills as a group.
- ▌ Videotape and critique group's volleyball skills.
- ▌ Participate as a group in a class volleyball tournament.

Group work activities:

- ▌ As a class, complete handout to identify five key points of the overhand serve.
- ▌ Briefly discuss handout; observe teacher as model.
- ▌ Assemble into groups of three; four groups are assigned to a court with two groups on a side serving across the net.
- ▌ Observer uses "five key points" handout to provide feedback.
- ▌ Groups on right side exchange with groups on left side; groups practice serving and try to hit a Hula Hoop® on the other side; groups keep track of number of successful serves.
- ▌ Groups play modified game, rotating servers after each rally.
- ▌ Groups of three meet and discuss which of the five key points was the most difficult.

▌ **Figure 9.3**　An example of a cooperative learning lesson.

initial scores. In cases in which students are clearly "faking it," their points for improvement shouldn't count.

In physical education, the sport education curriculum model (see chapter 3, pages 60-61) offers potential as a cooperative learning structure because it contains many cooperative learning features (Siedentop, 1994). Table 9.5 illustrates the "jigsaw" structure of the cooperative learning approach to interaction (Hurwitz, 1993a).

Table 9.5   "Jigsaw" Cooperative Learning Structure

Soccer outcomes		
Skills	**Knowledge**	**Attitudes and values**
Dribble	Rules	Enjoyment
Pass/kick	Defensive strategies	Helping others
Head	Offensive strategies	Responsibility
Trap	Skill analysis	Self-improvement

Step	Description
1. Introduction	Orient students to the content, objectives, and process to be used. Use motivating techniques. Form five teams according to skill level with 1 being the highest rank. Use past records or pre-tests to rank students. Distribute students as follows, after checking for racial and gender balance and adjusting accordingly: Team A: 1, 10, 11, 20, 21 Team B: 2, 9, 12, 19, 22 Team C: 3, 8, 13, 18, 23 Team D: 4, 7, 14, 17, 24 Team E: 5, 6, 15, 16, 25
2. Input	Establish "expert teams." Each expert team will be made up of one member from each of the teams. Since one expert team will work on dribbling, one on heading, one on the rules, and so on, the following strategy for forming the expert teams should be used: Put the most skilled student from each team on the expert team working on the hardest skill, the second most skilled student from each team on the expert team working on the second hardest skill, and so on. Using this strategy, the expert teams might be composed as follows: Dribbling: 1 (A), 2 (B), 3 (C), 4 (D), 5 (E) Heading: 6 (E), 7 (D), 8 (C), 9 (B), 10 (A) Trapping: 11 (A), 12 (B), 13 (C), 14 (D), 15 (E) Pass/kick: 16 (E), 17 (D), 18 (C), 19 (B), 20 (A) Rules: 21 (A), 22 (B), 23 (C), 24 (D), 25 (E)
3. Content interaction	Each expert team works together at a station to become "expert" in their skill or the rules. At each station are materials to help (printed material, posters, videotapes, films, handouts prepared by teacher). The materials focus on how to teach the skill or rules. Each station shows a schedule for when the teacher will be available to cover teaching hints and skill analysis pointers. When not involved in this activity, the teacher circulates to monitor expert team activity and help as needed. Students help each other develop greater expertise and devise teaching plans.
4. Input	Re-form teams. Assign the following roles within each team: Taskmaster: Keeps group on task; makes sure that each individual contributes. Encourager: Gets others to share ideas, give opinions, and help others; gets group to work hard. Cheerleader: Makes sure teammates know they are appreciated; has team celebrate when they make a gain. Gatekeeper: Makes sure each student has a turn and that all participate about equally. Checker: Makes sure everyone agrees with answer before group decision and that everyone understands.
5. Content interaction	Within the teams, each expert in turn teaches his skill or rules to the other team members. All of them help each other to learn and improve. The teacher circulates to monitor team progress and help as needed.

Step	Description
6. Assessment	Test skills and knowledge of rules. Each student's individual performance on the tests will count toward her own grade. But each team can earn team points according to how well the team does on each test. The following chart can be used to award team points, assuming skills on a 10-point scale and rules on a 50-point scale:

Average team score skill test	Average team score rules test	Team points
0-5	0-25	5
5.1-6	25.1-30	10
6.1-7	31.1-35	20
7.1-8	35.1-40	35
8.1-9	40.1-45	55
9.1-10	45.1-50	80

Step	Description
	At the end of the unit, team point totals can be used to reward teams with certificates, ribbons, choice of activities, notice in newsletter, picture on bulletin board, or some other appropriate reward.
7. Content interaction	Prepare for team play (modified or lead-up game). Each team is given resources to help them devise offensive and defensive strategies. The members of each team will work together, playing the roles of taskmaster, encourager, cheerleader, gatekeeper, and checker.
8. Content interaction	Teams play in some kind of tournament. Each team accumulates additional team points for their won–lost record and for a "team play rating" as recorded by the teacher. These team points are added to the points accumulated in the testing process.
9. Closure	Summative processing. Use discussion or processing forms within teams and as a large group to review the previous eight steps.
10. Closure	Reward the teams according to accumulated team points.

Accommodating Special Students

In this chapter we have established the importance of individualization. We suggested focusing on various student characteristics, such as preferred learning style, interests, abilities, and achievement level. Likewise, we justified interaction by its contributions to students' dignity, responsibility, and social development. Together, these patterns would seem to offer a sufficient set of alternatives to recognize the full range of individual differences. However, providing total equity in learning experiences is not an easy task. Chapter 2 analyzed the trends and issues of diversity, and table 2.2 (pages 41-42) identified the implications for physical education.

In reality, differences among certain students require consideration in terms of variety, adaptation, and treatment. This section will help you accommodate the needs of culturally diverse, at-risk, and gifted and talented students. We present the characteristics of each kind of student and offer suggestions for devising appropriate learning experiences. However, there is a great deal of overlap in two respects. First, culturally different students are often also at risk. Second, learning experiences that are appropriate for these "special" students are often useful for all students.

Culturally Diverse Students

As an extension of our multicultural society, multicultural education means that student differences are treated as strengths rather than as weaknesses. Regardless of cultural origin (e.g., Asian, Hispanic, African American, Native American), students deserve an equal opportunity to be physically educated. As a curriculum designer and teacher, your attitude toward culturally diverse learners makes a difference. The kinds of learning experiences you devise reflect the degree to which you accept these differences. All students expect equal opportunity, but they also have an obligation to treat others equally as they gain a multicultural perspective—a perspective intended to end prejudicial behavior and injustice (Hellison & Templin, 1991).

Minority students should not be thought of as "disadvantaged" or "culturally deprived," but rather should be seen as individuals experiencing cultural discontinuity. These students with particular sets of cultural values and norms find themselves in settings with very different values and norms (Glatthorn, 1993). For example, in physical education, an individualized and competitive group structure often predominates. This structure is contrary to the more cooperative norms of some cultures. Students from those cultures may withdraw from competition. Also, cognitive style differences (preferred ways of receiving and processing information) have been associated with culture. Students from certain cultures need to see the whole before understanding the parts. This has implications for the learning sequence of motor skills and the nature of inductive versus deductive learning experiences.

It is one thing to understand the nature of cultural discontinuity; it is another to be able to do something about it. With this in mind, we offer the following suggestions to help you provide a supportive and growth-enhancing environment for students from diverse cultural groups (Glatthorn, 1993):

- Empower students through learning experiences that involve decision making and social action skills; students from victimized groups will have higher expectations of themselves.

- Challenge students to take learning risks and expand their horizons through problem-solving tasks; don't focus unduly on the minority student's everyday world.

- Systematically vary the kinds of learning experiences. Cooperative learning has positive effects on achievement, particularly for students whose cultures emphasize group activities and peer assistance. Computer-assisted approaches are particularly effective for students lacking communication skills.

- Use alternative forms of assessment within learning experiences, such as shared responsibility (i.e., teacher and student as coevaluators) and portfolios (e.g., samples of products, logs, self-check sheets, peer criteria task sheets). Student portfolio systems can be effectively implemented throughout K-12 physical education programming as described previously in this chapter (pages 207-209).

Providing opportunities for students to share ideas and express concerns helps develop a cooperative learning environment.

At-Risk Students

The term *at-risk* identifies students who are in danger of failing to complete their education with an adequate level of skill or of dropping out of school before having achieved the skills needed for effective functioning in society. Several personal, family, school, and social factors are associated with this population: health problems, substance abuse, teen pregnancy, low self-esteem, low aspirations, suicide tendency, low socioeconomic status, single-parent homes, low parental support, neglect and abuse at home, low academic achievement, community beset with stress and conflict, unemployment, and incarceration.

Physical education teachers tend to believe that students inherently enjoy physical activity. In the case of at-risk learners, this is a faulty assumption (Sparks, 1993). The learning experiences devised by teachers often reinforce the socially maladjusted behaviors of at-risk students. Typically, in physical education, skills are developed progressively with complex levels dependent on success during early stages. At-risk learners often lack this prerequisite success because they resist common learning models. Therefore, the humanistic and social development curriculum model outlined in chapter 3 (pages 59-60), with its emphasis on self-responsibility and decision making may be helpful for at-risk learners (Hellison & Templin, 1991).

Learning deficits that are easiest to remediate are those that never occur in the first place. Although early prevention experiences are more effective than later intervention efforts (Slavin & Madden, 1989), access to effective early education programs is hardly a guarantee. In the absence of any primary prevention, some prescriptions can be suggested. The following four approaches seem to be effective in improving the performance of at-risk students (Glatthorn, 1993):

▌ *Reciprocal learning.* In this case, reciprocal learning means that students gradually assume the role of teacher. It goes beyond receiving and giving feedback by peers. The concept of "scaffolding" is advanced (a metaphor for support that is gradually removed when it is no longer needed). Emphasis is placed on the active role of the student.

▌ *Cooperative learning.* As described previously, cooperative learning has been shown to be highly effective in achieving a variety of outcomes important for at-risk students. Personal responsibility (individual accountability) and decision making are inherent to this approach.

▌ *Tutoring.* One-on-one tutoring by teachers or aides is effective for at-risk learners. Peer tutoring has also been established as an effective approach.

▌ *Use of technology.* The use of technology such as handheld and notebook computers, digital cameras, camcorders, DVDs, and CD-ROM equipment seems to be effective with at-risk learners. Technology enhances decision making through self-directed learning. Technology-assisted learning was illustrated previously as an approach to individualization.

Gifted and Talented

Traditionally, high IQ test scores indicated that students were especially talented or bright—usually labeled "gifted." However, the IQ test has been criticized because it is unreliable and invalid as a measure of intelligence, culturally biased, focused on lower mental processes, and insensitive to creativity and other types of intelligence. More recently, the concept of multiple intelligences has emerged. According to one theory (Gardner, 1993), seven independent intelligences exist: linguistic, musical, logical-mathematical, spatial, bodily-kinesthetic, interpersonal, and intrapersonal. For example, a gymnast might be gifted in bodily-kinesthetic intelligence but not in linguistic or musical intelligence.

It should be clear that this discussion on gifted students is limited to accommodations in a heterogeneous (mixed) setting; we are not addressing a segregated, special class for gifted students. Although unintentional, many physical educators discriminate in favor of highly skilled students at the expense of less skilled students. Physical educators should strive for an atmosphere of inclusion rather than an aura of elitism. We suggest that all physical educators use learning experiences that do not place gifted students at risk in their peer relationships because of special treatment or favoritism.

In the discussion of functional assessments in chapter 7, we noted that one purpose of conducting functional assessments was to reveal individual variations. Entry appraisal provides the means for identifying gifted learners. With this information, you have an obligation to devise learning experiences that will challenge gifted students in a heterogeneous setting. Glatthorn (1993) recommends two general strategies:

▌ *Accelerating the pace.* Enable gifted students to progress more rapidly through learning tasks. You may recall that pace options were described as a method of individualization. Learning modules can facilitate individual progress through self-directed tasks, contracting, programmed learning, learning activity packages, independent study, and technology-assisted learning, all of which have been covered previously.

■ *Providing for enrichment.* Devise learning experiences for gifted students that offer greater depth or breadth than regular experiences. Content options and level-of-difficulty options may be used for this purpose. Reciprocal learning can be effective if "cluster" groups are used. A small group of four to six gifted students can work together in a regular class on advanced topics or areas of special interest. Cooperative learning is beneficial to gifted students when used judiciously, ensuring that excessive use does not limit growth. The "jigsaw" structure is appropriate given the use of students as experts.

Summary

Learning experiences evoke the desired behaviors in students through the external conditions in the learning environment. They are considered valid if they create the intended outcomes—knowledge, understanding, social responses, healthy attitudes, strong values, and physical skills. All learning experiences, regardless of what they are called, contain some form of input (demonstration or explanation) and content interaction (involvement with what needs to be learned to meet objectives). Some useful criteria for selecting learning experiences include the purposes being served, abilities and interests of the students, potential for success, match with objectives, and student needs. Two broad patterns of learning experiences are individualization and interaction.

Individualized learning experiences (1) allow students to practice outcome behaviors; (2) consider students' interests, competencies, and needs;

(3) contribute to multiple outcomes such as thinking, feeling, and moving; and (4) provide positive feedback and reinforcement as a guide to learning. Teachers can foster individual pursuit of an objective by varying the pace, providing content choices, developing different approaches on the basis of difficulty, and creating learning style alternatives. Various approaches include exploration, self-directed tasks, learning packets, tutoring, independent study, and technology-assisted learning. Portfolios offer another approach to individualization that is naturalistic, authentic, and performance based.

The purpose of interaction in learning experiences is the process itself. The four critical elements, regardless of the approach, are (1) social skills (e.g., consideration for differences, respect for others, cooperation, teamwork), (2) grouping (e.g., mixed ability, status, size), (3) interdependence (e.g., shared equipment, different roles, group reward dependent on each member), and (4) accountability (i.e., each member must achieve). Various approaches include reciprocal learning, role-playing and simulation, and cooperative learning.

Although individualization and interaction patterns of learning experiences offer a full range of alternatives, other accommodations may be needed for special students characteristically known as culturally diverse, at-risk, and gifted and talented. For students from diverse cultural groups, learning experiences may involve decision making and social action skills, challenges through problem-solving tasks, various kinds of approaches, and alternative forms of assessment. At-risk students seem to respond favorably to reciprocal learning, cooperative learning, tutoring, and the use of technology. To challenge gifted students, learning experiences should be devised that accelerate the pace (e.g., self-directed tasks, contracting, learning packets) and provide for enrichment (e.g., content options, level-of-difficulty options).

Making It Work

Have you achieved the expected outcomes (see page 196) for this chapter? You should be able to devise learning experiences for the achievement-based physical education curriculum. Still, you may have some practical questions that need answers, such as the following:

■ *Why is so much attention given to the structure of learning experiences?* Physical education is known for its traditional teaching–learning sequence of demonstration, explanation, execution, and evaluation. In other words, you show students something, explain it, have them try it, and then test it. Although these steps are not wrong, they offer little opportunity for variety. Thinking in terms of alternative sources and types of input makes a more dynamic learning experience possible. Add to this the various means of content interaction, and students are more likely to show interest in physical education. If you consciously plan for how to create intended outcomes, and plan stimulating and varied opportunities, students will be more responsive.

- *How can a teacher really individualize instruction with so many different students in one class?* Developing individualized materials (e.g., contracts, learning packets, self-directed task cards, peer checklists, programmed learning guides, technology-assisted learning) is time consuming and mentally challenging. Once you build this foundation, the key becomes student self-direction and self-management. After you have created student interdependence and accountability, you will realize that the excuse of having too many students to individualize is a cop-out. Students need to be taught how to be self-directed and responsible. Once your system is in place, the high student–teacher ratios won't seem as great.

- *Does technology truly have the potential for improving learning experiences in physical education?* First, a teacher who has limited technology skill and experience may be less likely to take advantage of the technology opportunities afforded physical education. As a teaching professional, you should be competent in word processing; creating spreadsheets and graphs; creating databases; accessing and using the Internet and the World Wide Web; producing posters, banners, and awards using desktop publishing software; and creating hypermedia presentations. Second, you should recognize how technology can improve learning experiences for students. For example, various technologies provide immediate feedback during skill learning (digital and video cameras), show audiovisual instructional materials (DVD), serve as resource tools for student research (World Wide Web), serve as goal setting tools (heart rate monitors), and offer real-time data recording for authentic assessment tasks (PDA or handheld computer). Technology has become an integral part of physical education by helping manage the teacher's role, enhancing students' cognitive and skill learning, improving students' health and fitness levels, and showcasing students' learning (Hastie, 2003).

- *How can I manage physical education portfolios with so many students and so little time?* If you're going to use portfolios, don't create a system you can't manage. Pick out those aspects that fit your situation initially and then expand as you and your students become more comfortable. For example, if you're in an elementary school, first-graders might start out with only two or three parts of a portfolio. By the time they're fifth-graders, they could have what you consider to be a complete portfolio. Granted, physical education is not like a single, contained classroom. However, you can certainly create a context for portfolios. Maybe the physical education component of the student's portfolio can be kept with the classroom or homeroom teacher or within a learning resource center. By relying on technology and student self-management, you can solve, or at least reduce, many of your organization and management problems. However, students must be taught the skills of self-management. You can't just say, "Here, go do this on your own!" They need help and direction. Once you have built your system, high student–teacher ratios won't seem as great because you won't have to discipline and manage as much.

- *In physical education, will students willingly participate in some of the interaction approaches such as role-playing and cooperative learning?* Of course they will! Why not? The problem is that most students don't associate alternative patterns of interaction with physical education. They're so used to calisthenic warm-ups, followed by drills, followed by game playing that anything innovative is viewed as weird. Traditional expectations need to be broken, not just for the sake of change, but because of students' needs. It may take time to change attitudes, so start slowly, but be persistent. Physical education has been negatively stereotyped in terms of its contribution to interpersonal and social effects. You should now be able to see how progressive physical education can occur with careful planning.

- *Can the needs of all students be met given that culturally diverse, at-risk, and gifted students are all in the same class?* Many of the approaches that have been found to be effective with these groups are good for all students. Your attitude toward these "special" students makes a difference. Varying the patterns of learning experiences while keeping in mind the particular needs of these students should improve student performance. Remember, think of student differences as strengths, not weaknesses. Capitalize on diversity rather than view differences as an obstacle to reaching learning potential. Let students help decide how differences will be handled, both for their benefit and yours. The idea is to develop proactive experiences. You can build a sense of community right away through cooperative, noncompetitive games. However, you should be prepared to deal with racial or cultural remarks and disrespectful behavior. For example, you could talk to students one-on-one or in small conferences; use student mediators to handle disputes; and strictly enforce consequences for language, behavior, or clothing that is offensive for any reason (e.g., insulting to anyone's gender, race, socioeconomic status, cultural background, or ability level, whether limited or gifted).

ten

Planning for Learning and Teaching

Chandra is in second grade. She is an outgoing student who generally likes school and trying new things. Today is the start of a new unit in physical education, and Chandra is excited. She knows from the teacher's remarks at the end of the last class that they will be working on skipping. Chandra cannot skip, but she thinks she is ready this year.

At the start of class they do their normal warm-ups, and then Ms. Brown reviews the components of skipping and demonstrates what a mature skip should look like. Chandra and her friends are excited, and Chandra notes during the demonstration that Ms. Brown is really good at skipping. Chandra hopes that her skip looks like Ms. Brown's. The teacher then explains an activity that involves skipping, divides the class into groups, and tells them to go to work. During the activity Chandra tries to skip many times, but it just doesn't happen and she knows it. She looks around and sees that some of her friends can now skip, and a few others still cannot. The teacher stops the class periodically and points out a few students who are skipping well and gives some more instruction.

At the end of the class Chandra is a little disappointed. She really hoped that skipping would come this year, but it didn't. She talks with her friends after class. One friend, who can now skip, explains that it is just like magic. She could not skip last year, and this year she just tried to do what Ms. Brown demonstrated and she could suddenly skip. She adds, "Ms. Brown is the best PE teacher I ever had." Another friend agrees and says that is how she learned to gallop last year. Chandra says, "I know. I think Ms. Brown is the greatest too, but I just thought the magic was going to happen for me this year when it came to skipping."

If you were Chandra's teacher and could plan the next class on skipping, what would you do differently? What is Chandra's major obstacle? Here you have a student who is well behaved, excited about physical education, and wants to learn what you are teaching. What she does not understand is her role in learning new motor skills. She thinks they happen by magic. The teacher provided instruction and gave Chandra an opportunity to learn, but did not engage her in the learning process. Chandra does not understand how motor skills are acquired and her role in this process. She also does not blame the teacher because she thinks Ms. Brown has done what she is supposed to do. That is, she must be a good teacher because other students can skip. Because Chandra does not know what she can do to learn this skill, she just waits for the magic to happen.

EXPECTED OUTCOMES

This chapter will guide you through the decision-making processes involved in designing and creating teaching templates and student learning formats. After reading this chapter, you will be able to do the following:

1. Use student assessment data to create teaching templates and student learning formats
2. Recognize the key decisions that must be made in creating a teaching template
3. Create a teaching template
4. Develop activity lists for the objectives in your curriculum
5. Recognize the key decisions that must be made in creating a student learning format
6. Create a student learning format

The goal of this chapter is to teach you how to organize your instruction so that learning will occur. This is where you make the "magic" happen. That is, you organize how you will teach the content so that students learn and achieve the goals and objectives targeted for instruction in the curriculum. To plan at this level involves integrating what you have learned from the last four chapters. You should now know the following:

■ *What content should be taught for each grade level and within each instructional block for each grade level.* This information is identified in the yearly and block teaching and learning maps developed at the end of chapter 6 (see figures 6.11 and 6.13).

■ *How to assess the objectives targeted for instruction.* Procedures for creating objective definitions, assessment procedures, and score sheets for the objectives in the curriculum were defined in chapter 7.

■ *Your role as the teacher.* From chapter 8 you know that you need to provide a positive learning environment and use effective teaching strategies.

■ *How to design appropriate student learning experiences so that the students interact and are engaged with the content they are learning* (see chapter 9, figures 9.1 and 9.2).

Your challenge now is to integrate this information into teaching templates and student learning formats that guide your instruction and student learning when you teach. Teaching templates and student learning formats are used in place of traditional lesson plans. They highlight the importance of focusing on both teacher and student behaviors during instruction. A teaching template defines what a teacher does during implementation, and a student learning format defines what students do during instruction. Traditional lesson plans, on the other hand, address both of these functions simultaneously in one document. Because lesson plans are limited in scope, compromises are usually made in favor of a greater emphasis on teacher behaviors than on student behaviors.

Teaching Templates

Teaching templates define the overall structure and format of a lesson. The template defines all of the procedural and organizational decisions teachers make to produce an effective and positive learning environment. In most cases a teaching template can be used for more than one lesson and in some cases for an entire instructional block. One of the advantages of using teaching templates is that they provide structure and consistency to the overall instruction that is conducive to student learning and reduces the amount of lost instructional time that results from organizational and transition changes.

The first teaching template for each instructional block is an assessment template. Before you can plan what to teach on the objectives targeted for instruction, you must know what the students already know, can perform, and value as well as what they still need to learn on each objective. Therefore, the focus of the first block each year will be on assessing where the students are on the objectives targeted for instruction during that block. After the initial block, assessment of the objectives for future blocks can be integrated into each block so the information is available for planning at the start of the next block.

A teaching template can be created by addressing the following five fundamental questions, which will guide you through a series of decisions:

1. What are the standard managerial procedures?

2. What is the format of the lessons?

3. What content needs to be taught?

4. How will the content be presented and worked on?

5. How will the environment be organized for instruction?

The sample teaching template in figure 10.1 shows how these guiding questions are operationalized. There is nothing special about the format of the teaching template. What is important is that

it contains the requisite information. We encourage you to create template formats that meet your unique needs and preferences. The purpose of this section is to highlight the contents of a typical teaching template by answering the five fundamental questions.

What Are the Standard Managerial Procedures?

As discussed in chapter 8, creating a positive learning environment is a critical element in fostering student learning. All effective teachers have established rules, signals, routines, and procedures to manage the movement of individuals and groups efficiently. They also have established student behavior management systems that clearly communicate how students are expected to behave and the consequences when these expectations are not met. These standardized managerial procedures are usually established early in each program level and carried forward through each grade in the program. Usually teachers must allocate a small amount of instructional time to review these procedures at the start of the year and occasionally during the year if problems occur.

Most experienced teachers have well-established managerial procedures for their classes, but few actually write them down. This can be a serious problem when the teacher is absent and a substitute teacher is called to cover these classes. Much instructional time can be lost while the substitute teacher reinvents management procedures and the students work through these changes. As shown in the sample template in figure 10.1, these procedures can be abbreviated on the top of the form and then explained in more detail in an attachment in the teacher's working notebook (see appendix B, page 335, for the blank form). The presence of the abbreviated procedures at the top of the template communicates that the procedures exist. Substitute teachers can either refer to the attachment or use the abbreviations as a review with the class to establish that they will be following the same procedures.

What Is the Format of the Lessons?

As a teacher, the second issue you must address in creating a teaching template is the format for this block of lessons. You can define your own formats with as many or as few sections as you desire. The important thing is that you create and follow a standardized format for a block of lessons. Figure 10.1 shows a simple format with three sections: introduction, body, and closure. The primary function of the teaching template is to divide the instruction

ABC School District Teaching Template

Teacher: D. Wilson

Block: Third

Grade: Seventh

Start date: 10/20/03

Class: Ms. Jones

End date: 11/26/03

Start time: 10:15

Standard managerial procedures: See teacher workbook for standard class procedures. When students enter the gym from the locker room, they pick up their task cards and go to their assigned area and begin their stretching. Students are allowed to talk until the class begins.

Format	Objectives (minutes)	Instructional focus	Instructional cue	Learning experiences	Organization	Equipment	Transition
Introduction	Flexibility (7)	Static stretching without bouncing	"Reach and hold": shoulder reaches, sit and reach, hurdler's stretch, standing, bend and hang	Teacher directed. Teacher explains which muscles need to be stretched and warmed up for tennis. Student task cards explain what they should focus on for each stretch. Near the end teacher reviews the components of the overhead serve.	Scattered in assigned spaces	Student task cards	After stretching, students pick up rackets and balls and jog out to tennis courts.
Body	Orientation (15) Ball toss (15)	Feet position in relation to the service line Tossing the ball above head height and in a straight line	"Position" "Toss"	Teacher reviews tasks for each station. Students go to assigned stations and begin work. Two groups: Group 1 - Zach as model and Alysson, Libra, and Nick. Group 2 - Andrew as model and Juan, Maria, Erin, and Melissa. Students work on the full serve while focusing on the target components. Teacher spends 50% of time at each station assessing and providing instructional feedback.	Tennis court divided into two stations. Station 1 is on orientation and has footprints. Station 2 has a poster illustrating the correct ball toss.	10 rackets, 30 yarn balls, 30 tennis balls, 10 set of footprints	Students rotate between the stations every 5 minutes.
Closure	Orientation (2) Ball toss (2) Weight transfer (2) Racket back (2)	Review orientation and ball toss. Introduce weight transfer and racket back.	"Position" "Toss" "Weight back" "Racket back"	Students practice 10 serves while their partners give them cues. Students should position themselves close enough to the net so that 8 out of 10 serves go over the net. Move back one step when successful. Teacer assesses the students on the four target components.	Students in pairs spread around the courts on service line. Student pairing indicated on the student task cards: Alysson and Libra; Juan and Nick; Erin and Maria; Melissa, Zach, and Andrew.	10 rackets and 30 tennis balls	Students collect equipment and return to locker room. Task cards are put back in folders.

Reflections: _____

■ **Figure 10.1** Sample teaching template.

into manageable chunks. The simple example in figure 10.1 works well when the typical classes are only 30-45 minutes long. You would probably need a more complex format with several sections when block scheduling results in classes that are 90 minutes or longer.

What Content Needs to Be Taught?

The third issue to address when creating your templates is what content you will teach during this instructional block. Referring back to the end of chapter 6, you already have defined yearly and block teaching and learning maps for each of the grades you teach. Take a moment to review your own yearly and block teaching and learning maps or use the examples in figures 6.10 and 6.13. The block teaching and learning map identifies what objectives are to be worked on as well as the emphasis and the amount of instructional time each objective should receive during each block. The information from the block teaching and learning map is transferred into the "Objectives" column on the teaching template as shown in figure 10.1

How Will the Content Be Presented and Worked on?

Now that you know what objectives you are going to include in each lesson and the emphasis each should receive, the next question is how you should teach the objectives. The answer to this question involves several decisions. First and foremost, you must decide what specifically you want to focus on teaching for each objective targeted for instruction. This is an assessment-based decision, which means that you need student assessment data on each objective so that you can determine the appropriate instructional focus. In chapter 7 you developed assessment procedures for each objective in your curriculum. These procedures included conditions for administering the assessment, the creation of scoring criteria or rubrics, and the creation of a score sheet for collecting and recording the assessment data.

Figure 10.2 shows a completed sample score sheet with preassessment data for the overhead tennis serve. Note that in addition to collecting data on how the students performed the components of the serve, the score sheet also collects information on their attention, comprehension, and effort (ACE) during the assessment. These ratings provide important information about the accuracy of the assessment information collected as well as the unique learning needs of the students.

After you have collected the initial assessment data, you must review and analyze where the students are on the content to be taught and then make appropriate decisions regarding what the students need to learn next and how much they should be expected to learn during this instructional block. This is referred to as setting target learning expectations, which is important for both student and program evaluation. A simple procedure for performing this analysis is to use color highlighters. First, take one color such as yellow and highlight the next component of the objective each student should learn. Then use a second color highlighter (e.g., blue) to mark the number of components you think this student will learn during this instructional block. When setting target expectations, you should consider the student's ACE characteristics. Figure 10.3 (page 227) shows a sample score sheet for the tennis serve objective with initial and target performance expectations marked with different shading. Light gray is used to represent yellow and dark gray is used to represent blue.

Now that you have established initial and target learning expectations for each student on the score sheet, you can use this information to identify what components of the skill you should focus on in your instruction. You will also need to communicate this information to the students so they know what they are focusing on during instruction. This will be covered later in the section on student learning formats (pages 230-236).

Looking at the sample score sheet in figure 10.3, what component of the tennis serve do you believe you should focus on first? Clearly, many of the students need work on the correct orientation. This component is entered on the teaching template (figure 10.1) as an instructional focus in the section labeled "Body" under the column labeled "Instructional focus."

Once you have determined an instructional focus for a given objective, you then have to decide how you will address that focus in the lesson. This involves deciding appropriate instructional cues, your teaching method and student learning experiences (e.g., drills and games), how you will organize the class for instruction, the equipment you will need, and finally how the students will be transitioned into and out of this activity into the next phase of the lesson. Enter this information in the subsequent columns on the teaching template for each instructional focus.

On the sample teaching template (figure 10.1), the first instructional focus to be addressed in the "Body" of the lesson is correct body orientation to

ABC School District Class Performance Score Sheet—Tennis Overhead Serve

Teacher: E. Dunn

Mastery criterion: 8

Class: Third period—gold days

Start date: 02/03/03

Grade level: 8

End date: 03/14/03

Scoring rubric:
0 = not present
1 = emerging, but needs work
2 = demonstrates correct pattern consistently

ACE ratings:
a = above average
b = average
c = below average

Students	Appropriate grip (1)	Correct orientation (2)	Toss well above head (3)	Weight transfers back during toss (4)	Racket back (5)	Weight transfer forward (6)	Ball contact above head and in front of body (7)	Follow-through (8)	Attention (A)	Comprehension (C)	Effort (E)	Comments
Juan	2	0	1	0	0	0	0	0	b	b	a	Tries too hard
Zach	2	2	1	2	1	1	0	0	a	a	a	
Libra	2	0	1	0	1	0	0	0	b	b	a	
Alysson	0	0	0	0	0	0	0	0	b	c	c	Do not group with Maria
Maria	0	0	0	0	0	0	0	0	a	b	c	
Andrew	2	2	2	2	2	1	1	1	a	a	a	
Nick	2	0	0	0	0	0	0	0	b	c	c	
Erin	2	0	0	0	0	0	0	0	b	b	b	
Melissa	1	1	1	1	0	0	0	0	b	b	a	Needs to slow down

Evaluation Values

A	B	C	D	E	F

Directions: given a verbal request to serve, the student should perform an overhead serve demonstrating the correct components from behind the baseline into the service box on 2 out of 3 trials.

Administrative considerations: stand in front and to dominant side of the student to observe.

Reflections: _____

Figure 10.2 Overhead tennis serve score sheet.

ABC School District Class Performance Score Sheet—Tennis Overhead Serve

Teacher: E. Dunn

Class: Third period—gold days

Start date: 02/03/03

Grade level: 8

Mastery criterion: 8

End date: 03/14/03

Scoring rubric:
- 0 = not present
- 1 = emerging, but needs work
- 2 = demonstrates correct pattern consistently

ACE ratings:
- a = above average
- b = average
- c = below average

Students	1 Appropriate grip	2 Correct orientation	3 Toss well above head	4 Weight transfers back during toss	5 Racket back	6 Weight transfer forward	7 Ball contact above head and in front of body	8 Follow-through	A Attention	C Comprehension	E Effort	Comments	A	B	C	D	E	F
Juan	2	0	1	0	0	0	0	0	b	b	a	Tries too hard						
Zach	2	2	1	2	1	1	0	0	a	a	a							
Libra	2	0	1	0	1	0	0	0	b	b	a							
Alysson	0	0	0	0	0	0	0	0	b	c	c	Do not group with Maria						
Maria	0	0	0	0	0	0	0	0	a	b	c							
Andrew	2	2	2	2	2	1	1	1	a	a	a							
Nick	2	0	0	0	0	0	0	0	b	c	c							
Erin	2	0	0	0	0	0	0	0	b	b	b							
Melissa	1	1	1	1	0	0	0	0	b	b	a	Needs to slow down						

Evaluation values

Directions: given a verbal request to serve, the student should perform an overhead serve demonstrating the correct components from behind the baseline into the service box on two out of three trials.

Administrative considerations: stand in front and to the dominant side of the student to observe.

Reflections:

Shading key: light gray indicates the color yellow for each student's first component to be worked on. Dark gray indicates the color blue for the additional components each student is expected to learn.

■ **Figure 10.3** Sample tennis serve score sheet with initial and target performance expectations.

the service line for the overhead tennis serve. The teacher has selected the instructional cue "position" to remind the student how to perform this component. In the "Learning experiences" column the teacher has noted that she will use a lecture demonstration method to review this component. The students will then be divided into two instructional groups and assigned to stations. Based on the student assessment data, the teacher has purposefully formed the two groups and made sure each has a model (e.g., Zach and Andrew) who can demonstrate the correct performance. All the students will have task cards that specifically indicate what they should focus on for each component. Note the teacher will have set the stations up before class so that the footprints for station 1 and poster for station 2 are already in place. During the practice at the stations, the students will use yarn balls. Yarn balls are used because they do not roll or travel as far when hit so they are easier to collect and less time is lost than when chasing tennis balls.

Note that you can have multiple learning experiences for any given instructional focus. As you select your learning experiences, you must also plan and incorporate ways that allow you to continually assess and record the progress your students are making on each objective.

When it comes to selecting instructional cues and activities, do not waste time reinventing the wheel. A wealth of published resources list hundreds of activities. In fact, the bulk of many traditional physical education curricula are lists and copies of these activities. The important thing to understand at this point is how these learning experiences are used in the ABC model. You should select learning experiences based on the assessed needs of your students as a means of teaching them the components targeted for instruction. This is clearly different from just involving the students in an activity with an objective and hoping they learn something. The challenge then is not finding activities, but analyzing the activities and coding them to which components of the objectives they best complement. This is an area in which a wealth of teaching knowledge is frequently underutilized or wasted completely.

Many experienced teachers spend their entire careers identifying effective instructional cues and activities through trial and error. When they retire, what happens to all of this valuable information? In most cases, it leaves in the head of the teacher because none of it is written down. This can easily be prevented by using staff development time during the year for teachers to share their effective instruc-

tional cues and activities and to capture these ideas in writing so that all teachers can use them.

A simple worksheet like the example shown in figure 10.4 can be used to organize this activity. Teachers are divided into small work groups by program levels and asked to complete a worksheet on a given number of objectives. The worksheets are prepared in advance with the components of each objective listed down the left side of the worksheet. These are taken directly from the assessment score sheets created in chapter 7 (see figures 7.9 and 7.11).

For each component, teachers are asked to identify teaching cues and specific learning experiences that focus on this component. The instructional cues should be words or short phrases that communicate what the students should focus on. The learning experiences should be explained in enough detail so that other teachers can use them. If they are well-known games, only a name may be needed. If it is a unique game or drill created by a teacher, then it would need to be described in enough detail so that others can understand it and implement it. Again, do not waste time rewriting activities that already exist. If the activity is already described well somewhere, provide that reference and a photocopy of the activity. For example, when working on arm extension in the overhand throw, a teaching cue could be to "make a T with your arms before throwing." An activity could be playing the game Cleaning Out the Backyard with paper balls and a net. The net would be set high and the paper balls would be light, requiring the students to throw hard to get the balls over the net.

The worksheets are then duplicated and shared with all teachers at that level and stored in the teacher workbooks discussed in chapter 6. Each year when this activity is repeated, you can start with the previous worksheets and ask the new working groups to add to or refine the original activities. This activity can also be tied into the program evaluation activities discussed in chapter 12.

Once you have created these activity lists and coded them to the components of each objective, this part of creating the teaching template involves just reviewing the lists and selecting the instructional cues and activities that best address the assessed needs of the students. Figure 10.4 illustrates that for any given instructional focus, such as arm extension for the overhand throw, you typically have one instructional cue and multiple learning experiences (see appendix B, page 336, for the blank form). You may use one activity to introduce and review the component and highlight the instructional cue. You may then use additional activities such as

Instructional Cue and Activity Worksheet

Grade: _Seventh_

Objective: _Overhand throw_

Skill components	Instructional cues	Activities/drills/games
Eyes focused on the target, side orientation to direction of throw	Targets and footprints. "Look over your shoulder to see the target."	Throwing stations or simple relay games. Partner gives feedback.
Weight transfer to rear foot during windup; arm passes above shoulder	"Rock back." "Throw hard."	Cleaning Out the Backyard using a very high net
Near complete extension of throwing arm to the rear during windup	"Make a **T** before you throw." Put balls behind at waist level and have them reach back and grab a ball as they throw.	Any baseball game replacing batting with throwing
Weight transfer to foot opposite throwing arm as arm passes above shoulder	Footprints "Throw hard."	Cleaning Out the Backyard using a very high net
Hip-to-shoulder sequential rotation during windup and throwing	"Uncoil like a spring."	Use mirrors or video to give feedback.
Follow-through well beyond ball release toward direction of travel	Footprints. Throwing side foot should be pointing at the target after the throw.	Any baseball game replacing batting with throwing
Smooth, not mechanical or jerky, integration of above actions	Emphasize throwing hard and fast.	Any activity that provides multiple throwing trials

Figure 10.4 Sample learning experience teacher worksheet.

drills to practice this component and games to use this component in a realistic setting. You may also want to list in this box a few alternative activities in case some of your initial activities do not work out as intended.

How Will the Environment Be Organized for Instruction?

The last three columns of the teaching template (figure 10.1) provide more detailed information on how instruction will be managed. The "Organization" and "Equipment" columns are self-explanatory. You list how the students should be organized (e.g., pairs, groups, teams) and what equipment is required for the listed activity. The "Transition" column provides space to indicate how the students should be transitioned from this activity to the next one on your list. There is nothing magical about the transition activities.

The goal is to move the students from one activity to the next with the minimal amount of confusion and lost instructional time. This can involve putting away equipment or getting new equipment. You do not need to repeat the standardized management procedures already listed at the top of the teaching template. As you become more proficient, you can use these transitions to review and practice other objectives. For example, you could have students review or practice a locomotor skill as they move between two instructional stations at opposite ends of the gym.

The last component of the teaching template is space to write reflective comments. Although you should make every effort to make your teaching templates perfect, they rarely turn out that way—at least not initially. It is important to write notes on the template regarding what worked well and what did not so that you know what activities to repeat in the future and which ones to replace. It takes

It takes only a minute to note on your teaching template what worked and what did not.

only a minute to make a quick note of when an instructional cue was not effective or when a game bombed because it elicited a different performance than the one you wanted the students to focus on. Unfortunately, if you wait until the end of the year or the start of the next year, you will have forgotten much of this information and you will be prone to making the same errors again. The finished teaching templates should be stored in your working notebooks immediately behind your block teaching and learning maps for each grade.

Student Learning Formats

Now that you have a teaching template that defines what you are going to do during instruction, the next step is to identify how the students are going to interact with and learn the content being taught. The significance of this step in the planning process is that it allows you to view your instruction from the perspective of the student. The simple goal of this process is to ensure that all students know what they are doing during instruction. Although you may think that should be obvious from your teaching template, it may not be for the students unless you communicate it explicitly. The way to learn about your students' needs is through assessment. The more you work with the students, the more assess-

ment data you will collect and the more capable you will become at addressing their needs.

The purpose of the student learning format is to make sure your instruction matches the needs of the students. The format of the student learning format and how it is implemented can vary depending on the level of the students and your methodology. In the lower grades the student learning format is used to communicate the appropriate information to the students. In the upper grades the student learning format could take the form of an activity card or a student contract. Regardless of its format, a student learning format addresses the following six questions from the perspective of the student:

1. Where should I be?
2. Whom should I be working with?
3. What are my responsibilities during instruction?
4. How do I know if I am being successful?
5. What are the teacher's expectations for me?
6. What should I do if I cannot meet the teacher's expectation or when I do meet it?

Where Students Should Be

How do students know where they should be for each activity in your teaching template? Based on your student assessment data, should some students be positioned closer to the teacher during demonstrations or positioned with their backs to certain potential distractions? How will you communicate this information to the students? In the lower elementary grades you may use carpet squares or spots to make sure students are in the correct position during learning experiences. As the students get older, you will want to transfer this responsibility of positioning themselves during instruction to the students. You could do this with task cards or individual student contracts.

Whom Students Should Be Working With

How are students grouped for instruction during your learning experiences? In the absence of assessment data, the typical practice is just to divide the students into the desired number of groups by some efficient means such as counting off by numbers. However, when you have assessment data, you can use this information regarding their learning attributes, performance abilities, cognitive skills, and social abilities to guide the formation of your groups (see chapter 8, page 181). For example, if you are using learning stations as your activity, you may want to group students with similar needs at each station. Or, you may want to form groups that include a couple of students who have mastered a given component and can demonstrate it and a few students who are still working on that component.

Based on the student assessment data, you may also want to control the size of the instructional groups. A common practice is to use smaller instructional groups for students with the greatest needs so that they get more learning trials, and slightly larger groups for the higher-performing students. Groups can be formed and varied according to any combination of content interactions and learning factors as noted in figure 9.2. Take care when forming groups based on ability to avoid any stigmatization around grouping. No one wants to be in the lousy group.

Instructional grouping is a dynamic process that is ever changing as students learn and master new skills. Your job is to continually evaluate student performance and to make grouping changes as

needed to meet the learning needs of the students. Again, for lower elementary students grouping is typically controlled by the teacher. However, as the students mature, they should be given increasing responsibility for making their own grouping decisions.

Student Responsibility During Instruction

This is the most critical element of the student learning format. Think back to the scenario at the beginning of this chapter. How did Chandra think learning occurred? The purpose of the student learning format is to teach the students that they are in control of their learning and that it does not occur by magic! In other words, students need to be taught how to learn. When learning a motor skill, for example, the students need to know that all motor skills have key components that, when practiced correctly, will eventually result in being able to perform that skill. Learning a motor skill requires several pieces of information:

Higher-performing students can be placed in large groups and still learn effectively.

- What are the key components of the skill to be learned?
- Which ones can I already perform?
- Which ones do I need to work on?
- Of the ones I need to work on, which one should I work on first?
- What specifically do I need to do to perform this component correctly?
- How long should it take to learn this component if I practice it correctly?

Initially, the teacher is the source for all of this information. However, once the students are taught the process of how to learn skills, they can then begin to assume responsibility and control of their own learning. If a student understands the process and wants to learn a new skill, the first question she should ask should be, What are the key components of this skill? If a student is working on a component and not having success, he should know that he needs someone to assess him and give him feedback on what he is doing incorrectly. For students to acquire a skill, you must teach it, model it, and reinforce it.

Obviously the amount of information and degree of responsibility must be adjusted to the students' ability levels. Preschool students, for example, might be taught that each motor skill has three parts: a start, an action, and a stop. As the students mature, these generic labels for the skill components would be replaced with the specific components such as "preparatory position" or "weight transfer." The goal is not to move all of the responsibility to the students, but to create an environment in which the responsibility is shared as the students actively engage in the learning process.

How Students Know They Are Learning

The keys to efficient learning are assessment and feedback (see chapter 8, pages 192-193). All too often students actually spend the majority of their learning time practicing incorrect patterns. They think they are performing the pattern correctly and, in the absence of any feedback from the teacher, continue to perform the same pattern.

You must select learning experiences so that you are either free to assess and provide feedback or have designed activities that provide the students appropriate assessment and feedback information. Because there is only one teacher and many students, the ideal situation is to teach the students how to assess and give feedback to each other. To perform these functions, the students must know the key components of the skills, know what the desired performances look like, and be able to judge when a performance is incorrect. Whenever there is any confusion or uncertainty about the correctness of a performance, the students should be encouraged to ask you for assistance.

You can also embed assessment and feedback into your learning experiences. For example, you can put footprints on the ground to show the correct side orientation for the start, the weight transfer to the opposite foot, and the follow-through when performing an overhand throw. When performing the skill, if the students' feet do not step on the correct footprints, they know they have made an error. Again, knowing the unique learning attributes of your students from your assessment will allow you to match the appropriate instructional cues and feedback to the students' primary learning modalities.

Students have additional responsibilities with peer teaching models of instruction. Now not only are they responsible for their own learning, but they also must assume responsibility for assisting their peers. Peer teaching is not as simple as pairing the students up and telling them to help each other. Although peer teaching can be very effective, the students must have both the skills and the maturity to be peer teachers. In addition, students must also be taught how to communicate feedback to other students in a positive and supportive manner. To ensure that both students have positive learning experiences, you should use all of the assessment data that are available and make careful decisions about who to pair with whom. To implement peer teaching successfully, you must invest a tremendous amount of time and training into preparing your students to be peer teachers.

Teachers' Expectations for Students

The next factor students need for effective learning is a realistic target expectation for their learning (see chapter 8, pages 180-181). This is especially true for younger students. If the students do what you tell them to do for a given skill, how long or how many times do they have to do it before they will learn it? As a general rule, students depend on you to supply this information. If you do not, then they impose their own expectation based on their past experience, which may have a negative impact on performance.

Peer teaching is not as simple as pairing the students and telling them to help each other.

Most younger children, with limited experience learning new motor skills, tend to underestimate how long it will take to learn a new skill. As a result, they frequently become frustrated when they have not learned the skill after a few trials. At the other extreme are students who have experienced a lot of failure in trying to learn motor skills. These students envision that to learn a new skill would require an impossible number of trials, so they give up before they even try. The point here is that your job is to communicate reasonable expectations.

When selecting learning activities for students, you must also be careful about what the activity reinforces. In most cases, when teaching motor skills, the emphasis is initially on how to perform the movement correctly. Once students have learned the movement, the emphasis shifts to the products of the performance, such as accuracy and force. In tennis, for example, you would first focus on how to perform the overhead serve and then focus on hitting the ball hard or on ball placement during the serve. Unfortunately, many learning experiences focus the learners' attention on the products of performance rather than on the process of how

to perform. This produces a negative learning situation.

Consider, for example, a teacher who is working with a student on her overhand serve in tennis, particularly her weight transfer during the swing. The teacher elects to put the student on a regulation tennis court so that she sees the connection between the activity and the eventual use of this skill in the game. However, as this student practices the weight transfer during the overhand serve, what she begins to focus on is that the ball is not going over the net. To get the ball high enough to go over the net, the student starts to modify the skill until she is ultimately punching the ball with the racket. The teacher sees this pattern and comes over to find out what is going on. When he inquires, the student tells him that his method did not work and her method does because with her method the balls go over the net. Now after one day of practice this student's overhand serve is no better, and she now has to unlearn this punch serve. The mistakes this teacher made were that he didn't set a clear expectation for the student, and he selected an activity that provided inappropriate feedback.

What would you do to correct these mistakes? First, based on your knowledge of this student's ability, you would communicate an expectation of how long it should take her to learn the weight transfer while serving. You might say, for example, "It will take you a day or two before the weight transfer begins to feel comfortable while you are serving, and then it will probably take another three or four days of practice before you start to see how transferring your weight increases the power of your serve." The second thing you would probably do is change the serving activity to neutralize the knowledge-of-results feedback provided by the net. You could do this in a number of ways such as moving the student closer to the net, removing the net completely, or having the student serve to a wall. The take-home point here is that in addition to setting realistic learning expectations for your students, you must also ensure that the learning activities reinforce the appropriate aspect of their performance.

What Students Should Do When They Are Not Successful or When They Succeed

Once students know what they are supposed to be working on and have a realistic expectation of how long it should take to learn the specific task, they can play a more active role in their learning. For this to occur, however, you must create a positive and secure atmosphere in which they feel comfortable asking for assistance. Unfortunately, in many instructional situations students spend the majority of their time and effort trying to avoid being seen by the teacher. They are afraid that if the teacher sees them, she will see something they are doing wrong in their performance, and they will then have to try to fix it. If the teacher does not see them, then nothing is said and they can happily continue to do whatever it is they were doing.

There are two problems here. First, the efforts of the students are not focused on trying to learn. Second, while the students are avoiding being seen, no learning is occurring. Because you cannot be watching all of the students all of the time to determine who is succeeding and who is not, this is an area in which part of the responsibility can be shared with the students. For this to work, you must create a learning environment in which your students want your attention because they see you as a source of information that will allow them to learn and achieve their goals.

Once you have examined your instruction from the perspective of your students' needs, the last task is to organize this information into a student learning format. Again, there is nothing special about the form. Figure 10.5 displays a sample student learning format designed for the elementary level that employs a similar structure to the teaching template (see appendix B, page 337, for the blank form). Note that in this case there would be a student learning format for each part of the lesson: introduction, body, and closure. Because student learning is dynamic, you can expect to make changes to the student learning format on a daily basis. You can write minor changes right on the form, but you will need to create a new form for the next class if you make any major changes. Although you may need only one teaching template for all of your third grade classes for any given instructional block, you will need a student learning profile for each class to address their unique needs.

As teachers become more proficient in developing student learning profiles, many of them naturally gravitate toward using student task cards. A sample student task card is shown in figure 10.6 (page 236) for a tenth-grade student in a tennis instructional block. Task cards provide students with an individualized prescription for each class. Given the teacher time needed to manage these cards, they are usually used with upper elementary, middle, and high school students. In these cases, when you identify a change for the next class or reassesses the student, you just tell the student to record the information on his task card for the next class. The effective use and management of task cards requires preplanning and experience, but the benefits are usually worth it. At the end of the instructional block, you can collect all of the task cards and record the assessment information in your database.

Creating and managing teaching templates and student learning formats may initially appear to be very time consuming. However, you can save a lot of time by using a computer. For example, you can create a blank master form using the table function in your word processing program. Once you have created the master, you can easily duplicate it to make enough copies for each class. Once you have created the original template and student learning format for each class, you can simply copy and paste a lot of the information when you need new forms. Then you can make the necessary modifications on the new forms for the next class or instructional block. Between classes or after school all you need to do is pull up the appropriate form, make the necessary modifications, and then print, and you are ready for the next class.

ABC School District Student Learning Format

Teacher: D. Wilson

Block: Third

Grade: Second

Date: October 7, 2003

Class: Mrs. R. Williams

Format part: Introduction

Start time: 10:15

Groupings: Match Mary with Taeyou. Keep Jose and David apart. Other students can select their partners. Remind Virgil's partner to tap the beat on his arm.

Objective(s)	Focus	Cue	Groupings	Expectations	Feedback	Comments
Hop	Rhythm	Move to an even beat	Group students in pairs and instruct them to give each other feedback.Pair Taeyou with Mary so he has a good model of the correct pattern.Separate Jose and David. Before they start, have everyone clap to the beat. Stand near Virgil and make sure he has the beat.	Students should review their task cards and know what component to focus on. Students should do at least two laps and request specific feedback from their partners.	Specifically observe the following students and provide teacher feedback: John J., Carol, Lucy, Tanika, Melissa, Andrew, Zachary.	Check the speed of the music and slow it down if necessary to match the class' general performance levels.
Gallop	Rhythm	Move to an even beat	Keep the same pairing as for hopping. Virgil, Taeyou, and Samoan are not ready to gallop yet. Remind them that they should continue to work on their hopping during this activity. Make sure Virgil has the beat before he starts.	Students should review their task cards and know what component to focus on. Students should do at least two laps and request specific feedback from their partners.	Specifically observe and give feedback to: Leslie, Ana, Simon, Iva, Marty, Glenn, Arty, Kerry.	Check the speed of the music and slow it down if necessary to match the class' general performance levels.

Reflections: Learning activities worked well. Separate Zachary and Andew in small group activities. Add pictures to Taeyou's task card with emphasis on arm position when hopping. Give the student working with Taeyou more instruction on how to deal with his off-task behaviors.

▮ **Figure 10.5** Sample student learning format.

Physical Education Task Card

Student: Nick Reeves

Grade: Tenth

Block: Third—black

Partner: Dillon White

Date: April 1, 2004

Teacher: N. Patterson

General instructions: Do warm-ups and cool-downs with class. Work on skills for the first 40 minutes. Play games for the last 20 minutes focusing on applying skills and not on competition.

Instructional space: Court 11

Objective(s)	Focus	Cue	Expectations	Feedback	Comments
Forehand stroke	1. Putting topspin on the ball 2. Squaring shoulders and feet to net after each shot	1. "Swing low to high." 2. "Square the body."	1. Swing correctly 7 out of 10 times keeping the ball in play. 2. Get square after every shot without being prompted by partner.	Dillon will give you feedback after each shot. You need to observe Dillon's backhand and make sure he gets his racket back in time and that he transfers his weight forward when he hits the ball.	Keep the ball in play for as many strokes as possible. The goal today is to practice, not pass your partner.
Overhead serve	Tossing ball 3 feet above head and slightly in front of body	"Toss high."	Get used to the new timing. Make contact with almost complete extension of your arm on 8 out of 10 attempts.	Dillon should give you feedback on the height of your toss and the angle of your elbow when you make contact. Dillon needs work on the same component. You should give him the same type of feedback.	Your serves should generally be long rather than short and into the net. You both have a tendency to punch at the ball; you do not want to do this.

Figure 10.6 Sample student learning format using a student task card.

Summary

Many beginning teachers are a bit intimidated by the ABC implementation planning process. They wonder how they are going to pull all of this information together and then somehow communicate it to the students so they understand and learn. In fact, for most beginning teachers, there is a disconnect between what they know should be done and what they are capable of doing. Beginning teachers may create highly sophisticated teaching templates and student learning formats that would rival the quality produced by experienced teachers. However, when they go to implement them, they crash and burn. Why? Because they did not learn how to implement them.

Although how to teach is not the focus of this book, we want to emphasize that there is a progression of skills needed to become an effective teacher. As a teacher you must work through this progression and acquire the skills and experience firsthand (see chapter 8, page 187). For example, you must first have your classes under instructional control before you can teach them. When you watch experienced teachers, you rarely see them focusing on class management issues because they already have established the class management system and have the students under control. When you student teach in these classes, class management is usually not a problem because you are working within a system that has already been established and learned by the students. However, when you get your first job and go to teach your first class, you will probably find that class management is a major issue. This is true of many teaching behaviors such as assessing students or using any number of different teaching methods.

What the beginning teacher does not see is the process the experienced teachers had to go though to get to their current level. The same is true for the ABC processes. There is a lot of information to assimilate and integrate into your teaching templates and student learning formats. It is important to note at this point that teaching involves a complex set of skills all of which require a knowledge base, practice, feedback, and experience to achieve. If teaching were as simple as reading a few chapters in a book and reviewing a few examples, we would not need college preparation programs and lifelong staff development programs for teachers.

The point here is that you need to view developing your teaching skills in the same way you view your students' learning of motor skills. They do not just occur by magic. They involve a systematic process that must be planned, implemented, and continually evaluated. The second point is that you have to be realistic in your expectations of your proficiency as a teacher. Although everyone wants to be a master teacher right away, it just does not happen that way. Being a master teacher is a long-term goal that for most teachers requires years of practice and experience to obtain.

To move toward master teacher status, you could use the criteria established by the National Board of Professional Teaching Standards (1994) for physical education as your professional goals. You could then assess yourself and determine where you are in relation to achieving each goal. With this information you could systematically use your recertification credits and staff development opportunities to address your needs. More information is provided on this topic in chapter 13.

Making It Work

Have you achieved the expected outcomes (see page 222) for this chapter? You should now understand the decision-making processes involved in designing and creating teaching templates and student learning formats. Still, you may have some practical questions that need answers, such as the following:

■ *Is this detailed level of planning using both teaching templates and student learning formats really needed to be an effective physical educator?* This is a common question asked by beginning teachers particularly when they observe experienced teachers who appear to be effective and do not use lesson plans. The crux of the issue is what constitutes effective teaching. If effective teaching is defined as organizing activity so that the students are busy and happy, then the answer is probably no, you do not need detailed teaching templates and student learning formats. However, in the ABC model an effective teacher is defined as one who can use appropriate teaching strategies and create a positive learning environment so that all students achieve the objectives targeted for mastery in the curriculum. If you are responsible for ensuring that students learn specific objectives, then you must do more than just organize activities that expose them to the content. You need to assess the students' physical, motor, cognitive, and social abilities and be able to use this information to design instruction that is tailored to meet their unique learning needs.

▮ *I like the idea of peer teaching, cooperative learning, and the use of task cards and student contracts, but can kids really be trusted not to cheat?* This can be a problem if you do not implement these methods and techniques correctly. In chapter 8 we discussed creating a positive learning environment, which includes creating an atmosphere of respect and a culture of learning. If you want to transfer responsibilities for learning to students, you must first prepare them for these responsibilities and create a learning environment in which these attributes are valued. These are skills that must be assessed, taught, and mastered just like motor skills. Once your students have these skills, you can use these methods and techniques successfully, and they will make your teaching and student learning more efficient.

▮ *What happens when you are the only teacher trying to teach this way?* It is hard, but you should not use this as an excuse for not doing what you know is appropriate to meet the needs of your students. Unfortunately, many physical education teachers have not been evaluated and held accountable for the learning of their students in the past. In the absence of any external monitoring, many physical education programs have regressed from instructional programs to recreation programs. In light of the recent school reform efforts and emphasis on holding schools accountable for student learning, it is only a matter of time before physical education teachers are required to document their effectiveness. Using the ABC model planning processes will position you well for complying with these demands for accountability. It is not your job to convince or convert other teachers to use the ABC model. It is, however, your professional responsibility (see chapter 13 for more information on this topic) to share what you know with your peers when they express an interest. In the interim, use the Internet to connect with other physical educators who are using the ABC model and share your values. Use these teachers as your support group as you create your teaching templates and student learning formats.

▮ *I can buy into the concept of developing teaching plans and engaging students in learning, but how can I avoid spending so much class time on assessing the students?* There are two issues to be addressed here. First, assessing is a requirement, not an option. To design appropriate teaching templates and complementary student learning formats, you have to have accurate assessment data on the objectives to be taught. The real issue then is how you use class time during assessments. If you line the class up and assess each student one at a time while the rest of the class waits, then yes, this is poor use of class time. The alternative is not to view assessment as a separate process but instead to view it as an integral part of teaching and learning. Make sure that whenever students perform skills they are being assessed by someone so that they can receive feedback. Design your assessment activities so that they are integrated into your instruction. The time you spend on assessing is actually an investment that increases the efficiency of both teaching and learning.

PART IV

Evaluating and Communicating the Physical Education Curriculum

This final section of the book addresses three critical questions: Are the students learning and achieving the objectives targeted in the curriculum? Is the curriculum being implemented as intended? and, What are your responsibilities as a physical educator for advocating and promoting your program and the profession? Chapter 11 examines the role of student evaluation in the ABC model and how you can report evaluation data and use them to calculate student grades. Chapter 12 extends the evaluation process to the program level and looks at issues related to teacher effectiveness and how to identify and make revisions to the program. Finally, chapter 13 explores how you can use the ABC model and your evaluation data to promote your programs and your profession.

Chapter 11

Student Evaluation and Grading

Student evaluation is the process of determining and reporting the degree to which students are achieving the objectives targeted for achievement in the curriculum. In this chapter you will learn how to use your ongoing reassessment data to evaluate student progress and mastery of the objectives. You will also learn how to organize this information into meaningful reports that you can share with students and parents. Finally, we address the issue of student grading and provide examples to illustrate how you can use student evaluation data to calculate student grades.

Chapter 12

Program Evaluation

Program evaluation is designed to address three questions: (1) Is the program producing the desired results? (2) Is the program being implemented as intended? and (3) Is the program plan appropriate? In this chapter you will learn how to use student assessment and reassessment data, which you have already collected as part of your ongoing instruction, to answer these questions. Finally, you will learn how to organize and manage your student performance data so that you know how and when to make changes to your instruction and modifications to the program plan.

Chapter 13

Professionalism

The ABC model provides a blueprint for designing, implementing, and evaluating a dynamic, ever evolving physical education curriculum that is responsive to student needs as well as local, state, and national standards. For the program to be successful, you must do more than just teach your classes. You must be willing to embrace change, be a lifelong learner, and work cooperatively with others. This chapter examines the roles and responsibilities you need to fulfill to be an effective advocate for both your physical education program and your profession.

eleven

Student Evaluation and Grading

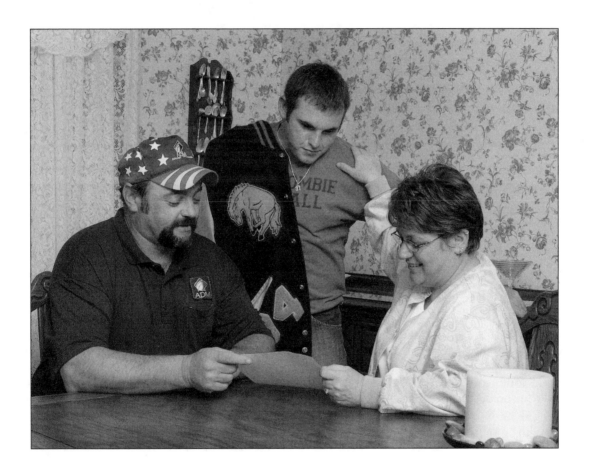

Yesterday Frank's parents received his report card and learned that he received a grade of C in physical education. Frank's parents are upset and concerned because Frank's low grades in physical education are having a negative impact on his grade point average, which they believe is going to adversely affect his chances of being admitted into the college of his choice. Unfortunately, instead of going to the physical education teacher for an explanation of how the grade was determined, the parents went directly to the superintendent and demanded an explanation. The superintendent met with the parents, acknowledged their concern, and promised to provide them with a prompt explanation of the grade within 24 hours. When the parents left, the superintendent called the principal of the high school and explained the situation. She stated that she wanted a written report explaining and justifying the grade assigned to this student in her office by 9:00 the next morning. The principal in turn contacted the physical education teacher and informed him that he would like to see the report at 8:00 before it is submitted to the superintendent.

If you were Frank's physical education teacher, what information would you provide the superintendent and principal to document the grades you have given in physical education? Would you perceive this as an opportunity to showcase your program and highlight your well-established curriculum-based evaluation system or as a potentially career-threatening encounter with your principal and superintendent? Take a moment now and write down the information you would anticipate having and being able to provide to the superintendent and principal in the morning.

EXPECTED OUTCOMES

This chapter will introduce you to student evaluation and grading and how you can use these processes to inform students and significant others about how students are progressing toward achieving the goals and objectives in the curriculum. After reading this chapter, you will be able to do the following:

1. Describe student evaluation and explain why it is an essential element of the ABC model

2. State the information that is needed for student evaluation and how this information is obtained

3. Identify the information that should be included in a student evaluation and explain why this information is relevant

4. Differentiate between student evaluation and student grading

5. Select the factors teachers should consider in determining student grades in physical education

6. Explain the role of computer technology in student evaluation and grading

---

This scenario identifies a number of important evaluation issues that will be addressed in this chapter. How should grades be determined? What should be included in physical education evaluation reports? Who should this information be communicated to? What forms of documentation should physical educators have to justify their grades? When should the information be communicated? To facilitate the presentation of the evaluation content, we have divided our discussion of evaluation into two chapters. This chapter will focus on student evaluation and grading, and chapter 12 will address program evaluation. Although presented in two chapters, it will be clear by the end of chapter 12 that evaluation is one continuous process.

As shown in the ABC model (see figure 11.1), the evaluation component informs the other components as to when and where modifications need

to be made. Student evaluation involves the process of determining and reporting the degree to which students have achieved targeted goals (see chapter 5) and corresponding instructional objectives (see chapter 6). Evaluation should be directly (explicitly) linked to (guided by) your goals and objectives. The key to student evaluation is collecting ongoing assessment data on how students are performing on the instructional objectives.

Student evaluation can be either formative or summative. Formative evaluation parallels ongoing assessment and focuses on the process and interpreting why certain results occur. For example, Ms. McKenna notices after repeated reassessments that Mary is not making any improvement in her skipping. She observes that Mary pays attention during instruction and understands what the components are that she should be working on. However, during

The Achievement-Based Curriculum Model

▌ Figure 11.1   Student evaluation is one component of the ABC model.

practice activities Ms. McKenna observes that Mary is a bit tentative and only gets in a couple of practice trials compared to the other students. As a result, Ms. McKenna decides to intervene by reorganizing the practice activities and by putting Mary in a smaller group where she will get more practice trials.

Summative evaluation, on the other hand, focuses more on the overall outcomes of instruction over time. For example, Ms. McKenna targeted on average that she expected the students in her class to learn 2 components of the skip during her instructional block. At the end of the instructional block she computes the average gain made by the class and finds that on average the class improved 2.2 components. Because this value is greater than her target expectations, she interprets this as a positive indication that her instructional block was effective.

Formative and summative evaluation should not be seen as two opposing methods but instead as two complementary forms of evaluation, each of which answers different questions. Formative evaluation should be done concurrently with ongoing assessment during instruction and should be used to make short-term instructional decisions such as whether students are receiving enough feedback or getting enough practice trials during a given activity. Summative evaluation is done periodically and is designed to address larger programmatic decisions

such as whether enough time is being allocated for a given objective to be mastered or whether students are mastering the objectives on schedule.

Assessment and Evaluation

The beauty of student evaluation is that it requires no additional information to be collected beyond what you are already collecting on a daily basis to provide effective instruction. Unfortunately, because of the time demands of recording assessment data, many teachers who are continually reassessing do not always record their assessments. Although this is understandable, we urge you to record at the minimum the students' entry-level and exit performances on each objective taught during an instructional period. We also strongly recommend, as discussed in chapter 10, that you set target expectations in terms of how much gain you expect students to make during an instructional period. Armed with these three values for each student on each objective taught, you have all of the information needed to evaluate student progress and program effectiveness and to develop a variety of meaningful evaluation reports.

Figure 11.2 shows a sample score sheet for the overhead tennis serve. The score sheet indicates where each student started on the objective (entry), the target expectations the teacher set for each student (target), and what each student had achieved

ABC School District Class Performance Score Sheet—Tennis Overhead Serve

Teacher: E. Dunn

Start date: 02/03/03   **Mastery criterion:** 8

Class: Third period—gold days

Grade level: 8   **End date:** 03/14/03

Scoring rubric:
- 0 = not present
- 1 = emerging, but needs work
- 2 = demonstrates correct pattern consistently

ACE ratings:
- a = above average
- b = average
- c = below average

Students	1 Appropriate grip	2 Correct orientation	3 Toss well above head	4 Weight transfers back during toss	5 Racket back	6 Weight transfer forward	7 Ball contact above head and in front of body	8 Follow-through	A Attention	C Comprehension	E Effort	Comments	A	B	C	D	E	F
Juan	2	2	2	2	0	0	0	0	b	b	a	Tries too hard	1	4	4	Y	N	.5
Zach	2	2	2	2	2	2	0	0	a	a	a		3	6	6	Y	N	.75
Libra	2	2	2	2	1	0	0	0	b	b	a		1	5	4	N	N	.5
Alysson	2	2	2	0	0	0	0	0	b	c	c	Do not group with Maria	0	3	3	Y	N	.38
Maria	2	2	2	0	0	0	0	0	a	b	c		0	3	3	Y	N	.38
Andrew	2	2	2	2	2	2	2	2	a	a	a		5	8	8	Y	Y	1.0
Nick	2	2	2	0	0	0	0	0	b	c	c		1	4	3	N	N	.38
Erin	2	2	2	2	2	0	0	0	b	b	b		1	5	5	Y	N	.63
Melissa	2	2	2	2	2	2	0	0	b	b	a	Needs to slow down	0	6	6	Y	N	.75

Evaluation values

Directions: given a verbal request to serve, the student should perform an overhead serve demonstrating the correct components from behind the baseline into the service box on two out of three trials.

Administrative considerations: stand in front and to the dominant side of the student to observe.

Reflections: Find new ball toss drills. This component key to other components. Correct drill is too time consuming.

A = Entry score—# of components achieved at the start of the unit
B = Target score—total # of components expected to be achieved by the end of the unit
C = Exit score—actual # of components achieved at the end of the unit
D = Target met—Yes, if exit score is ≥ target score; no, if exit score < target score
E = mastery—yes, if exit score is ≥ mastery criterion; no, if exit score < mastery criterion
F = % mastery—exit score divided by mastery criterion

Shading key: light gray indicates the color yellow for each student's first component to be worked on. Dark gray indicates the color blue for the additional components each student is expected to learn.

Figure 11.2 Sample tennis serve score sheet with entry, target, and exit scores.

The score sheet shown in figure 11.2 can be used to evaluate this student's overhead serve.

by the end of the instructional block (exit). These values are summarized in the columns on the far right of the score sheet. Note that the contents of each column are defined at the bottom of the sheet. The first three columns, "Entry," "Target," and "Exit," were just explained. The fourth column (D) contains either the letter *Y* for yes or *N* for no, indicating whether the student's exit performance level met the teacher's target expectation. The fifth column (E) also contains either *Y* or *N* depending on whether the student's exit performance level met or exceeded the mastery criterion established for the objective. The mastery criterion is listed in the top right corner of the score sheet. Finally, the last column (F) contains a percentage that indicates the mastery level the student had achieved as of this report. For example, if the mastery criterion for an objective was 8 and at the end of an instructional block a student had learned 6 of these components, her percent mastery would be 75% (i.e., 6 / 8 = .75).

When most teachers hear the term *student evaluation,* they think grading. Although these terms are related, they are not synonymous. *Evaluation* is a comprehensive term used to describe the process of interpreting performance data, reporting performance changes, and making decisions regarding what actions should be taken in response to the performance changes observed. Grading is just one example of how performance data can be reported.

A grade is a summative value used to indicate a relative measure of how the students did compared to an established set of criteria. Although a grade of A generally communicates that students did well, and a grade of F indicates they did poorly, the actual grade does not communicate what the student learned, how much progress the student made, or what areas still require more work. The same is true for numerical grades. Typically a numerical grade of 90 would be considered good, whereas a grade of 68 would be considered poor; however, neither communicates much more than a relative place on a continuum from unsatisfactory to excellent. In the ABC model we recommend that you use evaluation reports to communicate student progress and that grades can be one value included in the report if desired.

Student Evaluation Reports

Figure 11.3 shows a model student evaluation report that highlights the key components that should be included in an evaluation report (see appendix B, page 338, for the blank form). How the information is organized is up to the individual teacher. When transitioning from a pass/fail or letter grading system to progress reports, start with clear, well-documented reports. Anticipate that the initial evaluation report may seem overwhelming for some students and parents. Provide extra instructions (see figure 11.4 on page 247) with the initial reports as well as opportunities for students and parents to discuss the reports with you. Once students and parents understand how to read and interpret the reports, they will appreciate the detail and value these more comprehensive reports provide. The following sections address the essential elements you should include in a student evaluation report.

What Content Was Taught?

Although the students should know what content was taught, this is a critical piece of information to communicate to parents and others that read the report. Because only a couple of words can be used to identify each objective in the first column of the report (labeled "Objectives"), we recommend that you provide additional information that more fully describes each objective.

ABC School District Physical Education Student Evaluation Report

Student name: Brian McElroy

Grade level: 8

Number of students in class: 24

Report date: 06/10/03

Teacher: Luke Kelly

Objectives	Entry level	Target exit	Actual exit	Net change	Target met	Mastery criteria	% mastered	Class average	Teacher comments
Abdominal strength	25	35	37	12	Yes	40	92.50	31.25	Good progress—maintain program
Leg strength	8.20	7.80	7.70	0.50	Yes	7.80	100.00	8.52	Excellent
Cardiorespiratory endurance	629.00	607.00	548.00	81	Yes	600.00	100.00	713.45	Excellent
Forehand stroke	8	13	16	8	Yes	15	100.00	14.66	Excellent
Backhand stroke	6	12	12	6	Yes	15	80.00	14.41	Focus on racket preparation
Tennis serve	4	10	9	5	No	15	60.00	13.12	Focus on ball toss and slowing down
Knowledge of rules test	61.00	85.00	100	39.00	Yes	85.00	100.00	87.04	Excellent
Cooperative behavior	12	16	16	4	Yes	20	80.00	16.53	Good improvement
Tennis etiquette	8	18	20	12	Yes	20	100.00	17.65	Excellent

Figure 11.3 Model student evaluation report.

Instructions for Interpreting a Student Evaluation Report

Column heading	Explanation
1. Objectives	The first column of the report contains names or phrases used to label the objectives that were taught during this reporting period. For more detailed descriptions of the objectives, see the attached objective descriptions or consult the ABC School District Physical Education Curriculum.
2. Entry level	This column contains the student's entry performance level on each objective. Entry level indicated the performance level of the student prior to instruction. The entry level score is the basis for measuring improvement.
3. Target exit	This column contains the performance scores the teacher expects the student to achieve on each objective during this reporting period. Target achievement scores are set individually for each student.
4. Actual exit	This column contains the student's actual performance level on each objective at the end of the reporting period.
5. Net change	This column contains the difference between the student's entry and exit performance levels for each objective. This value is indicative of the amount of progress the student made on each objective during this reporting period.
6. Target met	This column contains either a yes or no depending on whether the student's actual exit performance on each objective was equal to or surpassed the target achievement score set by the teacher at the beginning of the unit for each objective.
7. Mastery criteria	This column contains the mastery criterion for each objective that has been established in the physical education curriculum that all students are expected to achieve.
8. % mastered	This column indicates what percentage of the mastery criterion the student has achieved to date on each objective. This value is calculated by dividing the student's actual exit performance score by the mastery criterion for each objective. Values over 100% are possible, but are reported as 100%.
9. Class average	This column contains the class average exit performance score for each objective. This value is provided to assist the reader in evaluating a student's performance in relation to the other students in the class. The class average exit value for each objective is the sum of the students' actual exit scores divided by the total number of students for each objective.
10. Teacher comments	This column may contain brief comments or codes provided by the teacher regarding the student's performance on the various objectives.

▌ **Figure 11.4**   Student evaluation report interpretation instructions.

Figure 11.5 shows an objective definition page that complements the student report shown in figure 11.3. Note that the first few sentences link the content in the report to the overall school physical education curriculum. The next section defines each of the objectives and how they are measured. It is critical that the unit of measure be explained. For example, the first objective in the report is abdominal strength. The description indicates that

to master this objective the student must be able to perform 40 curl-ups in 30 seconds.

You may be concerned that creating these documents will require a lot of work, but in reality you need to prepare only one of these forms for each reporting period for each grade level (assuming that the student reports are designed around the objectives for each year in the curriculum). Once you have created these documents for each year in

ABC School District Physical Education Student Evaluation Report
Description of Physical Education Objectives

The ABC School District physical education curriculum identifies 12 objectives to be mastered during the eighth grade. This report focuses on student progress on 9 of these objectives. For more information on these objectives or other objectives in the curriculum, please contact Mr. Kelly.

1. Abdominal strength (i.e., strength of the abdominal muscles) is a physical fitness objective measured by the number of curl-ups a student can perform in 30 seconds. The desired performance level of achievement (i.e., mastery) for all students is 40 curl-ups.

2. Leg strength is a physical fitness objective measured by the speed (in seconds) a student can run 50 yards. The desired level of achievement (i.e., mastery) is for all students to be able to run 50 yards in 7.8 seconds or less.

3. Cardiorespiratory endurance is a physical fitness objective designed to measure the efficiency of the heart, lungs, and circulatory system. Cardiorespiratory endurance is measured by the amount of time (in seconds) it takes a student to run a distance of one mile. The desired level of achievement (i.e., mastery) is for all students to be able to run one mile in 600 seconds (10 minutes) or less.

4. Forehand stroke is a tennis objective that is measured by whether the student demonstrates the 15 qualitative performance standards that are used to define the mature forehand tennis swing. The specific performance standards are defined in the physical education curriculum. The desired achievement level (i.e., mastery) is for all students to be able to perform all 15 standards.

5. Backhand stroke is a tennis objective that is measured by whether the student demonstrates the 15 qualitative performance standards that are used to define the mature backhand tennis swing. The specific performance standards are defined in the physical education curriculum. The desired achievement level (i.e., mastery) is for all students to be able to perform all 15 standards.

6. Overhead tennis serve is a tennis objective that is measured by whether the student demonstrates the 15 qualitative performance standards that are used to define the mature forehand tennis stroke. The specific performance standards are defined in the physical education curriculum. The desired achievement level (i.e., mastery) is for all students to be able to perform all 15 standards.

7. Knowledge of rules test is a cognitive objective designed to measure students' knowledge of the rules and strategies of the game of tennis. The test is composed of 50 multiple choice questions. Students' scores are the percentage of answers they get correct on a scale from 0 to 100. The desired level of achievement (i.e., mastery) is for all students to achieve a score of at least 85%.

8. Cooperative behavior is an affective objective designed to measure the degree to which students can work cooperatively with other students. This objective is rated on a scale with a range from 0 to 25. The desired level of achievement (i.e., mastery) is for all students to achieve a score of at least 20.

9. Tennis etiquette is a performance objective designed to measure whether students demonstrate correct tennis etiquette when they play tennis. This objective is rated on a scale with a range from 0 to 25. The desired level of achievement (i.e., mastery) is for all students to achieve a score of at least 20.

▌ **Figure 11.5** Sample objective definitions for student evaluation report.

the program, you can save them as computer files and reuse them as needed each year.

Where Was the Student Prior to Instruction?

The "Entry level" column of the report indicates where the student's performance was on each objective prior to instruction or at the start of the instructional block. These values are taken directly from the class score sheets. For example, the student in the sample report could perform 25 curl-ups in 30 seconds prior to instruction.

What Was the Student Expected to Learn During Instruction?

The "Target exit" column of the report indicates how much the teacher expected the student to learn during instruction. In chapter 10 you learned to set target expectations in terms of how much gain you expected students to make during the instructional period and to record these values on the class score sheet. These values are taken directly from the class score sheets for each objective. In the sample report in figure 11.3, the teacher expected this student to increase his abdominal strength so that he could perform 35 curl-ups in 30 seconds during this unit.

Where Was the Student's Performance at the End of Instruction?

The "Actual exit" column of the report indicates where the student's performance was on each objective at the end of instruction. These values are taken directly from the class score sheets. In the sample student progress report, this student was able to perform 37 curl-ups in 30 seconds at the end of the unit.

How Much Progress (Change) Did the Student Make?

The "Net change" column on the report indicates the difference between the student's entry and exit performances. Looking at the sample student progress report, this student's change score for abdominal strength was 12 (37 on exit – 25 on entry).

Was the Teacher's Target Expectation Met?

The "Target met" column indicates simply whether the student's progress during the instructional block

met the teacher's expectations. In the example, the teacher targeted this student to be able to do 35 curl-ups in 30 seconds. By the end of the block, the student could do 37 curl-ups in 30 seconds. Because he exceeded the teacher's expectation, the report indicates that he met the teacher's targeted achievement level as indicated by the yes.

What Are the Class-Level Expectations?

The "Mastery criteria" column indicates the performance level defined in the curriculum that all students are expected to master. For example, in the sample student report all students are expected to be able to perform 40 curl-ups in 30 seconds.

How Much Was Mastered?

The "% mastered" column indicates the amount of the objective the student has mastered to date. The student in the sample report can do 37 of the desired 40 curl-ups to date; he is currently at 92.5% mastery of this objective.

How Does the Student's Progress Compare to Others in the Class?

The "Class average" column allows you to compare the student to the other students in the class. You may or may not want to include this column in your report. Some teachers believe that student progress reports should be delimited to an individual student's performance, whereas others believe it is important to communicate how students are performing compared to the others in the class or even to other criteria such as state or national standards.

The "Class average" column indicates the average class exit performance level for each objective. This value can be compared to the student's actual exit value to see how he is doing compared to the other students. In this example, the sample student can perform 37 curl-ups and is at 92.5% mastery of this objective, whereas the rest of the class on average is performing only 31.25 curl-ups and is at only 78% mastery (31.25 / 40), indicating that this student is slightly ahead of the class.

Teacher Comments

The "Teacher comments" column is provided so that you can address any issues you have regarding the student's progress or lack thereof or to compliment the student's efforts. For example, if the student could not safely participate in class for half the instructional days because he failed to bring his sneakers, this would be important to communicate to his parents. You could also define participation as a learning objective and include it in the report.

Take a moment now to review the data in figures 11.3 and 11.5. Objectives were intentionally selected for this sample report to illustrate how to integrate different types of measurements (e.g., number of repetitions, time, qualitative components and percentiles) into a single report.

Keep in mind that the students' actual exit scores can exceed the mastery criteria. For example, the curriculum's criterion for mastery of the rules of tennis is 85%. The student in the sample report received a 100 on this test or scored 15% above the mastery criterion. In this case, his percentage mastery value would be 117.6% (100 / 85). In this sample report the program was designed to report all values equal to or greater than 100% as 100% to make the report easier to read and interpret.

Creating a Student Evaluation Report

Now that you have an idea of what student evaluation reports should look like, the next task is to learn how to produce them. These reports can be produced by following four steps.

Step 1: Collect the Necessary Information

As stated earlier in this chapter, the beauty of the ABC evaluation approach is that it uses the same information you have already collected as part of the ongoing assessment and instructional process. All of the data that are needed are already recorded on the class score sheets for each objective. The essential data are the students' entry, exit, and target performance scores for each objective taught. Assuming you have followed the recommendations presented in chapter 7 on designing your score sheets, you should already have score sheets containing these values for each objective in your curriculum.

Step 2: Organize the Information so It Can Be Manipulated

One of major reasons physical educators have traditionally done so little evaluation is that what little data we have collected has been lost in piles of paper. Although teachers can certainly produce

significant student evaluation reports by hand, the most practical solution is to harness computer technology to organize and manipulate data. Fortunately, computers are readily available in our schools today, and most come with database applications that we can use to organize data (Kelly, 1987). More information is presented at the end of this chapter on how to create databases.

The major challenge for physical educators is getting the data from the score sheets into database files so that they can then be manipulated by database management programs. Example commercial database programs that could be used are Microsoft® Access®, Microsoft® FoxPro®, StarOffice Base, and Visual dBase. The ideal solution would be to record the entry assessment data, target expectations, and exit performance data on a personal digital assistant (PDA). You could then periodically upload the data from the recording device to a computer and add them to the database.

If you do not have the luxury of the latest hand-held computer devices, you will need to be creative in how you transfer your data from paper-and-pencil score sheets into the computer. A common solution is to ask volunteers such as senior citizens, parents, or high school students (as elementary or middle school helpers) to enter the data. These volunteers must be given a little training on data entry and respecting the confidentiality of student data. Make sure you reinforce and reward the efforts of your better volunteers so they will continue to volunteer for you.

Step 3: Interpret the Performance Data in Terms of Established Criteria

Once you have entered the necessary data into a computer database, your next challenge is to manipulate them so that they can be used to answer questions. Typical questions related to student evaluation are, How much have the students learned? and, What percentage of the students have mastered a given objective? The advantage of using the computer is that it can quickly collect and sort student data and accurately calculate averages and produce percentages for entire classes in a matter of seconds. Performing these same manipulations by hand would be so time consuming that they would never get done. You can define in a report in the database the evaluation criteria that you ultimately decide to use in any given student evaluation report. Earlier in this chapter we presented the following 10 essential questions for student evaluation reports:

Using a PDA is the ideal method for recording student assessment data so it can be used for evaluation.

1. What content was taught?

2. Where was the student prior to instruction?

3. What was the student expected to learn during instruction?

4. Where was the student's performance at the end of instruction?

5. How much progress (change) did the student make?

6. Was the teacher's target expectation met?

7. What were the class-level expectations?

8. How much was mastered?

9. How does the student's progress compare to others in the class?

10. What are the teacher's comments?

You can also use the database to ask exploratory questions to better understand the progress students are making and the factors that may be influencing progress. For example, What is the relationship between student attendance and performance gains? Which students made the most and the least progress? Are there gender differences in performance on given objectives? Are classes within the same grade level performing differently from others? Questions like these are discussed in more detail in chapter 12, which addresses program evaluation. The bottom line is that once you have entered the essential data (i.e., entry, exit, and target scores) in the database, you can make any logical comparison.

Step 4: Report the Evaluation Results in a Meaningful and Informative Fashion

The final task is to present the student evaluation data in a meaningful and easy-to-interpret format. Again, what information is included in the report and how it is formatted is up to you. Database management programs will allow you to define the format of the report and decide which values to include; you can also program them to do a variety of mathematical manipulations to produce unique values as percentages and averages. Figure 11.2 shows a standard column report that is typically produced by database management programs. This same information could also be presented graphically as shown in figure 11.6.

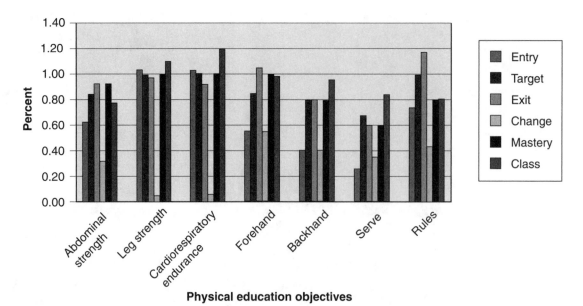

Figure 11.6   Student report presented in graphic format.

When students with disabilities are appropriately placed in physical education, everyone's needs can be addressed.

As a general rule, keep the report short (i.e., one page is ideal) and as simple as possible. Include only the information your intended audience will need. Now reflect back to the scenario presented at the beginning of this chapter. Wouldn't it be nice to be able to produce a report like the one in figure 11.3 and fax it to the principal and superintendent five minutes after they requested information about the student's grade?

We highly recommend that you file copies of each student's annual report in your school permanent folders. Occasionally, schools limit the amount of content that can be filed in the permanent folder. Although it would be worth arguing that all physical education reports should be included in the permanent file, another option is to create a cumulative report for each program level. Figure 11.7 shows a simple cumulative report that can be completed by hand and includes all of the objectives targeted for instruction for an elementary K-5 physical education program (see appendix B, page 339, for the blank form).

Many students with disabilities are included in regular physical education programs. The regular

Individual Student Cumulative Progress Report

Student: Ryan McCellan

Class: 2003

P.E. teacher: Eileen McElroy

School: Lockville Elementary

Each objective has a specific number of components. The numbers represent the number of components the student has demonstrated.

Key: Pr = Pre = number of components the student could perform before instruction.
P = Post = number of components the student could perform after instruction.
M = Mastery: y = student mastered this objective; n = student has not mastered this objective.

Objective—Name and #	1.1 Run (4)			1.2 Gallop (5)			2.1 Underhand roll (4)			4.1 Non-locomotor (5)			4.2 Body awareness (5)			4.3 Spatial awareness (3)			4.11 Changing run speed (3)		
	Pr	P	M	Pr	P	M	Pr	P	M	Pr	P	M	Pr	P	M	Pr	P	M	Pr	P	M
Grade K 1997-1998	2	4	y	2	5	y	1	4	y	2	5	y	3	5	y	1	3	y	1	3	y

Objective—Name and #	1.4 Jump (3)			1.6 Slide (3)			1.7 Skip (4)			2.3 Underhand throw (3)			4.4 Use of space (4)			4.5 Quality of movement (3)			4.10 Balance beam (4)		
	Pr	P	M	Pr	P	M	Pr	P	M	Pr	P	M	Pr	P	M	Pr	P	M	Pr	P	M
Grade 1 1998-1999	1	3	y	1	3	y	0	4	y	1	3	y	2	4	y	1	3	y	1	4	y

Objective—Name and #	1.5 Hop (4)			2.2 Bounce (4)			3.3 Flexibility (5)			3.7 Agility (6)			4.7 Forward roll (6)			4.8 Rope jump (5)			4.9 Rhythmic movement (3)		
	Pr	P	M	Pr	P	M	Pr	P	M	Pr	P	M	Pr	P	M	Pr	P	M	Pr	P	M
Grade 2 1999-2000	2	4	y	1	4	y	2	5	y	2	6	y	2	6	y	3	5	y	1	3	y

Objective—Name and #	1.8 Leap (3)			2.7 Sidearm strike (7)			2.10 Chest pass (5)			2.11 Bounce pass (6)			2.14 Overhead pass (5)			3.4 Abdominal strength (4)			3.6 Arm/shoulder strength (3)		
	Pr	P	M	Pr	P	M	Pr	P	M	Pr	P	M	Pr	P	M	Pr	P	M	Pr	P	M
Grade 3 2000-2001	1	3	y	4	7	y	2	5	y	3	6	y	2	5	y	1	4	y	1	3	y

Objective—Name and #	1.3 Horizontal jump (6)			2.4 Overhand throw (6)			2.8 Catch (5)			2.9 Underhand strike (4)			3.5 Mile run (4)			4.6 Basic dance pattern (4)					
	Pr	P	M	Pr	P	M	Pr	P	M	Pr	P	M	Pr	P	M	Pr	P	M	Pr	P	M
Grade 4 2001-2002	2	6	y	3	6	y	1	5	y	1	4	y	2	4	y	2	4	y			

Objective—Name and #	2.5 Kick (6)			2.6 Punt (6)			2.12 Forehand strike (7)			2.13 Soccer dribble (5)			3.1 Knowledge of physical fitness (13)			3.2 Fitness concepts (13)					
	Pr	P	M	Pr	P	M	Pr	P	M	Pr	P	M	Pr	P	M	Pr	P	M	Pr	P	M
Grade 5 2002-2003	3	6	y	2	6	y	1	7	y	3	5	y	7	13	y	4	13	y			

Figure 11.7 Sample cumulative progress report for an elementary program.

physical education curriculum and setting are appropriate for most of these students. Some special education students, however, may be placed in regular physical education settings but will work on different objectives or on a subset of the objectives the other students are working on. These students by law are required to have IEPs, which must be formally reviewed at least once a year. For these meetings committee members need data so that they can evaluate student progress, develop objectives for the next year, and determine the least restrictive environment for working on these objectives.

Given their case loads, many regular physical educators have difficulty providing IEP committees with the necessary data and attending the IEP meetings for the special education students in their classes. The same student evaluation reports discussed earlier can easily be adapted for use with special education students in physical education. In most cases only minor modifications need to be made in the objectives and possibly the mastery criteria. These reports can be used to communicate progress to the IEP committee. The committee can also easily see how this student is performing compared to the other students in the class.

Grading Students

Think back to the scenario at the beginning of this chapter. What things did you write down as the evidence and rationale you would provide the superintendent to justify the grade you had given? Most grading systems have two components: the behaviors that will be evaluated (e.g., knowledge, performance, and attitudes or values) and how each evaluated behavior will be weighted in the calculation of the final grade. Obviously, if you are using a database to manage your student evaluation data, you already have identified and defined the behaviors you will be evaluating. To convert the performance of these behaviors into a grade, all you need to do is determine how each behavior should be weighted in the final grade.

Although your initial reaction may be to just weight everything equally to avoid any additional mathematical calculations, this is not always appropriate. In most physical education units some objectives require more effort and time to learn than others do. These proportions of time and effort should be reflected in how each objective is weighted in the calculation of the final grade.

A challenge teachers face when developing a grading plan is deciding how progress and mastery should be weighted for each objective in the determination of the final grade. Figure 11.8 illustrates

the relationship between these two factors. Progress is a relative measure defined in terms of how much gain a student has made in relation to the teacher's expectations. Mastery is an absolute measure defined as a percentage of the final performance level defined in the curriculum that the student can currently demonstrate. As a general rule, an emphasis on progress favors the lower-performing students, whereas an emphasis on mastery favors the higher-performing students.

The data in figure 11.8 reveal that Maria has only one of the five required components of the volleyball set. During the unit, the teacher targeted that she should learn two additional components. At the end of the unit, she met this expectation and now has a total of three components. In terms of progress, Maria made 100% progress (two components targeted and two learned). In terms of mastery, she started at 20% mastery (i.e., she had only one of the five components) and finished at 60% mastery (i.e., she had three of the five components). Although she improved 40% (progress), she is still only at 60% mastery of this objective as it is defined in the curriculum. Maria also started relatively low on the other objectives in this unit and made good progress but mastered only one of these objectives (i.e., volleyball rules).

Figure 11.8 shows that if Maria's grades were based on just progress on these objectives, she would have an average of 92 and would earn a grade of A–. If she were graded just on mastery, she would have an average of 81 and would earn a grade of B–. Lashauna, on the other hand, has the opposite profile. She starts out with high entry scores and has very little room to show progress. If graded only on mastery, she would earn a grade of A–. However, if graded on only progress, she would earn a grade of F. The final column in figure 11.8 illustrates the impact of averaging (i.e., equally weighting) progress and mastery in the calculation of student grades. When this is done, Maria earns a grade of B–, and Lashauna earns a grade of C.

The purpose of this example is to illustrate that the way factors are weighted when calculating student grades can have a dramatic impact on the grades obtained. Because mastery is defined in the objective, it functions as an absolute value. Grading systems based on mastery tend not to motivate low-performing students because these students do not believe they can reach these standards. On the other hand, mastery grading systems may also not adequately motivate high-performing students because many will start the unit with a high or passing grade. Progress-based grading systems are more relative and based on teacher judgments.

Student: Maria

Objective	Entry	Target	Exit	Mastery criteria	% progress	% mastery	Average
Volleyball set	1	2	3	5	100	60	80
Cooperation	60	80	75	90	75	83	79
Volleyball rules	50	80	85	80	100	100	100
Average					92	81	86
Letter grade					A-	B-	B

Student: Lashauna

Objective	Entry	Target	Exit	Mastery criteria	% progress	% mastery	Average
Volleyball set	4	1	4	5	0	80	40
Cooperation	75	95	90	90	75	100	88
Volleyball rules	80	90	90	80	100	100	100
Average					58	93	76
Letter grade					F	A-	C

▌ **Figure 11.8**   The impact of considering progress and mastery in calculating student grades.

Because progress systems can be individualized, they tend to favor the low-performing students because appropriate standards can be set to match the needs and abilities of each student. Regardless of which system or combination of systems you use, you should make sure your students know how the various factors of their grades are weighted so they can allocate their effort accordingly.

A simple grading grid like those shown in figure 11.8 can be made in a computer spreadsheet program such as Microsoft® Excel® (see figure 11.9). (See appendix B, page 340, for the reproducible form.) The advantage of using a spreadsheet is that instead of putting actual values in all of the cells, some cells can contain formulas. In figure 11.9 the dark gray cells actually contain formulas, and the results of the formulas are shown in the cells. The values shown in the light gray cells are actual numbers. The advantage of using the formulas is that you can change any of the values in the light gray cells, and in less than a second all of the formulas are recalculated and the results displayed in the dotted cells. For example, if you change the percent progress (cell D4) from 50 to 20, the mastery = % (cell F4) would change from 50 to 80, and the averages in the last column would change to cell I9 = 68.00, I10 = 81.67, I11 = 100.00, and I13 = 83.22, respectively. If you want to create this spreadsheet, here are the formulas for the respective cells:

Cell	Formula
F4	$(100 - D4)$
G9	$\{[(E9 - C9) / D9] \times 100\}$
G10	$\{[(E10 - C10) / D10] \times 100\}$
G11	$\{[(E11 - C11) / D11] \times 100\}$
G13	$\{[(E13 - C13) / D13] \times 100\}$
H9	$[(E9 / F9) \times 100]$
H10	$[(E10 / F10) \times 100]$
H11	$[(E11 / F11) \times 100]$
H13	$[(E13 / F13) \times 100]$
I9	$\{[(D4 / 100) \times G9] + [(F4 / 100) \times H9]\}$
I10	$\{[(D4 / 100) \times G10] + [(F4 / 100) \times H10]\}$
I11	$\{[(D4 / 100) \times G11] + [(F4 / 100) \times H11]\}$
I13	$\{[(D4 / 100) \times G13] + [(F4 / 100) \times H13]\}$

To illustrate how grading systems affect decision making and effort, consider the following situation. Mary is a night person who really does not get in gear until around noon. She is quiet and somewhat introverted. She likes to socialize with her friends but generally is withdrawn in large groups. Mary needs to take one more course and earn a B grade or higher to raise her GPA enough to graduate. Historically, Mary has done well in classes that employ multiple choice tests and very poorly in classes that involve papers and essay type exams. The two sections of the course she needs to graduate are both offered at 8:00 A.M. on Tuesday and Thursday. One section is taught by a really dynamic professor, Dr. Riddel, who does a lot of creative activities in class. The other course is taught by Dr. Kobel, who is pretty boring and basically lectures the entire time.

Do you require any additional information, or do you already know which section of this course Mary should enroll in? What other information would be important for you to know? Do you just need to know how letter grades will be assigned? Table 11.1 shows the letter grade distributions used by each teacher. Do you now have enough information to make a decision?

What do you need to know to make an informed decision for Mary? How about the evaluation criteria for each course? You need to know what factors (i.e., assignments, activities, exams) will be used in

	A	B	C	D	E	F	G	H	I
1									
2									
3									
4			Progress=	50	Mastery=	50			
5									
6	Student A								
7		Objectives	Entry	Target	Exit	Mastery criterion	Progress	Mastery	Average
8		--------	-------	-------	-------	---------	--------	--------	--------
9		Volleyball set	1	2	3	5	100.00	60.00	80.00
10		Cooperation	60	20	75	90	75.00	83.33	79.17
11		Volleyball rules	50	30	80	80	100.00	100.00	100.00
12		--------	-------	-------	-------	---------	--------	--------	--------
13		Average					91.67	81.11	86.39
14									
15									
16									
17									

▌ **Figure 11.9** Exploring different weights for progress and mastery on final averages.

Table 11.1 Hypothetical Letter Grade Distributions for Drs. Riddel and Kobel

Dr. Riddel		Dr. Kobel	
Grade	Average	Grade	Average
A	90-100	A	92-100
B	80-89.9	B	84-91.9
C	70-79.9	C	76-83.9
D	60-69.9	D	68-75.9
F	00-59.9	F	00-67.9

the calculation of Mary's final grade and how much each contributes to the final grade. Table 11.2 shows evaluation criteria for both teachers.

Based on this information, what course section should Mary take, and how did you reach this decision? First, you assessed Mary's strengths and weaknesses, and then you compared them to the grading criteria to determine where she would do the best. Given the likelihood that Mary would oversleep and miss a number of classes, would probably not participate much in a large group, and does poorly on written work, she would probably not do as well in Dr. Riddel's class. However, because Dr. Kobel does not take credit away for missing class or not participating and evaluates solely by using multiple choice tests, Mary is likely to fare better in this class. Grading aside, which class do you think Mary might learn more in? What happens when the grading system used focuses students' efforts more on getting acceptable grades than on learning?

The point here is that evaluation criteria serve three purposes. First, they communicate to the students what the teacher values and believes is important for them to learn. Second, they communicate how students should focus their effort and attention. Third, they communicate how the factors will be combined and weighted to determine grades.

Using the previous example, what are some of the things communicated by Dr. Riddel's criteria? First, she believes students should be in class and should interact actively with the content. Second, the use of essay exams and the paper communicate that she is interested not only in the students knowing the facts but also in their being able to analyze, synthesize, and apply this information. Dr. Riddel's weighting of the criteria indicate that all of the factors are approximately of equal importance with a little more weight being given to the final exam.

Dr. Kobel's criteria communicate that she is interested primarily in the students learning factual information. Apparently, because class attendance and participation are not required, she expects that the students will be able to learn the content from other sources (i.e., class reading assignments) and not solely from her lectures. The equal weighting of the two exams and the exclusive use of multiple choice questions communicates that all of the content has approximately equal importance and that she is concerned primarily with students learning facts.

Now let's consider what we communicate to students and parents by the factors we use to evaluate performance in physical education. Reflect back to the scenario at the start of the chapter. What criteria did you write down when you were going to explain Frank's grade to the principal and superintendent?

Attendance

Prepared for class (dressed out)

Attitude

Effort

Participation

Knowledge

Performance

What do factors such as attendance, being prepared for class, attitude, or effort communicate to students and parents? How much credit do students typically receive in other subject areas such as math and science for showing up to class on time with a pen and paper and a smile on their faces? Although these factors are important for learning to occur, they are prerequisites, not objectives. It is the student's responsibility to come to class, to be dressed appropriately, and to be ready to learn.

Students are smart. If they can earn a passing or acceptable grade simply by showing up and not misbehaving, then that is what they are going to do. If the only way they can earn a passing grade is by demonstrating certain knowledge and performance on the objectives defined in the curriculum,

Table 11.2   Course Evaluation Criteria for Drs. Riddel and Kobel

Criteria	Dr. Riddel	Dr. Kobel
Attendance	15%	0%
Participation	15%	0%
Midterm	20% (essay exam)	50% (multiple choice)
Project	20% (10-page paper)	0%
Final	30% (take-home essay)	50% (multiple choice)

then that is where they will focus their efforts. Your responsibility is to make sure that your evaluation criteria match what you want your students to focus on. (Please note that attitude and effort as used in the previous example refer to subjective judgments made by the teacher. These should not be misinterpreted as being the same as the learning objectives related to attitude and persistence that are defined in the curriculum.)

To calculate and document letter and numerical grades, you must have data. Over the years, many physical education programs have stopped giving letter and numerical grades and have regressed to pass/fail, satisfactory/unsatisfactory, credit/no credit, or other simple dichotomous grading systems. Unfortunately, most schools have moved to these simple systems not because they believed they are the most appropriate to communicate progress to students and parents, but because they lacked the data needed to support more comprehensive and informative grading systems. The end result of these changes is that we have erroneously lowered the academic rigor associated with physical education. If we want to maintain our appropriate place in the overall school curriculum, we must have comparable standards and expectations for students.

Creating Database Applications

It should be clear by now that computer technology is necessary for managing student performance data and producing meaningful and professional student evaluation reports. You may also be asking yourself whether you have the computer skills needed to set up a computer database and create the reports needed for student evaluation. Do not panic; there are practical solutions to these challenges.

Database applications can be created at a number of different levels. At one extreme would be to create one district-wide database accessible to all of the physical education teachers. This centralized approach has many advantages. For example, it would require the creation of only one database application that would contain all of the curricula and student information, and this information would only need to be entered once. This database would be located on one of the school's computer servers and could be accessed by the teachers using appropriate security protocols via their school's intranet.

At the other end of the continuum is a decentralized approach in which teachers have their own databases. The advantage of the decentralized approach is that all teachers would have ready access to their data as long as they had access to their computers. The down side of this approach is that there is the potential for a lot of duplication of effort in terms of creating the individual databases. For example, each teacher would probably be responsible for entering their curriculum objectives and the descriptive information on their students into the database. This duplication of effort could be reduced by systematically creating the individual databases. For example, one basic database structure could be created and then loaded with the appropriate objectives for the different program levels (i.e., elementary, middle, and high school), thereby producing three databases. Each of these databases could then be copied and distributed to the teachers at each program level.

Where you start on the continuum from centralized to decentralized data management will be a function of your computer skills and how your school district is currently managing student performance data in other content areas. Regardless of which approach you use, the two critical tasks are defining the database structure and entering the curriculum objectives into the database. Once the database is created, the student information can be imported from existing databases. You then just need to enter your entry, target, and exit scores for each student on each objective, and you are ready to begin producing reports.

Regardless of whether you use a centralized or distributed process, it is critical that you play a major role in defining the database structure, the data entry templates, and the basic report templates. In most cases, the school district already has one or more staff members who are employed to create database applications for administrative functions. The ideal solution is to use these professionals to address your database needs. As with all computer applications, the application you get is only as good as the information you put in. What this means is that you will need to carefully explain to these programmers exactly what you want the application to do. The more detailed information you can provide them, the better-quality product they will produce.

If for some reason you cannot tap into the programmers used by the central administration, the next best approach is to find the faculty member who teaches database applications at the high school level. This faculty member may be able to use the development of the physical education database as a class project in one of the advanced computer applications courses.

In most cases, it is not an efficient use of physical educators' time to try to learn and develop these applications on their own. The physical educators' time would be better spent collecting ongoing assessment data and getting these data into the database. The creation of the database applications should be allocated to professionals who can efficiently develop these applications.

Your real challenge is getting your performance data (entry, target, and exit scores) into these database programs. Although you could enter your own data, in most cases it would be advantageous to find volunteers to assist in this process. There are usually adults in the community, particularly senior citizens, who would like to help in the local schools but do not want to interact directly with the students. These volunteers make excellent data entry individuals.

You should make, or have made by the database programmer, data entry forms. These are user-friendly applications that control how data are entered into the database. If you have ever filled out a survey or a registration form on the Internet that incorporates pull-down menus and click-on responses, you were actually using a data entry form for a database. The advantage of using a data entry form is that you can program in safety controls to make sure that key fields are completed and to check that the data entered are accurate. Another advantage of using data entry forms is that users can only enter data; they cannot access any of the other database functions.

You may find the idea of managing all of your data using a computer overwhelming. If this is the case, you can always start small and then gradually increase the amount of information you manage. One technique is to have a small group of physical educators take the responsibility for working with the other school personnel to create a database and the related forms. Once the database is available, it is introduced to all the physical educators during a summer workshop. After the workshop each teacher is responsible for managing either one grade level or one class per grade level for the coming year. Input on problems is requested from all teachers in the spring, and another workshop is held in the summer to address any identified problems. The next year, teachers are responsible for adding an additional grade. This process is repeated until all of the grades or classes are being managed.

Summary

You should now understand the role of student evaluation and how it informs the other components of the ABC model. It should be clear now that although grading is a component of student evaluation, a grade, by itself, does not communicate much meaningful information. A student progress report is a better way to communicate what content was taught, what the student was expected to learn, how much learning occurred, the degree to which the student has mastered the content, and how the student's performance compares to that of others in the class. You should also understand that although summative grades communicate little, the grading criteria used to calculate student grades communicates a lot about what you value and expect from your students. Finally, it should be apparent that to harness the power and potential of student evaluation, you must use computer technology to help you manage your data.

Making It Work

Have you achieved the expected outcomes (see page 242) for this chapter? You should now understand what is involved in student evaluation and grading and what decisions teachers must make to implement these processes. Still, you may have some practical questions that need answers, such as the following:

▌ *Are parents really going to be interested in reading physical education progress reports, and if they are, will they be able to understand them?* Parents are always interested in knowing how their children are doing, particularly when they are doing exceptionally well and when they are having problems. When dichotomous grades such as pass/fail and satisfactory/unsatisfactory are used, parents do not have much information to work with and students can frequently explain away bad grades by saying that the teacher only likes athletes. When a comprehensive student evaluation report, such as the one proposed in the ABC model, is used, both of these issues are addressed. Parents now know exactly what the students were expected to learn, where they started and where they finished, as well as how their performances compare to the established mastery standard and to those of the other students in the class. Parents may have a little difficulty interpreting the first report you send home, but after you address those issues, they will be looking forward to the next one.

- *If you grade students on progress toward achieving the objectives in the curriculum, wouldn't the more advanced students get bored?* Keeping students on task and actively engaged in learning is more a function of using assessment information and appropriate implementation planning. However, grades can serve as an extrinsic motivator for some students. In these cases, grading only on progress would probably stress these students. Remember, because these more advanced students would probably start out with many of the components of most of the objectives, they would have less room to show improvement. In some cases some of these students may have already demonstrated the mastery level at the start of the instruction block. You can challenge these students by extending the performance criteria to make the skills more challenging or by replacing the skills with more advanced skills.

- *If my school has already adopted an satisfactory/unsatisfactory grading system for physical education, do I really need to worry about student evaluation and grading?* Yes, first you need to start using student evaluation reports to supplement the current grading system. Second, you need to begin lobbying, with the other physical educators, to have the grading for physical education put on the same grading system as the other content areas. Fortunately, the student evaluation reports will provide you with all the documentation you need to demonstrate and justify to the school administration and school board that numerical and letter grades are appropriate for physical education.

- *If time is an issue in both collecting assessment data and doing all of the calculations for the student reports, could I save time by just collecting and using exit scores?* You may save a little time, but you will lose a lot of important information. If you collect only exit data, you have no way of knowing how much learning actually occurred as a result of your instruction. It may very well be that the students learned nothing, and what you have as their exit performance is the same as their entry performance. In addition, if you do not collect entry data, you will not have any information to guide the planning of your instruction or to provide students with feedback.

- *I am computer phobic. I will never be able to make all of these reports and forms, so what do I do about student evaluation and grading?* Not every teacher has to be a computer expert and independently create all of the needed reports and forms. The sensible thing to do would be for the physical education staff to get together and work on these tasks in small groups so that they can take advantage of everyone's talents. Some teachers, for example, are good at designing forms, whereas others have the computer skills to actually make them. Another option would be to learn how to use computer technology and overcome your fear of computers. You could start your evaluation efforts by making simple reports by hand and then slowly converting them to computerized forms. Because the use of technology in schools is only going to increase over time, there is no time like the present to start learning to use it so you can benefit from the advantages it provides.

twelve

Program Evaluation

As a result of economic conditions and reduced local and state tax revenues the school board is anticipating a 10 to 15% cut in their budget for next year. Although all programs are being examined, the word is that the board is particularly looking at physical education. The president of the school board has contacted you because her kids go to your school. She asks you to give a brief 10- to 15-minute presentation at the next board meeting. She stresses in her request to you that the school board knows that physical activity is important for kids. What they are interested in is evidence that the school district's physical education program is actually effective and that students are achieving and leaving with these benefits. The next school board meeting is in a week.

What information could you present on your program to convince the school board that the students in your school are achieving and leaving the program with the benefits physical education is supposed to produce? What sort of uniform and consistent information do you think you could collect from the other physical educators in your district to make a case for the overall effectiveness of the district's physical education program? How would you proceed to organize your presentation?

EXPECTED OUTCOMES

This chapter will provide you with the knowledge and tools you need to document how effective both your and the school district's overall physical education curriculum is in meeting its goals and objectives. After reading this chapter, you will be able to do the following:

1. Differentiate between student and program evaluation
2. Explain the three questions ABC evaluation is designed to answer and what actions should be taken based on these answers
3. Identify the information needed for program evaluation reports and explain how to obtain this information
4. Decide what information should be included in a program evaluation report, how it should be organized, and why it is relevant
5. Describe the role of computer technology in program evaluation

---

Is the request made by the president of the school board in the preceding scenario unrealistic? Is it unreasonable for administrators and parents to expect physical educators to provide data showing their effectiveness? Assuming that all physical education programs have some form of curriculum that indicates what content is covered in the program at the various program levels and grades, what information would be reasonable for teachers running these programs to be able to report to their consumers? Would it be unreasonable for a principal to ask at the end of a unit, year, or program level what percentage of the students achieved the grade-level benchmarks targeted for mastery in the curriculum? How many physical educators do you think could answer these questions and support their answers with data?

How are ongoing changes made to the overall physical education curriculum? Assuming that the initial curriculum was created based on the staff's best estimates, is it reasonable to assume that when the program is implemented some changes are going to be needed? For example, after implementing the curriculum, teachers may notice that students need more time to achieve some objectives at their target grade levels or that some objectives may need to be moved up or down in the curriculum to match the developmental level of the students in the program. How are these issues identified, and how are these decisions made?

These are just a few examples of the types of questions program evaluation in the ABC model is designed to address. ABC program evaluation is the process of determining and communicating program merit and areas that need to be reviewed for potential revisions. Unfortunately, formal program evaluation procedures are absent in most school physical education programs.

This is not to imply that teachers do not reflect on their teaching and the impact of their programs. Most teachers do, but this form of evaluation is typically teacher dependent, subjective, not systematic, and not based on student performance data. Most teachers can recall at the end of a year which units appeared to go well and which ones bombed. Some can remember a few activities, games, or drills that were really successful and a few that were not. But because there are usually no procedures to record this information and integrate it into the program plan, much of this information is lost each year.

The primary reason most programs do not have formal program evaluation procedures is the lack of student performance data. If teachers do not collect—at a minimum—student pre- and postperformance data on the objectives taught in the program each year, then they lack the information needed to evaluate their programs formally.

The major difference between program evaluation and student evaluation is the unit of comparison. During student evaluation, the data used are specific to an individual student and comparisons are made between the individual student's performance and established criteria such as target achievement levels or mastery performance levels. In program evaluation, the unit of comparison tends to be larger (e.g., class level, grade level). Instead of looking just at an individual student's performance, program evaluation looks for changes and trends over time on larger units such as all of the students in a class or grade level or all of the teachers working on a given objective.

Program evaluation in the ABC model is a straightforward process: The program's organization, implementation, and evaluation are based on program objectives. As discussed in chapter 11, teachers evaluate student progress to determine the degree to which stated instructional objectives are achieved. Student gain is simply the student's entry performance (preassessment) subtracted from their exit performance (postassessment). Program evaluation concerns itself with the number of students enrolled in the program and their collective gains on the objectives taught. If the proportion of gains is large enough, then the program can be said to be effective; if insufficient gains occur, then some aspect of the program is in need of revision.

Data-Based Decision Making

To determine if your program is producing the desired results, you can use the data you have already collected in your ongoing implementation of the program. The student change data you will need to determine program effectiveness are already available in your assessment and reassessment records.

Figure 12.1 shows a completed class performance score sheet (CPSS) for the overhead tennis serve. The score sheet indicates the students' actual assessment and reassessment data as well as several summative values in columns down the right side of the sheet. The first three columns reflect the students' entry performance scores (column A), target achievement scores (column B), and exit performance scores (column C). Columns D through F were discussed in chapter 11 under student evaluation. Column D indicates whether the students met their target expectations, and column E indicates whether the students have achieved mastery of the objective. Column F shows the percentage of mastery the students have achieved. This value is calculated by dividing each student's exit score by the mastery criterion for that objective.

The data in columns A through F can also be used for program evaluation. Instead of analyzing the individual student scores, program evaluation analyzes the sums of these respective values for all of the students in the class. Using this summative data, you can calculate three values to assist in program evaluation. The first of these values is class mean gain (CMG). This value is calculated by subtracting the sum of the entry scores (column G) from the sum of the exit scores (column I) and dividing the result by the total number of students in the class. This value indicates the average amount of learning that occurred during the unit. This value can be used to interpret whether the time allocated for a given objective in the program plan is appropriate.

A second indicator of program effectiveness is class average percentage of mastery (CAM). This value is calculated by dividing the sum of the percentage of mastery (column J) by the total number of students in the class. This value indicates how close or far away the class is on average from mastering the objective being evaluated. This value combined with the class mean gain value can be used to evaluate whether enough time is allocated in the program for the students to achieve mastery.

Let's assume there is a fitness objective composed of 10 components in the program that has been targeted to be mastered by working on it during two units a year for two years. After the first year, the class mean gain is 1.5 components, and the class average percentage of mastery is 3.5 components. Assuming that the students continue to progress at the same rate (i.e., 1.5 components per unit or 3.0 components per year), these values would indicate that there is probably insufficient time left in the second year for these students to master this objective. That is, if the class starts the second year at an average of 3.5 components and improves only 1.5 components in each of the units in year 2, the class will attain a total gain of 3 components in the second year. The class as a whole will complete their time on this objective at only 65% mastery (6.5 of the 10 components). Having this information after the first and second units would allow you to identify this problem and make appropriate adjustments so that the class could achieve mastery in the second year.

The third value is teacher effectiveness (TE), which indicates the teacher's effectiveness in reaching the target expectations. This value is calculated by dividing the sum of the exit scores (column I) by the sum of the target scores (column H). Although the teacher effectiveness value is a good indicator of whether the program is having the desired effect, keep in mind that this value is dependent

ABC School District Class Performance Score Sheet—Tennis Overhead Serve

Teacher: E. Dunn   **Start date:** 02/03/03   **Mastery criterion:** 8

Class: Third period—gold days   **Grade level:** 8   **End date:** 03/14/03

Scoring rubric: 0 = not present
    1 = emerging, but needs work
    2 = demonstrates correct pattern consistently

ACE ratings: a = above average
    b = average
    c = below average

Students	1 Appropriate grip	2 Correct orientation	3 Toss well above head	4 Weight transfers back during toss	5 Racket back	6 Weight transfer forward	7 Ball contact above head and in front of body	8 Follow-through	A Attention	C Comprehension	E Effort	Comments	A	B	C	D	E	F
Juan	2	2	2	2	0	0	0	0	b	b	a	Tries too hard	1	4	4	Y	N	.5
Zach	2	2	2	2	2	2	0	0	a	a	a		3	6	6	Y	N	.75
Libra	2	2	2	2	1	0	0	0	b	b	a		1	5	4	N	N	.5
Alysson	2	2	2	0	0	0	0	0	b	c	c	Do not group with Maria	0	3	3	Y	N	.38
Maria	2	2	0	2	0	0	0	0	a	b	c		0	3	3	Y	N	.38
Andrew	2	2	2	2	2	2	2	2	a	a	a		5	8	8	Y	Y	1.0
Nick	2	2	2	0	0	0	0	0	b	c	c		1	4	3	N	N	.38
Erin	2	2	2	2	2	0	0	0	b	b	b		1	5	5	Y	N	.63
Melissa	2	2	2	2	2	2	0	0	b	b	a	Needs to slow down	0	6	6	Y	N	.75
													G (12)	**H** (44)	**I** (42)			**J** (5.27)

Evaluation values

Directions: given a verbal request to serve, the student should perform an overhead serve demonstrating the correct components from behind the baseline into the service box on two out of three trials.

Administrative considerations: stand in front and to the dominant side of the student to observe.

Reflections: Find new ball toss drills. This component key to other components. Correct drill is too time consuming.

A = Entry score—# of components achieved at the start of the unit
B = Target score—total # of components expected to be achieved by the end of the unit
C = Exit score—actual # of components achieved at the end of the unit
D = Target met—yes, if exit score is ≥ target score; no, if exit score < target score
E = mastery—yes, if exit score is ≥ mastery criterion; no, if exit score < mastery criterion
Teacher effectiveness = sum of exit scores (I) / sum of target scores (H)

F = % mastery—exit score divided by mastery criterion
G = Sum of entry scores
H = Sum of target scores
I = Sum of exit scores
J = Sum of % mastery scores

Class mean gain = sum of exit scores (I) − sum of entry scores (G) / total number of students
Class average % mastery = sum of the % mastery (J) / total number of students

Shading key: light gray indicates the color yellow for each student's first component to be worked on. Dark gray indicates the color blue for the additional components each student is expected to learn.

■ Figure 12.1   A completed class performance score sheet (CPSS) with evaluation columns added.

on the teacher's ability to set appropriate target expectancy levels for each student. If the teacher consistently underestimates each student's achievement and sets a lower expectation, the effectiveness value achieved would be proportionally too high. Conversely, the opposite would occur if the teacher consistently sets expectations that are too high. The accuracy of the teacher effectiveness value can be interpreted by using it in conjunction with the class mean gain and class average percentage of mastery values. High teacher effectiveness values should be considered exemplary when they are also producing high class mean gains and high class average percentage of mastery values. Table 12.1 summarizes how these values can be calculated using the data from the class performance score sheet.

The key to successful program evaluation is the maximum use of available information. Although you can generate valuable evaluation information by using your class score sheets and simple hand calculations, there are limitations to how much evaluation you can do by hand. Clearly, using computers and database management programs will allow you to perform more timely and comprehensive evaluations of your programs. Not having access to computer technology, however, should not be used as an excuse for not doing program evaluation. If you must do evaluations by hand, systematically sample objectives across your program. You may choose, for example, to use only one class per objective for evaluation purposes and then generalize the results found for that class to all of the other classes working on the same objective.

Given the availability of computers in the schools, you should be able to harness the power of computer technology to help you in your evaluation efforts. Figure 12.2 shows a sample computer-generated class evaluation report for all of the objectives a teacher taught to one class of students (see appendix B, page 341, for the blank form).

Table 12.1   Formulas for Calculating CMG, CAM, and TE

Label description	Class mean gain (CMG)	Class average % mastery (CAM)	Teacher effectiveness (TE)
Formula	CMG = [(sum exit scores – sum entry scores) / # of students in the class]	CAM = (sum of % mastery / # of students in the class)	TE = (sum of exit scores / sum of target scores)
Column reference	CMG = (I – G) / N	CAM = (J / N)	TE = (I / H)
Example: (Values taken from figure 12.1.)	3.33 = (42 – 12) / 9	.58 = 5.27 / 9	95.45% = 42 / 44

If you must do program evaluation by hand, systematically sample objectives across your program.

ABC School District Physical Education Class Evaluation Report

Teacher: E. Dunn

Number of students in class: 32

Grade level: 8

Class: Third period—gold days

Report date: 6/10/03

Objectives	Class mean entry	Class mean target	Class mean exit	Class mean gain	% class meeting target	Mastery criteria	% class meeting mastery	Class average % mastery
Abdominal strength	25.20	35.42	37.56	12.36	90.25	40.00	75.00	93.90
Leg strength	8.20	7.91	7.80	0.40	80.36	7.60	100.00	97.40
Cardiorespiratory endurance	629.00	609.00	604.66	24.34	98.60	600.00	95.71	99.23
Forehand stroke	8.10	13.77	14.29	6.19	92.83	15.00	100.00	95.26
Backhand stroke	6.88	12.13	12.91	6.03	84.41	15.00	80.00	40.20
Tennis serve	4.79	10.32	9.98	5.19	78.26	15.00	60.00	66.53
Knowledge and rules test	61.00	85.00	100.00	39.00	100.00	85.00	100.00	100.00
Cooperative behavior	11.20	15.60	16.53	5.33	96.23	20.00	83.22	82.65
Tennis etiquette	9.12	14.02	17.65	8.53	96.71	20.00	85.69	88.26

■ **Figure 12.2** A computerized class report: one class by objectives.

This report parallels the student evaluation report discussed in chapter 11 (figure 11.3) and contains several of the same values calculated earlier in the hand-generated report. The major differences are that the computer-generated report contains all of the objectives included in a reporting period (i.e., a unit or year), each value in the report represents the class average, and two additional columns have been added: percentage of the class meeting the target and percentage of the class meeting mastery. The percentage of the class meeting target indicates the percentage of students who have achieved their individual performance levels targeted by the teacher at the start of the unit. This value is comparable to the teacher effectiveness value discussed earlier. The percentage of the class meeting mastery value represents the percentage of students in the class who have met or exceeded the mastery criterion for a given objective.

To understand how to interpret these values, let's examine the data for the first objective—abdominal strength. The data reveal that the class on average could do 25 (class mean entry) curl-ups at the start of the unit. The teacher on average targeted the class to improve by 10 curl-ups (class mean target [35] minus class mean entry [25]), and by the end of the unit the class on average had increased their number of curl-ups to 37 (class mean exit), indicating an average improvement of 12 curl-ups (class mean gain). The percentage of the class meeting target value of 90 indicates that 90% of the students met or exceeded their individual target expectations set by

the teacher. Using the mastery criterion of 40 curl-ups, it appears that only 75% of the class is currently able to do 40 or more curl-ups. The 93.90% average percentage of mastery indicates that the majority of the class is making good progress and is close to achieving the mastery criterion of 40 curl-ups.

Data-Based Program Evaluation

Now that it is clear that you can fairly easily group, analyze, and summarize student assessment and reassessment data in reports, the next issue is learning how to use this information to evaluate the program. Figure 12.3 shows the ABC model with the evaluation component highlighted. Program evaluation is necessary to identify program merit and to systematically improve the procedures of planning, implementing, and evaluating instruction. Program evaluation in the ABC model addresses three basic questions:

1. Is the program producing the desired results?
2. Is the program being implemented as intended?
3. Is the program plan appropriate?

Fortunately, you can answer most of these questions with the data you have already collected as part of your ongoing assessment process. The other data you may need can easily be collected during the course of your normal instructional routine.

The Achievement-Based Curriculum Model

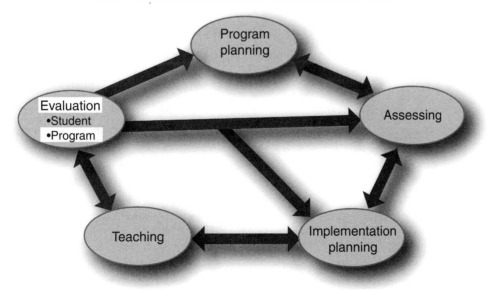

■ **Figure 12.3** Program evaluation is one component of the ABC model.

Is the Program Producing the Desired Results?

This question is concerned with student outcomes. Are the students learning the objectives targeted for each grade level, and are students leaving the program having achieved the program goals? Although this question can be examined at the teacher level, it is usually most informative when examined at the district level. If all of the student data are in one central database, you can generate this report directly from the combined data. If the student data are decentralized at the program, school, or teacher level, you could generate reports at each level and then view them collectively.

Figure 12.4 shows a sample elementary program report. The grades included in the program are listed across the top, and selected objectives to be achieved are listed down the left side. For each grade level one value is reported in the chart—the average percentage of mastery. The grade level at which each objective was targeted to be mastered is indicated by shading.

The data in figure 12.4 reveal that the students are on target for three objectives (i.e., greater than 90% of the students are shown to have mastered the target objectives by the end of the appropriate grade). The data also reveal a serious problem with one of the objectives, the skip, because only 55% of the students have demonstrated mastery by the target grade. This finding would warrant further investigation to determine the cause of this lack of

progress. The teachers could further analyze the data to determine if all teachers are having difficulty with this objective or if some teachers are experiencing success.

Figure 12.5 shows a report of teachers by objective. In this report the class data for all teachers are shown for one objective in the curriculum. In this example the objective is the forehand tennis stroke. If all teachers are found to be having difficulty, that would suggest that either more time needs to be allocated to this objective or that the objective should be placed later in the program.

The data in figure 12.4 also reveal that for one objective, the gallop, the majority of the students actually achieved this objective ahead of schedule. These data suggest that mastery for this objective could be moved earlier in the curriculum, or that some of the time allocated for this objective could be reallocated to other objectives that need more time.

Figure 12.4 illustrates just one sample report that could be generated to evaluate whether the program is producing the desired results. Using the same variables discussed earlier in the sample class report, the same grade-by-objective format shown in figure 12.4 could be used to produce reports that focus on other indicators such as average target change, average exit, average mean gain, or the percentage of students meeting target expectations. If the students are found not to be achieving one or more of the target objectives, the next step would be to examine how the program was implemented.

ABC School District Physical Education Evaluation Report
Average % Mastery by Grade and Program Objective

Report date: June 12, 2002

Total number of students: 2,321

Objectives	K	1	2	3	4	5
			Grades			
Run	96.5	100	100	100	100	100
Gallop	95.2	99.2	100	100	100	100
Hop	68.9	97.6	100	100	100	100
Skip	23.1	37.9	55.2	81.3	96.7	100

■ **Figure 12.4** Sample report of average percentage of mastery by grade and objective. Mastery targets are shaded.

ABC School District Physical Education Report
Multiple Teachers by One Objective Report

Objective: Forehand tennis stroke

Report date: 06/10/03

Number of teachers included in report: 7

Grade: Second

Total number of students: 232

Physical education teachers	Class mean entry	Class mean target	Class mean exit	Class mean gain	% class meeting target	Mastery criteria	% class meeting mastery	Class average % mastery
M. Britton	0.8	3.0	3.1	2.3	93.7	7	51.6	44.4
D. Jones	1.3	3.5	4.3	3.0	97.1	7	59.7	61.5
M. Clark	1.4	3.6	3.8	2.4	96.6	7	55.0	53.9
P. Kamide	1.3	3.9	4.1	2.8	95.6	7	58.5	58.8
J. Kowalski	0.9	3.0	3.7	2.8	84.5	7	56.1	52.6
B. Brennan	1.1	2.8	2.8	1.7	97.3	7	22.6	39.8
L. St. John	2.2	4.5	5.3	3.1	99.4	7	63.3	75.3

▌ **Figure 12.5** Sample report of teachers by objective.

Is the Program Being Implemented As Intended?

This question focuses on whether the teachers are implementing the program as defined in the program plan and their subsequent yearly and block teaching and learning maps. Common questions would be: Are the appropriate objectives being taught? Is enough time being spent on the objectives? Are appropriate instructional techniques and activities being used? and, Are students being provided with sufficient practice and feedback?

Program implementation evaluation is typically performed at the individual teacher level. This is not to imply that it cannot be done at the grade or program level. What would be different would be the focus. At the teacher level, the purpose is to identify areas in which students are not progressing as expected and then to determine why and what the teacher can do to correct the problem. At the program level, the purpose would be to identify larger problems that are shared by several teachers with the intent then of providing some form of support or assistance for these teachers such as a staff development workshop.

The initial reaction of many teachers when they view their class evaluation data and learn that their students are not progressing as expected is to blame the students. Although the students bear some of the responsibility for their own learning, particularly as they get older, they should not be used as scapegoats. It is after all the teacher's job to teach the appropriate content, organize the environment so that it is conducive to learning, and motivate the students to

learn. Barring any long-term absences or other situations that prevented students from participating in class, it should be expected that if they were there for the instruction, they should have learned.

The goal then is to identify who is not progressing as expected and then to determine why. The first step would be to generate a class evaluation report to analyze how the students are progressing. Using the class evaluation report in figure 12.2, which objective do you think the teacher needs to focus on? Look at the data for the tennis serve. This objective has the lowest average percentage of mastery of any of the objectives taught. In addition, this objective also has the lowest percentage of the class meeting their target objectives. Further review reveals that the students' entry levels and the teacher's expectations (class mean target) for the serve appear comparable to those of the other tennis objectives. However, a review of the class mean exit and class mean gain values reveals that students made much less progress on the serve.

The next step would be to review the students' actual assessment data to see if the cause of this performance deficit can be identified. Figure 12.1 shows the CPSS for the tennis serve. Take a moment to review the data and see if you can find an explanation for the lack of progress. It appears that one group of students was making progress as expected, and another group was not. The students who were not making progress appear to share a common problem: They have trouble with the toss to initiate the serve. Because an appropriate toss is needed to perform the other components of the skill, this is the component that is holding them back.

Program implementation evaluation is performed at the individual teacher level.

The teacher's job now is to go to back to her teaching templates and student learning formats and review how she addressed this component. How did she assess this component? How did she teach it? How much time did she spend on it? What activities and drills did she use? How were the students given feedback? The teacher should identify one or more things that she believes should be done differently the next time she teaches this component. She should then write these changes on the teaching template so they will be there the next time she goes to teach this unit.

Although student performance data are critical for identifying implementation problems, additional information is usually needed to find the cause and fix the problems. In the preceding tennis serve example, the teacher needs to go back and analyze her teaching templates and student learning formats. What would happen if this teacher did not have written records of what she had taught? She would have nowhere to go back to. She would probably just hope that she remembered this problem the next time she taught this objective. Odds are that when she does teach this objective again, she will not remember this problem and more than likely will teach this skill the way she did in the past, repeating the same error.

The key to avoiding this vicious cycle is to start with written teaching templates and student learning formats and then to continually modify them based on student assessment and evaluation data. Figure 12.6 shows a model teaching template. Note that all the teacher has done is write simple notes on the template so that she knows what aspects of the template to repeat and what aspects to change.

Another way to evaluate implementation problems is to examine who is having trouble learning a given objective. All data-based management programs have options that allow you to search and sort the data on selected parameters. The ability to disaggregate the data is important to any intervention process. For example, you could easily search your class data and view their performance on a given objective sorted by

▌ demographics (e.g., socioeconomics, gender, race),

▌ those who did and did not achieve their target expectations,

▌ those who are above and below a given percentage of mastery, or

▌ those who showed no improvement during the unit.

Basically, you can sort the data on any defined variable and divide them into two or more subgroups. Most database programs will also allow you to combine several variables in one sort (e.g., which students were present for all classes, met their target expectations, but are still performing at less than 50% mastery). This information tells you which students were having the greatest difficulty with a given objective and allows you to examine your teaching strategies in terms of how to specifically address the needs of these students in future lessons. If after analyzing and refining your teaching methods you still find that a majority of your students are having difficulty mastering the target objectives as scheduled, then your efforts should turn to evaluating the appropriateness of the program plan.

Is the Program Plan Appropriate?

This question is designed to look at the big picture and addresses questions such as, Should the number of objectives in the program be increased or decreased? Should the sequence or placement of any of the objectives in the program be changed? and, Are the program goals still achievable or do they need to be revised? Although implementation evaluation is primarily done at the individual teacher level, evaluation of the program plan is typically done by the entire staff collectively or by a representative subgroup of the staff. Recall that when the ABC program plan was initially developed, it was built on the experience and best estimates of the staff. As such, the initial plan was the first step in the dynamic evolution of a functional physical education curriculum. Periodic evaluation of the program plan is the process that gradually shapes and refines the program over time so that it achieves its stated goals.

Once the student performance data are in the database, you can use evaluation reports to group and organize the data in many different ways. Figure 12.7 (page 273) depicts a summary report that collectively shows how all of the students in eighth grade performed on the objectives targeted to be achieved in that grade. In this example, the values in the table represent the average of 232 students taught by seven different teachers. What does this report say about how the students in this district are doing on achieving the objectives in the program targeted to be achieved in eighth grade? Overall, they appear to be doing very well. The last two columns indicate that the majority of students have achieved mastery and the majority of the remaining students are close to achieving mastery.

ABC School District Teaching Template

Teacher: D. Wilson   **Grade:** Second   **Class:** Ms. Williams   **Start time:** 10:15

Block: Third   **Start date:** 10/07/02   **End date:** 11/21/02

Standard managerial procedures: See teacher workbook for standard class procedures. Students have assigned spots on the floor and know to go to their spots when they enter the gym. When the teacher raises her arms over her head, the students know to go to their spots. Bruce has special needs and should be kept close to the teacher so that he attends and stays on task.

Format	Objectives (time)	Instructional focus	Instructional cue	Instructional activities	Organization	Equipment	Transition
Introduction	Hop (4) Gallop (4)	Rhythm	"Move to the beat"	Teacher directed, students move around the gym. Teacher plays music with a strong, even beat. Teacher reviews components of hop and gallop, observes, and gives feedback.	Cones placed in corners of gym. Students move around outside edge of gym.	4 cones	To start, teacher gives "go" signal. At end, teacher raises arms; students go to their spots.
Body	Catch (4)	Preparatory position	"Flex" to be ready to catch	Teacher demonstrates all catch components and emphasizes the preparatory position.	On spots in front of teacher	One 8-inch playground ball	NA
	Catch (10)	Preparatory position Arms extended Hand contact Arms absorb Smooth integration	"Flex" "Reach" "Fingers" "Retract" "Fluid"	Students get task cards on teacher's signal. Cards indicate who the students work with and what each student should focus on at each station. Teacher moves around assessing and giving feedback.	Gym divided in advance into 5 stations—one for each component. Signs are posted and equipment is set up. Students signaled to change stations every 2 minutes.	Balls are at each station: one for every 2 students.	At end of 10 minutes teacher raises arms—students return to their spaces.
Closure	Catch and personal space (8)	Review catch components	"Flex" "Reach" "Fingers" "Retract" "Fluid	Play game Catching Hot Potatoes (see teaching notebook for game description). Teacher reviews and stresses respect for personal space.	Scattered formation around the gym	More balls than there are students	Arms-up signal at end. Students line up to leave from their spaces.

Reflections: Add changing directions to locomotor skills in intro. When setting up the stations, move the station focusing on prep position so it is in front of the wall with the mirrors. Prompt the students to self-check their "flex." Add a second game to the closure—8 minutes was too long for Catching Hot Potatoes.

ABC School District Physical Education Report
Grade by Curriculum Objectives

Grade: Eighth

Report date: 06/10/03

Teachers included in report: M. Britton, D. Jones, M. Clark, P. Kamide, J. Kowalski, B. Brennan, L. St. John,

Number of students in class: 232

Objectives	Class mean entry	Class mean target	Class mean exit	Class mean gain	% class meeting target	Mastery criteria	% class meeting mastery	Class average % mastery
Abdominal strength	32.10	39.24	39.64	7.54	100.0	40.00	99.54	99.11
Leg strength	8.25	7.71	7.66	0.59	97.16	7.60	99.33	99.37
Cardiorespiratory endurance	652.13	628.8	626.03	26.10	98.67	600.00	92.67	95.60
Forehand stroke	9.36	14.61	14.79	5.43	99.45	15.00	96.94	98.63
Backhand stroke	8.77	14.28	14.24	5.47	97.94	15.00	93.73	94.92
Tennis serve	8.21	14.19	14.32	6.11	98.67	15.00	95.17	95.55
Knowledge of rules test	66.39	94.57	89.60	23.21	96.61	100.00	87.29	89.67

■ **Figure 12.7** Sample report of summary grade by objectives.

Think back to the school board president's request presented in the scenario at the beginning of this chapter. Wouldn't it be nice to be able to just go to your computer and generate a report like this that you could give to the president 10 minutes after her request? You could also prepare a report that shows collectively how students are doing on more global standards and benchmarks.

The report in figure 12.5 uses the same column headings but highlights seven different teachers' class data on one program objective—the forehand tennis stroke. The physical education staff could use this type of report to facilitate staff development. For example, teachers who are having less success on this particular objective could be paired up with teachers who are having high success to discuss methods and exchange ideas.

Obviously, once the student performance data are computerized, your imagination is the only limitation regarding how you can organize the data to answer evaluation questions. Although the sample forms include the most common elements used in evaluation reports, we encourage you to define your own reports and use values that are most meaningful to you and your target audiences. In addition to evaluating student and teacher performance, you can also use evaluation data to explore a variety of issues confronting your programs. Here are some common issues faced by physical education programs that could be easily examined by defining new reports and organizing the student data accordingly:

▌ What effect does class size have on student achievement?

▌ What effect does class length (one 90-minute class versus two 45-minute classes) have on student achievement?

▌ What effect does team teaching (two classes combined with two teachers) have on student achievement?

▌ What effects do self-directed, individual, paired, or group activities have on the achievement of various objectives?

▌ What effect does different teaching environments (full versus split gyms, indoor versus outdoor, split gyms with and without dividers, etc.) have on student achievement?

These are just a few of the many evaluation questions you could begin to address once you have your student performance data computerized. The bottom line is that you can always defend your program better with data-based arguments docu-mented with professionally designed reports than you can with subjective emotional arguments.

Student performance data can be used to identify problem areas, but teacher implementation data are needed to interpret the problems and formulate solutions. Just as student performance data are collected as an integral part of the ABC assessment process, teacher implementation data should be collected as a routine part of the ABC instructional planning and teaching processes. As already discussed, some of this data can be collected by simply writing comments on the teaching template. For program evaluation we recommend that teachers be required to complete a formal evaluation form on each objective they teach each year. If the objective is taught across the entire year, they would complete it at the end of the year. If the objective is taught in a self-contained instructional block during the year, then teachers should complete the form at the end of the block. Figure 12.8 shows a sample objective evaluation worksheet (see appendix B, page 342, for the reproducible form). A form such as this would be completed by all teachers and submitted to the physical education curriculum committee for review and analysis.

Figure 12.9 (page 276) displays a second end-of-year worksheet designed to collect summary information on all of the objectives each teacher taught during the year (see appendix B, page 343, for the blank form). To complete this form, teachers would need to supply information from both their class evaluation reports and their lesson evaluations. The first column ("Objectives") lists the program blocks and related objectives scheduled for a given year. The next column indicates the total amount of time allocated for each objective in the program plan for that year. The third column indicates the amount of time spent. Data for this column are obtained from the teachers' comments recorded on either the teaching templates or the class performance score sheets. The fourth column ("Time difference") gives the difference between the planned and actual time columns. Class mean gain and class average percentage of mastery values were calculated from the class performance score sheets as depicted in figure 12.1 (page 264).

This composite of time use and student progress provides a clear picture of the program's implementation effectiveness from which strengths and weaknesses can be identified. Where expectations were met, the teachers can then attempt to refine the program so that the same results can be achieved with less time, effort, or cost. Where expectations were not met, the teachers must determine why and

ABC School District
End-of-Instruction Objective Evaluation Worksheet

Objective:_____   Teacher: _____

Time allocated in program plan: _____

Actual amount of time spent:_____

How effective do you feel you were in teaching this objective?

1	2	3	4	5
Low		Medium		High

How would you describe your students' progress on this objective?

1	2	3	4	5
Behind schedule		On schedule		Ahead of schedule

List any factors that are negatively affecting your ability to teach this objective.

_____

_____

_____

_____

_____

List any great teaching techniques or activities you use that are very effective for teaching this objective.

_____

_____

_____

_____

_____

Other comments or suggestions regarding this objective:

_____

_____

_____

_____

▍ **Figure 12.8**   End-of-instruction objective evaluation worksheet to be completed by the teachers.

ABC School District End-of-Year Objective Evaluation Worksheet

Teacher: Eileen McElroy   Program level or grade(s): Third grade

Objectives targeted for mastery this year

Objectives	Time allocated	Actual time spent	Time difference	Class mean gain	Class average % mastery
Skip	440	400	-40	100%	98%
Catch	460	500	+40	97%	95%
Self-discipline	300	250	-50	92%	94%

Objectives scheduled to be introduced or worked on

Objectives	Time allocated	Actual time spent	Time difference	Class mean gain	Class average % mastery
Overhand throw	280	310	+30	93%	65%
2-hand strike	280	300	+20	76%	58%
Cooperation	184	184	0	89%	72%

▮ Figure 12.9 End-of-year curriculum objective evaluation.

initiate appropriate changes. When the program begins to produce consistent positive results, the teachers can start a good public relations program by advertising the quality of the program. Program evaluation summary data should be reported annually to all relevant audiences (i.e., administrators, school board members, and other teachers).

We want to stress at this point that documenting needs and recording changes are the two keys to successful program evaluation. The goal of program evaluation is to identify effective practices so that they can be repeated and ineffective practices so that they can be replaced. The key is that the changes must be written down. One of the greatest wastes in our profession is that we constantly reinvent the wheel. Thousands of veteran physical education teachers have spent 30 or more years of trial and error developing and refining their "in the head" physical education programs and teaching techniques. When they retire, their programs and all their tried-and-true techniques leave with them. New teachers right out of school are typically hired to replace them, and what do they have to start with? A bottom-up curriculum developed by a curriculum committee several years earlier that no one follows. From an accounting perspective

this is a crime. School districts have invested over a million dollars in each of these veteran teachers over the course of 30 years, and they have nothing to show for it.

Program evaluation can and should also be applied to the ongoing and required annual evaluation of physical education IEPs for students with special needs. Although the achievement of the short-term objectives in the IEP for the current year were discussed in chapter 11, program evaluation would look at the students' overall performance across their objectives in relation to overall goals for their individual programs. The questions are the same as those posed at the beginning of this section for the overall physical education program: Should the number of objectives in the program be increased or decreased? Should the sequence or placement of any of the objectives in the program be changed? Are the program goals still achievable or do they need to be revised? The only difference is the scope of the program. The decisions now relate to the specific program designed to meet individual students' physical and motor needs.

Program evaluation would look at the student's performance and rate of progress over several years to determine the appropriateness of the program goals. If the student is progressing ahead of schedule, then his program goals could be expanded. If the student is progressing more slowly than expected, then there are a number of possible options. You would first need to analyze the efficacy of the instruction and make improvements where warranted. If you find that instruction is appropriate, the next option would be to see if you could increase the amount of time allocated for physical education for this student. If the student is receiving the maximum amount of time possible, then the last option would be to further delimit the program goals so that the student can achieve them based on his current rate of progress and the maximum amount of instructional time possible.

Summary

This chapter's description of program evaluation represents a marked departure from how evaluation has traditionally been addressed in physical education. Program evaluation has typically been viewed as an external process imposed on teachers by an outside group—typically the administration. As such, the evaluation is done by individuals, usually the school principal, for purposes such as completing required school staff evaluations. Although these evaluations may include a brief review of curriculum materials and observations of teachers' instruction, they are usually guided by criteria that have little bearing on the quality of the program or the teachers' ability to meet the program objectives. That is, these evaluations focus on ascriptive criteria such as the following:

▌ Organization of equipment

▌ Organization of students

▌ Discipline and control

▌ Safety

▌ Student dress

Physical education programs may be evaluated by principals based on the perceived administrative costs. Poor programs would be characterized by large numbers of parent complaints, discipline problems, or frequent student injuries. Conversely, a good program might be characterized as one in which there were no parent complaints, discipline was handled by the teacher in the gym, and there were few student injuries. Because this form of evaluation does not provide teachers with any substantive information regarding either their own effectiveness or the effectiveness of the program, teachers historically have not valued evaluation.

Program evaluation as presented here in the ABC model is designed to be a positive and proactive process that will ensure that students achieve the targeted objectives and goals in the program and that instruction is effective and efficient. Given the discrepancy between what has traditionally been done under the guise of evaluation and what is recommended by the ABC model, you should anticipate some misunderstanding and resistance when you first introduce the ABC evaluation model.

Evaluation is a powerful tool that you can use to evaluate your performance and the effectiveness of your programs and document and advertise that effectiveness to others. Although program evaluation does provide all of these benefits, you must use it and manage it wisely. We recommend that you evaluate your effectiveness for a while before you begin to advertise how good you are. Many teachers are initially surprised by their lack of effectiveness when the evaluation process starts. This should not be surprising because teachers have had little or no information in the past to help them be effective. The good news is that once teachers begin to analyze their performance, they typically tend to improve their effectiveness quickly.

Keep in mind too that evaluation data can be used for different purposes by different groups. Although the intent of evaluation in the ABC model is for it to be teacher controlled and used to improve instruction and program effectiveness, the same data can be used administratively to identify and sanction ineffective teachers or to reduce resources for programs that are not effective. Again, we suggest that you get the program evaluation system up and running and producing desirable results before advertising it publicly.

Although the district level is the most desirable level of evaluation, program evaluation can be started at any level and then slowly expanded to the district level. The goal is to start evaluating. If organizing a district-wide evaluation program is not feasible for some reason, it can be started at the individual teacher level. If evaluating all of the students on all of the objectives in a given program level is too much to handle, then start smaller. One approach would be to start in the first year just managing the data on all of the objectives for one year for one class. The one class should be in the lowest grade level for that program (i.e., kindergarten for elementary or sixth grade for middle school). The second year you could expand your evaluation to include all of the classes in the first grade level of your program and to add one class at the next grade level. Follow this progression until you have included all of the classes for all of the grades in your program.

Finally, evaluation is a process. How it is used depends on who uses it and their intentions. Evaluation by itself will not make students learn more, teachers teach better, or poor programs produce exemplary results. What a good program evaluation process will do is identify areas of merit and concern. You must be committed to analyzing and using this information to ensure student achievement of program objectives and to refine the overall program so that all students achieve the program goals.

Evaluation, unfortunately, is not always kind. It is not always easy to accept that your instruction on a given objective was not effective or that half of your instructional time for a given objective was lost because of poor class management. However, once you know this information, you have a choice. You can blame someone else or pretend that it was an unusual year and then just hope things go better next year, or you can embrace the evaluation process by analyzing your instruction and identifying and making changes. In the end, you get back what you put into the evaluation process. Given the tight economic conditions facing our schools, there will be increasing emphasis on accountability as people ask, What is the school getting for its money? The ultimate question, then, is not whether evaluation should be done, but who is going to design and implement the evaluation process that looks at your teaching and the effectiveness of your program.

Making It Work

Have you achieved the expected outcomes (see page 262) for this chapter? You should now understand what is involved in program evaluation and what decisions you must make to implement this process. Still, you may have some practical questions that need answers, such as the following:

▌ *How would program evaluation inform me that an objective was not developmentally sequenced correctly in the curriculum?* One of the features of program evaluation is that it allows you to look at big questions involving multiple factors over time. In this case, program evaluation would look at the percentage of students achieving mastery of the targeted objectives in the curriculum. If this analysis reveals that some objectives, independent of school and teacher, are consistently either being mastered early or not being mastered on schedule, then this would suggest that maybe these objectives are not appropriately developmentally sequenced in the curriculum.

▌ *When I observe a lack of gain, where should I look first for the problem?* When you produce a program evaluation report and observe a trend in your students' performance that indicates they are not learning as expected, the initial reaction is frequently to think, I wonder what is wrong with these kids? In reality, the problem and solution are usually closer to home. That is, most trends that are great enough that they involve multiple students are usually the result of an instructional problem. You need to look at factors such as how you taught this particular objective, how much time you allocated, how you grouped the students, or whether any events interfered with instruction. For example, Ms. Jubak taught the catch and throw objectives together, allocating equal amounts of time to each objective. When she ran her program evaluation report, she noted that the students in all of her classes made substantial gains on the throw, which were consistently above her expectations. However, when she viewed the catch data, she found that the students consistently did not meet her expectations. A review of teaching and learning maps and teaching templates revealed that she had allocated an equal amount of time to both objectives. In this case, the problem turned out to be working on throwing and catching together. When throwing is paired with catching, the students tend to have more success with throwing and therefore focus more on this skill. This is because throwing is initiated by the learner, and the object is projected out into space. For catching, the performance is initiated by the person throwing the ball, and the person catching must respond to this stimuli. If the person throwing the ball cannot control the force of the throw or is inaccurate, then this has a negative impact on the learning of the student doing the catching.

■ *What is the relationship among class average percentage of mastery, class mean gain, and teacher effectiveness values, and why is it recommended that all three of these values be used to evaluate a teacher's performance?* When doing program evaluation, you must summarize the data into a few values that you can use to get an overall feel for the degree to which the students are achieving the targeted objectives and whether the instruction is being implemented as intended. To this end, three values are calculated: class average percentage of mastery (CAM), class mean gain (CMG), and teacher effectiveness (TE). The CAM is an absolute indicator. This value informs teachers on average how close their students are to achieving the mastery standard set in the curriculum. Although it communicates whether the students are achieving the desired outcome, it does not communicate how much progress they have made. The CMG and TE values focus more on student progress. The CMG indicates the percentage of gain or change in the students' performance. This value is informative, but it is negatively influenced by the students' entry levels. That is, the higher you start, the less room you have to improve. The TE value indicates the ratio between the students' exit performance and what the teacher expected them to learn. This is the most subjective measure of the three because it incorporates the teacher's judgments of what students are expected or targeted to learn. If the teacher sets low expectations for the students, then this value will be falsely inflated. Although each value by itself provides useful information, if used alone it could be misinterpreted or lead to erroneous conclusions regarding the program or teacher effectiveness. However, if used in concert, these three values provide an accurate view of both student progress and teacher effectiveness.

■ *If we plan our program around the time and teaching conditions we have, how can we use evaluation data to show we need more time or smaller class sizes?* There are two strategies for responding to this question. First, you need to be able to document how effective your program can be with the resources you currently have allocated. In other words, with the time, facilities, equipment, and class sizes you currently have, you can teach a certain number of objectives, which will result in all students achieving a certain number of goals. You could then make the case that your program could do so much more for the students (i.e., they could achieve more goals) if you had more resources. A second option would be to work with your school administration and conduct a pilot study. For example, let's say you wanted to demonstrate that class size is negatively affecting achievement in physical education. You could arrange with your administration to have one class scheduled with the ideal size. You would then teach the students in that class the same content as the students in the other classes and then compare the achievement data. Ideally, you should be able to show that small class size results in greater student achievement.

■ *When using the ABC model, why is it recommended that you not immediately offer to publicly disseminate your program evaluation results?* Most physical educators are conscientious and work hard on their teaching. In the absence of evaluation data, they assume that they are effective and that their students are learning the content they have taught. When they see the potential power and potential uses of program evaluation reports for disseminating the effectiveness of their programs, they naturally get excited. This excitement can lead them to make promises to produce reports showing exemplary results before seeing the initial data. Caution is suggested here because teachers do not always achieve the results they anticipate during the first few years. As a general rule, it takes teachers two or three years of implementation to integrate the ABC assessing, planning, and teaching behaviors into their programs before they start producing the results they want. It also takes time to create the student databases and to create and refine the program evaluation reports. A more reasonable technique is to forecast that after three years of implementation, you will have the systems in place to produce these exemplary reports. If you are able to achieve the results you want to disseminate sooner, you can always start producing the reports earlier than planned.

thirteen

Professionalism

You are being considered for the job of physical education teacher in a district that has a staff of 30 physical educators. During your interview, the assistant superintendent of instruction asks you how you would go about revising the district's physical education curriculum to bring it in line with the latest national and state standards. You, of course, explain how you would use the ABC model. Soon after you are hired, the assistant superintendent asks you to conduct a three-hour inservice during the physical education staff development time scheduled at the beginning of the year. She explains that you just have to explain the ABC model so the staff can determine whether it is interested in pursuing this model for revising the physical education curriculum.

You have mixed reactions to this request. You are flattered that the assistant superintendent has asked you to do such an important presentation. On the other hand, you are apprehensive about what the veteran teachers might think of you, the new teacher right out of school showing up and telling them what they should be doing. Because you cannot think of a way to graciously turn down the assistant superintendent, you say yes. After a little reflection, you realize that this presentation will not be that bad. You just have to explain the ABC model, which the other teachers should like because it is designed to develop functional and accountable programs.

On the specified date, you give your presentation and leave some time at the end for questions. A veteran teacher, who was talking during most of your presentation, stands up and asks why the staff should waste time revising the curriculum again. He states that no one ever follows the curriculum. He has been involved in a dozen revisions over the past 25 years and is still teaching the same curriculum he has always taught; what is the difference this time? He sits down to applause from a few other teachers. Another teacher asks what are they going to get if they do all the additional work you have described related to this new model. This question gets another group of teachers complaining about how overworked and underappreciated they are by the administration. After the inservice ends, a couple of teachers come up to you and compliment you on your presentation and tell you they would like to learn more about some of the ideas you presented. They tell you not to worry about those other teachers. They do not like anything that involves change.

You have mixed emotions about the teachers' reactions. Worse yet, you know the assistant superintendent is going to call you and ask how it went. How do you explain the behavior and responses of the teachers without potentially damaging the physical education program? How would you respond to the assistant superintendent when she calls to see how the presentation went?

EXPECTED OUTCOMES

This chapter will help you understand your responsibilities as a professional physical educator. After reading this chapter, you will be able to do the following:

1. Explain how the ABC model can be used to promote your program and educate others regarding the benefits of a functional physical education curriculum
2. Accept your individual responsibilities as a professional
3. Plan and develop your own long-term professional development plan
4. Recognize your responsibilities as a member of your school physical education staff and as a member of your profession
5. Design and implement plans to promote and advocate for your program within the school and community political systems

The ABC process is a means to enable physical educators to develop functional and accountable physical education programs. Many of the ABC recommended planning, assessing, implementing, and evaluating procedures are marked departures from traditional practice. As such, you should be cognizant of the different ways these changes may be perceived by other physical educators, teachers, and administrators. As illustrated in the preceding scenario, teachers commonly react in several ways when changes are proposed. Some teachers become excited just because they like a new challenge. Others react negatively because they find changes threatening. Back in chapter 1 we discussed the fact that change provokes loss, challenges competence, creates confusion, and causes conflict (Evans, 1996).

Changing requires some risk and usually additional effort. Teachers must leave the comfort of doing things their way, being in control, and knowing they can succeed to try a new way in which they are not in control and could possibly fail. On top of the risk, teachers also have to learn and practice new skills and behaviors. For change to work in most situations, the benefits need to at least equal the perceived risks or costs for those involved.

In terms of teachers and curriculum changes, there are numerous potential benefits such as ensuring all students are achieving, meeting program goals and objectives, program justification, accountability, and job security. Some common risks or costs could be loss of reputation, failure, frustration, and demands for additional time and effort. Although it may appear that the benefits of change easily outweigh the costs, this unfortunately is not always the case. Many teachers already feel undercompensated, overworked, and underappreciated. When asked to change voluntarily, they frequently assert that they should be compensated for their time or released from other responsibilities.

Unfortunately, there are typically very few external incentives to motivate teachers to make ongoing curriculum revisions. Given the current pay and reward systems in the public schools, the motivation for making curriculum changes, as recommended by the ABC model, will almost exclusively be intrinsic. Although every effort should be made to improve teacher pay, the primary motivation for ongoing curriculum evaluation and revisions is and will always be professionalism. However, curriculum revision efforts are often linked to a school district's continual planning model, a common practice in today's standards-based, high-stakes testing environment. Personnel and operating costs for these ongoing improvement processes are frequently supported financially through district or state funds.

Accepting and embracing change is part of being a professional. As a professional in the field of physical education you have many responsibilities in addition to showing up and teaching your classes. You are responsible for staying up-to-date on the latest advances and developments in the field so that your teaching is effective. You are also responsible for being an involved citizen in your school governance and community. Finally, you are responsible for being an advocate for both your physical education program and your profession. In addition to your personal responsibilities, you also have responsibilities as a member of the physical education staff in your district. Because your program is only a piece of the total curriculum, you must work with the other physical education staff to ensure that the overall curriculum is effective. Once you have a successful curriculum, you must then work with the other members of the staff to continually evaluate, revise, and promote the program. Some of the common individual and collective responsibilities of physical educators are shown in table 13.1.

Individual Professional Responsibilities

Before you can be a contributing member of a physical education staff you must be sure you are meeting your individual professional responsibilities. Your primary responsibility is to do your job to the best of your ability. In addition, you have a number of other responsibilities as a professional educator.

Table 13.1   Professional Responsibilities of a Physical Educator

Individual	Collective
Do your job to the best of your ability.	Make the curriculum the best it can be.
Stay up-to-date.	Create and participate on a district curriculum evaluation committee.
Be active in your profession.	Promote and advocate for the program.
Be an active school citizen.	Create and implement a promotion plan.
Serve as an advocate for physical education in your school.	Educate your administration about the physical education curriculum.
Develop and implement a professional development plan.	Establish a system so that physical education is represented at all school board meetings.
	Know the budget process and have standing requests for resources.
	Integrate the physical education program into the community.

Stay Up-to-Date and Active in Your Profession

Your first responsibility is to stay up-to-date on the latest research, developments, and trends in the field of physical education. You can do this by being a member of your national, state, and local professional organizations. The most common national organization is the American Alliance for Health, Physical Education, Recreation and Dance (www.aahperd.org). As a member of these organizations, you can stay up to date by reading professional journals, attending professional conferences, or regularly checking professional Web sites.

Membership in a professional organization is a two-way street. In addition to taking advantage of the resources that are available to maximize your efficacy, you should also share what you know and have developed to assist other members of your profession. This does not mean that you have to write a journal article or a book, although you could. You could contribute through computer listservs by responding to questions posed by other teachers on Web sites such as PE Central (http://pe.central.org) and PE-talk (www.pelinks4u.org), or you could share your expertise and experience by giving presentations at state and national conferences.

Be an Active School Citizen

In addition to being active in your profession, you must also be an active citizen in your own school and community. Being an active school citizen is also a two-way street. Serving on school committees and participating in school events provides opportunities to both educate others about physical education and the benefits it provides to the students, and also to learn about other school issues and the values of the other teachers and members of the community. One of the benefits of being an active citizen is that teachers whose initiatives you supported in the past will be likely to support you when you need it. You can also sometimes launch an initiative of your own while solving a school need if your timing is good.

Consider the situation of an elementary school physical education teacher who wanted to run a fitness club before school. He knew he needed some volunteer help and a small budget to get the program started. At a faculty meeting an issue arose about problems managing the children who were being dropped off early in the morning because their parents needed to go to work. The principal told the teachers that although a few parents had volunteered to help, they did not think they had the skills to manage all of the students. The principal

All the physical educators must accept and share responsibility for maintaining the physical education curriculum.

was leaning toward reallocating some of the teacher aides to address this problem. This of course was not received well by the classroom teachers who were not excited about losing their aides. At this point the physical educator spoke up and volunteered to handle the problem by involving these students in the fitness club he was creating. All he needed were the parents who already volunteered to help and a small budget to support his new program. As you might suspect, the other teachers were more than willing to support this new program and even the supplemental budget.

Serve As an Advocate for Physical Education in Your School

Being part of school committees can also provide insights into the misconceptions other teachers may have about physical education. Many physical educators report that other teachers in their schools do not think that they teach or follow a curriculum. In essence, some teachers perceive physical education as fun and games and, although they think it may be good for the students, they do not think it is as important as their subject areas. These misconceptions occur when teachers assume that the school's physical education program is the same as the physical education programs they went through 20 or more years ago.

These misconceptions prevail because there is frequently no one at the various school meetings to set them straight. Because the teachers think they know what is done in physical education, they do not inquire about the specifics of the school's physical education program. By just being in attendance at these various meetings you will have numerous opportunities to highlight various aspects of the physical education curriculum and to correct any misconceptions that may arise. When these opportunities to educate others about physical education arise, you need to be prepared to respond in a positive, nondefensive manner. Here are a few simple rules to follow when being a good school citizen:

1. Listen and show respect for the views of others even when you disagree with them.

2. Show other committee members the same respect that you want them to show you.

3. When discussing an issue, particularly when you are presenting an opposing view, do not personalize your arguments.

4. Remember that you are all on the same team with the same objective—meeting the educational needs of the students in your school.

5. Do your homework and be prepared for the issues that will be discussed.

6. Present and argue your views to the best of your ability during the discussion on an issue. However, once the group reaches a decision, accept and support the decision of the group.

Teachers must leave the comfort of doing things their way, being in control, and knowing they can succeed to try a new way in which they are not in control and could fail.

Develop and Implement a Professional Development Plan

Although physical educators are typically not paid for their individual professional activities, these activities can be counted in other ways. Many of these professional activities can be used to satisfy requirements for tenure, licensing, and recertification. For example, many school districts require that teachers develop and implement individual professional development plans that are reviewed and approved by the school principal. For these plans to be most beneficial for teachers, they should be guided by long-term goals. Each year's staff development plan should build on the previous plan and ultimately culminate in the achievement of some goal.

Say you want to eventually be recognized by the National Board for Professional Teaching Standards (NBPTS) (see chapter 1, page 12) as a master teacher. Using the ABC planning process, the NBPTS physical education standards would become your goals. You would then task analyze these goals down into a series of objectives you would need to achieve to document achievement of each standard. These objectives could then be distributed over five, eight, or ten years based on the nature of the objectives and the amount of time you could devote to each. Each year of this long-range plan would then become one of your annual staff development plans. You would use your own ongoing assessment of your progress as well as the external administrative evaluations you receive to evaluate your progress and to make necessary revisions to your plan.

In addition to having a well-thought-out plan, you must also have an efficient way to organize and manage the required documents or artifacts you will need to demonstrate that you met each standard. One of the most efficient ways to manage these materials is to develop a professional portfolio (Melograno, 1998). Table 13.2 illustrates several professional teaching standards and possible artifacts that you could use as documentation.

Collective Professional Responsibilities

As stated throughout this book, the ABC model is a process. For the process to work, it requires a committed group of teachers. Developing, implementing, evaluating, and modifying the physical education curriculum is not one person's job; it is everyone's job. Your curriculum is like a car; if you

do not continually invest in its maintenance, it will eventually break down and not meet your needs. In the case of a district-wide physical education curriculum, you have multiple people using the same car. All of the teachers should participate in, share, and accept responsibility for the maintenance of the curriculum. Although many of the staff collective responsibilities discussed in this section parallel the individual professional responsibilities, they differ in terms of their complexity and magnitude. The two major collective responsibilities a physical education staff has are (1) to make sure the physical education program is the best it can be and (2) to promote and advocate for the physical education program.

Making the Curriculum the Best It Can Be

As discussed in chapter 12, no physical education curriculum is ever perfect. The curriculum evolves from the collective experience and best estimates of the staff. As the program is implemented, it is continually evaluated, and the evaluation information is used to make revisions as needed. For this to occur, two processes must be in place. First, there must be a mechanism by which the curriculum can be reviewed and revised by the staff on some periodic basis. Seco nd, there must be a dynamic staff development program that can assist and guide teachers in addressing and resolving problems and issues related to the curriculum.

Creating a Curriculum Evaluation Committee

One method of operationalizing a dynamic curriculum evaluation system is to create a standing curriculum committee (Kelly, 1988). How the committee is formed will depend on local school policies and procedures. A common method is to elect representatives on staggered three-year terms from each of the program levels included in the program. The terms are staggered by program level to ensure continuity between years and to limit the time needed to bring new members up to speed.

Although representation and involvement are important considerations, the committee should also be kept to a manageable size for practical reasons. A typical committee for a comprehensive K-12 program might have six members: two from each program level (elementary, middle, and high school). Membership on this committee should

Table 13.2   Teaching Standards and Physical Education Artifacts

	Supporting standards	Possible artifacts
Core Proposition 1: Teachers are committed to students and their learning.	(a) Teachers recognize individual differences in their students and adjust their practice accordingly. (b) Teachers have an understanding of how students develop and learn. (c) Teachers treat students equitably. (d) Teachers' mission extends beyond developing the [psychomotor] capacity of their students.	(a) Reflective journal describing accommodations and response to self-control strategies for five students with mild behavior disabilities in a sport education teaching unit. (b) Project for a graduate course titled "How Children Learn Motor Skills" showing how principles and concepts are applied to an elementary physical education program. (c) Case studies showing development in physical education for a student of cultural origin different from most members of a class, a student at-risk, and a student who is gifted and talented. (d) Observational checklists for determining students' tendencies toward self-responsibility, respect for others, sense of fair play, and higher-order thinking in movement awareness activities.
Core proposition 2: Teachers know the subjects they teach and how to teach those subjects to students.	(a) Teachers appreciate how knowledge in their subjects is created, organized, and linked to other disciplines. (b) Teachers command specialized knowledge of how to convey a subject to students. (c) Teachers generate multiple paths to [learning].	(a) Integrated unit plan with language arts and speech titled "Communicating Through Movement." (b) Self-appraisal worksheets and inventories for health-related components of fitness (i.e., cardiorespiratory endurance, muscular strength and endurance, flexibility, body composition). (c) Videotape of series of teaching episodes in which a variety of instructional strategies is used (e.g., problem solving, simulations, self-check, reciprocal).
Core proposition 3: Teachers are responsible for managing and monitoring student learning.	(a) Teachers call on multiple methods to meet their goals. (b) Teachers orchestrate learning in group settings. (c) Teachers place a premium on student engagement. (d) Teachers regularly assess student progress. (e) Teachers are mindful of their principal objectives.	(a) Student portfolio work samples representing different intelligences (e.g., linguistic, mathematical, kinesthetic, spatial, personal, musical) for a six-week unit on "Creative Use of Leisure Time." (b) Guidelines for group work at fitness stations, participation in team drills, and role-playing a sensitive problem (e.g., mocking others' ability, respecting officiating calls of opponent). (c) Floor plans and setups for gymnasium and outdoor space showing arrangement of equipment and materials and location of students that maximize active learning. (d) Scoring rubrics for a set of sequential lessons on manipulative skills (e.g., dribbling, kicking, throwing, catching, volleying, striking). (e) Lesson plans that link explicit learning objectives with specific student activities and performance standards.
Core proposition 4: Teachers think systematically about their practice and learn from experience.	(a) Teachers are continually making difficult choices that test their judgment. (b) Teachers seek the advice of others and draw on education research and scholarship to improve their practice.	(a) Descriptions of how the rules and strategies of traditional games (e.g., soccer, volleyball, basketball) are modified to encourage greater participation and teamwork. (b) Annotated bibliography of the principles and applications of "cooperative learning" specific to physical education instruction at the middle school level.
Core proposition 5: Teachers are members of learning communities.	(a) Teachers contribute to school effectiveness by collaborating with other professionals. (b) Teachers work collaboratively with parents. (c) Teachers take advantage of community resources.	(a) Individualized Education Plans (IEPs) showing the motor development component for a group of students with learning disabilities. (b) Reflection sheet for use by parents to review and comment on a videotape of a choreographed dance routine. (c) Photographs from an elective course conducted at a local state park titled "Outdoor Pursuits" (e.g., camping, backpacking, hiking, orienteering, cross-country skiing).

initially be delimited to physical educators until the program is producing the desired results. Once the staff is pleased with the overall effectiveness of the program, the curriculum committee should be expanded to include a central administration representative and a parent representative.

Teachers can earn staff development hours or points for serving on this committee. Many school districts will also pay these teachers to meet for several days during the summer to work on the curriculum revisions. This committee would be charged with collecting objective evaluation forms (see figures 12.8 and 12.9) from all teachers each year. This information along with the program evaluation reports discussed in chapter 12 would be reviewed and analyzed to identify implementation problems and determine needed modifications to the program plan.

The committee would also be charged with planning appropriate staff development activities to remediate any implementation problems they identify. Staff development activities could range from bringing in outside experts to work with the entire staff on issues shared by a majority of the staff to individualized plans to address the needs of specific teachers. A common approach is to create a peer consultation model in which teachers are paired each year with teachers with different strengths and weaknesses. These teachers meet throughout the year on staff development days to share and discuss their implementation strategies. If funding is available, these teachers can also be released once or twice during the year from their classes to observe each other teach. Finally, the curriculum committee would be responsible for making all of the necessary revisions to the curriculum and sharing these changes with the staff. The revisions are usually given and explained to the staff in August during a staff development meeting prior to the start of the next school year.

The key to developing and maintaining a dynamic physical education program is having an established and well-supported curriculum committee. Serving on this committee should be perceived as an honor and not as a burden. How to gain support for this committee is discussed in the next section on promoting and advocating for the program.

Promoting the Program

Some physical educators believe that their job is to teach and that someone else is responsible for handling the public relations and school politics. The reality, however, is that if physical educators do not promote, defend, and fight for their programs, no one else is going to do it for them.

Once the ABC process has been implemented, one of the key components for promoting a program is in place—data to document that the program is effective. However, having the program in place and working is not enough. Remember that many other educators, administrators, and parents do not understand what a comprehensive high-quality physical education program is. They think they know all they need to know about physical education based on the physical education they had when they were in school, and these opinions are not always accurate or favorable.

A good starting point when developing a promotional plan for the physical education program is to market it as something radically new. Promoting the physical education program should not be viewed as a one-time or occasional activity. This is an ongoing process. There is no one best way to promote your program. The best approach is to use a variety of methods. Once the program is well established, the nature of the promotional activities will change, but you will always need to promote the program. Obviously, some promotional efforts are conducted at the school level by the individual physical education teachers. Following are some common promotional activities:

- Student progress reports
- Open houses
- Newsletters
- Web sites
- Features in local newspapers

Sending home student progress reports (see figure 11.3) to parents and sharing program evaluation data with the school principal will communicate some important information about the program. You can also use traditional promotional activities such as open houses and newsletters. In addition, your physical education staff should always be looking for new ways to communicate information about both the scope and sequence of the program and its effectiveness. Developing a physical education program Web site, for example, is an excellent way to promote the program and program activities. You can also use the Web site to solicit input and feedback from parents and students about the program.

A good promotion program requires both boldness and creativity. Most local newspapers devote space to human interest stories and local events. There are hundreds of success stories in physical education every week waiting to be told. Contact a few local reporters and develop a relationship with them. Find out what they are looking for in a story and educate them about the features of your program and the unique experiences that students have in the program. When you eventually hit on a story, make sure you take full advantage of the educational and political opportunities the story presents. Emphasize the unique aspects of your program that afford the experiences being highlighted in the story. Also be gracious in sharing the credit for your successes. Recognize the administration and school board for their support as well as any local service groups that have contributed resources to your program. Use as many names as you can. Everyone likes to see their name in print.

Advocating for the Program

In addition to promotional activities, your physical education staff must also be proactive in how they advocate for their program. Nowhere is this more important than in how they communicate with the school board and central administration. Unfortunately, in many school districts there are no established lines of communication between the physical education program and these decision-making bodies. In these cases, it is not uncommon for these groups to make decisions that negatively affect physical education without any input or participation from the physical education staff. How could this happen? Here is an actual scenario:

The state had instituted a new statewide testing program to evaluate how schools were doing in regard to the state performance standards. At least 80% of the students in each grade had to achieve the standards for the school to be reaccredited. Schools had three years to remediate any weaknesses that were found.

After the first year of testing, one local school district found that its elementary students were performing well below the 80% mark in both language arts and math. At the next school board meeting, the board asked the superintendent what the problem was and what could be done to address it. The superintendent responded that the teachers thought they did not have enough time to cover all of the content included in the standards. Someone on the board suggested that they could cut physical education, which currently was being provided five times a week for 30 minutes each class, to twice a week. This change would give the teachers

an additional hour and a half each week. Everyone at the meeting seemed to think this was a reasonable suggestion. They decided to think it over and bring it to a vote at next month's meeting.

A week before the next meeting, the school board published its agenda as it was required to do. A local radio station reported the agenda as part of its public service announcements. A physical educator heard it on the radio on the way to school. When she got to school, she called some of the other physical educators to find out what was going on. No one knew! Eventually, a group of teachers got together after school and called some school board members to find out what was happening. They learned that they could speak out against the motion before the vote at the next meeting. They also found out that the suggestion to reduce physical education was made by a school board member who didn't believe physical education was important. He apparently had had a negative experience in physical education when he was in school and didn't think much has changed in physical education. The physical educators contacted a bunch of parents and asked them to speak in favor of physical education at the meeting.

The night of the meeting a dozen physical education teachers gave emotional speeches focusing on the damage cutting physical education time would have on the program and the students. Unfortunately, they did not have an ABC-based program and subsequently did not have any data to support their arguments. In addition, about 25 parents spoke in support of the program. Sensing that this was a politically sensitive issue, the superintendent spoke up after the public comments and commended the physical educators for their fine programs and all of the contributions they make to the students and their schools. He then explained that the district was in a difficult position and that they all had to pull together as a team and do something to address their poor tests scores. He offered a compromise: Instead of cutting physical education from five to two days as recommended by the school board, he suggested that it only be reduced to three days given the strong arguments made by the parents and the teachers. After a short discussion the school board accepted the compromise and unanimously approved it.

After the meeting the physical educators were really upset. Most of the parents were upset too, but some believed that they had had a positive effect because physical education was only reduced to three days. A month after the meeting everyone had accepted the change and was back to doing their jobs as usual.

Although this may seem like a rather extreme example, unfortunately, situations like this are quite common. The real problem in this scenario was not that physical education was attacked at the expense of the academic subjects; that unfortunately will probably always happen. The real problem was that physical education was not in the decision-making loop. The physical educators found out about the issue only after an action had been decided on and a vote was scheduled. Reversing an action is usually much harder than stopping it from becoming an issue.

Establishing a Connection With the School Board

A proactive approach that would allow physical educators to avoid the previous scenario would involve establishing an ongoing connection with the school board. The school board in the scenario should have been well informed about the physical education program and the time needed to support a quality program before any issues regarding time came up. When a member did suggested that physical education time be reduced, other members of the board should have known enough about the program to anticipate the impact it would have. Finally, if someone from the physical education staff were at every school board meeting, there would have been someone there to inform and educate the school board members on the issue before they committed to an action.

Accomplishing all of this may sound complicated, but it is really quite simple. Instead of waiting for physical education to be attacked for resources, the proactive thing to do would be for the physical education staff to meet periodically with the school board, particularly after new members are added, to explain the physical education program. Each board member should be given a copy of the curriculum along with a recent set of program evaluation reports. These tasks could be added to the responsibilities of the curriculum revision committee discussed earlier.

A second strategy is to have a representative of the physical education staff at every school board meeting. This person would introduce her- or himself to the board members, particularly the chair, before the meeting and let them know she or he is there and is available if any concerns or questions should arise about physical education. This strategy accomplishes two things. First, it ensures that there is a member of the staff present to educate the board on any issues that arise. Second, it communicates to the board that the physical education program is well organized and actively engaged in the district's governance process. Most school boards meet only once a month. If you have a physical education staff of 30, each member would have to attend a meeting only once every two and a half years.

Being Involved in the Budget Process

Your physical education program should always have a request for additional resources on the table for consideration by the school board. Requesting additional resources is a good sign. Most dynamic and effective programs are constantly improving, trying to expand, and exploring new methods. These activities require resources in various forms such as additional staff, equipment, time, space, or staff development funds.

Requesting resources is also an educational opportunity. Most requests for resources require a justification or rationale. You can use this justification statement as an opportunity to educate the school board about a specific aspect of your physical education program. Of course in this justification you would focus on the needs of the students and document your request with data from your evaluation reports. The best-case scenario would be that you educate the board regarding a specific need and they agree to fund your request. The worst case is that you educate the board about a need and leave them feeling responsible for the need not being addressed because they cannot supply the funding. This is a psychological tactic. When budget problems arise, the board will already believe it has cut your program by not addressing this need, which may shield your programs from additional cuts. With nothing on the table, however, physical education would most likely be one of the first areas targeted for a cut.

The format for resource requests varies widely across districts. In most cases they are relatively short, usually one to three pages in length. Figure 13.1 shows a few guidelines for preparing a resource request (see appendix B, page 344, for the reproducible form).

Consider the following scenario:

Analysis of your physical education program data for the past five years shows an increase

1. Clearly define the problem this resource request is designed to address.

2. Focus the request on the needs of the students. You want the board to understand that whatever you are requesting will directly affect the students and assist them in achieving an established goal in the program.

3. Provide concrete data from your program and the literature to justify your request. You do not want the board to perceive your request as just a novel idea. Support it with enough data and literature to suggest that it will address the need you have identified.

4. Show that you have exhausted what you can do with your existing resources (e.g., you have already developed and run a pilot program and now need resources to make it available to all students).

5. Give an accurate budget that is sufficient to address the need you have identified and shows that you are being fiscally responsible and prudent.

▌**Figure 13.1**   Guidelines for preparing a resource request.

in the risk for obesity in K-2 students district-wide from 15 to 19%. These same students are also showing marked delays in their acquisition of the motor skill objectives in the curriculum. A review of the recent research literature reveals that inactivity in children is a vicious cycle. Inactivity leads to weight gain, which in turn makes physical activity less attractive. Over time avoidance of physical activity and subsequent weight gain makes learning new motor skills even more difficult. If no intervention is provided, most children eventually lack the motor skills needed to participate in lifetime sport skills and to maintain their fitness at levels needed to be healthy. High levels of obesity and low motor skills have also been shown to correlate with lower academic performance in the classroom. The research shows that there are two keys to reversing this cycle. First, intervention must start early before children experience too great a delay in motor skill acquisition. Second, children and their parents need to be aware of the children's low activity levels.

Over the past three years, the physical education staff at your school has tried a number of innovative strategies and initiatives to address this problem. For instance, last month's Sunday paper featured a story on the parent–child fitness clubs at the elementary schools. What you have found from these programs is that in many cases children and their parents are just unaware of how low the children's activity levels actually were and that they

have no way of accurately monitoring it. You have discovered activity monitors to be effective in providing students with regular individualized feedback.

Based on this information, your physical education staff recently attended a workshop on how to use the latest activity monitor made by Acme Products. With some funds solicited from the local Elks Club, the staff purchased three activity monitors and piloted using them in three elementary schools. The findings to date have been very encouraging and parallel what was found in the literature. Student activity levels have increased significantly. The parents of the pilot students have also responded very positively particularly to being able to monitor and reinforce their children for their increased activity.

Your staff would like to begin using activity monitors with all elementary students found to be "at-risk" of inactivity. You need a total of $23,800 to buy 200 activity monitors at $119 apiece. You have already contacted the Acme company to see whether they will give you a discount. They have informed you that if you buy 200 monitors and allow them to use your district as a model, they will sell them to you for $59 apiece. Finally, the local Elks Club is really excited about this program and has agreed to donate another $1,800 toward getting it up and running. Therefore your staff is requesting $10,000 to buy the activity monitors needed to run this program. The monitors are warranted for 10 years and are solar powered. Over this 10-year period the monitors will be used by over 2,000 students (200 students per year × 10 years) for an average cost of $5 per student. You believe this is a reasonable investment to offset the potentially severe health risks to your students associated with inactivity.

Again the format and process for making resource requests will vary. The important point is that one way to protect your current resources is to make well-justified requests for additional resources. In addition to requesting resources, a request like the one in the example above also provides another opportunity to publicly promote and justify the effectiveness of your program.

Integrating Your Program Into the Community

Your final collective responsibility is to integrate your program into the community. One of the most effective ways to educate people about your program is to get them involved in it. Because resources are usually hard to come by from within the school district, an alternative is to tap community resources. Most communities have service organizations such as the Lions, Elks, and Kiwanis clubs. These clubs are dedicated to performing community service and are usually composed of influential members of the community. They are good sources for volunteers and for resources. If you need funds to build a climbing wall, these organizations can help you raise the funds. You of course would acknowledge their support by naming the wall after them or running a special program to introduce the members of the club to the climbing wall and explaining to them how it is used in achieving the goals and objectives of the physical education curriculum.

Another community resource you could tap is a local college or university, which can supply volunteers and student teachers. Make sure the benefits are mutual. If your program is used as a placement for training students, what does your program get from it? You could, for example, ask the college supervisor to periodically make a public presentation at a school board meeting. In this presentation he would acknowledge the quality of the physical education program, the excellence of role models provided by the physical education staff, and the critical role both of these factors play in the training of college students.

Self-Reflection

One way to evaluate how the ABC model prepares you for your professional responsibilities is to com-

pare the abilities you have using the ABC model to an established standard. Danielson (1996) identified the four components of professional responsibility shown in table 13.3. For each component she identified a few key elements and then described the four levels of performance from unsatisfactory to distinguished. Take a few moments to review these criteria and analyze how the ABC model has prepared you to meet each component and each key event. If you implement the ABC model as presented in this text, your performance should consistently be in the proficient and distinguished categories.

Summary

After reading this chapter, you should understand that professionalism is the key to your success as a physical educator. The ABC model provides a blueprint for designing, implementing, and evaluating a dynamic, ever evolving physical education curriculum that is responsive to student needs as well as to local, state, and national standards. Your dedication as a professional in implementing the ABC model will determine whether the program is successful. Clearly, you cannot do everything by yourself; you must also be able to work collaboratively with the other physical educators in your district so that the overall program is successful in meeting its goals.

You should also now understand that you are an integral part of the physical education profession. The profession is not some abstract concept; it is the application of our scientific body of knowledge to addressing the physical and motor needs of our students so that they can live active and healthy lives. The value of our profession is ultimately defined by the impact it has on the students it serves. We are at a critical junction in our profession where we need to do a better job communicating and documenting the benefits physical education provides for society. The future of our profession is in your hands. The students you educate today are the taxpayers and school board members of the future. Given the ever increasing demands on school time and for increased accountability, physical education will only be retained in our schools if we can document its effectiveness and if consumers value the benefits provided by the program.

Finally, remember that change starts with you and your commitment to your profession. With the ABC model and your preparation in the scientific core of your field, you have the tools needed to be successful. Use these tools to address the needs of your students, and measure your success by the success of your lowest-performing students.

Table 13.3   Danielson's Four Components of Professional Responsibility

	Component 4a: Reflecting on teaching			
Element	**Unsatisfactory performance**	**Basic performance**	**Proficient performance**	**Distinguished performance**
Accuracy	Teacher does not know if a lesson was effective or achieved its goals, or profoundly misjudges the success of a lesson.	Teacher has a generally accurate impression of a lesson's effectiveness and the extent to which instructional goals were met.	Teacher makes an accurate assessment of a lesson's effectiveness and the extent to which it achieved its goals, and she can cite general references to support the judgment.	Teacher makes a thoughtful and accurate assessment of a lesson's effectiveness and the extent to which it achieved its goals, citing many specific examples from the lesson and weighing the relative strength of each.
Use in future teaching	Teacher has no suggestions for how a lesson may be improved another time.	Teacher makes general suggestions about how a lesson may be improved.	Teacher makes a few specific suggestion of what he may try another time.	Drawing on an extensive repertoire of skills, the teacher offers specific alternative actions, complete with probable successes of different approaches.
	Component 4b: Maintaining accurate records			
Student completion of assignments	Teacher's system for maintaining information on student completion of assignments is in disarray.	Teacher's system for maintaining information on student completion of assignments is rudimentary and only partially effective.	Teacher's system for maintaining information on student completion of assignments is fully effective.	Teacher's system for maintaining information on student completion of assignments is fully effective. Students participate in the maintenance of records.
Student progress in learning	Teacher has no system for maintaining information on student progress in learning, or the system is in disarray.	Teacher's system for maintaining information on student progress in learning is rudimentary and partially effective.	Teacher's system for maintaining information on student progress in learning is effective.	Teacher's system for maintaining information on student progress in learning is fully effective. Students contribute information and interpretation of the records.
Noninstructional records	Teacher's records for noninstructional activities are in disarray, resulting in errors and confusion.	Teacher's records for noninstructional activities are adequate, but they require frequent monitoring to avoid error.	Teacher's system for maintaining information on noninstructional activities is fully effective.	Teacher's system for maintaining information on noninstructional activities is highly effective, and students contribute to its maintenance.

(continued)

Table 13.3 *(continued)*

	Component 4c: Communicating with families			
Element	**Unsatisfactory performance**	**Basic performance**	**Proficient performance**	**Distinguished performance**
Information about the instructional program	Teacher provides little information about the instructional program to families.	Teacher participates in the school's activities for parent communication but offers little additional information.	Teacher provides frequent information to parents, as appropriate, about the instructional program.	Teacher provides frequent information to parents, as appropriate, about the instructional program. Students participate in preparing materials for their families.
Information about individual students	Teacher provides minimal information to parents and does not respond or responds insensitively to parent concerns about students.	Teacher adheres to the school's required procedures for communicating to parents. Responses to parent concerns are minimal.	Teacher communicates with parents about students' progress on a regular basis and is available as needed to respond to parent concerns.	Teacher provides information to parents frequently on both positive and negative aspects of student progress. Response to parent concerns is handled with great sensitivity.
Engagement of families in the instructional program	Teacher makes no attempt to engage families in the instructional program, or such attempts are inappropriate.	Teacher makes modest and inconsistently successful attempts to engage families in the instructional program.	Teacher's efforts to engage families in the instructional program are frequent and successful.	Teacher's efforts to engage families in the instructional program are frequent and successful. Students contribute ideas for projects that will be enhanced by family participation.
	Component 4d: Contributing to the school and the district			
Relationships with colleagues	Teacher's relationships with colleagues are negative or self-serving.	Teacher maintains cordial relationships with colleagues to fulfill the duties that the school or district requires.	Support and cooperation characterize relationships with colleagues.	Support and cooperation characterize relationships with colleagues. Teacher takes initiative in assuming leadership among the faculty.
Service to the school	Teacher avoids becoming involved in school events.	Teacher participates in school events when specifically asked.	Teacher volunteers to participate in school events, making a substantial contribution.	Teacher volunteers to participate in school events, making a substantial contribution, and assumes a leadership role in at least some aspect of school life.
Participation in school and district projects	Teacher avoids becoming involved in school and district projects.	Teacher participates in school and district projects when specifically asked.	Teacher volunteers to participate in school and district projects, making a substantial contribution.	Teacher volunteers to participate in school and district projects, making a substantial contribution, and assumes a leadership role in a major school or district project.

Reprinted, by permission, from C. Danielson, 1996, *Enhancing professional practice: A framework for teaching* (Alexandria, VA: ASCD).

Making It Work

Have you achieved the expected outcomes (page 282) for this chapter? You should understand your role as a professional relative to both your individual and collective responsibilities. Still, you may have some practical questions that need answers, such as the following:

■ *What do I do if other teachers, school staff, or administrators communicate inaccurate perceptions of physical education?* Many classroom teachers, for example, seem to value physical education only because it gives them a planning period, not because they believe physical education is important for their students. Such attitudes should be interpreted as misconceptions and not personal attacks on you or your program. Try to avoid taking these comments personally and focus on the issue. What may make teachers think this way? What do they actually see of your program? What do they know about how your physical education program is designed and implemented? What do they base their perceptions on? Most teachers see only brief segments of your program usually at the beginning or end of your classes or hear random comments from their students when they return to class. Although you may have your students actively engaged in practicing a given component of an objective, outsiders may think that the students are just playing a game and having fun. Many classroom teachers take these observations and mesh them with their childhood experiences in physical education and then form their judgments. Once you have an understanding of why teachers may have misconceptions regarding physical education, the solution is to correct these misconceptions through education.

Our first mistake as physical educators is to assume that others are going to take the initiative to learn about our programs. We have to take the first step and start the conversation. This could be done by asking the principal if you could have time at the next faculty meeting to present an overview of the physical education program and what the students will be working on this year. You could then follow up your presentation with regular updates to the teachers via the school newsletter, e-mail, or Web page. At the end of each grading period, you could provide each teacher with a copy of their students' individual physical education progress reports and then offer to meet with them to discuss how their students are doing. Educating others on the value of physical education and what you are doing in your program should be an ongoing and ever evolving process. Never assume that someone knows; tell them and be sure. Also, work with other teachers on integrated curriculum projects such as science and physical education, math and physical education, or history and physical education.

■ *Shouldn't my school provide inservice programs on new educational developments and trends to keep all of the teachers up to date?* Yes, and most will offer a variety of inservice staff development programs to try to address the needs of their teachers, but these will probably not be sufficient to keep you up to date on all you need to know. Most staff development programs offered at the beginning of the year before school or on teacher work days during the year tend to be short one-time presentations designed to address broad educational issues that affect all teachers. Even inservice programs offered in the various content areas tend to be awareness presentations designed to provide an overview on a given topic. To stay up to date on the latest developments in your field, you will need to be directly involved with your profession via one or more professional organizations. These organizations produce journals, hold conferences, and support Web sites that can provide you with more detailed "how to" information on the latest developments in your field. Also, new technology mediums such as CD-ROMs, the Internet, and distance education courses provide alternative ways to access the latest developments and information in your field.

■ *Isn't it the responsibility of the leaders in the field of physical education to advocate for our profession and educate the public about the value of physical education for all students?* Yes it is, but who are the leaders in our field? Are the leaders the college and university faculty that publish research articles, write textbooks, and give presentations at national conferences, or are our leaders the teachers who can effectively teach our difficult content to a diverse population of students? The point here is that the commitment you make to your profession, not the level at which you teach, determines whether you are a leader. When you see a need or an issue, the question should not be, I wonder who is going to address this? but, What can I do to address this? It could be something as simple as posting a question on one of the profession's Web sites to find out whether other members of the profession are having the same problem. A simple question can often spark a professional discussion that eventually results in a conference presentation or journal article.

■ *What if a new student comes into my physical education class with a note from his parents asking me to excuse him from physical education for the year because he is an elite junior tennis player who is in excellent physical condition. The note asks that instead of going to physical education the student be allowed to do his homework because it is hard for him to get all of his schoolwork done on the weekends when he is involved in traveling to and playing in tournaments. How should I respond to this request? What are the underlying issues?* First, the parents have equated being skilled and fit in one activity with being physically educated. Second, they are looking for time during the school day for the student to do his homework. It is probably also safe to assume that the student involved would probably prefer to be in physical education than in a study hall doing homework. One possible way to address this situation would be to meet the parents halfway. Your goal is to educate them so that they understand that there is more to physical education than proficiency in one lifetime sport. At the same time, you want to let them know that you are sensitive to their concern about their child having sufficient time to do his homework. First, you would explain that being skilled and fit in tennis does not fulfill all of the objectives targeted to be achieved in the physical education curriculum for their child. This should prompt them to ask what is required. This would then open the door to bringing out your ABC curriculum and explaining the scope and sequence of the physical education program and the full range of competencies the student would be expected to demonstrate by the end of the program to meet the local, state, and national standards for physical education. Once you have established that physical education cannot be waived, you could then offer to assist them in working with the school guidance counselor to find some flexibility in the student's schedule so he can have some time to work on his homework.

■ *All of this talk about working collaboratively with the other physical education teachers sounds great, but what happens if the physical education teachers do not get along with each other?* Although unfortunate, this situation is not uncommon and should be anticipated. What is important to understand at the outset is what your expectations are in terms of collaboration. If your expectation is that everyone will agree, socialize together, and act like one big happy family, then you probably are going to be disappointed. Most physical education staffs are composed of a wide range of individuals with diverse backgrounds, personal situations, personalities, and needs. For example, some of the staff will be single, some may be married and just starting to have a family, and others could be starting to think of retirement. What you have to focus on is building on common bonds. To start, everyone on the staff has a common interest in physical education. They have all invested at least four years studying this area in college and have chosen to pursue this field for their careers. Second, using the ABC planning process will have provided you with a good foundation. You will be working with a curriculum that the entire staff played an equal role in developing. Third, everyone likes to be successful and to be associated with a successful program. Fourth, everyone has different strengths and interests. Focus on what each staff member can do and can contribute and not on what they cannot. Show everyone the same respect you would want them to show you. Conflicts and disagreements are inevitable. Agree to disagree, but do not personalize it. Finally, always leave the door open. Remember that change is very challenging for some individuals. Don't lock them out or alienate them. Each time there is a new opportunity, invite them to participate. In most cases, they eventually will want to be part of the group if the group is respectful and positive.

Appendix A
Program Planning Case Study

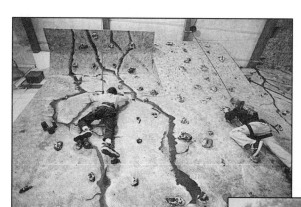

This case study of the Meta School is designed to illustrate the first nine steps in the ABC planning-down process. This is a hypothetical example intentionally limited in scope to minimize the size of the example and the complexity of the tables. The goal is to illustrate the worksheets and products produced for each of these steps in the planning process. The nine ABC planning steps covered in this example are summarized in table A.1 and keyed to the chapters in which they are addressed.

Table A.1   Nine ABC Planning Steps

Steps	Chapter	Key processes	Product
1	5	Developing the curriculum philosophy statement: Forming a curriculum committee; conducting a needs assessment; aligning the curriculum with national, state, and local recommendations and needs; and integrating with the school philosophy and curriculum.	A written philosophy statement that includes links to the overall school mission and philosophy, a statement of the underlying values and beliefs that serve as the foundation for the physical education curriculum, and a summary of the processes used to develop the curriculum as well as the members of the curriculum development committee
2	5	Defining the curriculum goals: incorporating the planning-down concept, identifying program outcomes, justifying curriculum outcomes, building consensus	A rank-ordered list of curriculum goals that indicates what students will achieve by the end of the program. Each goal is supported by a series of justification statements.
3	5	Determining policies and resources: reviewing the resources and school policies needed to implement the curriculum successfully	A written statement of the resources and polices needed to implement the curriculum
4	6	Delineating objectives for each goal: incorporating the planning-down concept, task analyzing goals, defining preliminary objectives, building consensus, rank-ordering objectives	A rank-ordered list of objectives for each goal based on their significance to the goal
5	6	Establishing program goal emphasis: determining the emphasis each goal should receive by program level, interaction of planning down and implementing up, building consensus	A table that illustrates the percentage of time that will be devoted to each curriculum goal by grade and program level across the curriculum
6	6	Calculating available instructional time: identifying the amount of instructional time available by program level, identifying the amount of lost instructional time	A table that illustrates the actual amount of instructional time available by program level and the total number of hours available for the entire program
7	6	Calculating an average objective mastery time: estimating mastery times for each goal, building consensus, reviewing objective definitions and the concept of mastery, calculating weighted estimates for each goal	A single time estimate that represents the amount of time needed to teach and achieve mastery of an average objective in the curriculum

Steps	Chapter	Key processes	Product
8	6	Calculating the total number of objectives in the curriculum: using the results of steps 6 and 7 to determine the total number of objectives that can be included in the curriculum, using the program emphasis table to determine the number of objectives for each goal	A table that illustrates the number of objectives that will be included in the curriculum for each curriculum goal
9	6	Sequencing the objectives across the curriculum: using the ranked lists of objectives for each goal to determine the specific objectives that will be included, using developmental principles and the implementing-up concept, determining when instruction will be initiated and when mastery is expected	A program plan that indicates at what grade levels all of the objectives in the curriculum will be initiated and mastered to achieve the stated curriculum goals at the end of the program

Step 1: Program Philosophy

Normally the process would be to have the staff investigate the underlying philosophies of the teachers and integrate these with the overall school philosophy and the values of the community. This typically involves forming a curriculum team and then planning and conducting a needs assessment. In our hypothetical situation, these issues have been streamlined and defined by the school's headmaster. Here is the situation:

The Meta School is a private school that includes grades 1-12. The school offers required physical education in all grades twice a week for 30 minutes a session. The headmaster of the school has surveyed the teachers, parents, and students to determine what they believe should be the focus and outcomes of the school's physical education curriculum. She has determined, based on this input, that all students leaving the required grade 1-12 program should be proficient in tennis and volleyball as well as have the fitness, social, and cognitive skills needed to maintain a healthy and active lifestyle. The headmaster appoints a curriculum committee composed of all three of the physical education teachers as well as the school's curriculum director, a member of the school's board of directors, a parent,

and a student. This committee is charged with creating an achievement-based physical education curriculum to achieve these goals. The headmaster also communicates that the physical education staff will have the facilities and equipment needed to teach the content in the curriculum. They will also have an ideal student-to-teacher ratio of 18 to 1. The only restriction the headmaster imposes is that the curriculum must be achievable in the time currently allocated to physical education in the school day.

The physical education staff believes that students should be exposed to many other important skills and lifetime activities in physical education in addition to tennis, volleyball, and fitness. The headmaster informs the staff that her goals for the program are consistent with the NASPE standards and that they can work on any additional skills or sports they believe are appropriate as long as all students leave the program with the competencies she has specified.

The physical education curriculum committee convenes and completes the ABC philosophy worksheet (see worksheet A.1). Based on the information collected in the philosophy worksheet, the committee drafts the philosophy statement (see figure A.1) for their curriculum.

Achievement-Based Curriculum Philosophy Worksheet

This worksheet is designed to help curriculum development committees identify major points that should be included in a curriculum philosophy statement. These prompts are provided as guidelines. Depending on the local needs and interests, some points may need to be emphasized more or less than others. In the current scenario many of the issues were addressed by the headmaster.

State why all students need physical education:

The staff searched the Web sites of AAHPERD and the surgeon general for quotes supporting the need for physical education.

State the benefits gained from physical education:

The staff searched Web sites, particularly that of the Centers for Disease Control and Prevention, for quotes to support the benefits of physical education.

State how the physical education curriculum is linked to the school curriculum or mission:

The staff reviewed the school's curriculum and found statements that supported the value of physical education in the total education of students.

State how the physical education curriculum is linked to community interests and values:

The headmaster surveyed parents and students to determine what they valued and believed should be taught in physical education

State the time required to effectively implement the physical education curriculum:

The headmaster guaranteed that at least an hour a week (two 30-minute sessions) would be allocated to physical education as well as an hour a day for student recreation time.

State the teacher qualifications needed to implement the curriculum:

The headmaster stipulated that certified physical education teachers would be employed to implement the curriculum.

State the class size and instructional space the curriculum was designed to accommodate:

The headmaster promised the physical education staff a student-to-teacher ratio of 18 to 1 and the necessary equipment and facilities to implement the curriculum.

State the policies and resources (in general terms) needed to effectively implement the curriculum:

Because the physical education program is well supported by the administration and required for each grade in the curriculum, no additional policies or resources were required.

State who was involved in the physical education curriculum development process:

The headmaster appointed a representative committee composed of all three of the physical education teachers as well as the school's curriculum director, a member of the school's board of directors, a parent, and a student.

State the process used by the curriculum committee to develop the curriculum:

The curriculum committee used the ABC planning process.

State the goals that will be achieved by the students when they complete the curriculum:

1. The students will be able to play a functional game of tennis employing all of the fundamental strokes, rules, and strategies.

2. The students will be able to play as a member of a team a functional game of volleyball demonstrating all of the appropriate skills, strategies, and rules.

3. The students will demonstrate the ability to design, implement, and adhere to a personal fitness program designed to develop and maintain health.

4. The students will demonstrate responsible social behavior and respect for individual differences in all physical activity settings.

State the rationales and benefits for students achieving these goals:

See worksheet A.2 (pages 302-303).

▊ **Worksheet A.1**

Physical Education Philosophy Statement

Physical education at the Meta School is an integral part of the overall school curriculum and an essential part of the development of all students. This balance between exercise and learning has long been recognized as exemplified by this quote from Thomas Jefferson: "Give about two hours every day to exercise, for health must not be sacrificed to learning. A strong body makes the mind strong." The need for physical education and activity is greater today than in the past as evidenced by this quote regarding physical activity and health from the surgeon general: "Nearly half of young people 12-21 years of age are not vigorously active; moreover, physical activity sharply declines during adolescence. Childhood and adolescence may thus be pivotal times for preventing sedentary behavior among adults by maintaining the habit of physical activity throughout the school years. School-based interventions have been shown to be successful in increasing physical activity levels." In addition, the Centers for Disease Control and Prevention has reported that "modest, regular physical activity substantially reduces the risk of dying from coronary heart disease (the nation's leading cause of death) and decreases the risk for colon cancer, diabetes, and high blood pressure. Physical activity also helps to control weight; contributes to healthy bones, muscles, and joints; helps to relieve the pain of arthritis; and reduces symptoms of anxiety and depression." To reap the benefits of exercise and physical activity, students must master the fundamental and advanced motor skills required for successful participation in these activities. In light of these findings, the Meta School requires that physical education instruction be provided for all students by a certified physical educator twice a week for 30 minutes across the entire grade 1 through grade 12 continuum. In addition, students at the the Meta School are provided an hour of recreation time each day during which they are encouraged to participate in the physical activities they have been taught in physical education. It is expected that at the completion of the Meta School physical education curriculum all students will at a minimum have achieved the following goals:

1. Be able to play a functional game of tennis employing all of the fundamental strokes, rules, and strategies

2. Be able to play as a member of a team a functional game of volleyball demonstrating all of the appropriate skills, strategies, and rules

(continued)

▊ **Figure A.1** Meta School philosophy statement.

3. Will demonstrate the ability to design, implement, and adhere to a personal fitness program designed to develop and maintain health

4. Will demonstrate responsible social behavior and respect for individual differences in all physical activity settings

This statement was developed by the physical education curriculum committee, which was composed of the following members:

Vivian Johnson, physical educator (chair)

Don White, physical educator

Melissa Fellow, physical educator

Robert Gonzalez, school board member

Lucy Brown, student member

William Rodenbaugh, parent

❚ **Figure A.1**   *(continued)*

Step 2: Defining the Curriculum Goals

In this step the curriculum committee identifies and then rank-orders all of the potential goals that can be addressed in the program. As part of this process, each committee member typically completes the program goals and supporting rationales worksheet (worksheet A.2). These worksheets are then used to create a composite list of all of the goals identified by the committee members. The consensus-building technique is then used to prioritize the goals from highest to lowest. In this case study, the goals were set by the headmaster and adopted by the staff. Note that the staff did add two additional lifetime sport goals in the hope that once the goals set by the headmaster are achieved, there would be time left to work on these goals.

The program goals and supporting rationales worksheet (A.2) that follows contains a summary of the information generated by the Meta School physical education teachers.

Once the goals are identified, the next task is to rank-order them. To rank order the goals the Meta School physical education curriculum committee follows the consensus-building technique described in chapter 5. Each committee member first independently rates each goal from 1 to 6 with the rating of 1 being assigned to the highest priority goal. The ratings for each goal provided by the various committee members are then averaged, and the average rating is reported in worksheet A.3 (page 304). After reviewing and discussing the summary values, the committee independently rates them again. This process is repeated until the absolute ranking of each goal does not change between rounds. Note that the goal with the lowest average rating is the

---

Program Goals and Supporting Rationales

1. Goal statement: <u>All students will be able to play a functional game of tennis employing all of the fundamental strokes, rules, and strategies.</u>

    Rationale statements:

    a. <u>Tennis is a lifetime sport that can be played throughout the life span.</u>

    b. <u>Tennis involves minimal equipment and can be played on courts that are generally available to the public at little or no cost.</u>

    c. <u>Tennis is a good activity for maintaining health and fitness.</u>

2. Goal statement: <u>All students will be able to play as a member of a team a functional game of volleyball demonstrating all of the appropriate skills, strategies, and rules.</u>

   Rationale statements:

   a. <u>Volleyball is a lifetime sport that can be played with teams in varying sizes from two to six players.</u>

   b. <u>Volleyball involves minimal equipment and can easily be set up and played in a variety of public and recreational settings.</u>

   c. <u>Volleyball is a good activity for maintaining health and fitness.</u>

3. Goal statement: <u>All students will demonstrate the ability to design, implement, and adhere to a personal fitness program designed to develop and maintain health.</u>

   Rationale statements:

   a. <u>Everyone needs a fitness routine to maintain strength, flexibility, and cardiorespiratory endurance.</u>

   b. <u>Affordable health clubs are readily available in most communities.</u>

   c. <u>The ability to correctly use exercise equipment is a prerequisite to being able to use it to obtain fitness benefits.</u>

4. Goal statement: <u>All students will demonstrate responsible social behavior and respect for individual differences in all physical activity settings.</u>

   Rationale statements:

   a. <u>To successfully participate with others in sport or fitness settings, participants must be responsible for their own behavior.</u>

   b. <u>To successfully participate with others in sport or fitness settings, participants must be able to follow established rules and procedures.</u>

   c. <u>To successfully participate with others in sport or fitness settings, participants must understand and respect individual similarities and differences.</u>

5. Goal statement: <u>All students will be able to play as a member of a team a functional game of basketball demonstrating all of the appropriate skills, strategies, and rules.</u>

   Rationale statements:

   a. <u>Basketball is a lifetime sport that can be played with teams in varying sizes from one to five players.</u>

   b. <u>Basketball involves minimal equipment and can be played on courts that are generally available to the public at little or no cost.</u>

   c. <u>Basketball is a good activity for maintaining health and fitness.</u>

6. Goal statement: <u>All students will be able to play a functional game of golf employing all of the fundamental strokes, rules, and strategies.</u>

   Rationale statements:

   a. <u>Golf is a lifetime sport that can be played throughout the life span.</u>

   b. <u>Golf involves minimal equipment and can be played on public courses available in most communities.</u>

   c. <u>Golf is a good activity for maintaining health and fitness.</u>

❚ Worksheet A.2

Goal Ranking Worksheet

Goals	Ranking Rounds				
	1	**2**	**3**	**4**	**Final**
1. Tennis	1.75(1)*	2.50(3)	2.00(2)	2.00(2)	(2)
2. Volleyball	2.50(3)	2.25(2)	2.50(3)	2.50(3)	(3)
3. Fitness	2.25(2)	1.50(1)	1.50(1)	1.50(1)	(1)
4. Social responsibility	4.00(4)	4.25(4)	4.50(4)	4.50(4)	(4)
5. Basketball	5.00(5)	5.00(5)	5.00(5)	5.00(5)	(5)
6. Golf	5.50(6)	5.50(6)	5.50(6)	5.50(6)	(6)

*The first value is the average of the teachers' ratings for that goal in that round. The value in parentheses is the relative rank of that goal in relation to the other goals for that round. For example, the average rating of the teachers for tennis in the first round was 1.75. This rating was the lowest compared to the other goals so its relative ranking is (1).

▌ Worksheet A.3

highest priority goal (i.e., fitness). The absolute ranking of each goal based on the average ratings is shown in parentheses.

Step 3: Identifying the Policies and Resources Needed to Successfully Implement the Curriculum

In this case study there was no additional need for policies or resources because the headmaster offered full support for the physical education program. Most schools have numerous issues such as grading, waivers for physical education, scheduling, and access to facilities and equipment that can affect the implementation of the curriculum. These issues are addressed in more detail in chapter 5. These issues would be discussed as part of the process of developing the philosophy for the program and then integrated into the final philosophy statement.

Step 4: Delineating Objectives for Each Program Goal

The goal of this step is to create a rank-ordered list of objectives for each program goal. This is the stage at which the planning-down part of the planning is performed. Each goal is task analyzed to identify all of the subskills or objectives needed to achieve the goal. After creating the lists, the curriculum committee members rank the objectives from most (rank = 1) to least important in terms of their contribution to the goal. The committee then uses the consensus-building technique to produce an overall ranking for the objectives within each goal. For individual and team sport goals the prerequisite objectives are typically listed in subcategories such as body awareness, locomotor, and object control skills. After creating the separate lists for each goal, the committee compares the lists, removing duplicate objectives and distributing them proportionally across the respective goals. At the end of this step there should be a list of objectives for each goal ranked from 1 (highest priority) to x, where x represents the number of objectives for that goal. Worksheets A.4.1 through A.4.6 show the final ranked objective lists created by the curriculum committee at the Meta School. Note that the duplicate objectives have also already been removed. For example, catching would have appeared as an object control objective for the tennis, volleyball, and basketball goals. Because catching only needs to be learned once, the duplications have been removed.

Objectives by Goal Delineations

Goal: Tennis

Total number of objectives = 21

Category	Objective	Rank
Body awareness	Body parts	1
	Personal space	2
	Body actions	3
Locomotor skills	Running forward	4
	Hopping	5
	Running backward	6
	Galloping	7
	Sliding	8
Object control skills	Underhand toss	9
	Catch	10
	Forehand strike	11
	Backhand strike	12
Advanced skills	Forehand strike with racket	13
	Backhand strike with racket	14
	Overhead serve with racket	15
	Backhand slice with racket	16
	Forehand slice with racket	17
	Top spin serve with racket	18
	Volley with racket	19
	Tennis drop shot	20
	Slice serve with racket	21

❙ **Worksheet A.4.1**

Objectives by Goal Delineations

Goal: Volleyball

Total number of objectives = 18

Category	Objectives	Rank
Body awareness	Spatial awareness	1
	Balance	2
	Directionality	4
	Shoulder roll	10
Locomotor skills	Skipping	3
	Lateral movement	5
	Changing directions	8
	Vertical jump	9
	Combination skills	11
Object control skills	Overhand throw	6
	Underhand strike	7
	Overhand strike	12
Advanced skills	Volleyball bump (two-arm pass)	13
	Volleyball set	14
	Underhand serve	15
	Overhead serve	16
	Spike	17
	Blocking	18

❚ **Worksheet A.4.2**

Objectives by Goal Delineations

Goal: Physical fitness
Total number of objectives = 14

Category	Objectives	Rank
Flexibility	Trunk/lower back	1
	Leg	8
	Shoulder	9
Strength	Abdominal	2
	Arm	3
	Lower back	6
	Leg	7
	Shoulder	10
	Upper back	11
Cardiorespiratory endurance	Treadmill	4
	Exercise bikes	5
	Stair climber	12
	Rowing	13
	Cross-country skiing simulators	14

▌ **Worksheet A.4.3**

Objectives by Goal Delineations

Goal: Social and cognitive skills
Total number of objectives = 31

Category	Objectives	Rank
Social	Respect for others	1
	Following instructions	2
	Following rules	3
	Self-advocacy	4
	Respect for equipment	5
	Teamwork	6
	Cooperation	7
Cognitive	Tennis rules	8
	Volleyball rules	9
	Tennis strategy	10
	Volleyball strategy	11
	Working and resting heart rates	12
	Measuring heart rate	13
	Training routines and techniques	14
	Tennis scoring	15
	Volleyball scoring	16
	Weightlifting safety	17
	Tennis etiquette	18
	Volleyball etiquette	19
	Tennis doubles play	20
	Overload principles	21
	Weightlifting technique	22
	ACSM guidelines	23
	Circuit training	24
	Golf rules	28
	Golf etiquette	29
	Golf scoring	31
	Basketball rules	27
	Basketball defense	30

■ **Worksheet A.4.4**

Objectives by Goal Delineations

Goal: Basketball

Total number of objectives = 7

Category	Objectives	Rank
Object control	Bounce	1
	Chest pass	2
	Bounce pass	4
	Set shot	3
Advanced skills	Dribbling	5
	Layup	6
	Jump shot	7

■ Worksheet A.4.5

Objectives by Goal Delineations

Goal: Golf

Total number of objectives = 5

Category	Objectives	Rank
Advanced	Putting stroke	1
	Swing—woods	4
	Swing—low irons	2
	Swing—high irons	3
	Pitching	5

■ Worksheet A.4.6

Step 5: Establishing Program Goal Emphasis

The purpose of this step is to determine how much emphasis each program goal should receive in the program. The program percentage goal emphasis in turn will determine how much content can be included in the curriculum for each goal. To do this step, the Meta School curriculum committee created a chart with the goals listed down the left side and the grades in the program listed across the top (see worksheet A.5). Note that the prerequisite areas (i.e., body awareness, locomotor skills, and object control skills) for the lifetime sport goals have been nested within the lifetime goals. Each committee member independently completes the chart indicating how much emphasis to give to each goal at each grade. Only 100% can be allocated in each column or grade across the goals. As discussed in chapter 6, a simple spreadsheet can be created in Microsoft® Excel® to simplify summing the numbers and getting the correct totals for each column.

To achieve consensus, the committee averages the individual values and uses the consensus-building technique. To compute the final program weight for each goal, they sum the values across each row and then divide by the number of grades. The sum of the emphasis values for fitness is 265. They divide this value by 12, the number of grade levels in the program, and arrive at a program weight of 22%. Note that the teachers in the Meta School added two additional goals they hope to work on if time allows. No emphasis is assigned to these goals at this time. If later in the process they find they have time to work on additional content, they can come back to this step and add the appropriate amount of emphasis.

Percentage Goal Emphasis Worksheet

Goal	1	2	3	4	5	6	7	8	9	10	11	12	Program weight
Fitness	10	10	10	10	15	15	25	30	30	30	30	50	22
Tennis (includes body awareness, locomotor, and object control skills)	30	40	40	35	30	35	25	20	20	20	20	10	27
Volleyball (includes body awareness, locomotor, and object control skills)	30	40	40	35	35	30	25	20	20	20	20	10	27
Basketball													0
Golf													0
Social/cognitive	30	10	10	20	20	20	25	30	30	30	30	30	24
Sum = 100%	100	100	100	100	100	100	100	100	100	100	100	100	100

* Each value in the chart represents the average of all of the committee members' ratings.

■ Worksheet A.5

Step 6: Calculating Available Instructional Time

Now the curriculum committee of the Meta School needs to calculate how much time they have available in physical education for the total program. To do this, they complete the instructional time worksheet (worksheet A.6). At the Meta School the amount of time allocated for physical education is consistent across all years of the program, so doing the calculation by program level was probably not necessary. However, in most school districts the length of physical education classes and the frequency typically vary by program level. After determining the total number of minutes for each program level, the committee subtracts 10% for uncontrolled lost instructional time. After completing their calculations, the Meta School curriculum committee learns that they have a total of 388.8 hours of instructional time across 12 years.

Step 7: Calculating Average Objective Mastery Time

The Meta School physical education curriculum committee now needs to figure out how long it takes the physical education teachers to teach an average objective in their curriculum. To accomplish this task, they complete worksheet A.7. Because the Meta School has only six goals, they decide to select a sample objective from each goal area to use for this estimate. Part B of the worksheet shows the time estimated by each teacher to teach mastery of the sample objective for each goal. The last column to the right in this table shows the average of the teachers' estimates for each goal area. This average value for each goal area is then entered in the table in part C and multiplied by the number of objectives in each goal. These values are then summed and divided by the total number of objectives to produce the averaged weighted time need to teach a typical objective in this curriculum. For the Meta School that is 388.8 minutes, or 6.5 hours.

Instructional Time by Program Level

Program Level	Grades	# weeks per year	# min per class	# classes per week	Total minutes	Minus 10%	Total hours available	Hours per year
Elementary school	5	36	30	2	10,800	–1,080	162.0	32.4
Middle school	3	36	30	2	6,480	–648	97.2	32.4
High school	4	36	30	2	8,640	–864	129.6	32.4
Totals	12				25,920	–2,592	388.8	32.4

▌ Worksheet A.6

Using Weighted Estimates to Calculate an Overall Mastery Time

A. Review the objectives listed in your goal or objective delineations and either create a row for each goal or identify three to five categories that can be used to group all of the objectives (e.g., fitness, social, cognitive, and motor skill).

B. Pick one representative objective from each category and list it in the following table. Now have all the teachers individually estimate how long it would take to teach all of the students in one of their classes mastery of this objective and put this value in the table. Values should be in 10-minute intervals.

Category	Sample objective	Teacher ratings 1	2	3	Average
Fitness	Develop abdominal strength	280	400	500	393
Tennis	Learn the overhead serve	390	550	520	487
Social/ cognitive	Learn the strategies involved in tennis singles	260	220	280	253
Volleyball	Learn the forearm pass	340	450	420	403
Basketball	Learn how to perform a layup	420	600	510	510
Golf	Learn to putt	560	750	510	607

C. Now you need to weight the average you have calculated for each category by the number of objectives in each category. To do this, you need to multiply the number of objectives in each category by the average estimate calculated for each category in part B.

Category	(a) Estimated average from step 2	(b) Number of objectives in this category	(c) Weighted average (the product of column a × column b)
Fitness	393	14	5,502
Tennis	487	21	10,227
Social/cognitive	253	31	7,843
Volleyball	403	18	7,254
Basketball	510	7	3,570
Golf	607	5	3,035
Sum		96	37,431

D. Divide the sum at the bottom of column (c) in part C by the sum at the bottom of column (b) in part C. The quotient is the overall mastery time for your curriculum: Sum of column (c) [37,431] / sum of column (b) [96] = 389.9 minutes, or 6.5 hours.

▌ **Worksheet A.7**

Step 8: Calculating How Much Content Can Be Included in the Curriculum

Now that the Meta School physical education curriculum committee knows how much time is available in their program and how long it takes to teach a typical objective, they can calculate how much content can be included in their curriculum. Part A of worksheet A.8 shows the process the committee used. From this process they learn that they can teach a total of 60 objectives in their program. Now they need to determine which 60 objectives of the total 96 they have identified should be included. Fortunately, this is a simple process using the results of the previous planning steps. As shown in part B of worksheet A.8, the number of objectives for each goal is determined by multiplying the percentage goal emphasis for each goal determined in step 5 by the total number of objectives in the program.

Note that the number of objectives calculated for each goal in part B will usually be a whole number plus a fraction (e.g., 12.1). Because it is preferable to use whole numbers, these numbers should be rounded up or down systematically so that you end up with the correct number of objectives at the end of your calculations. In the Meta School example, all of the values were rounded down, resulting in a sum of 59. The one additional objective was then added to the tennis goal.

Now the Meta School curriculum committee knows exactly how many objectives can be included in their curriculum for each of their goals. They now just need to go back to the rank-ordered lists of objectives for each goal created in step 2 and select the appropriate number of objectives. For example, the top 17 ranked objectives for the tennis goal can be included in the curriculum. The curriculum members go back to worksheet A.4.1 and include all of the objectives from body parts (ranked #1) through the forehand slice with racket (ranked #17). They repeat this process for all of the goals until they have identified the appropriate 60 objectives. The end result is a table of objectives as shown in part C of worksheet A.8. Note that the ranks were left on the objectives for illustrative purposes. All the committee really needs to put in the table are the names of the appropriate objectives.

Calculating How Much Content
Can Be Included in the Curriculum

A. Calculate the number of objectives that can be included in the curriculum based on the instructional time available (step 6) and the average objective mastery time (step 7).

Total instructional time / average objective mastery time = total # of objectives

388.8 hours / 6.5 hours = 60 objectives

B. Calculate how many objectives can be taught in each goal area by multiplying the % goal emphasis estimates for each goal (calculated in step 5) by the total number of objectives in the program (calculated in part A of this worksheet).

Goal	% goal emphasis	Total # of program objectives	# of objectives for this goal
Fitness	22.0	60	13
Tennis	27.0	60	17
Volleyball	27.0	60	16
Basketball	00.0	60	0
Golf	00.0	60	0
Social/cognitive	24.0	60	14

C. Select the top-ranked objectives for each goal using the values calculated in step 8, part B.

Fitness	Tennis	Volleyball	Social/cognitive
Flexibility: trunk/lower back (1)	Body parts (1)	Spatial awareness (1)	Respect for others (1)
Flexibility: leg (8)	Personal space (2)	Balance (2)	Following instructions (2)
Flexibility: shoulder (9)	Body actions (3)	Directionality (4)	Following rules (3)
Strength: abdominal (2)	Running forward (4)	Shoulder roll (10)	Self-advocacy (4)
Strength: arm (3)	Hopping (5)	Skipping (3)	Respect for equipment (5)
Strength: lower back (6)	Running backward (6)	Lateral movement (5)	Teamwork (6)
Strength: leg (7)	Galloping (7)	Changing directions (8)	Cooperation (7)
Strength: shoulder (10)	Sliding (8)	Vertical jump (9)	Fair play (25)
Strength: upper back (11)	Underhand toss (9)	Combination skills (11)	Leadership (26)
CRE: treadmill (4)	Catch (10)	Overhand throw (6)	Tennis rules (8)
CRE: Lifecycles (5)	Forehand strike (11)	Underhand strike (7)	Volleyball rules (9)
CRE: stair climber (12)	Backhand strike (12)	Overhand strike (12)	Tennis strategy (10)
CRE: rowing (13)	Forehand strike with racket (13)	Volleyball bump (two-arm pass) (13)	Volleyball strategy (11)
	Backhand strike with racket (14)	Volleyball set (14)	Working and resting heart rates (12)
	Overhead serve with racket (15)	Underhand serve (15)	Measuring heart rate (13)
	Backhand slice with racket (16)	Overhead serve (16)	Training routines and techniques (14)
	Forehand slice with racket (17)		

CRE = Cardiorespiratory endurance.

Step 9: Sequencing the Content Across the Curriculum

Now that the Meta School physical education curriculum committee knows the content that will be included in the curriculum, the next step is to sequence the objectives across the grades developmentally so that it will be taught at the appropriate time. Although development frequently influences how objectives are ranked within goals, this is not always a valid assumption, particularly with more advanced skills.

Using the objective lists created in part C of worksheet A.8, the curriculum committee now must distribute the objectives across the years in the program. Using the percentage goal emphasis worksheet created in step 5 (worksheet A.5) as a guide and having subdivided the motor skill goals (i.e., tennis and volleyball) into the prerequisite categories back in step 4, they are now ready to distribute the objectives across the program. It is recommended that the prerequisite motor skill areas (e.g., locomotor skills) be used as grouping categories in the scope and sequence chart to reflect the elementary level content. The goals or objectives should be listed down the left side of the table and the grades across the top (see worksheet A.9). For each objective three codes are entered into the table: when instruction should start (- -), when the objective is expected to be mastered (**), and, if appropriate, when time will be allocated for review (R). These categories are discussed in more detail in chapter 6. The other rule for this table is that a certain number of objectives should be targeted for mastery during each year. The Meta School has 32.4 hours of instructional time each year, and they estimated that it would require approximately 6.5 hours to master an average objective. Using these values, they should target 5 (4.98 rounded up) objectives for mastery each year. Rather than using the consensus-building technique, the Meta School curriculum committee just makes a table on a blackboard and discusses where each objective should be placed. The final results are shown in worksheet A.9.

Meta School Scope and Sequence

Goal area	Objective	Grades											
		1	2	3	4	5	6	7	8	9	10	11	12
Body awareness	Body parts	**	R										
	Personal space	**	R										
	Body actions	- -	**	R									
	Spatial awareness	- -	**	R									
	Balance	- -	- -	**	R								
	Directionality	- -	- -	**	R								
	Shoulder roll						- -	**	R				
Locomotor	Running forward	**	R										
	Hopping	- -	**	R									
	Running backward	- -	**	R									
	Galloping	- -	- -	**									
	Sliding		- -	**									
	Skipping		- -	- -	**								
	Lateral movements		- -	- -	**	R							
	Changing directions		- -	- -	- -	**	R						
	Vertical jump			- -	- -	**	R						
	Combination skills		- -	- -	- -	- -	**	R					
Object control	Catch	- -	- -	**	R		R						
	Underhand toss	**	R										
	Overhand throw		- -	- -	- -	**	R		R				
	Underhand strike		- -	- -	**	R							
	Overhand strike			- -	- -	**	R						
	Forehand strike				- -	- -	**	R					
	Backhand strike				- -	- -	**	R					
Fitness Flexibility	Trunk/lower back		- -	- -	**	R							R
Flexibility	Leg			- -	- -	- -	- -	- -	- -	- -	- -	**	R
Flexibility	Shoulder				- -	- -	**	R		R		R	
Strength	Abdominal		- -	- -	**		R		R		R		
Strength	Arm				- -	- -	**		R		R		

■ Worksheet A.9

Goal area	Objective												
		1	**2**	**3**	**4**	**5**	**6**	**7**	**8**	**9**	**10**	**11**	**12**
Strength	Lower back							- -	- -	- -	**		R
Strength	Leg									- -	- -	- -	**
Strength	Shoulder									- -	- -	- -	**
Strength	Upper back								- -	- -	**	R	
CRE	Treadmill								- -	- -	**	R	
CRE	Lifecycles											- -	**
CRE	Stair climber										- -	**	
CRE	Rowing										- -	**	
	Working and resting heart rates				- -	- -	- -	- -	- -	**		R	
	Measuring heart rate				- -	- -	- -	- -	- -	**	R		
	Training routines and techniques									- -	- -	**	R
Tennis	Forehand stroke					- -	- -	**					
	Backhand stroke						- -	- -	**				
	Overhead serve						- -	- -	**				
	Backhand slice							- -	- -	**			
	Forehand slice							- -	- -	**			
	Rules					- -	- -	**	R	R			
	Strategy								- -	- -	- -	**	R
Volleyball	Bump					- -	- -	**	R				
	Set						- -	- -	**	R			
	Underhand serve						- -	- -	**				
	Overhead serve						- -	- -	**	R	R		
	Rules					- -	- -	**	R				
	Strategy								- -	- -	**	R	
Social/ cognitive	Respect for others	- -	**	R	R	R	R	R	R	R	R	R	R
	Following instructions	**	R	R	R	R	R	R	R	R	R	R	R
	Self-advocacy	- -	- -	- -	- -	- -	- -	- -	- -	- -	- -	- -	**
	Respect for equipment	- -	- -	- -	- -	- -	- -	- -	- -	- -	**	R	R
	Teamwork					- -	- -	- -	- -	- -	- -	**	
	Cooperation	- -	- -	- -	- -	- -	- -	- -	- -	- -	- -	- -	**
	Follow rules	- -	- -	- -	- -	**	R	R	R	R	R	R	

Header over grade columns: **Grades**

** Mastery expected by the end of this grade.
- - Objective is introduced or worked on during this grade.
R Objective is reviewed or time is allocated for maintenance.
CRE = Cardiorespiratory endurance.

Now that the scope and sequence of the curriculum has been determined, the Meta School teachers can now begin to develop their yearly and block teaching and learning maps as discussed in chapter 6.

Epilogue

This initial physical education program plan created by the Meta School using the ABC planning process is the foundation for an ongoing and dynamic process. The physical education curriculum is based on the Meta School teachers' best educational estimates for a host of variables. When they implement their curriculum, they can validate or revise these estimates as needed based on program evaluation.

Appendix B

Program Planning Worksheets

Achievement-Based Curriculum Philosophy Worksheet

This worksheet is designed to help you identify major points that may be included in a curriculum philosophy statement. These prompts are provided as guidelines. You may want to emphasize some points more or less than others, depending on the local needs and interests.

State why all students need physical education:

_____

_____

_____

State the benefits gained from physical education:

_____

_____

_____

State how the physical education curriculum is linked to the school curriculum or mission:

_____

_____

_____

State how the physical education curriculum is linked to community interests and values:

_____

_____

_____

State the time required to effectively implement the physical education curriculum:

_____

_____

_____

State the teacher qualifications needed to implement the curriculum:

_____

(continued)

(continued)

_____

_____

State the class size and instructional space the curriculum was designed to accommodate:

_____

_____

_____

State the policies and resources (in general terms) needed to effectively implement the curriculum:

_____

_____

_____

List those who were involved in the physical education curriculum development process:

_____

_____

_____

State the process used by the curriculum committee to develop the curriculum:

_____

_____

_____

State the goals the students will have achieved when they complete the curriculum:

_____

_____

_____

State the rationale and benefits for students achieving these goals:

_____

_____

_____

Consensus-Building Technique

1. List the competing items or issues and assign each a unique number from 1 to x (where x is the number of the last item in the list).

2. Have each member independently rate, or rank, the items from highest priority (1) to lowest priority (x). All items must be ranked, and all items must be assigned a unique rank—no ties.

3. Collect the individual rankings, compute the average ranks for each item, and then relist the items in rank order from 1 to x based on the calculated average ranks.

4. Provide members a timed individual opportunity to address why they believe any item should either be moved farther up or down the list. All comments must be directed to the content in question; no personal references to the comments of other members should be allowed. Depending on the complexity of the issue, a time limit should be placed on the individual comments ranging from 1 to 3 minutes. Each member should systematically be provided with an opportunity to speak to the rankings. This process is specifically designed to rein in the domineering, overly verbal members and to encourage the quiet, less verbal members to participate.

5. After the comment period, all members again rerank the items. This process allows individuals to reflect on the insights, new information, and comments that have been made and to indicate the impact on their ranking of the items.

6. Compute average ranks for each item and then relist the items in rank order from 1 to x based on the calculated average ranks.

7. Repeat steps 4 through 6 until the relative rankings stabilize. Although the actual average ranks (values) will vary after each reranking, as soon as the items stay in the same order for two rankings, consensus has been reached. Once a consensus is reached, the issue is closed to further discussion during the planning process.

From *Developing the Physical Education Curriculum* by Luke E. Kelly and Vincent J. Melograno, 2004, Champaign, IL: Human Kinetics.

Program Goals and Supporting Rationales

Goal statement: All students will be able to play a functional game of tennis using appropriate strokes, rules, and strategies.

Rationale statements:
1. Tennis is a lifetime sport that can be played throughout the life span.
2. Tennis involves minimal equipment and can be played on courts that are generally available to the public at little or no cost.
3. Tennis is a good activity for maintaining health and fitness.

Goal statement: _____

_____

_____

Rationale statements:

1. _____

_____

2. _____

_____

3. _____

_____

Goal statement: _____

_____

_____

Rationale statements:

1. _____

_____

2. _____

_____

3. _____

_____

Goal Ranking Worksheet

Ranking Rounds

Goals	1	2	3	4	Final
1. _____	_____	_____	_____	_____	_____
2. _____	_____	_____	_____	_____	_____
3. _____	_____	_____	_____	_____	_____
4. _____	_____	_____	_____	_____	_____
5. _____	_____	_____	_____	_____	_____
6. _____	_____	_____	_____	_____	_____
7. _____	_____	_____	_____	_____	_____
9. _____	_____	_____	_____	_____	_____
10. _____	_____	_____	_____	_____	_____
11. _____	_____	_____	_____	_____	_____
12. _____	_____	_____	_____	_____	_____
13. _____	_____	_____	_____	_____	_____
14. _____	_____	_____	_____	_____	_____
15. _____	_____	_____	_____	_____	_____
16. _____	_____	_____	_____	_____	_____
17. _____	_____	_____	_____	_____	_____
18. _____	_____	_____	_____	_____	_____

From *Developing the Physical Education Curriculum* by Luke E. Kelly and Vincent J. Melograno, 2004, Champaign, IL: Human Kinetics.

Goal and Objective Ranking Worksheet

Program goal: _____

Summative ratings and relative (ranks)*

	Rounds		
	1	**2**	**3**

Sport-specific objectives

	1	2	3
_____	_____	_____	_____
_____	_____	_____	_____
_____	_____	_____	_____
_____	_____	_____	_____
_____	_____	_____	_____
_____	_____	_____	_____
_____	_____	_____	_____

Prerequisite objectives

	1	2	3
_____	_____	_____	_____
_____	_____	_____	_____
_____	_____	_____	_____
_____	_____	_____	_____
_____	_____	_____	_____
_____	_____	_____	_____
_____	_____	_____	_____

Object control skills

	1	2	3
_____	_____	_____	_____
_____	_____	_____	_____
_____	_____	_____	_____
_____	_____	_____	_____

*Initially, each teacher would complete this form individually. The teachers would rank each objective in the list from 1 to x with 1 being assigned to the most important objective and x the least important. The individual teacher ratings would be averaged to produce a summative rating for each objective. These average ratings are shown in the three columns for each of the three rounds. For example (see figure 6.3), 13.4 is the average ranking for the forehand strike objective received in the first round. These ratings would then be rank-ordered to produce a relative ranking for the objectives. The relative rank is shown in parentheses next to the average ranking. For example, the relative rank for the forehand strike was (14). This means of the 20 objectives, this objective was the 14th most important. When the relative rankings stay the same between rounds, consensus has been reached.

Percentage Goal Emphasis Worksheet

Goal	K	1	2	3	4	5	6	7	8	9	10	11	12	Program weight
Sum = 100%														

* Each value in the chart represents the average of all teachers' ratings.

Instructional Time by Program Level Worksheet

Level	# grades	Weeks per year	# min per class	# classes per week	Total minutes	Minus 10%	Total hours available	Hours per year
Elementary								
Middle school								
High school								
Totals								

From *Developing the Physical Education Curriculum* by Luke E. Kelly and Vincent J. Melograno, 2004, Champaign, IL: Human Kinetics.

Using Weighted Estimates to Calculate an Overall Mastery Time Worksheet

A. Review the objectives listed in your goal and objective delineations and identify three to five categories that you can use to group all of the objectives (e.g., fitness, social, cognitive, and motor skill).

B. Pick one representative objective from each category and list it in the following table. Now have all the teachers individually estimate how long it would take to teach all of the students in one of their classes mastery of this objective and put their values in the table. Values should be in 10-minute intervals.

Category	Sample objective	Teacher ratings					Average
		1	2	3	4	5	

C. Now you need to weight the average you have calculated for each category by the number of objectives in each category. To do this, you need to multiple the number of objectives in each category by the average estimate calculated for each category in step 6.

Category	(a) Estimated average from step 2	(b) Number of objectives in this category	(c) Weighted average (the product of column a × column b)
Sum			

D. Divide the sum at the bottom of column (c) in step C by the sum at the bottom of column (b) in step C. The quotient is the overall mastery time for your curriculum: sum of column (c) (42,750) / sum of column (b) (114) = 375 minutes or 6.25 hours

Calculating How Much Content Can Be Included in the Curriculum Worksheet

A. Calculate the number of objectives to include in the curriculum based on the instructional time available (step 6) and the average objective mastery time (step 7).

   Total instructional time / average objective mastery time = total number of objectives

B. Calculate how many objectives to teach in each goal area by multiplying the percent goal emphasis for each goal (calculated in step 5) by the total number of objectives in the program (calculated in part A).

Goal	% goal weight	Total # of program objectives	# of objectives for this goal

C. Select the top-ranked objectives for each goal using the values calculated in step 8, part B.

Calculating the Number of Objectives by Grade and Program Level Worksheet

Program level	Time per year (hours)	Average mastery time (hours)	# of objectives per year (time / mastery)*	# of years in program level	Total # of objectives per level
Elementary					
Middle					
Secondary					

*This value is calculated by dividing the time per year (column 2) by the average mastery time (column 3). Note that the quotient from this calculation will usually be a whole number plus a fraction (e.g., 5.18). Because it is preferable to use whole numbers, these numbers should be rounded up or down systematically so that you end up with the correct number of objectives at the end of your calculations. In the example in figure 6.10, the elementary and secondary values were each rounded down and the middle school level was rounded up. The resulting sum of all the objectives by level equals 113, which is one short of the total 114. In this case, one additional objective would be added in one of the secondary years to make up for the rounding error.

From *Developing the Physical Education Curriculum* by Luke E. Kelly and Vincent J. Melograno, 2004, Champaign, IL: Human Kinetics.

Elementary Objectives Scope and Sequence

Goal area	Objective	Grades					
		K	1	2	3	4	5

**= Mastery expected by the end of this grade
- - = Objective is introduced or worked on during this grade
R = Objective is reviewed or time is allocated for maintenance

TLM Matrix of Block Themes by Objectives

Teacher: _____ **Program level:** _____ **Grade:** _____

Objectives for This Year

	Mastery (minutes)	Work on (minutes)	Review (minutes)

Theme blocks

Sample Spreadsheet Format for TLM Matrix Calculations

Objectives	Time available (in minutes)	Blocks										Time used (in minutes)

ABC School District Class Performance Score Sheet

Teacher: _____

Class: _____

Start date: _____

Grade level: _____

Mastery criterion: _____

End date: _____

Scoring rubric:
- 0 = not present
- 1 = emerging, but needs work
- 2 = demonstrates correct pattern consistently

ACE ratings:
- a = above average
- b = average
- c = below average

Students	1	2	3	4	5	6	7	8	Attention A	Comprehension C	Effort E	Comments	A	B	C	D	E	F
														G	H	I			J

Evaluation values

Directions: _____

Administrative considerations: _____

Reflections: _____

A = Entry score—# of components achieved at the start of the unit
B = Target score—total # of components expected to be achieved by the end of the unit
C = Exit score—actual # of components achieved at the end of the unit
D = Target met—yes, if exit score is ≥ target score; no, if exit score < target score
E = mastery—yes, if exit score is ≥ mastery criterion; no, if exit score < mastery criterion
F = % mastery—exit score divided by mastery criterion
G = Sum of entry scores
H = Sum of target scores
I = Sum of exit scores
J = Sum of % mastery scores
Teacher effectiveness = sum of exit scores (I) / sum of target scores (H)
Class mean gain = sum of exit scores (I) – sum of entry (G) / total number of students
Class average % mastery = sum of the % mastery (J) / total number of students

ABC School District Teaching Template

Teacher: _____   Grade: _____   Class: _____   Start time: _____

Block: _____   Start date: _____   End date: _____

Standard managerial procedures: _____

Format	Objectives (minutes)	Instructional focus	Instructional cue	Learning experiences	Organization	Equipment	Transition

Reflections: _____

Instructional Cue and Activity Worksheet

Grade: _____

Objective: _____

Skill components	Instructional cues	Activities/drills/games

ABC School District Student Learning Format

Teacher: _____   Grade: _____   Class: _____   Start time: _____

Block: _____   Date: _____   Format part: _____

Groupings: _____

Objective(s)	Focus	Cue	Groupings	Expectations	Feedback	Comments

Reflections: _____

_____

_____

_____

_____

_____

ABC School District Physical Education Class Evaluation Report

Student name: _____ Number of students in class: _____ Teacher: _____

Grade level: _____ Report date: _____

Objectives	Entry level	Target exit	Actual exit	Net change	Target met	Mastery criteria	% Mastered	Class average	Teacher comments

From *Developing the Physical Education Curriculum* by Luke E. Kelly and Vincent J. Melograno, 2004, Champaign, IL: Human Kinetics.

Individual Student Cumulative Progress Report

Student: _____

Class: _____

P.E. teacher: _____

School: _____

Key: Pr = Pre
     P = Post

Each objective has a specific number of components. The numbers represent the number of components the student has demonstrated.

M = Mastery

Objective—Name and #	1.1 Run (4)			1.2 Gallop (5)			2.1 Underhand roll (4)			4.1 Non-locomotor (5)			4.2 Body awareness (5)			4.3 Spatial awareness (3)			4.11 Changing run speed (3)		
	Pr	P	M	Pr	P	M	Pr	P	M	Pr	P	M	Pr	P	M	Pr	P	M	Pr	P	M

Objective—Name and #	1.4 Jump (3)			1.6 Slide (3)			1.7 Skip (4)			2.3 Underhand throw (3)			4.4 Use of space (4)			4.5 Quality of movement (3)			4.10 Balance beam (4)		
	Pr	P	M	Pr	P	M	Pr	P	M	Pr	P	M	Pr	P	M	Pr	P	M	Pr	P	M

Objective—Name and #	1.5 Hop (4)			2.2 Bounce (4)			3.3 Flexibility (5)			3.7 Agility (6)			4.7 Forward roll (6)			4.8 Rope jump (5)			4.9 Rhythmic movement (3)		
	Pr	P	M	Pr	P	M	Pr	P	M	Pr	P	M	Pr	P	M	Pr	P	M	Pr	P	M

Objective—Name and #	1.8 Leap (3)			2.7 Sidearm strike (7)			2.10 Chest pass (5)			2.11 Bounce pass (6)			2.14 Overhead pass (5)			3.4 Abdominal strength (4)			3.6 Arm/shoulder strength (3)		
	Pr	P	M	Pr	P	M	Pr	P	M	Pr	P	M	Pr	P	M	Pr	P	M	Pr	P	M

Objective—Name and #	1.3 Horizontal jump (6)			2.4 Overhand throw (6)			2.8 Catch (5)			2.9 Underhand strike (4)			3.5 Mile run (4)			4.6 Basic dance pattern (4)		
	Pr	P	M	Pr	P	M	Pr	P	M	Pr	P	M	Pr	P	M	Pr	P	M

Objective—Name and #	2.5 Kick (6)			2.6 Punt (6)			2.12 Forehand strike (7)			2.13 Soccer dribble (5)			3.1 Knowledge of physical fitness (13)			3.2 Fitness concepts (13)		
	Pr	P	M	Pr	P	M	Pr	P	M	Pr	P	M	Pr	P	M	Pr	P	M

Progress and Mastery Weights Worksheet

	A	B	C	D	E	F	G	H	I
1									
2									
3									
4			Progress=	50	Mastery=	50			
5									
6	Student A								
7		Objectives	Entry	Target	Exit	Mastery criterion	Progress	Mastery	Average
8		--------	--------	--------	--------	--------	--------	--------	--------
9		Volleyball set	1	2	3	5	100.00	60.00	80.00
10		Cooperation	60	20	75	90	75.00	83.33	79.17
11		Volleyball rules	50	30	80	80	100.00	100.00	100.00
12		--------	--------	--------	--------	--------	--------	--------	--------
13		Average					91.67	81.11	86.39
14									
15									
16									
17									

ABC School District Physical Education Class Evaluation Report

Teacher: _____

Class: _____

Number of students in class: _____

Report date: _____

Grade level: _____

Objectives	Class mean entry	Class mean target	Class mean exit	Class mean gain	% class meeting target	Mastery criteria	% class meeting mastery	Class average % mastery

From *Developing the Physical Education Curriculum* by Luke E. Kelly and Vincent J. Melograno, 2004, Champaign, IL: Human Kinetics.

ABC School District
End-of-Instruction Objective Evaluation Worksheet

Objective:_____   Teacher: _____

Time allocated in program plan: _____

Actual amount of time spent:_____

How effective do you feel you were in teaching this objective?

1	2	3	4	5
Low		Medium		High

How would you describe your students' progress on this objective?

1	2	3	4	5
Behind schedule		On schedule		Ahead of schedule

List any factors that are negatively affecting your ability to teach this objective.

_____

_____

_____

_____

_____

List any great teaching techniques or activities you use that are very effective for teaching this objective.

_____

_____

_____

_____

_____

Other comments or suggestions regarding this objective:

_____

_____

_____

_____

ABC School District End-of-Year Objective Evaluation Worksheet

Teacher: _____   Program level or grade(s): _____

Objectives targeted for mastery this year

Objectives	Time allocated	Actual time spent	Time difference	Class average gain	Class average % mastery

Objectives scheduled to be introduced or worked on

Objectives	Time allocated	Actual time spent	Time difference	Class average gain	Class average % mastery

Guidelines for Requesting Resources

1. Clearly define the problem this resource request is designed to address.

2. Focus the request on the needs of the students. You want the board to understand that whatever you are requesting will directly affect the students and assist them in achieving an established goal in the program.

3. Provide concrete data from your program and the literature to justify your request. You do not want the board to perceive your request as just a novel idea. Support it with enough data and literature to suggest that it will address the need you have identified.

4. Show that you have exhausted what you can do with your existing resources (e.g., you have already developed and run a pilot program and now need resources to make it available to all students).

5. Give an accurate budget that is sufficient to address the need you have identified and shows that you are being fiscally responsible and prudent.

References

American Alliance for Health, Physical Education, Recreation and Dance. (1987). *Basic stuff: Series I and II*. Reston, VA: Author.

Annarino, A.A. (1978). Operational taxonomy for physical education objectives. *Journal of Physical Education and Recreation, 49* (1), 54-55.

Annarino, A.A., Cowell, C.C., & Hazelton, H.W. (1980). *Curriculum theory and design in physical education* (2nd ed.). St. Louis: Mosby.

Block, M.E. (1994). *A teacher's guide to including students with disabilities in regular physical education*. Baltimore: Paul H. Brookes.

Bolt, B.R. (2000). Using computers for qualitative analysis of movement. *Journal of Physical Education and Recreation, 71* (3), 15-18.

Bucher, C.A. (1983). *Foundations of physical education & sport* (9th ed.). St. Louis: Mosby.

Carnegie Task Force on Teaching as a Profession. (1986). *A nation prepared: Teachers for the 21st century*. New York: Author.

Chepyator-Thomson, J.R. (Ed.). (1994). Multicultural education: Culturally responsive teaching. *Journal of Physical Education, Recreation & Dance, 65* (9), 31-36, 61-74.

Christie, B. (2000). Topic teamwork: A collaborative integrative model for increasing student-centered learning in grades K-12. *Journal of Physical Education, Recreation & Dance, 71* (8), 28-32, 37.

Craft, D.H. (Ed.). (1994). Inclusion: Physical education for all. *Journal of Physical Education, Recreation & Dance, 65* (1), 22-56.

Danielson, C. (1996). *Enhancing professional practice: A framework for teaching*. Alexandria, VA: Association for Supervision and Curriculum Development.

Darling-Hammond, L. (Ed.). (1992). *Model standards for beginning teacher licensing and development: A resource for state dialogue*. Washington, DC: Council of Chief State School Officers, Interstate New Teacher Assessment and Support Consortium.

Doolittle, S., & Fay, T. (2000). *Authentic assessment of physical activity for high school students (NASPE Assessment Series)*. Reston, VA: National Association for Sport and Physical Education.

Dunn, S.E., & Wilson, R. (1991). Cooperative learning in the physical education classroom. *Journal of Physical Education, Recreation & Dance, 62* (6), 22-28.

Evans, R. (1996). *The human side of school change: Reform, resistance, and the real-life problems of innovation*. San Francisco: Jossey-Bass.

Franck, M., Graham, G., Lawson, H., Loughrey, T., Ritson, R., Sanborn, M., & Seefeldt, V. (1992). *Outcomes of quality physical education programs*. Reston, VA: National Association for Sport and Physical Education.

Freeman, W.H. (1982). *Physical education and sport in a changing society* (2nd ed.). Minneapolis: Burgess.

Gardner, H. (1993). *Multiple intelligences: The theory in practice*. New York: HarperCollins.

Glatthorn, A.A. (1993). *Learning twice: An introduction to the methods of teaching*. New York: HarperCollins.

Glatthorn, A.A. (1994). *Developing a quality curriculum*. Alexandria, VA: Association for Supervision and Curriculum Development.

Glatthorn, A.A. (1998). *Performance assessment and standards-based curricula: The achievement cycle*. Larchmont, NY: Eye on Education.

Goodlad, J.I. (1979). *Curriculum inquiry: The study of curriculum practice*. New York: McGraw-Hill.

Graham, G. (Ed.). (1992). Developmentally appropriate physical education for children. *Journal of Physical Education, Recreation & Dance, 63* (6), 29-60.

Graham, G. (2001). *Teaching children physical education: Becoming a master teacher* (2nd ed.). Champaign, IL: Human Kinetics.

Graham, G., Castenada, R., Hopple, C., Manross, M., & Sanders, S. (1992). *Developmentally appropriate physical education practices for children*. Reston, VA: National Association for Sport and Physical Education, Council on Physical Education for Children.

Hammersley, C.H. (1992). If we win, I win—Adventure education in physical education and recreation. *Journal of Physical Education, Recreation & Dance, 63* (9), 63-67, 72.

Harrison, J.M., Blakemore, C.L., & Buck, M.M. (2001). *Instructional strategies for secondary school physical education* (5th ed.). Boston: McGraw-Hill.

Hastie, P. (2003). *Teaching for lifetime physical activity through quality high school physical education*. San Francisco: Benjamin Cummings.

Hellison, D. (1995). *Teaching responsibility through physical activity*. Champaign, IL: Human Kinetics.

Hellison, D.R., & Templin, T.J. (1991). *A reflective approach to teaching physical education*. Champaign, IL: Human Kinetics.

Hopple, C.J. (1995). *Teaching for outcomes in elementary physical education: A guide for curriculum and assessment*. Champaign, IL: Human Kinetics.

Hurwitz, R. (1993a). *Cooperative learning sample units: Soccer.* Unpublished manuscript, Cleveland State University, HPERD Department.

Hurwitz, R. (1993b). *Role playing instructional strategy.* Unpublished manuscript, Cleveland State University, HPERD Department.

Hurwitz, R. (2002). *Learning experiences.* Unpublished manuscript, Cleveland State University, HPERD Department.

Jacobs, H.H. (Ed.). (1989). *Interdisciplinary curriculum: Design and implementation.* Alexandria, VA: Association for Supervision and Curriculum Development.

Jacobs, H.H. (1997). *Mapping the big picture: Integrating curriculum and assessment K-12.* Alexandria, VA: Association for Supervision and Curriculum Development.

Jewett, A.E., Bain, L.L., & Ennis, C.D. (1995). *The curriculum process in physical education* (2nd ed.). Boston: WCB/McGraw-Hill.

Jewett, A.E., & Mullan, M.R. (1977). *Curriculum design: Purposes and processes in physical education teaching-learning.* Washington, DC: American Alliance for Health, Physical Education and Recreation.

Kelly, L.E. (1987). Computer assisted instruction: Applications for physical education. *Journal of Physical Education, Recreation & Dance, 58,* 74-79.

Kelly, L.E. (1988). Curriculum design model: A university-public school model for designing a district-wide elementary physical education curriculum. *Journal of Physical Education, Recreation & Dance, 59,* 26-32.

Kelly, L.E. (1989). Instructional time: The overlooked factor in PE curriculum development. *Journal of Physical Education, Recreation & Dance, 89,* 29-32.

Kirchner, G. (1992). *Physical education for elementary school children* (8th ed.). Dubuque, IA: Brown.

Kounin, J.S. (1970). *Discipline and group management in classrooms.* New York: Holt, Rinehart & Winston.

Lavay, B.W., French, R., & Henderson, H.L. (1997). *Positive behavior management strategies for physical educators.* Champaign, IL: Human Kinetics

Lawson, H.A., & Placek, J.H. (1981). *Physical education in the secondary schools: Curricular alternatives.* Boston: Allyn & Bacon.

Locke, L.F., & Lambdin, D. (1976). Teacher behavior. In *American Alliance for Health, Physical Education and Recreation, Personalized learning in physical education* (pp. 9-33). Washington, DC: American Alliance for Health, Physical Education and Recreation.

Long Beach Unified School District. (2000). *Physical education content standards and benchmarks.* Long Beach, CA: Author. Retrieved January 15, 2003, from the World Wide Web: www.lbusd.k12.ca.us/curriculum/site_map.htm.

Lund, J.L. (2000). *Creating rubrics for physical education (NASPE Assessment Series).* Reston, VA: National Association for Sport and Physical Education.

Melograno, V.J. (1994). Portfolio assessment: Documenting authentic student learning. *Journal of Physical Education, Recreation & Dance, 65* (8), 50-55, 58-61.

Melograno, V.J. (1996). *Designing the physical education curriculum* (3rd ed.). Champaign, IL: Human Kinetics.

Melograno, V.J. (1997). Integrating assessment into physical education teaching. *Journal of Physical Education, Recreation & Dance, 68* (7), 34-37.

Melograno, V.J. (1998). *Professional and student portfolios for physical education.* Champaign, IL: Human Kinetics.

Melograno, V.J. (2000a). *Portfolio assessment for K-12 physical education (NASPE Assessment Series).* Reston, VA: National Association for Sport and Physical Education.

Melograno, V.J. (2000b). Designing a portfolio system for K-12 physical education: A step-by-step process. *Measurement in Physical Education and Exercise Science, 4* (2), 97-115.

Michigan Governor's Council on Physical Fitness, Health and Sports. (2000). *Exemplary physical education curriculum: Changing the shape of Michigan's youth.* Lansing, MI: Author. Retrieved January 15, 2003, from the World Wide Web: www.michiganfitness.org.

Mohnsen, B.S. (2001). *Using technology in physical education* (3rd ed.). Cerritos, CA: Bonnie's Fitware.

Mosston, M., & Ashworth, S. (2002). *Teaching physical education* (5th ed.). San Francisco: Benjamin Cummings.

Mosston, M., & Mueller, R. (1974). Mission, omission and submission in physical education. In G.H. Glynn (Ed.), *Issues in physical education and sports* (pp. 97-106). Palo Alto, CA: National Press Books.

National Association for Sport and Physical Education. (2002). *2001 Shape of the nation report.* Reston, VA: Author.

National Board for Professional Teaching Standards. (1994). *What teachers should know and be able to do.* Southfield, MI: Author.

National Commission on Excellence in Education. (1983). *A nation at risk: The imperative of educational reform.* Washington, DC: U.S. Government Printing Office.

National Commission on Teaching & America's Future. (1996). *What matters most: Teaching for America's future (summary report).* Woodbridge, VA: Author.

Ohio Department of Education. (1999). *Ohio's model for competency-based physical education.* Columbus, OH: Author. Retrieved March 17, 2001, from the World Wide Web: www.ode.state.oh.us/ohio_hpe_model.htm.

O'Sullivan, M., & Henninger, M. (2000). *Assessing student responsibility and teamwork (NASPE Assessment Series)*. Reston, VA: National Association for Sport and Physical Education.

Rink, J., Dotson, C., Franck, M., Hensley, L., Holt-Hale, S., Lund, J., Payne, G., & Wood, T. (1995). *National standards for physical education: A guide to content and assessment*. St. Louis: Mosby.

Senge, P., Kleiner, A., Roberts, C., Ross, R., Roth, G., and Smith, B. (1999). *The dance of change: The challenges of sustaining momentum in learning organizations*. New York: Doubleday.

Sherrill, C. (1998). *Adapted physical activity, recreation and sport: Crossdisciplinary and lifespan* (5th ed.). Boston: WCB/McGraw-Hill.

Siedentop, D. (1991). *Developing teaching skills in physical education* (3rd ed.). Mountain View, CA: Mayfield.

Siedentop, D. (1994). *Sport education*. Champaign, IL: Human Kinetics.

Siedentop. D. (2004). *Introduction to physical education, fitness, and sport* (5th ed.). Boston: McGraw-Hill.

Siedentop, D., Mand, C., & Taggart, A. (1986). *Physical education: Teaching and curriculum strategies for grades 5-12*. Mountain View, CA: Mayfield.

Slavin, R. E. (1990). *Cooperative learning: Theory, research, and practice*. Englewood Cliffs, NJ: Prentice Hall.

Slavin, R.E., & Madden, N.A. (1989). What works for students at risk: A research synthesis. *Educational Leadership, 46* (5), 4-13.

Sparks, W.G. (1993). Promoting self-responsibility and decision making with at-risk students. *Journal of Physical Education, Recreation & Dance, 64* (2), 74-78.

Ulrich, D.A. (2000). *The test of gross motor development examiner's manual* (2nd ed.). Austin, TX: Pro-Ed.

U.S. Department of Education. (1991). *America 2000: An education strategy*. Washington, DC: Author.

U.S. Department of Health and Human Services. (1996). *Physical activity and health: A report of the Surgeon General*. Atlanta, GA: Author.

Villa, R., & Thousand, J. (1990). Administrative supports to promote inclusive schooling. In W. Stainback & S. Stainback (Eds.), *Support networks for inclusive schooling: Integrated interdependent education* (pp. 201-218). Baltimore: Paul H. Brookes.

Villegas, A.M. (1991). *Culturally responsive pedagogy for the 1990s and beyond* (Trends and Issues Paper No. 6). Washington, DC: ERIC Clearinghouse on Teacher Education.

Virginia Department of Education. (2001). *Proposed physical education standards of learning for Virginia public schools*. Richmond, VA: Author. Retrieved January 15, 2003, from the World Wide Web: www.pen.k12.va.us/VDOE/Instruction/sol.html.

Wessel, J.A. (1976). *I CAN primary skills*. Northbrook, IL: Hubbard.

Wessel, J.A., & Kelly, L. (1986). *Achievement-based curriculum development in physical education*. Philadelphia: Lea & Febiger.

Wiggins, G., & McTighe, J. (1998). *Understanding by design*. Alexandria, VA: Association for Supervision and Curriculum Development.

Wong, H.K., & Wong, R.T. (1998). *The first days of school: How to be an effective teacher*. Mountain View, CA: Harry K. Wong Publications.

Index

Note: The italicized *f* and *t* following page numbers refer to figures and tables, respectively.

About the Authors

Luke E. Kelly, PhD, is a professor of kinesiology at the University of Virginia. Dr. Kelly has 25 years of experience working with public schools in evaluating and revising their physical education curricula to meet the needs of students with disabilities. He has coauthored two books with Janet Wessel relating to the achievement-based curriculum (ABC) approach, and he has also written numerous articles on the topic. He and coauthor Janet Wessel were the ones to introduce the ABC process to the physical education profession in 1986.

Since 1986, Dr. Kelly has been awarded federal grants to disseminate the ABC process. He has served as the president of the National Consortium for Physical Education and Recreation for Individuals with Disabilities and has served as chair for VAHPERD and for the AAHPERD Adapted Physical Activity Council. He also directed the NCPERID national standards project from 1992 to 1999.

In 1999 Dr. Kelly was inducted as a fellow in the American Academy of Kinesiology and Physical Education. He has also received the G. Lawrence Rarick Research Award and the William H. Hillman Distinguished Service Award from the NCPERID. His hobbies and interests include fly-fishing, reforestation, and carpentry.

Vincent J. Melograno, EdD, is chairperson and professor in the department of health, physical education, recreation, and dance at Cleveland State University. Dr. Melograno has authored four textbooks on curriculum design, two other books on portfolio assessment and fitness, several chapters in books, and numerous articles and monographs. He also has presented nationally and internationally and has been awarded several research and training grants.

Dr. Melograno has a doctorate in curriculum and instruction from Temple University. He has served as a department chair for 20 years. He also has served as chair for NASPE's Curriculum and Instruction Academy; Ohio AAHPERD president; visiting lecturer at Seoul National University; and external examiner in 2002-04 for the National Institute of Education, Nanyang Technological University (Singapore). In addition, Dr. Melograno is in the International Who's Who in Sport Pedagogy Theory and Research, awarded by the International Association for Physical Education in Higher Education. Dr. Melograno enjoys tennis, fitness training, and softball in his spare time.

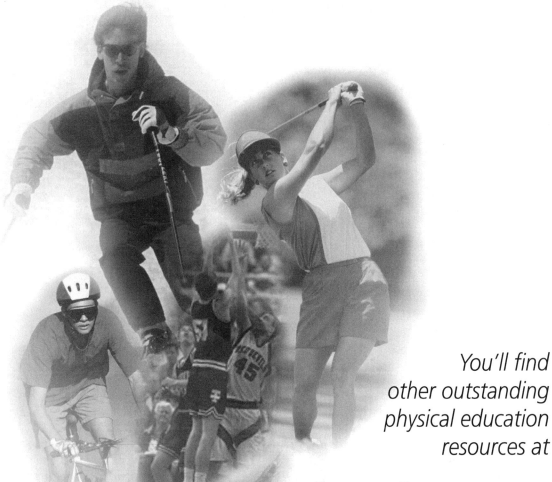